REFLECTIONS ON COMMUNITY ORGANIZATION

REFLECTIONS ON COMMUNITY ORGANIZATION

Enduring Themes and Critical Issues

Edited by Jack Rothman
University of California, Los Angeles

F. E. Peacock Publishers, Inc.
Itasca, Illinois

The Smith Richardson Foundation provided valuable assistance by supporting a conference at the University of North Carolina, at which the contributing authors were able to critique their work and seek unifying themes.

The School of Public Policy and Social Research, UCLA, provided clerical and material aid to facilitate manuscript review and communication with the team of contributing authors.

All royalties from this book will be assigned to the Journal of Community Practice, *an official publication of the Association for Community Organization and Social Administration.*

*To Andrew Jordan Rothman and other newly
arrived grandchildren everywhere. May they, in
these ill-tempered times, engender an outbreak
of innocence and gentility throughout the world.*

—Jack Rothman

Contents

PART ONE

SETTING THE STAGE

Intent and Content

Jack Rothman

INTENT

This has been a tough time for social work and its natural allies and supporters—liberals, progressives, and the left generally. I think it has been especially tough for Community Organization, which typically has been the forward arm for advocacy and social reform in the social work profession. *Turning Back* is the title Stephen Steinberg (1995) gave his book describing the contemporary "liberal retreat" from hard-hitting progressive policies. But I sense this has not necessarily been a voluntary retreat. Bill Clinton, I presume, thought he needed to swaddle himself ideologically in a patchwork "New Democrat" mantle to be elected president. Everywhere we look there are low resources and weak public support for the poor, human services, governmental programs, affirmative action, and the politics of change.

Clearly, innovative thinking and powerful strategies are needed to break through the contemporary impediments to shaping a more just and compassionate community. I can think of a variety of sources of vital ideas—grassroots activists, research, experts, the young, emerging successful initiatives. But one means among others, the one that animated

3

me in composing this book, is to scrutinize the historical past for insights and approaches that can help guide the future (Berkhofer, 1995).

For these insights, I turned to a core of leaders and innovators who have profoundly influenced the field of community organization theory and practice since the end of World War II. An enormous transformation took place in this field after that pivotal moment just before midcentury. The GI Bill and postwar environment brought a flood of newcomers into social work and Community Organization—people who had different backgrounds, experiences, and outlooks from those who had come before. The subsequent civil rights revolution, War on Poverty, population migrations, deterioration of the urban centers, mushrooming of the suburbs, and technological breakthroughs, among other portentous events, made severe demands on—and evoked creative responses, practical and intellectual, from—these professionals. This new breed forged a sea of change in the character and structure of the field, as well as on American communities, over the last half century—the lessons of which are not readily at hand for those about to enter the fray.

Twelve senior scholars, teachers, and activists, colleagues and contemporaries of mine, whose lives and endeavors traverse this entire time period, and who have viewed it from different angles and in different roles, agreed to write reflective narratives that recall their experiences and insights. Some are currently active, others are in varied stages of retirement, and each speaks from a unique vantage point, identifying dominant events, ideas, forces, persons, organizations and tactics, and crystallizing what they all learned about battles fought and those still to come. They identify the enduring themes and critical issues that permeate this field. Composition of the circle of reflection authors was set by space limitations and an attempt to balance factors such as background, gender, and type of practice activity.

This generation of remarkable professionals left an indelible mark. They engaged in such projects as directing Mobilization for Youth, a pathsetting community action program that helped spark the War on Poverty; spearheaded local efforts to bring about national motor/voter legislation and the Welfare Rights movement; headed the National Federation of Settlements through a critical time; reorganized and resuscitated a moribund National Association of Social Workers; and stimulated widely used community-based approaches to combat youth gangs.

They established the first contemporary community organization graduate specialization in social work; formulated fundamental theoretical constructs in the field; and conducted international comparative research on the workings of voluntary associations.

Reviewing the challenges these innovators faced and the solutions they forged offers us clues for engaging in the struggles of today. Also, in a time characterized by a politics of exhaustion plaguing the left, the story of their quest and commitment could serve to generate new energy and re-solve. Ironically, I have found few similar sources in our field—where the wisdom of pioneers of change, who influenced the past in a profound way, has been distilled and codified through autobiography and personalized analysis to be passed on to those who want to accomplish the same in the future. (There have been parallel projects in other fields: For example, *Reflections on Community Studies* [Vidich, Bensman, and Stein, 1964] registers the reminiscences of the major researchers who carried out community-based ethnographic field work.)

The narratives in this book are individual stories, written in autobiographical, first-person style, and immersed in the verities of direct engagement. All are original and crafted specifically for this volume. Each author provides a concise set of bibliographic references that illuminate and detail the issues that are discussed, so that practitioners and students can obtain further information and analysis on the subject. But the presentations are not burdened by the usual trappings of academic discourse. For this project, the emphasis is on quality and relevance, and fluidity of communication, rather than on the protocols of formal scholarship.

When the first drafts of these narratives were completed, they were shared among all the writers, and the participants were brought together in a conference to offer critiques, suggestions, and clarifications, and to work toward achieving greater coherence and meaning in the overall set of presentations. This conference took place at the University of North Carolina in Chapel Hill in May of 1997, under the good offices of Dean Emeritus John Turner of the School of Social Work, who acquired funding from the Smith Richardson Foundation and co-chaired the event. Faculty and students of the School attended, as well as a few other invitees, including Florence Stier and Preston Wilcox, whose remarks made a valuable contribution to the quality of the discussion.

I believe that rooting the narratives in specific events and social missions has immense value for a book on practice intervention. But it could also lead to a melange of encapsulated battlefield stories. To guard against this, I have asked scholars from several allied disciplines to provide analytic commentaries across the presentations—"reflections on the reflections"—in order to objectify and enrich the dialogue. These reactive commentaries are through the lenses of a political scientist (Clarke), a community psychologist (Fawcett), a historian and social work educator (Fisher), and a sociologist (Zald). Also, a mid-career community organization educator and practitioner (Gutiérrez) responded to the reflections, offering the outlook—and a view toward the future—of someone currently active in the field. These commentaries are scholarly treatments that integrate and expand the pool of ideas, drawing on diverse theoretical perspectives.

In remarks in his chapter, Austin states that social workers have operated in an atmosphere of "intellectual isolation" within the profession, and tend "to talk only with others who are part of our conceptual community." Such separation can close out both criticism and creativity, and stymie self-improvement and professional advancement. I hope that the commentaries on the reflections serve as an antidote to the insularity about which Austin warns us.

CONTENT

In format, following the two introductory chapters that set the stage in Part 1, there will be the narrative reflections, which comprise Part 2 and are the core of the book. Then, in Part 3, there follow the five responsive commentaries that seek to bring special meaning, from diverse vantage points, to the reflective pieces.

I visualize the core reflective papers in two dimensions that serve to provide a structure and a conceptual frame for readers. The first dimension concerns the varied *domains* of endeavor of the authors, such as practice, the profession as an organized system, and university training. The second refers to the key *themes and issues* that the authors dealt with in their narratives. Using these two dimensions, I will shine a spotlight on the reflections from distinct angles and illuminate them differently. Further, and different, ways of seeing and interpreting the reflective narratives flow from the subsequent analyses of the commentators.

On setting the stage, this first introductory chapter discusses the reflections with reference to the structure of the book; the second introductory chapter places the reflections in their historical context, delineating the political and economic parameters and long-term social currents that helped shape the actions described in the reflections.

Domains

The types of endeavor that the authors engaged in are varied and distinctive. But they also cluster within four domains. One domain focuses on strategies and programs employed to impact community problems. A second, while also concerned with practice, is best seen as addressing the wider social and economic context surrounding intervention. A third involves effort directed at advancing the professional underpinnings of the field—its theoretical foundations and the professional association that reflects and represents social work. The final domain involves professional preparation for this field—or calling—particularly establishing and managing graduate education. These domains provide a conceptual frame, and also the basic outline, for the autobiographical reflections.

The discussion of domains can be visualized with ease in this way:

Strategies and Programs
    Advocacy and Social Action
    Neighborhood and Community Development
    Rational Planning on Concrete Problems
The Broader Context of Practice
The Organized Professional System
Academic Programs and Professional Training

Strategies and Programs

Within the first domain, the authors of the reflections deal with a range of problems, including poverty, delinquency, housing, urban redevelopment, health, and others. But their interventive approaches can be placed roughly into three categories of action: advocacy and social change, neighborhood and community development, and rational planning to solve concrete problems. Those who are acquainted with my work will detect here the familiar "Three Models"—a conceptual formulation that has stood me in good stead over the years. It was introduced exactly 30 years ago as of this writing, and I will call upon it once again to reign in practice phenomena that often appear highly disparate and jumbled (Rothman, 1968). The three modalities, as I have stressed in my writings, often overlap and intertwine, and the narratives that follow reflect that reality too.

Advocacy and Social Action. The two pieces involving advocacy are by Brager and Perlman. Brager describes the drive of Mobilization for Youth on the Lower East Side of New York to open up opportunities for poor and minority young people and their families. A range of actions that clearly can be identified as radical or militant were carried out by the program, including rent strikes, confrontations with schools and service agencies, and competition with city officials for control of resources. These initiatives provoked strong counteractions, and Brager details a jarring case study of an agency at the vortex of an abrasive community conflict and under severe stress.

Perlman helped staff Action for Boston Community Development, which aimed at widespread changes in the city of Boston, especially changes in deeply entrenched programs such as the public schools. A key goal was to goad service delivery systems into becoming more responsive to poor and disadvantaged people, or to establish innovative delivery systems outside of the established service network. To achieve this, ABCD employed a combination of bargaining, incentives and political pressure in what can be described as a brand of "advocacy planning" (Davidoff, 1965).

Internal organizational contradictions apparently blunted the change aims of the project. The complex mix of strategies that evolved resulted in a somewhat muted action thrust and end result. Perlman portrays these complications in what I found to be a fascinating and candid dissection of urban political dynamics.

Neighborhood and Community Development. The section on neighborhood work and locality development also has two narratives (as do all the other subparts of the book), one by Turner on bringing together citizens in several Cleveland localities to tackle common problems collaboratively, and the other by Berry on developments in the settlement house movement. Turner's narrative discusses locality-focused practice in two different community settings. He describes a study he conducted of a low-income central city neighborhood council composed of social agencies, religious and educational institutions, indigenous streets clubs, and neighborhood organizations. He also reports his work in the middle-class, multiracial Glenville area. Turner points out some of the difficulties in fostering citizen participation, noting differences among different class groups, but he also acknowledges instances of his success in nurturing grassroots leadership.

The practitioner engaged in neighborhood work, Turner indicates, must often play the part of coach and role model to motivate low-income residents to participate effectively, while serving more as a consultant in middle-income communities. Turner also brings into view wider societal factors that impact and constrain the practice of locality development.

Tracing historical trends in neighborhood work within the settlement house field, Berry shows fluctuations in some basic features of the movement over time: localism, citizen self-help, cooperation and inclusiveness, the worker's enabling role, and a group work emphasis. She brings us into the corrosive controversy surrounding the local community control issue that dominated the field in the sixties, showing its disrupting effects on board governance and agency decision making. An overriding theme here, and in the field generally, is the tension between change and service goals.

Rational Planning on Concrete Problems. Aspects of social planning are highlighted by Spergel and Barry. Spergel recounts his career-long effort to contend with the interrelated problem of delinquency, youth gangs, and drugs, showing how manifestations of this problem changed over time. His intervention approaches, likewise, shifted and expanded in response to these developments. In an informative and compelling way, Spergel describes these programmatic changes and his rationale for making them. Accounts of the bumpy road he encountered in trying to coordinate relevant community institutions are absorbing. A constant theme, and I think a most valuable one, is his consistent use of research to understand the focal problem, with the application of empirical findings in a systematic way to design subsequent intervention plans.

Barry also relied heavily on data in her work. Most of her career was in the health and welfare planning field, with a strong emphasis on health issues. She gives a vivid and layered description of the planning process in connection with the Health Goals Project of the Cleveland Community Planning Federation, for which she provided staff service. A crucial feature of the project was drawing on the technical input of highly informed health experts from around the country. As in several of the other reflections, Barry tells of her professional transition from group work to community organization.

The Broader Context of Practice

Community Organization concentrates on the local social space where people ordinarily function on a daily basis, and where they can fairly easily interact with one another (Warren, 1972). But in a highly interdependent society and global economic system, locally based systems are impacted by wider potent forces. Both Cloward and Piven, and Austin, identify some of these forces. The Cloward and Piven piece highlights political power and its operations, especially with regard to poor people and their chances for improving their lives. They discuss the nature of electoral politics, including electoral stability, the cohesion of dominant political coalitions, and the effects on power elites of destabilizing events, such as economic crises, mass civil disobedience, and widespread industrial strikes.

Austin takes us along on a longitudinal tour of his professional life, including his actions at the local, state, and national levels. He observes at every stage that broad macro influences played a determining part in the programs he was able to mount and the results he was able to achieve. In his view, racial and ethnic considerations were the dominant factors in his practice. Segregated housing patterns, racial animosities, rapidly changing neighborhoods, inner-city economic decline, and biased employment practices all come into view as conditions and deterrents in his work.

The Organized Professional System

A profession requires a theoretical base to guide it intellectually and to gain legitimacy and an aura of competency with the public. It also needs an organizational base to do its collective business and garner resources. In this section, I discuss the former and Alexander the latter. In my piece, I outline theoretical developments in community organization, beginning with writers such as Pray and Newstetter, who were significant at the time I entered the field in the early fifties. I then look back to earlier important contributors, such as Lindeman and Steiner, and to later scholars such as Ross,

Specht, and Brager. The overall trend in scholarship, I show, is toward greater complexity, specificity and sophistication over time.

Alexander, who was executive secretary of NASW during a pivotal period in its development, describes his thinking and his involvements in rebuilding the organization. He entered into his position at a time of crisis, when the organization was in financial stress and under severe criticism from many sides. His role was that of a community organizer in a formal organization context, using the NASW as an action system to represent and enable the broader professional community of social workers. Alexander's approach and tactical actions make a fascinating story that has not been reported elsewhere.

Academic Programs and Professional Training

As in other practicing social professions, such as urban planning and nursing, educational preparation was located initially in organizational and community settings where the practice was taking place (McGlothlin, 1960). Social agencies were the original source for equipping social workers, and gradually the training moved into higher education circles. Social casework became the focus of such training, and only later did community organization obtain some solid footing.

Schwartz describes the process involved in establishing the first contemporary two-year specialization at the University of Pittsburgh. He sets forth the rationale he used to justify the program and describes the curriculum structure that he put in place. Of special note is his discussion of field instruction issues and developments, and also his use of his own practice and consulting experiences to enrich his teaching. Schwartz also details his work in disseminating this program to other schools around the country.

In some ways, community organization education has had a shaky place in schools of social work. It is outside of the more traditional and dominant clinical practice culture, and it needs to contend for acceptance and support in an often unsympathetic environment. On the other hand, community organization students are often volatile and challenging, bringing their critical view of established institutions and their propensity to seek structural change to bear on the educational institution providing their training. The Berkeley situation characterizes such student unrest and protest, and Kramer rises to the task of constructing (or reconstructing) this case study—portraying the issues, events, and consequences of the Berkeley experience with CO education.

Enduring Themes and Critical Issues

We now move on to the second dimension that I am using to integrate and interpret the reflections. There is a series of significant themes and issues running through these narratives, sometimes reiterated by several different authors, sometimes brought forward in a single reflection. These themes are at the heart of the book, for they constitute underlying philosophical and strategic concerns that have challenged CO practitioners in the past, and will tug at them in the future. Let us revisit the reflections, this time using a different spotlight—one that illuminates them from a thematic perspective.

The Limits of Advocacy

The first theme in this section, introduced by Brager, considers the tactics, demands and risks of social action, using the Mobilization for Youth experience as a case study. It reveals the propensity of power elites to respond in force when threatened, and the kinds of pressures they can apply to thwart social advocacy.

Mobilization focused on opening opportunities for low-income youth and for residents of poor communities. This involved confronting obstacles standing in the way of this advance, including institutions blocking needed improvements in education, housing, employment, and law enforcement. For example, mobilization staff aided residents in carrying grievances to school officials, to police precincts having abusive officers, and concerning slum landlords, and also helped to develop leadership skills among residents so they themselves could demand redress of their grievances.

Predictably, there was a reaction from establishment groups. The city government, heads of institutional areas like schools and the police, and the right-wing press became alarmed over this grassroots empowerment, and all combined to clamp down on the action thrust. Mobilization staff were publicly and vociferously labeled as subversives engaged in such dubious acts as distributing incendiary leaflets, fomenting rent strikes, and promoting racial disorder. Opponents called for a political means test for all staff members, which, at bottom, would weed out those most committed to the militancy and neutralize the others. A special counsel was appointed by the board chairman to examine staff backgrounds, and the City Department of Investigation also undertook an inquiry. While the agency fought back—by lobbying influentials, holding rallies, and conducting a petition drive—these efforts were not sufficient to overcome the virulence of the onslaught.

Change advocates have to keep in mind that elites will lash out when they perceive that their interests are challenged and that these forces have the will and power to use punishing hardball tactics. I think a key lesson is that activists, to the greatest degree possible, need to calculate the strength of these potential counterattacks, and to assess their own ability to defend against them. Having said this, it is also obvious that social action inherently has political ramifications that cannot be predicted precisely, and that risk is a constant companion of strong advocacy that imperils the status quo.

Brager's review brings us to the issue of the kinds of goals that are possible in advocacy organizations. Perlman frames the issue specifically in terms of idealistic goals versus practical realities, and makes this the central theme of his narrative. He connects the personal and the public domains, linking his professional goals back to his own values, derived from his family background, college influences, union participation, and experiences in World War II. This resulted in an overriding personal commitment to social justice, which drove his professional actions.

The dynamics of the goals/realities dilemma is portrayed through Perlman's experience in Action for Boston Community Development (ABCD). The aims of the program were ambitious, involving large-scale changes in the pattern of service delivery in Boston in order to advance the interests of poor and minority populations. Based on his own assessment of the results, and analyses of the program by others in several scholarly reviews, Perlman feels that ABCD did not live up to its intentions. In part, this shortfall resulted from the conflicting expectations of funders and sponsors of the program. There were also differences between the funders and local groups. Ultimately, the organization may have lacked the legitimacy and mandate needed for its far-reaching undertaking.

In retrospect, Perlman feels that his expectations were unrealistic and even simplistic. He underestimated the complexity of the problems and the resistance that would be generated. He did not, he says, take into account the degree of political competition that would be generated. Process considerations involving representations and participation may have been given too much sway. A key point Perlman makes is that significant change takes substantial time, and that substantial outcomes can accrue only in the long run.

This issue is complex because setting goals that are too small may result in overly narrow gains, while pursuing goals that are too grand may lead to frustration and defeatism. Morris and Binstock (1966) take the position that goals involve neither "a utopian scheme" nor "affirmation of the status quo," but need to conform to the criterion of feasibility. Brager suggests a useful principle here: Push the parameters of the feasible resolutely to the maximum achievable end point. I like the name Michael Harrington (1989) gave to this strategic notion—*visionary gradualism*.

Social Changes Versus Social Services

There has been a historic debate in community organization, and in social work generally, about whether the profession should focus on changing detrimental social conditions or providing aid to those absorbing the "slings and arrows" of societal default. In a landmark argument in 1929,

Porter Lee posed the question in the rather either/or terms of "cause" versus "function." He asked whether social work should pursue reformist causes or carry out traditional professional function in an orderly society—that of helping individuals and families live a better life.

The functionalist position, in Lee's view, is correlated with the high road of professionalism, and the alternative with zealous political movements (see Lee, 1937). In their scathing and impassioned critique in *Unfaithful Angels*, Specht and Courtney (1994) chastise social work for largely abandoning the reformist path and going overboard for micro-ameliorative practices, in particular psychotherapy.

I saw some of these issues unfolding in Turner's account of his activities and observations in neighborhood councils. On the one hand, he describes a series of modest local successes, but, on the other, he writes of limited results emanating from broader social forces that his projects did not engage. Most of the council efforts brought about small improvements in the immediate life circumstances of residents: obtaining a new corner traffic light, achieving some reduction in juvenile crime and disruption, gaining access to city functionaries, achieving greater civic assertiveness, confidence and conviviality among residents. Turner describes one council as serving as a form of civic "800" number for registering complaints about city services, which were then brought by council officers to the attention of public officials.

These were important benefits for the local people, Turner feels, but the program and the service enhancements it achieved did not have a critical impact on the group status of the poor or minorities, or on their material conditions relative to housing, education, and employment. In his view, something acts to keep minorities locked into second-class citizenship and to keep the poor remaining poor. That something is embedded in corporate and political policies outside the purview of the neighborhood. Turner believes that upgrading local city services and social agency programs through typical neighborhood council actions can improve the lives of residents in various ways, and is a valuable contribution; nevertheless, this leaves a largely untouched backlog of need and inequity. Berry addresses this question from a vantage point providing greater scope. She served for over a decade as the executive director of the National Federation of Settlements, historically the major impetus and voice for neighborhood organizing and citizen participation in the United States.

From its earliest days, the settlement house movement had a duality of purpose. The movement initiated varied helping services in poor neighborhoods: It brought neighbors together to get to know each other better; established clinics, milk stations, and nursing services; opened kindergartens and libraries; and created programs for teaching citizenship skills. At the same time, settlements spearheaded legislation outlawing child labor, improving housing conditions for the poor, upgrading public sanitation—and birthing the federal Children's Bureau.

In different time periods, one or the other of these tendencies predominated. Beginning in the twenties, after the pioneering stalwarts of social advocacy had passed on, a more conservative mode developed. Technicians replaced muckrakers and concentrated on institution building through improving the administration, financing, and staffing of settlements and neighborhood centers. After World War II and into the fifties, group workers flooded the field, focusing on furthering the personal development of clients and inculcating the skills of democratic living. The settlement field in this period also became absorbed with the micro issues of multiproblem families, the aging, and hard-to-reach youth.

The sixties brought a sharp swing in direction. The civil rights movement, urban protests, and OEO (Office of Economic Opportunity) programming placed a renewed emphasis on neighborhoods. The settlements were already there and in the thick of it. In this situation, local minority groups and urban activists pushed neighborhood centers hard toward tactical militancy and structural change aims. In countervailing fashion, their funders in Community Chests/United Ways steered them in the direction of conventional social services, as did the nonpolitical requirements of their tax exemption status. In this ferment, searing ideological cleavages within the movement froze the staff into continuing debate and turmoil.

A mandate to go in one or other of these directions, Berry feels, is a false choice. Reform is a necessary objective, and at the same time Band-Aid services are valid when a Band-Aid is needed. Perlman comments on the basic dilemma by recognizing "the difficulty of combining these…and the difficulty of separating them." In Berry's view, changing society and aiding individuals are simply two sides of the same coin.

To me, this position seems reasonable and persuasive. But I detect within it a dilemma that has to be watched. Social workers and humanists are drawn naturally to relieving the tangible hardships and discomforts suffered by individuals. And that service inclination, over time, can have a long-term—largely unseen—corrosive effect on the impetus for reform.

Berry believes that incremental change is what is possible and desirable, and, as an example, holds that during times of agonizing and dangerous urban agitation, such as rioting, the proper role is to calm the waters and prevent harm to innocents. As we shall see later, Cloward and Piven take a drastically different position on this.

The Scope and Methods of Planning

Planning is a prominent feature of contemporary society, used both to bring about deliberate, controlled change and to keep ongoing community programs and processes on a stable, orderly course. There is a strong rationalistic tone to modern planning (Simon, 1957), which leads to a comprehensive cast to the design of plans, as well as the systematic use of research data to guide their development (Friedmann, 1987).

I see these elements, in the narratives of Spergel and Barry. Spergel depicts his early activities in working with street gangs, where he started out by emphasizing a personalistic approach through group work, counseling, and efforts to foster individual development on the part of group members. Over time, he began to realize that gang-related acting out behavior did not merely comprise the antisocial tendencies of youth, but was linked to surrounding societal and community influences. Indeed, gang delinquency was an indicator of the defects of various social institutions and arrangements, and gang structures, to some degree, were improvised mechanisms to substitute for more legitimate instrumentalities that were missing or failing.

As he proceeded, Spergel began to involve a range of relevant entities in collaborative planning on the problem: schools, the police, business and employment organizations, the courts, and human service agencies. He also engaged indigenous community groups, such as neighborhood councils, churches, and civic associations. Teamwork in providing and planning services became salient, including the combining of social control and youth development approaches.

Community organization was essential in this, and in opening up new opportunities for youth. Spergel's strategy went from a rather narrow, single-factor approach to one that was much more complex and holistic. As I mentioned earlier, research data were generated and applied throughout to modify the design of plans.

A different aspect of planning is portrayed in Barry's exposition. In her work with the Cleveland Federation for Community Planning, the design of health services was a central focus. Her experiences took place in the sixties and seventies, at a time when community planning in the social work field, historically, was undergoing a pronounced change.

Community planning councils, most often affiliated with Chest/United Way agencies, typically engaged in a rather parochial and low-keyed kind of operation. Those organizations, I personally observed at the time, ordinarily confined themselves to the programs of voluntary agencies that were members of the Chest, without involving the large public sector in any appreciable way. Much of their effort was given over to coordination and information sharing among these private agencies. In many councils, considerable time was devoted to reviewing individual social agency programs in connection with budget hearings and the allocation of funds within the Chest. The scope was restricted and the planning methods were rudimentary.

In her work, Barry developed a health goals model that was highly sophisticated and data-rich. It encompassed broad multisector planning, with a focus on the problem as manifested in the community, rather than a focus on agencies and their programmatic preoccupations. A rigorous conceptual frame was constructed for categorizing health components and for drawing conclusions based, as she says, "upon predictable results from the application of knowledge and experience."

The staff systematically invoked expertise, nationally and internationally. Thirty health areas were delineated, and 29 position papers were commissioned from technical experts worldwide to illuminate the targeted health areas factually. In addition, a survey was conducted to develop an empirical profile of the health system in the local area.

The resulting findings were reviewed by panels involving 339 community professionals, academics, and citizens. The project resulted in a series of program spin-offs in such areas as aging, alcoholism, and dental health. The Cleveland experience influenced health planning nationally, and was a stimulus for moving social work community planning in a more adequate and rigorous direction.

These examples illustrate social work's engagement in comprehensive and research-based planning. However, not all planning theorists favor a highly rationalistic approach. Rittel and Webber (1973) believe that, in the contemporary world, rationalism in planning is too rigid and unrealistic a concept. This is because planning has to confront "wicked problems," not neat and well-defined ones that bow to closely reasoned plan designs. Therefore, they believe, planning has to be ad hoc, incremental, flexible, and sensitive to political conflict and rancor.

In my view, this position has a great deal of merit. But we need to take into account the particular starting point in the professional field we are discussing. In social work—where community planning was often elementary, constricted, and intensely attuned to process concerns—I believe the movement toward increased technical precision and broader scope had a balancing influence at the time. Continuing discretion must be used to keep the balance right.

Times and Conditions for Social Change

The writings of Cloward and Piven, and of Austin, are consistent with views of Rittel and Webber about the politically charged—and "wicked"—character of the change process. This perspective on disorderliness in the politics of social policy is detailed graphically by Weir (1992). Cloward and Piven in their analysis focus on the nature of those times when significant change is possible, indicating that these periods come rarely and in irregular historical cycles, and Austin reports from the front lines on the conflictual political, economic, and racial environment impinging on change efforts.

According to the Cloward and Piven analysis, meaningful change in favor of the poor came only twice in this century, within five-year time spans—one in the midst of the depression and the other during the civil rights revolution and urban upheavals of the sixties. In their view, political and economic elites yield power and make concessions only when faced with conditions they cannot control: urban riots, industrial strike waves, civil disobedience, rent strikes—events producing discord on a mass scale—sufficient to evoke a sense of crisis and the breakdown of key institutions. Normative community organizing and electoral campaigning efforts do not create such pressures for change; rather, significant transformations require "disruptive dissensus."

During such unstable periods, the authors advise, change agents ought to mobilize people in a way that feeds and furthers the turmoil. During other periods, more typical community organizing should be carried out to keep alive both hope for the future and the ideal of social justice, which provides a base for disruptive mobilization.

In Austin's narrative, I found some points of compatibility with the writing of Cloward and Piven. For example, in his research on developments in Ford Foundation urban projects, Austin discovered that *contested* change campaigns that "pushed the envelope" relative to the prevailing consensus were often more effective in achieving such things as school integration than were *uncontested* change initiatives. In his research on War on Poverty programs of community action, he concluded that only where confrontation took place between residents of low-income neighborhoods and established institutions did citizen participation spark discernable improvements in the local pattern of discrimination and poverty. Obviously, the contextual factors that Austin emphasizes matter a great deal, but, as these results suggest, so do choices made by organizers about advocacy actions, choices often involving risk and uncertainty.

Austin identifies some of the contextual forces that he found were critical in affecting and shaping the results of his work at the local level: "the political economy of the larger arena, including presidential politics, political struggles around race and control of education at the city level, the influence of national foundations like the Ford Foundation, the impact of the south to north migration of Afro-American families, the impact of urban renewal within cities, and the pervasive impact of economics on neighborhood reality." Political power analysis, he concluded, was a more important strategizing tool than rationalistic needs assessment surveys.

The Tension Between Building the Professional Association and Building CO Theory

The pair of narratives by Alexander and me can be analyzed from the standpoint of the sociology of the professions. All professions need a body of knowledge to legitimate and guide their functions in society, and they need a professional association to represent and protect their interests

(Abbot, 1990; Larson, 1977). These components are most often in harmony, but sometimes they can be out of kilter.

In my discussion of the development of the theoretical and intellectual base in community organization, I point out some of the sticking points and conceptual shifts in the evolution of CO theory over time. Early practitioner/thinkers such as Jane Addams emphasized activism and social reform. Some later theorists gave weight to balancing community needs and resources, to coordinating agency programs, and to using a nondirective intervention mode. These theorists decried political involvements and militant advocacy for being unduly rancorous and lacking in professional decorum.

A good deal of energy has gone into making CO theory cognitively compatible with social work, which in practical terms meant consistency with the dominant casework perspective. Over time this changed, a multimodel CO paradigm gained acceptance, and casework itself followed by embracing a variety of approaches to practice beyond Freud.

Shifting to Alexander, he indicates that for NASW, organizational development became a vital necessity as a financial and operational crisis emerged in the early sixties. He describes a series of actions he took to resuscitate the association, using organizational development and community organization tools as a means of revitalizing the association, and through it, the broader social work functional community.

In a situation wracked with dissension, Alexander found ways to facilitate communication and cooperation among divergent elements. By bringing the membership back to founding principles and to agreed-upon priorities, he helped establish a sense of order and direction. Alexander takes us through the steps he used in strengthening the board of directors, staff performance, membership services, professional standards, and community outreach.

I detect an interesting point of tension in these two presentations. Alexander assumes the merit of the association as a given, as well as its significance in supporting all divisions of practice, including CO. In my piece, I point out some negative features of the tie between Community Organization and the social work profession: CO's marginal position in the profession as a perplexing and rambunctious stepchild; its constant struggle to gain legitimacy and resources; and the strain to put CO theory into the mold of overriding clinical theory—in turn patterned after psychoanalytic theory.

I think macro practice subordination is symbolized by the profession's conception of clinical practice as "direct service" (to individuals and families), and macro practice's designation as "indirect service." My CO colleagues, though, generally view themselves as giving *direct service* to communities—enhancing the community's cohesion, problem-solving competency, institutional relations, and public attitudes. The endeavor to conceptualize CO practice roles does not benefit from needing to be filtered always through the individualized service lens.

On my part, I ruminate about letting CO be CO in its intellectual endeavors, and ask whether CO interests might better be served in an organizational setting outside of NASW, and an academic climate outside of CSWE. Note that clinical practitioners have set up their own federation to pursue what they view as their best interests.

Educational Innovation and Change in Graduate Community Practice Training

The narratives by Schwartz and Kramer are case studies in educational innovation and change in university settings (Cameron, 1984; Rothman, 1987), and reflect processes in the field of organizational innovation generally (Zaltman, Duncan, and Holbeck, 1984). Schwartz reports on his role in instituting the first contemporary two-year specialization in CO at the University of Pittsburgh, and Kramer recounts the tumultuous events at Berkeley that shook and transformed the school.

In my view, the literature on innovation gives us the best window for understanding why the pioneering two-year specialization took hold in the Pittsburgh situation, and how it spread. For example, we know that a forceful executive committed to innovation is a facilitating element, and, at Pittsburgh, Wilbur Newstetter—decidedly a strong dean—favored the new program, putting his influence firmly behind it. Also, organizations that have innovated successfully in the past are those that are more likely to undertake further innovation. Pittsburgh, it happens, had been a major center for pathbreaking group work curriculum development. Consistent with validated innovation practices, Schwartz used materials and entreaties that were clearly communicated and in tune with the language and culture of the group (social work/casework) that the innovator is seeking to win over.

The literature points to the significant role, in successful diffusion, of a champion of innovation, a single individual devoted to propagating a new idea or program. Schwartz promoted the two-year specialization at numerous national and state social work professional and educational organizations, on agency boards, in committees, through consulting with schools of social work, and in endless discussions, including formal talks and papers on 33 separate occasions over a three-year period.

Schwartz states it pointedly in his narrative: "I publicized CO up and down the country and circulated our curriculum materials to any school of social work that requested it. I published a number of articles in a variety of journals, and believe that my efforts may have led to the certification of the two-year CO curriculum by the CSWE." This is obviously a graphic depiction of the champion-of-innovation concept in action.

The literature makes it clear that innovations are not always accepted en toto and for all time. A process of reinvention and transformation frequently occurs, and this is dramatized in Kramer's review of the experience at Berkeley. He indicates that initially the CO program was viewed as "pioneering and innovative," but, as we know, for a novel initiative in an organization to take hold, it must be viewed by members as compatible with its culture.

The CO program at Berkeley took on a social action flavor that was extremely militant and used highly disruptive tactics. What the Berkeley experience illustrates, it seems to me, is that an educational program that includes excessively militant tactics cannot be sustained in a university setting, and especially when the tactics are turned against faculty members and the university itself.

Universities are generally conservative in nature, using normative procedures for discourse and change that are deliberative, genteel, and slow-paced. When a university-sponsored entity propagates highly radical and abrasive actions—as opposed to ideas—either inside or outside of the institution, there is a culture clash that "pushes the envelope" too far, and makes continuation of the program untenable. In a sense, this narrative may be a counterpart to Brager's discourse: Brager deals with the limits of militancy in the community context; Kramer treats the limits of militancy in the university context.

What seems to have happened here is that a macro concentration featuring a militant social action form of CO self-destructed, then shifted and reconstituted itself as a macro program featuring the social planning component of CO coupled with administration. This is not rare, for, in my experience, CO exists in varied forms currently in schools of social work, including, among others: CO as a stand-alone specialization; CO as grassroots practice in combination with planning; CO as grassroots practice in combination with administration; and CO as planning in combination with administration (the current arrangement at Berkeley). CO also is sometimes blended indistinctly into a macro generic program or an overall generic curriculum.

CSWE in its enrollment statistics lists community practice in three categories: (1) CO and Planning, (2) CO and Planning with Administration/Management, and (3) Direct Practice with CO and Planning (Lennon, 1993). So the forms for CO training are diverse—and irregular—and the possibilities for shifting and reconfiguring, as in the Berkeley case, are multiple. I believe that these sundry and mingled forms of CO representation in schools of social work may result in an underestimation, nationally, of CO presence in the curriculum and student body.

These themes are embedded in individual papers, but not always pinpointed, or put at center stage. The themes emerge in the context of frontline practice demands and obstacles, the personal and professional life histories of the writers, and the press of other ideas that deserve consideration and attention. The commentaries that follow the reflections in the book highlight other themes and construe themes differently. Here, I have given my own take as the editor—ruminations and interpretations that I hope will be useful in their own terms, and which will stimulate in the mind of you, the reader, other ways of organizing and understanding the store of ideas in these documents.

COMMENTARIES ON THE REFLECTIONS

This introduction has centered on the reflections, but I want to discuss the commentaries briefly also. The commentaries in Part 3 examine the actions and concepts in the narratives from the perspectives of different fields of study. The aim is to bring an interdisciplinary framework to the analysis of community intervention, to enrich our understanding of the content of the reflections, and to avoid a professionally insular interpretation of the text.

Clarke speaks as a political scientist, and does us the service of emphasizing the importance of ideas in setting the agenda in community politics. With the contemporary academic focus on the role of power in community affairs, awareness of the power of ideas as a change force can easily get lost. Clarke shows, for example, how ideas from the social sciences contributed to the concept of Mobilization for Youth, and how the implemental ideas in that program stimulated the creation of similar projects elsewhere.

I appreciate Clarke's position and believe change agents should be highly sensitive to the salience of good ideas, for community activists generally are not connected to power centers in society. But through their contacts, experiences, and access to information, they are positioned to generate potent ways of thinking. The vitality of their ideas is one available means for counterbalancing their usual deficit of formal economic and political power. In her analysis Clarke, rightly, indicates that ideas, to be actualized, have to be linked strategically to windows of opportunity, to the response patterns of elites, and to the shifting attitudes of the general public.

Community psychologist Fawcett does us a different kind of service. He draws on the reflections to extract a set of "lessons"—intervention principles or guidelines—that are embedded in the writings. Most of the commentators are attracted enthusiastically to the ideas of the authors, but in my view, Fawcett's concern with practical intervention derivatives makes its own special contribution, particularly in a book that will be used in preparing students for professional practice roles.

Fawcett presents lessons from the reflections under a set of useful rubrics. A few examples will convey the character of the analysis. Under *community context* are these: Multiple practice models are necessary to deal with contextual variations; crosscutting issues are useful; intervention cannot be divorced from politics or conflict. Under *community action and mobilization* we find the following lessons: There are strong leaders even in the most deprived communities; community practitioners should never "get used to" the terrible conditions they see in their work; practice demands often take us beyond what we know and require inventive decisions. Under *intervention and the maintenance of efforts*, lessons include: The strategy has to fit the situation; external support may be a necessity, but also trap that constrains options; organizing requires small interim wins to sustain the effort. While these lessons provide a compendium of answers about what to do in varied practice situations, Fawcett concludes by aptly noting, "...leadership in community work may begin with a *few good questions.*"

Fisher, an urban historian/social work educator, examines a variety of historical issues related to CO in his commentary. "History matters" is his keynote, and he goes on to show why that is so. He treats history in terms of collective memory and context (as I do in the next chapter), but goes beyond that. In his discussion, he views the reflections not merely as memory, but as a record of history-in-the-making. In this connection, he focuses on power as a critical variable in producing change, balancing off Clarke's endorsement of the importance of ideas.

Fisher devotes the bulk of his commentary to the concept of history as context, particularly the contextual influence of national events and trends on local programs. He illustrates this in detail through a description of the particular growth of community development corporations (CDCs) in the contemporary conservative political climate. Fisher also usefully locates specific reflections in specific contexts, according to factors such as geography, class, race, and gender.

Zald applies the tools of sociological analysis to dissect and reconceptualize the narratives, leaning on theoretical notions from the sociology of the professions and organizational behavior. Several points particularly caught my attention in his multifaceted and penetrating interpretations. Zald identifies the reflection authors as the second generation in instituting social work in university settings. This cohort leaned more heavily on research and theory than the previous one, which rooted its teaching in wisdom garnered from practice. At the same time, Zald conjectures, social science may offer less to a practice-oriented field like this than "a relentlessly problem-oriented approach" that scans all possible sources of intelligence, regardless of their academic "fashionableness."

Zald takes note, correctly, I think, of the widespread growth of community organizing programs that are run and staffed by indigenous racial, ethnic, and special-interest groups. Most of these fall outside of the field of social welfare and the profession of social work. The skills required in these programs, he contends, can best be learned in the neighborhood and on the street. For this reason, grassroots advocacy may not overlap very much with social work, and from the standpoint of grassroots organizations, Zald states, "the MSW in CO may look increasingly irrelevant" in the future. I encountered several other provocative analyses in his discussion that I believe will generate further deliberation and debate among scholars and practitioners.

The final commentary, and the concluding article in the book, is by a current midcareer educator and practitioner, Lorraine Gutiérrez. Her contribution is distinctive and well placed in the book, in that her essay drives our discourse forward to the future. She gives attention to emerging trends and issues in CO practice. Among the developments she foresees are the devolution of programs and services from the federal to the state and local level, with its potential for community-based planning; increased inequality in our society, with its implications for advocacy and economic opportunity actions; and a more multicultural composition of our society, with its relevance to "ethnic agency" programming and cross-cultural coalition-building.

Gutiérrez predicts increased CO involvement in the child welfare field, and in the creation of community-based collaboratives in areas such as homelessness, community violence, and substance abuse. Other scholars have also outlined prospects for community intervention, especially Wenocur and Soifer (1997), and Khinduka (1996). I was taken by Wenocur and Soifer's vision of a national and international data base of community organizing efforts.

Several of the commentary authors, in keeping with the flavor of the book, included autobiographical material in order to share with readers the origins of their thinking and the influences that shaped them. However, their presentations are by design solidly academic in character, and abundantly referenced, using standard bibliographic form (ASA). The reflections, although memoirs and less referenced, use the same bibliographic form, with the inclusion of endnotes in addition to the bibliography when appropriate. (There are two exceptions among the reflections, the Cloward and Piven and Rothman pieces, where the narrative calls for heavy documentation. In those instances, endnote numbering is used throughout the text so that the narrative flow is not broken up by frequent author/date notations.)

CONCLUDING REMARKS

I started the chapter rather glumly, decrying the conservative and right-wing climate hanging over us today and obstructing progressive causes.

When we are in the middle of one of these epochs, it feels as though there will be no end—that it will go on forever. But the truth is that there are zigzagging cycles in human affairs: A revolutionary period inevitably is followed by a reactionary one, and a conservative era always, over time, gives way to a reformative one. Usually some combination of a disruption in the political economy together with organized advocacy brings about these transformations. The Great Depression and the growth of trade union activism were a large part of what led into the New Deal; the physical and economic breakdown of the inner city together with concerted civil rights militancy gave rise to the Great Society programs. Cloward and Piven speak of these matters in their piece, and the next chapter of the book specifically treats historical forces and trends.

When I began my practice career in 1951, it was a time of conformity, complacency, and inquisitory terror. McCarthyism was rampant in the land, bludgeoning any voices proposing even mildly liberal initiatives. Speaking up for pro-black or pro-union positions during that Cold War delirium put you in serious jeopardy of being labeled a Communist and a subversive, with repercussions of losing your job and career, your legitimacy, and your good name. Invasive loyalty oaths were widespread, together with blacklists and invidious informal scrutinizing and screening methods at the workplace and in community groups.

At that time, my friend's sister, who had been a Communist Party member and was also a competent and responsible social worker employed by the city government, felt compelled to dispose of her personal library, without burning the books. She beseeched me to take some of her left-wing volumes. That's how I acquired a copy of *Das Kapital* as well as some other classic writings by Marx and similar dissent philosophers and social critics.

After weighing the proposition intently, I had decided to take a chance on this because, while I held socialist beliefs—nondoctrinaire in character—my "bourgeois" commitment to liberal political democracy kept me apart from involvements with the Communist camp. But it was a risky thing to do, and there were a lot of other things that I was careful to avoid risking—signing certain petitions, or joining groups I didn't know much about. Young people today would find it utterly impossible—and unreal—to comprehend the degree of fear abroad in the nation about freely expressing progressive ideas.

Still, within a ten-year period, a powerful civil rights revolution had begun, the student movement was stirring, and John Kennedy had defeated Red-hunting Richard Nixon for the presidency and, with his brother Robert, was mapping innovative urban programs for the poor. A measure of optimism, I would say, is not a totally irrational trait, especially when it is combined with a resolve to make good things happen.

The dilemma I described about accepting books illustrates how the history of the times generates a climate enveloping our thinking, and how that is tightly interwoven with the actions we take (personally and professionally), or opt not to take. In this chapter, my endeavor has been to set the stage for your reading of the reflections by erecting a conceptual scaffolding for navigating the different domains and themes. To complete that endeavor, I am convinced, it is important also to put in place the historical backdrop, which is accomplished in the next chapter.

BIBLIOGRAPHY

Abbot, Andrew. 1990. *The System of Professions: An Essay on the Division of Expert Labor*. Chicago: The University of Chicago Press.

Berkhofer, R. 1995. *Beyond the Great Story: History as Text and Discourse*. Cambridge, MA: Harvard University Press.

Cameron, K. S. 1984. "Organizational Adaption and Higher Education." *Journal of Higher Education* 54, 359–380.

Davidoff, Paul. 1965. "Advocacy and Pluralism in Planning." *Journal of the American Institute of Planners* (November), 31(4):331–338.

Friedman, John. 1987. *Planning in the Public Domain: From Knowledge to Action*. Princeton, NJ: Princeton University Press.

Harrington, Michael. 1989. *Socialism: Past and Future*. New York: Arcade Publishing.

Khinduka, Shanti. 1996. "Community Service—Today and Tomorrow." Keynote address presented at 1995 Midwest Deans & Directors Leadership Retreat at the Mandel School of Applied Social Sciences, Case Western Reserve University, Cleveland, OH.

Larson, Magali Sarfatti. 1977. *The Rise of Professionalism: A Sociological Analysis*. Berkeley: University of California Press.

Lee, Porter R. 1937. *Social Work as Cause and Function and Other Papers*. New York: Columbia University Press.

Lennon, Todd M. 1993. *Statistics on Social Work Education in the United States: 1993*. Alexandria, VA: Council on Social Work Education.

McGlothlin, William J. 1960. *Patterns of Professional Education*. New York: G. P. Putnam's Sons.

Morris, Robert, and Robert H. Binstock. 1966. *Feasible Planning for Social Change*. New York: Columbia University Press.

Rittel, Horst, and Melvin M. Webber. 1973. "Dilemmas in a General Theory of Planning." *Political Sciences* (June), 4(2):155–169.

For their helpful reading of the drafts of the introductory chapters I would like to thank Robert Fisher, Judy Rothman, Jon Sager, Leonard Schneiderman, and Harry Wasserman.

Rothman, Jack. 1968. "Three Models of Community Organization Practice," from National Conference on Social Welfare. *Social Work Practice*. New York: Columbia University Press.

Rothman, Jack. 1987. "Disseminating Curriculum Innovations Among Schools of Social Work." In *The Chronically Mentally Ill in Rural Areas: Model Curricula for Social Work Education*, edited by M. P. Keenan. Washington, DC: The Council on Social Work Education.

Simon, Herbert A. 1957. *Models of Man: Social and Rational*. New York: John Wiley & Sons.

Specht, Harry, and Mark E. Courtney. 1994. *Unfaithful Angels: How Social Work Has Abandoned Its Mission*. New York: The Free Press.

Steinberg, Stephen. 1995. *Turning Back*. Boston: Beacon Press.

Weir, Margaret. 1992. *Politics and Jobs*. Princeton, NJ: Princeton University Press.

Vidich, Arthur J., Joseph Bensman, and Maurice R. Stein. 1964. *Reflections on Community Studies*. New York: John Wiley & Sons.

Warren, Roland L. 1972. *The Community in America*. Chicago: Rand McNally & Company.

Wenocur, Stanley, and Steven Soifer. 1997. "Prospects for Community Organization." In *Social Work in the 21st Century*, edited by Michael Reisch and Eileen Gambrill. Thousand Oaks, CA: Pine Forge Press.

Zaltman, G., R. Duncan, and J. Holbeck. 1984. *Innovations & Organizations* (1st ed., 1973). Malabar, FL: Robert E. Kreiger Publishing Co.

Historical Context in Community Intervention

Jack Rothman

The authors of the reflections did the bulk of their work in the time period between the end of World War II and the early 1970s, although some began their careers prior to the war, and others have been professionally vigorous to this moment. Nevertheless, the narratives concentrate on actions in the decade of the fifties (when most were starting out and having their early, memorable practice experiences) and the sixties (a period of intense activity, excitement, and perplexity). I will focus on that time frame in this historical review.

History, if you think about it, can be two things. It can be memory of events and acts, and it can be an analysis of the context of these events. I picture historical memory as the story of what happened in a particular place at a particular time, usually involving people in a struggle with their social and physical environment. The reflections in this book are such a story, or chapters of the story. They provide an institutional memory of a very important epoch in the professional history of social work and Community Organization.

The basic themes and issues that the authors highlight in their stories are generic and timeless. They are at the core of this project. But they take on a different coloration in different temporal contexts, and need to be understood from that standpoint.

These narratives resemble the stuff of oral history archives, but because the participants are highly literate, and articulate authors, the documents are in written form. This kind of institutional memory provides a record for recall, a source for extracting learnings, and a means of identifying heroes and villains. In his commentary, Bob Fisher makes the point that such a collective memory can serve to make people toiling at the cutting edge of dissent and innovation feel less marginal and alone.

As context, and this is the predominant way I will be using history in this discussion, history provides the wider backdrop surrounding the story. It describes the political currents, economic conditions, cultural climate, and environmental circumstances that help shape and explain the story. Hallinan (1998) states the proposition succinctly: "...social behavior is constrained by the context in which it occurs...contextual factors and the actions of individuals interact in a dynamic and reciprocal manner to influence social events" (p. 6). In this case, the authors are human actors—change agents—producing event outcomes in context, or sometimes failing in their efforts to do so.

It is not possible to appreciate the time period in question without taking into account the immediate postwar period. This, of necessity, will be a rough sketch—brief, selective, and somewhat of a montage. Parenthetically, in portions of his book, *Let the People Decide*, Fisher (1984)—one of our reactive commentators—treats the history of the relevant time period cogently, and I will draw on that analysis in this discussion.

I should note that, in outlining the national sociopolitical context, I discovered, rather unexpectedly, that I had to include a substantial description of the wider geopolitical context. I found myself inadvertently drawn into grappling with salient Big Power issues of international scale, and with the connection of these to the local community organization scene.

THE POSTWAR FORTIES

The period immediately following WWII was the most exhilarating time I have lived through. The Great War was over, and from battlefields all around the globe husbands, fathers, and sons, representing virtually every family and neighborhood, were returning home. So were our first-ever servicewomen, who were part of the WACS, WAVES, and SPARS. We had overcome the Fascists, a monstrously evil and omnipotent force, in a devastating and unconditional defeat. Facing what we knew to be a real threat to our survival and values, we worked together—all of us—courageously and with genuine patriotic spirit, to triumph for democracy, and we were proud of ourselves as a nation. Even an entrenched skeptic like Howard

Zinn (1973) designates this one of "America's unquestionably virtuous wars" (p. 7), and Studs Terkel (1984) calls it "The Good War" in his oral history book.

We now set out to build a sane and safe world community, spreading President Roosevelt's Four Freedoms far and wide, with universal peace as the cornerstone of the future. One of the very first public events to take place as the war drew to an end in the spring of 1945 was the creation of the United Nations at a conference in San Francisco.

Within the country, there were challenges and opportunities everywhere. Good-bye to the rationing of eggs, sugar, and gasoline; women could even buy nylon stockings again. Automobiles, put on hold during the war years, were now beginning to spin off the assembly lines, and who wouldn't covet one? Factories also spewed forth washing machines, refrigerators, toasters, and dozens of other appliances that had been displaced by machine guns and ammunition. And people had money to buy these things, for they had been on forced savings during the wartime era of empty shop shelves.

The GI Bill offered a chance to go to college for millions of veterans—myself included—many of whom wouldn't have been able to afford advanced education, and we streamed resolutely into colleges and universities everywhere to make up for lost time. Reunited families, together with a multitude of newlywed families, were desperate for a place to live, and this resulted in an extensive home-building endeavor, both in the cities and in the emerging suburbs. These families would shortly produce a booming supply of babies.

A spirit of idealism and bonhomie was in the air. Black soldiers—together with other minorities—had fought, side by side with whites, the good fight against tyranny abroad, and they were anticipating an upgrade in equality and life chances at home. Many women had aided the war effort by working in factories to make the tanks and shells that spelled victory, many enjoying their new flexibility and pocket money and looking forward to more of the same. Too many of these minority and feminist hopes were to be short-changed in the decade ahead, but at the time they soared.

The compassionate voice of Eleanor Roosevelt was heard widely, perhaps in an even more influential way after the death of her husband. Progressive organizations of many kinds sprouted, including the newly formed American Veterans Committee, which I joined and which challenged the more established and conservative veterans groups. Unions had gained unprecedented strength during the war—including the successful "Operation Dixie" drive in the South—rising by 1945, to a robust force of 15 million members, who were poised to advance the welfare of working people. Before long, a Fair Deal program was proposed by Truman to carry forward key elements of Roosevelt's New Deal.

Overseas, former colonial nations were at last gaining their independence, as exhausted imperial powers such as Britain and France relinquished control. Ghandi, in particular, was an inspiration because of his successful nonviolent campaign to liberate India. The founding of the state of Israel, after the abomination of the holocaust and almost 2,000 years of Jewish exile, was a source of jubilation for Jews and others. Close Allied collaboration during the war led to American–Soviet friendship organizations, and in this atmosphere there was a pluralistic array of progressive political groups, even some having communist or socialist ideas.

Many of the authors of the reflections state that the educational opportunity and ideological inspiration that sprung from this time served to pave their way into social work. Similar to other fields and institutions, social work had come to somewhat of a standstill during the war years, with many social workers in the service, or providing social or emotional support to armed service personnel. In the immediate aftermath, the field was somewhat amorphous and engaged in an effort to rediscover and reconstitute itself. During this period, it focused on training a new cadre of professionals who would shape its future, among them the reflection authors.

Behind the general elation was a specter that would come to dominate and distort social life nationally and on a global scale. When the war ended, there was a sea of devastation everywhere, with two giants standing above it all. Most of Europe and other nations around the world were in ruins physically and economically, and had suffered massive loss of life. However, the United States escaped with little physical damage and few civilian casualties, emerging as an economic behemoth through its wartime role as the "arsenal of democracy." While we quickly dismantled much of our armed forces, the atomic bomb gave us fearsome military might.

The Soviet Union had suffered much of the brunt of the war, with Hitler's ferocious juggernaut rolling over much of the countryside and causing, it is estimated, at least ten million military and civilian fatalities. But the Soviet Union still had an enormous land army as well as dominance over Eastern European countries, and part of Germany, that it had occupied during the fighting. The war had churned up two superpowers, with the United States at the top of the heap.

These two nations did what dominant powers have done throughout history. They tried, out of self-interest, to create spheres of influence, which are basically mechanisms to provide self-defense internally, and to promote the economic exploitation of resources, markets, and labor externally. Using the advantages each had at hand, the Soviet Union relied heavily on blunt military penetration of surrounding nations (supplemented by ideological penetration), while the United States used more subtle and sophisticated economic penetration (also supplemented by ideological penetration). With the distance of an ocean between us and most strategically placed nations, the United States lacked proximate and in-your-face mechanisms of influence, even if it wanted to use them, and pretty much had to depend on indirect leverage.

During the war and immediately afterward, each side tried to bargain for an arrangement that would promote its own interests: For example, the United States argued for a revitalized Germany that would provide markets and constitute a buffer against the Soviets, while the Soviet Union advocated a neutered Germany that would never again be a threat to the East, and would pay heavy reparations for the damage it had done to the Soviet homeland. (The current efforts of the United States to extend NATO almost to the border of the new and enfeebled Russia is a continuation of that kind of Big Power maneuvering.)

At Teheran, Yalta, and Potsdam, intense bargaining took place around sphere-of-influence issues, but the national interests of the parties were at such variance and distrust was so strong that contention and jockeying became institutionalized. There was a steady escalation of conflict leading up to a "Cold War," fueled by a set of moves and countermoves involving, among others, Soviet obstinacy in occupied areas such as Iran and Eastern Europe; a menacing speech by Stalin in early 1946 in which he hinted at the inevitability of war; Churchill's "Iron Curtain" address soon after in Fulton, Missouri; the Truman Doctrine; the Marshall Plan; the Berlin Blockade; and NATO.

The situation is described aptly by Goodman and Gatell (1972):

> So each side, Russia and America (East and West) girded for battle in a Cold War. Each went on the "defensive," convinced that the other was threatening its vital interests. Fear fed fear, and hostility intensified, as Russia adopted a policy of *Consolidation and Probing* and America pursued a policy of *Containment*. The United States regarded any change in the status quo...as a threat to the balance of power, while the Soviet, possessing for the first time the power to act on their fears, would no longer tolerate being surrounded by hostile, capitalist nations. (p. 561)

Both sides rapidly adopted a strategy of drawing lines in the sand, rather than straining for accommodation, each thinking the other fundamentally intractable and deceitful. The strident tone of the Cold War in the United States, as well as its major instrumentalities, I would note, was put in place by the Democrats under Truman, with the bipartisan support of the Republicans. The intense Cold War atmosphere rapidly came to smother the liberalism, fellowship, and openness in American life that had flourished immediately after the war.

Although I have made it sound here as though the Cold War was inevitable, I don't think that's necessarily true. There is evidence that Roosevelt was more disposed to give and take in negotiating with the Soviets than was Churchill or Truman, and more confident about his skills in deal-making with Stalin. We know that the Soviets did withdraw troops from Iran in 1946 when pressed, and kept their pledge not to intervene to aid the Greek rebels. We will never know if Roosevelt could have come to terms with the stolid Stalin, or if Stalin would have stood behind his word. But in the realm of speculation, these are surely possibilities.

THE FIFTIES

The geopolitics of the Cold War fundamentally shaped the social climate of the fifties at home, leading to vast economic growth, together with political repression and conformity. All of this influenced the nature of community organization approaches and programs in that decade. Economic prosperity was the keynote, in the context of an "affluent society," where people sought material benefits and lifestyle advances under the beguiling rule of President Eisenhower. According to Diggins (1988), the American people were "preoccupied with their own lives and largely nonpolitical," the overriding goal being "the pursuit of happiness" (p. 177). This blithe national mindset did not take cognizance of a host of poor at the bottom of the barrel and minorities located outside of the mainstream.

The driving force behind the economy was a massive military build-up to contain the Soviets, supplemented by an immense foreign aid program of exports and credits to allies, friends, and marginal Third World countries. "Military Keynesianism" was the economic engine of prosperity, with federal deficit spending providing leverage for unprecedented industrial expansion of both the military and consumer type.

Consumerism spiraled as personal income rose and the credit card revolution encouraged delayed payments on purchases ranging from automobiles to TVs to stereos to flights to Europe. Television, an all-powerful communication medium and rival to the movies as a cultural arbiter, blanketed the nation. A slew of innovative industries came into being: electronics, petrochemicals, aerospace, nuclear physics applications, and others. Newly instituted discount houses such as Korvette's and Grant's made buying accessible and cheap. And a slick advertising network kept demand in high gear. Many of us began to notice that this eruption of industrial energy brought with it the unfortunate by-product of substantial environmental spoilage and pollution.

As incomes rose, more and more people moved to the suburbs, where developers, using mass-production technologies, were able to construct a profusion of Levittown-type communities, together with related schools, shopping centers, swimming pools, and other amenities. The nuclear, male-dominated family, in *Father Knows Best* style, prevailed—at least on television. A gigantic federal highway construction program was undertaken in 1956 to link the proliferating suburban communities to downtown, to one another, and to other parts of the country. This constituted a policy decision to downplay public transportation and rather to provide lavish support to private means of transport. In the suburbs, shopping malls and industrial parks sprung up, together with drive-in hamburger joints and outdoor movies, while downtown areas disintegrated as places for shopping and employment.

As people with rising incomes departed the inner cities for suburbia, the vacated undesirable areas were occupied increasingly by low-income racial minorities, many migrating from the rural and urban South to seek economic opportunities. The agricultural South was fast becoming obsolete for many African Americans who worked the land. Farms were becoming more mechanized, larger, and geared to new crops. Accordingly, tenant farmers and farm hands were rapidly displaced and, blocked by discrimination in southern industries, they headed north for jobs, and to the inner cities for cheap, unrestricted housing. Thus began one of the largest internal migrations, ever, in United States history.

Services and physical conditions deteriorated markedly in these core urban areas. At the same time, jobs became scarce there as businesses and industrial plants also joined the march to better locations offering more space and greenery—leaving the tax base of the city, where minorities were concentrated, in shambles.

Such racially based population shifts were aided and abetted by federal policies that offered low-interest, insured FHA loans to those flooding the outskirts, while tacitly making inner city neighborhoods ineligible, and relegating them to negligence and abandonment. John Kenneth Galbraith (1958) in his book, *The Affluent Society*, documented the lavish lifestyle of many in the fifties, but also took note of a large impoverished population in the land, warning, presciently, that—if ignored—they would one day be a source of protest and disorder. The comfortable and even opulent style of living of many individuals he compared to a widespread condition of "public squalor."

Going hand in hand with the fifties of prosperity and good times was a fifties of hysteria and repression. A pervasive Red Scare dominated public life and stifled free speech and progressive politics. I would say that the causes of this were multiple and tangled, and cannot be simplified.

There was genuine fear of the Soviet Union because of both its strength and its alien, undemocratic system. It now had the hydrogen bomb, and Stalin had shown himself to be a ruthless and bloody dictator, both in his own country and in countries that he took over. The Communists appeared as an internal as well as external threat to us because of their assumed capability to use American citizens as spies, political agitators, and potential saboteurs.

This natural fear was heightened and intensified by efforts of political leaders to mobilize our citizenry in the battle against the Soviet system. Approval by the public of astronomical expenditures of public funds for military purposes and foreign aid required more than a mild commitment to national interest, it required an emotional dread and adhorrence of an evil and threatening outside force. Chafe (1986) comments that the two Cold War protagonists closed ranks, "with both sides using moralistic rhetoric and ideological denunciation to pillory the other" (p. 77).

Eisenhower's secretary of state, John Foster Dulles, had ratcheted up *Containment* to *Massive Retaliation*. Adding to the frenzy in this situation were the regular A-bomb air raid drills that were held, with children hiding under their desks at schools, and families building bomb shelters in the basements of their homes. In 1957, the Soviets heightened America's alarm even more by launching Sputnik. As this Soviet intruder circled over our heads, we realized that the time had come when the Atlantic Ocean was no longer our dependable shield and protector.

Public apprehension may have been pumped up for more self-seeking reasons as well. The industrial defense conglomerate generated untold profits for corporate elites in munitions and related fields, and was a general spur for the economy. It was to the benefit of corporate and political leaders to keep anxiety high and the industrial machinery rolling.

To maximize the commitment to large-scale defense spending, though, would necessitate more than rallying people to this cause through education and propaganda. It would also require clamping down on any and all political opinion running counter to the Cold War mentality.

The result of all of this was the development in American life of a widespread paranoia that came to betray our traditional principles of free expression. Truman incited a witch-hunting mood as early as 1947 by instituting a loyalty check of all federal employees, which evolved into a security check also. Suspicion and concern mounted when Alger Hiss was accused of spying in the State Department, and the Rosenbergs were convicted and sentenced to death for stealing atom bomb secrets.

As safeguards, we employed the Internal Security Act for general political surveillance, the resuscitated Smith Act to try communist leaders, the McCarran Act to monitor immigrants, House Un-American Activities Committee hearings to expose Hollywood screenwriters, the Red Channels newsletter to pry into TV programs and personalities, blacklists by employers to formally and informally keep suspected applicants out of jobs, J. Edgar Hoover's FBI to snoop everywhere and prepare dossiers on ordinary citizens, and a spate of similar intrusions into personal beliefs and activities. One insidious result of this intense scrutiny was that progressives began to engage in self-censorship, suppressing their own ideas and novel ways of thinking about issues, a reflex that many of us have carried forward to this day.

The epitome of all of this was Senator Joseph McCarthy, who saturated the media with vague lists of alleged spies and subversives infiltrating every crevice of American society. McCarthyism represented the high point of the witch-hunt, but he went too far—eventually discrediting the repression campaign when he detected subversion in the army high command, the Republican administration, and even in President Eisenhower's oval office. But many people's lives and careers had been ruined and American principles of free speech and civil liberties had been ravaged, with lingering consequences. All of us who were then on the liberal or left side of things remember that time as a bleak and frightening nightmare.

With this backdrop, I think we will better understand the character of Community Organization during the fifties decade. Eisenhower was a moderate Republican who supported business and corporate interests, but he took no strong actions to dismantle major New Deal welfare and social security provisions. Community Organization was basically conservative and constrained in this atmosphere. With economic conditions good overall, there was little public dissatisfaction, and no inclination to stir things up. As I point out in my reflective narrative, the major theorists of that time (Pray, Newstetter, Ross) unanimously projected a concept of Community Organization that featured self-help, client self-determination, an enabling role for the practitioner, process goals, and a consensus modus operandi. Engaging in even conventional politics was often frowned upon as being unprofessional and crude. Militant advocacy was totally out of the question.

Settlement houses put a great deal of emphasis on group work and engaged in neighborhood work that emphasized the building of relationships and problem-solving capacities among neighbors (as described by Berry in her narrative). Several of the reflection authors, such as Turner and Austin—and myself—report practice involvements aimed at stabilizing racially changing neighborhoods, or providing services to deal with the aftermath of large-scale population shifts to the suburbs.

I saw almost no radical organizing going on at the time. Community people, in large measure, were very cautious about joining any organizations or rocking the boat during the McCarthy era. Alinsky, who had published *Reveille for Radicals* in the forties and mobilized the dynamic Back of the Yards organization then, went into retreat. This was the time when the CIO expelled its more militant affiliates and, in 1955, joined the conservative, Cold War boostering AFL.

The main avenues of advocacy were in the area of civil rights. The NAACP was engaged in a highly effective campaign emphasizing legal redress, rather than social or political advocacy, which in 1954 led to the *Brown v. Board of Education* Supreme Court ruling. This decision threw out the "Separate But Equal" doctrine that was the mainstay for Jim Crow going back to the 1896 *Plessy v. Ferguson* case. During 1955–56, Martin Luther King came to national attention as a leader of the Montgomery bus boycott, which ended discrimination on public transportation in that city. This was a nonviolent, well-disciplined, and restrained campaign carried out on a high moral plane. It laid the groundwork for broader and more militant actions that would materialize later.

Community welfare councils carried out traditional programs, eschewing the governmental sector and touting "voluntarism," focusing heavily on coordinating the activities of social service agencies strictly in the private sector. There are descriptions of work in such settings in narratives by Barry and Austin, and also by Schwartz in a Jewish Welfare Council. Vigorous community-wide planned change during this period hardly existed and was not identified by any of the reflection authors.

Some social workers took part in the United Community Defense Services (UCDS) program, which was sponsored by Community Chests and Councils of America and the National Social Welfare Assembly. Berry describes her observations of this program in her narrative. The objective of this extensive project was to help with social aspects of development in 227 "critical defense areas," small communities mainly in the South and West that were targeted for defense mobilization. The aim was to quell the social turmoil involved in abruptly expanding small communities to encompass sizable defense plants, hydrogen bomb facilities, and armed forces bases. The work in its practice components called for genuine grassroots involvement with people and institutions in planning services and creating communities.

The program was, in many respects, an application of social work to the Cold War context. We can discern this connection, at least tacitly, in the writings of Elizabeth Wickenden, a social work leader in the UCDS, as follows: "a [country's] program of military defense…must be considered to exist for all its people… No sharp distinctions can properly be made in this situation between considerations affecting people's 'welfare' and those affecting their 'defense,' for defense has become an accepted safeguard to their welfare" (Wickenden, 1955). Not all social workers were carried along by the Cold War flow. For example, Bertha Capens Reynolds in 1953 presented a dissenting paper on "Fear in Our culture," and another on "McCathyism vs. Social Work" in 1954 (*Ongoing*, 1997).

During the fifties a great deal of locally based organizing took place overseas in community development (CD) projects in newly emerging independent countries such as India and nations of Africa. Arthur Dunham, my colleague at the University of Michigan, was a leading academic in this field, as I note in my reflection. These developing nations needed support in nurturing grassroots democracy and local problem solving at the village level. There was some social work representation here, but not a vast amount.

Clearly, there was a great deal of merit in helping to improve the functioning of impoverished colonial people who had been denied the opportunity to learn the skills of self-government, but there were Cold War reverberations in this also. The United States, through the Administration for International Development (AID), was a major promoter of CD, providing funds and training assistance to thirty countries, with the aim of improving living conditions and attitudes in these areas, while serving to bolster their resistance to communist propaganda and influence. The Peace Corps was a later expression of the same strategy.

A large amount of organizing took place in the fifties with little social work involvement. This was in neighborhood improvement associations that sprung up across the country in conjunction with the burgeoning affluent suburbs. These organizations were outside of the social work/social welfare institutional framework and went under names such as homeowners' associations, property owners' associations, and civic clubs. They were essentially neighborhood protection groups, aiming to guard against entry into the neighborhood of racial minorities and lower-class families, and to stave off commercial development. All of this was meant to preserve property values and neighborhood homogeneity in the face of potential invasion by perceived undesirable elements.

These organizations also looked after the beauty and comfort of the community and sought to secure necessary public services, while also striving to hold down taxes. They engaged in self-help projects of various kinds, often attending to the needs of children in connection with education and recreation. Leadership and staffing were indigenous and voluntary, comprised ordinarily of a small group of lawyers, realtors, and businessmen. Because of the conservatism, with clear racist overtones, of these groups, it was my observation that social workers—including the reflection authors—basically avoided them.

THE SIXTIES

The fifties have been viewed by many as a tranquil time with a ubiquitous conservative consensus. The "silent generation" we were called—those of us who went to college during this time—put to sleep by Eisenhower and scared out of our wits by Joseph McCarthy and the FBI. But as other analysts, David Halberstam (1993) included, point out, many of the seeds sprouting in the sixties were planted in the fifties.

In the writings of Jack Kerouac, Allen Ginsberg, and William Burroughs, the "Beat Generation" was veering headlong away from the mainstream. Critics of "mass society," such as C. Wright Mills and Erich Fromm, were spreading doubts about the "men in the grey flannel suit" mentality. Dorothy Day and Michael Harrington, among others, were voicing a divergent left-wing politics, a position that appeared in print in small but feisty publications such as *The Catholic Worker, I.F. Stone's Weekly, The Nation*, and *Dissent* magazine.

While *Leave It to Beaver* and *Ozzie and Harriet* projected a saccharin picture of America on TV, a different image came through on the big screen in films such as *Rebel Without a Cause* and *The Wild Ones*. Interestingly, it was also during this relatively quiescent time that Meyer Schwartz established a highly innovative two-year concentration in Community Organization, which served as the groundwork for the outpouring of such educational programs in the next decade. There were other dominant historical forces of the fifties that flowed over into the sixties.

As before, I will discuss political and economic trends of the decade first and then relate them to the unfolding of Community Organization practice. The Cold War, with its "spheres of influence" confrontations, continued at full throttle, focusing on Cuba early in the new decade and later much more intensively and tragically on Vietnam. Military expenditures, aided by deficit spending, continued to zoom and to propel American economic development at home and expansion abroad. More new products and new technologies streamed into the market and consumerism expanded, all linked to a rising standard of living and the upward climb of real wages and real income.

The earlier migratory pattern of south to north and city to suburbs, heavily racial in character, persisted. Inner cities were becoming ever more bleak and suburbs more opulent. The benefits of prosperity were distributed in an increasingly lopsided fashion, with wealth highly concentrated at the top and many people feeling left out, particularly African Americans and other minorities. Inner-city communities were burdened by a tangle of impediments and disabilities: unemployment, deteriorating housing, inadequate and run-down schools, drugs, crime, teenage pregnancy, poor health services, high infant mortality rates—the pervasive injustices and pathologies of racism. An "underclass" was in the making.

Soon after the sixties broke, Michael Harrington (1962) in *The Other America: Poverty in the United States* dramatically unmasked the extent of economic deprivation, documenting the existence of millions of "invisible" poor—blacks, the elderly, the young, and others—overlooked and by-passed by Wall Street types speeding home to the Westchester Counties of the nation. This same form of blindness to class and race inequity was widespread in the land. The poor and minorities, however, were not unaware of the affluence that both surrounded and eluded them, and their anger was beginning to build.

The decade started on an upbeat note with the election of John F. Kennedy to the presidency, with his promise to "get America moving again" after the humdrum Eisenhower regime. But with an uncooperative

Congress and Kennedy's inclination, I believe, to be more the politico than the crusader, movement was slow paced.

But outside of Washington, sparks of change were beginning to ignite. On campuses in Ann Arbor, Berkeley, and Madison we began to see the student movement emerging, in particular, Students for a Democratic Society. With their motto of "participatory democracy" and their disdain for "the establishment," these young people committed themselves passionately to fundamental change and to social justice. Todd Gitlin (1989), in his book *The Sixties: Years of Hope, Days of Rage*, points out that many of the New Left students were children of liberals and radicals who were disappointed and outraged that their parents had caved in to right wing repression. For them, simply taking action was an imperative—it made a statement—even if the action was insufficiently planned or unsuccessful. Action *in itself* was change, change from the passivity and submission of the Old Left during the fifties.

During these same early years of the sixties, black students in the South were initiating "freedom rides" and lunch counter protests to force change in racist practices. They linked different campus groups together to organize the Student Nonviolent Coordinating Committee in order to push these actions forward more vigorously and to expand into voter registration drives. SNCC was inspired by the Montgomery bus boycott and Martin Luther King's continuing work. During SNCC's valorous protests in the face of brutal southern resistance, the oppressed status of African Americans was broadcast to the whole country through TV and the press. Both the civil rights and Students for a Democratic Society arms of the student movement emphasized a community organizing strategy that was community-based, advocacy-oriented, focused on democratic participation, and nonviolent in character.

In these same early years, certain formal institutions began to develop programs and strategies aimed at shaking up established social welfare ways of doing business. This included the National Institute of Mental Health, the Ford Foundation, and The President's Committee on Youth Crime and Delinquency. These efforts gave rise to Mobilization for Youth in New York City, an innovative agency geared to promoting the interests of the poor through unconventional means. There are detailed descriptions of these events in reflections by Brager, Perlman, and others, and I also alluded to them in the previous chapter.

The assassination of President Kennedy on a fateful November day in 1963, together with mounting demonstrations and urban disorders in inner-city areas, tipped the scales in the direction of muscular programs favoring the disadvantaged. President Lyndon Johnson, building on a national sense of loss, in combination with his awesome political skills, pushed through a banquet of legislation, including the 1964 and 1965 civil rights/affirmative action and voting rights statutes and the 1964 War on Poverty, with its Community Action Program (CAP), which Fisher (1984) calls the largest neighborhood organizing project ever mounted in the United States. To some degree, the CAP framework was based on the ideas and experiences of Mobilization for Youth, and it was an initiative that I believe is of supreme importance for the organizational efforts described in this book.

CAP was a direct response to widespread urban disorders starting in 1963 and continuing through 1968, and had the dual (and somewhat contradictory) aims of addressing the needs and inequities that were being surfaced and, at the same time, bringing calm to the situation that was disturbing the status quo—somewhat akin to what the New Deal tried to accomplish during the depression years of the thirties. But it also had a more direct political aim, one that I venture to say is not commonly recognized—that of solidifying votes in the urban ghettos to compensate for the loss of Democratic strongholds in the South to the Republicans and the States' Rights Party.

The official poverty program organizations were designated to receive funds directly from Washington, thus bypassing state and municipal officials. These organizations would also gain power and autonomy through the requirement of "maximum feasible participation" of target areas residents on governance boards. The CAAs, Party strategists in Washington thought, could become new political vehicles in the inner cities to gain the loyalties of blacks and ensure their votes at election time. In this conception, community organization and politics merged and intertwined on a grand scale, and in a way that I believe is unprecedented.

To some extent, the program worked too well. CAAs were more militant and assertive, more change oriented, more promotive of minority interests, and more threatening to establishment Democratic mayors and local Party leaders than anyone had anticipated. Internal tensions within Party circles boiled over as mayors strained to gain increased control over the program and its local operations.

The new agencies, moreover, brought trouble onto themselves, as inexperienced residents struggled to learn administrative skills, competed with one another for leadership and spoils, mismanaged and misappropriated funds, and created havoc as they devised alternative organizational forms. An extended time period and a nurturing environment, in my view, was essential to process such a far-reaching change. This was not granted and probably couldn't be. The program, as I see it, contained a basic contradiction, for elites will not extend funds or support (or patience) on behalf of those who are seeking to diminish or overturn their power. Surely, this is an iron law of political sociology.

Washington, before long, put regulations in place to curtail these new bodies, through clearing the funding of grants through municipal officials, restricting partisan activities, and making mandatory a larger number of categorical service programs such as multiservice centers and Upward Bound. This closed off discretionary funds that could be used for advocacy. Most important, by 1967, the Green Amendment cut the heart out of the program by eliminating the need for the majority of the governing boards to be local residents, thereby gutting the fundamental principle of maximum feasible participation.

The real end of this remarkable program, and of many other facets of Johnson's Great Society, came with the election of Nixon to the presidency in 1968. Nixon won, in part, because of public anguish over the war in Vietnam (he had a "secret" plan to end it), and the new Republican Congress had little interest in catering to the poor in inner cities and rural areas. Their constituency was elsewhere.

In 1972, Nixon would institute a personal-services-without-advocacy "New Federalism," involving block grants and revenue sharing channeled through city and state formal bureaucratic structures. The language of citizen participation remained in the legislation, but this was illusionary. While calling an end to the Great Society, Nixon took care to keep military expenditures at a high level, pushing through an Antiballistic Missile Program of some heft. By this time the steam was out of the protest movement, as concessions cooled off emotions, and leaders were co-opted into more conventional, and often more lucrative, modes of participation.

Concurrent with these developments, coalitions were being formed in cities across the country to deal with blight and physical disintegration in the central city. These pro-growth coalitions sought to clear and rejuvenate the civic center, bringing together for this purpose business and industrial interests, city politicians, liberal reformers, and real estate and construction representatives. They promoted large-scale urban redevelopment, improved transportation, and refigured city financing. But, as I observed around me, the urban reconstruction projects often resulted in wholesale displacement and dispersion of the poor, what Jane Jacobs (1961) termed "slum shifting."

As the decade proceeded, the democratically oriented, humanist, and nonviolent thrust of the student movement subsided, and others employed strategies that were more jarring and vexing, culminating in the "days of rage" that Gitlin identified. There were urban eruptions—with mass rioting—resulting in devastation of property and lives, menacing posturing by the Black Panthers, and wild acting out by The Weathermen. Simultaneously, hopeful points of light such as Martin Luther King Jr. and Robert Kennedy were snuffed out toward the end of the decade in wrenching fashion. Malcolm X, growing as a force for both racial justice and racial reconciliation, had been assassinated in 1965.

Advocates for social change, in a remarkable achievement, had blunted the momentum of the war in Vietnam and brought down Lyndon Johnson. But in his place there came Richard Nixon to lay the groundwork for a new and much more conservative decade. What, we may ask then, had the sixties accomplished, and what specially was the role of community organization in the sixties from a social work vantage point?

I am persuaded that the sixties represented a high point for Community Organization in the United States, and in social work. To start with, a multiplicity of new two-year CO specializations were put in place at social work schools nationwide, building on Meyer Schwartz's work at Pittsburgh. There were substantially more CO programs and students at schools then than at any time before or after. Ralph Kramer depicts one such program in his narrative, a program that was especially volatile, but which illustrates the sense of excitement, idealism, and movement, and the expansion of racial minorities and women in the student body, characterizing most programs in those years.

Some social workers were substantially involved in the War on Poverty, in particular the Community Action Program, from the start. They had taken part in the earlier initiatives created through NIMH, The Ford Foundation, and the President's Committee on Youth Crime and Delinquency, which were forerunners and models for CAP. Perlman and Brager record these early events and programs in connection with Action for Boston Community Development and Mobilization for Youth. Austin portrays CAP programming from his position as a professor at Brandeis University, where he conducted research on actions and outcomes at sites across the country.

Many social workers were involved in offshoots and reverberations of this effort in settlement houses and other programs serving minorities and the poor, and were caught up in issues related to local community control, governance, and advocacy—as Berry spells out in her narrative. They also played a role in establishing alternative or innovative specialized agencies, for example, to serve abused women or, as Spergel illustrates, gang members in low-income neighborhoods. In this same connection, Perlman tells of his work in forming innovative neighborhood multisector centers.

Welfare rights groups began to form in CAAs across the country, and in late 1996 they were brought together under the impetus of George Wiley to establish the National Welfare Rights Organization. Cloward and Piven were instrumental in providing ideas and leadership to NWRO, and they describe the course of events in their report. As I recall, another social worker, Tim Sampson, had a key role alongside Wiley at the inception of the organization. Alexander, in his narrative, gives an account of his dealings with NWRO in his role as executive head of NASW.

Social workers were also active in related federally sponsored programs of the time, such as VISTA—Volunteers in Service to America (whose director was a social worker)—and the Peace Corps (of which a number of directors in different nations and international regions were social workers). The Peace Corps became a recruiting ground for social work as numerous returning volunteers without formal training applied to schools in order to continue and strengthen their work. I had many of them in my classes, and found their dedication and experience to be a major plus.

As I mentioned, urban coalitions of business and political elites undertook massive urban renewal projects in the city centers during this time, and social workers found themselves participating in efforts to redirect or halt some of these operations. Local citizens became alarmed and mobilized in order to block projects that they learned would tear down their homes or run freeways through their neighborhoods. Most of these actions were spontaneous and indigenous, although social workers also staffed many of them as, for example, in the kinds of neighborhood councils discussed by Turner.

The Alinsky Industrial Areas program also engaged in many such protests, thwarting city hall and real estate developers in cities around the country and demanding better municipal services. Spergel reports on his encounters with the Alinsky organization in Chicago in his narrative. Because of Alinsky's antipathy toward social workers, there was little participation from our field in his campaigns.

Under the Kennedy-Johnson administrations, federal social programs and expenditures to support them expanded enormously—far beyond only locally oriented organizing approaches. A multiplicity of categorical services were mandated, but with requirements calling for the careful planning and concerted delivery of the services. Specifically, social policy initiatives called for planning to be integrated into service delivery, including the use of well-defined methods of program development, management, and evaluation (Gruber, 1981). The wide range of programs promoted by the federal government in this way included community mental health, housing and community development, job training, medical care, income maintenance, child welfare, and many others.

This had a decided impact on planning at the local community level. "A new pluralistic planning environment had been created, with alternative centers of planning for different, specific problem areas and open competition for scarce resources and space on the public agenda" (Wenocur, 1997, p. 628). CO professionals quickly began to occupy positions in these new categorical service planning centers.

Community welfare councils and United Ways were forced to react to the new reality that surrounded them. They could no longer claim to be the sole or preeminent hub for planning at the community level or to view the voluntary sector as the essence of social welfare planning. Barry, in her reflection, informs us of how councils widened their scope, meshed with the governmental sector, and began to use more sophisticated planning methods. She and other social worker practitioners played a part in facilitating this shift of focus in councils (although I observed that United Ways were beginning to turn to MBA types more and more to fill executive positions).

Social workers were much less prominent or active in other important movements and programs of the time. For example, there were few social workers in the student movement, although SDS, through its ERAP—Economic Research and Action Program project (which was partially funded through the United Auto Workers)—carried out basic community organizing functions on the grassroots level. These projects were conducted in inner-city districts in Newark, Cleveland, and Chicago, among other locations.

As I saw it, there was a basic tension between the outlook of the student movement and of social work teachers and practitioners. I mentioned earlier that the students felt the taking of action to be an imperative in its own right. And they wanted full, round-the-clock discussion and consensus, in true participatory democracy form, before making a strategy decision. These endless rounds of discussion were both exhilarating and draining. The quality and amount of participation seemed to be more important than the quality and rationale of the action.

Moreover, participation and action-taking were more important than any particular outcome (a failed action would simply, and happily, provide the basis for a new action). Within this context, organizational forms and leadership, students believed, ought to be dispersed, informal, and loose—counter to the rigidity and power tripping found in established organizations. In her analysis of the New Left, Evans (1980) takes to task this counter-organizational form of organizational operation and the preoccupation with process rather than task goals in social struggle.

From an up-front vantage point, I can tell you that this student activist perspective contrasted sharply with the stringent efforts of CO teachers then in schools of social work to legitimate this practice area within the profession. Social work educators wanted the practice to be based on the careful design of strategies, the use of well-conceived structures and sophisticated leadership to attain goals, and the effective and accountable reaching of outcomes. Calculated strategizing was a cardinal principle, they believed, that applied to all forms of community intervention, from militant advocacy to service delivery.

Add to the divergence the fact that students felt it essential for actions to invariably confront and affront establishment elites, because power wielders, in their view, would respond only to intense pressure, whereas CO social workers felt that confrontation should be used when needed and avoided if not critical for a given end. There was a clash of concept and tone here that, in my experience, could not readily be resolved. A similar stand-off occurred between Old Left radicals and the New Left students, to the detriment of the entire progressive camp.

Regarding the SNCC branch of the student movement, there was some degree of participation by social workers, but not extensively or in key leadership roles. This movement, in essence, was strongly regional, indigenous, and self-directed. Similarly, with regard to Martin Luther King Jr.'s activities in both the South and the North, social workers participated mainly by joining the string of public marches and demonstrations that were held.

As the decade proceeded, the student movement became less political and more cultural in character. Their perceived failure to make a discernable dent in either universities or the wider community arena led many students to adopt a more personal form of change activity, which became known as "the cultural revolution." Rather than relying on organized political mobilization, they employed individual acts of defiance and transformation in lifestyle. This involved deviant forms of dress, music, sexual relations, speech, recreational drug use, and the like, symbolized by the "hippie" image.

Instead of seeking to influence policy decisions in order to bring about change, people created the change immediately and on the spot, one by one, simply through cumulative behavioral adaptation. As an unorganized movement, the cultural revolution was propelled by various charismatic individuals (such as Jerry Rubin), making heavy use of the media as a form of communication, and modeling outlandishly rather than verbalizing what they advocated. There was little formal leadership here, by either social workers or others.

This movement, it seems to me, was a complex and variegated composite, involving the mix of individuals who were idealistic and dedicated, together with those who were self-indulgent and superficial ("flaky" was the usual descriptor). But it has had a significant carry-through effect, as shown in the much greater informality, flexibility, and diversity in social practices we see around us today.

The Vietnam antiwar movement was one of the most sweeping and powerful citizen actions of the century, in that it derailed a president and stymied the indomitable military-industrial complex. Many social workers took part in marches, public meetings, and political initiatives geared to ending the war, but relatively few participated in a professional staff capacity. As an example of this, a fellow social work faculty member and I were part of a small action group that planned the first "teach-in" against the war at the University of Michigan in March of 1965. The teach-in format had an enormous impact and was duplicated by countless universities across the nation. This type of private, civic engagement in antiwar actions typified social workers widely. Additionally, the Peace Committee of NASW mobilized social workers to participate as members—organizational banners and all—in community-coalition-sponsored peace demonstrations around the country. This grew out of the vote of the national Delegate Assembly to go on record as opposed to war.

Much community action during the decade was emergent, spontaneous, and informal—including early feminist endeavors, the La Raza Latino organization, and the American Indian Movement (AIM). These groupings were essentially voluntary and indigenous rather than professional and salaried. To the degree that social workers were engaged, it was more likely to be as participants than staff members.

A SUMMING UP

In retrospect, the postwar forties had an enormous influence on the rest of the century, particularly in terms of very broad international and economic forces that have molded American society in general. Also, the war experience changed the expectations of racial minorities and women about their role and status, perceptual shifts that were deeply felt and sustained over time. Although the sedate fifties were a time of incubation, some people feel that frustrated hopes helped ignite the conflagration of change that exploded later. For me, the legacy of the fifties is somewhat indistinct in regard to its substantive contributions for those of us in social work concerned with CO. It was a time when things were simmering, rather obscurely and on a low burner.

The sixties, on the other hand, packed a wallop, leaving an imprint on America, and on social work and community organization, that was profound and lasting. But the sixties created so much noise and motion that it isn't always easy to sort things out.

I found the sixties an enormously ebullient and confusing time. There were many different things blowing in the wind. Many of the people, whose aims I fervently shared, used methods I seriously questioned. I had always though of myself as a cutting-edge progressive, and I began to feel my identity crumbling. I couldn't go along with many who claimed to hold the cutting edge: Weathermen who opted to continue their argument by smashing shop windows in the street; long-haired cultural revolutionists who went about without changing their clothing and needing a bath; the fanatic who blew up a science laboratory at the University of Wisconsin; and others who simply believed that being uncivil and surly was the true mark of the change advocate. Much of what we all reached for during that period was not attained, yet things will never be the same.

In social work, due to the efforts of CO practitioners, including the authors in this book, Community Organization was put on the map, establishing a lasting benchmark for future reference. The concept of participatory democracy, an elemental CO precept from the start, has entered the vernacular and become a rallying cry for disadvantaged people. Advanced and technically refined social planning methods, developed in federal programs, carried over in social work CO as basic tools leading, additionally, to the advent of policy practice. Many substantive service programs, such as Medicare, have become permanent artifacts of our society.

The War on Poverty was brought to a halt, not won. But a magnificent accomplishment of the Community Action Program was the training of a corps of African Americans (and other minorities) in the arts of politics and community advocacy resulting, for blacks, in a new political class, a constellation of advocacy organizations, a significant body of professionals, and a substantial middle class. Some of the roots of the contemporary feminist movement, also, can be traced to this era. Civil rights legislation of the Johnson administration still forms the basis for affirmative action to this day. In their narrative, Cloward and Piven identify a window of time in the sixties as one of only two periods during this century when the poor and minorities made significant gains.

Rather than trying to make a comprehensive assessment, let me tick off some of the accomplishments that Gitlin (1989) mentions in his review:

A greater sense by those in power of the need to be accountable

More open cultural mores, including greater sexual freedom

Public aversion to military intervention and adventurism

The transmutation of idealistic principles into activists' private lives

The continuation of active social movements and local organizing

Gitlin makes the point that we live in a more conservative time now, but part of what we are conserving are the breakthroughs of the sixties. I submit that this notion applies equally to breakthroughs in the field of social work community organization.

As you peruse the reflections, the different sociopolitical environments of each decade—the late forties, the fifties, and the sixties—hover in the background. But the themes that the authors present and act on in their narratives transcend historical periods. They represent fundamental strategic and philosophical issues that impinge on practice whenever and wherever conducted. Whether to strike for large goals or more accessible ones; emphasize services or social reform; design plans that are comprehensive and precise or ad hoc; call for calm or fan discontent during times of upheaval and crisis—these are choices and conundrums that have always been with us.

The authors recount how they thought these issues through in the doing, and they reassess their actions in retrospect. The particulars of their encounters are set by distinct temporal and circumstantial factors, but the relevance of the issues to concerns of practice applies very broadly. The best way to scrutinize these narratives is with conceptual bifocals that simultaneously look backward and forward.

With that, I wish you an enjoyable read and a meaningful encounter with the writers and their ideas. And, taking a long view of history, I look ahead hopefully into the new century, when, with your help, humankind's social and moral competency in community life and human relationships will make sure strides in keeping pace with our glittering technological accomplishments.

BIBLIOGRAPHY

Alinsky, S. D. 1946. *Reveille for Radicals*. Chicago: University of Chicago Press.

Chafe, W. D. 1986. *The Unfinished Journey: America Since World War II*. New York: Oxford University Press.

Diggins, J. P. 1988. *The Proud Decades: America in War and in Peace/1941–1960*. New York: W. W. Norton.

Evans, S. M. 1980. *Personal Politics: The Roots of Women's Liberation in the Civil Rights Movement and the New Left*. New York: Vintage Books.

Fisher, R. 1984. *Let the People Decide: Neighborhood Organizing in America*. Boston: Twain Publishers.

Galbraith, J. K. 1958. *The Affluent Society*. Boston: Houghton Mifflin.

Gitlin, T. 1989. *The Sixties: Years of Hope, Days of Rage*. New York: Bantam.

Goodman, P., and F. O. Gatell. 1972. *USA: An American Record*. New York: Holt, Rinehart and Winston, Inc.

Gruber, M. L. ed. 1981. *Management Systems in the Human Services*. Philadelphia: Temple University Press.

Halberstam, D. 1993. *The Fifties*. New York: Villard Books.

Hallinan, M. 1998. "Sociology and the Goal of Generalization." *Footnotes* 26(1):6.

Harrington, M. 1962. *The Other America: Poverty in the United States*. New York: Macmillan.

Jacobs, J. 1961. *The Death and Life of Great American Cities*. New York: Random House.

Ongoing (Summer/Fall, 1997). University of Michigan School of Social Work, Ann Arbor, MI.

Piven, F. F., and Richard A. Cloward. 1971. *Regulating the Poor: The Functions of Public Welfare*. New York: Random House.

Terkel, S. 1984. *The Good War: An Oral History of World War Two*. New York: Pantheon Books.

Wenocur, S. 1997. "Social Planning in the Voluntary Sector." *Encyclopedia of Social Work*. 18th ed. Vol. 2. Anne Minahan, Editor in Chief. Washington, DC: National Association of Social Workers, pp. 625–632.

Wickenden, E. (August 1955) "Military Defense and Social Welfare." (National Association of Social Welfare MSS, Social Welfare History Archive.)

Zinn, H. 1973. *Postwar America: 1945–1971*. Indianapolis: The Bobbs-Merrill Company.

PART TWO

THE REFLECTIONS: DOMAINS AND THEMES

INTERVENTION
STRATEGIES AND
PROGRAMS

Advocacy and
Social Change

Agency Under Attack: The Risks, Demands, and Rewards of Community Activism

George Brager

In the early 1950s, the initial years of my work life, community organization referred largely to the coordination and collaboration of social agencies and/or to a cooperative planning process conducted by professionals with an educated, largely middle-class citizenry. The participation of low-income service users in influencing institutional decision making was at best a peripheral element in the field, and although "grassroots" organizing took place in the country, it was not by and large considered a part of social work. It was not until the concept of citizen participation emerged as a major idea—a prized value and the great nuisance of the social legislation of the 1960s—that organizing low-income consumers of services found currency as a mode of practice in schools of social work. A significant contributor to this development was Mobilization for Youth (MFY), an agency on the Lower East Side of New York City.

This paper focuses on one aspect of the Mobilization for Youth experience: a virulent attack on the agency by New York City officials and the right-wing press. MFY's social change–oriented community program was the primary target of the onslaught, and the experience illustrates some of the risks, demands, and perhaps the rewards of community activism.

Mobilization for Youth was designed to demonstrate ways of helping residents of an inner-city slum to deal with problems caused by living under the corrosive conditions of poverty, deprivation, and discrimination. Initially planned as an attempt to combat delinquency through interventions involving an entire community, it became the model for the War on Poverty. It is not hyperbole to assert that the Economic Opportunity Act of 1964 and the many programs that sprang up to implement it stemmed in considerable measure from the MFY experience. In *Maximum Feasible Misunderstanding*, a book by Daniel Patrick Moynihan that is hardly laudatory about community action programs in general or Mobilization for Youth in particular, he writes:

> The first OEO Community Action Guide…clearly shows the influence of MFY. Preschool education (such as Head Start), legal aid for the poor (not just to defend them, but to serve them as plaintiffs), a theory of community organization, an emphasis on research and evaluation, and most especially the insistence on the involvement of the poor, all these were the legacy of Mobilization for Youth.[1]

Mobilization's program was based on opportunity theory, as developed by Richard Cloward and Lloyd Ohlin. To reduce delinquency, it was held, it is necessary to expand objective opportunities available to impoverished youth; thus youth employment and education became major components of the program. It was also necessary, in this schema, to attack factors that prevent youth from taking advantage of whatever opportunities do exist; a network of specialized services to individuals, group members, and their families was therefore included as well.

But Mobilization's mandate was to develop programs that represented innovation in content, method, structure, or auspices. It does not require theoretical sophistication to hold that poor youngsters need jobs, that their education should be better, or that individuals in trouble require help in order to maximize their life changes. Nor does espousal of these notions guarantee programmatic innovation. A primary source of MFY's innovation stemmed from the rather simple idea that if services were to be organized meaningfully, social class variables had to be taken into account in program planning. An understanding in class terms of reciprocal relationship between the "defects" of the clients and those of the institutions with which they interact suggests specific targets for intervention.

The engagement of the low-income community was featured in most MFY's activities, but in none was it more emphasized than in its community organizing program. According to Mobilization philosophy, poverty was viewed as the problem, and power, in the hands of those suffering the consequences of poverty, was necessary for its solution. Power, in the sense of the ability to affect one's life chances, can be provided to an individual through a network of services. It is also possible to try to vest power in a group, the group with the most at stake. With power, citizens can press for additional or improved services, express and demand redress of grievances from public and private institutions, develop leadership skills, and offer their youth some optimistic evidence of what the future might hold. A challenging social action program was viewed as the vehicle by which this might be accomplished.

The social action program was a lightning rod that drew controversy to the agency. Slightly more than two years after operations had gotten underway, on Sunday, August 16, 1964, blazoned in bold capital letters on the front page of the New York *Daily News*, then a right-wing tabloid, were the headlines: "YOUTH AGENCY EYED FOR REDS: City Cuts Off Project's Funds." Two days later, in similarly dramatic style, front-page headlines read: "CITY TO PROBE YOUTH AGENCY: Mayor Reveals Curb on Cash," and the next day again, "LIST 45 LEFTIES IN YOUTH GROUP." Thus began an intense attack on the agency that continued unrelentingly for the next five months. Featured on the front pages of New York's seven dailies, some of which were friendly and some stridently negative, the organization was ultimately transformed.

In the maelstrom of August 1964 to January 1965, as a codirector of the agency, I was absorbed—immersed—all day, every day, whether at work or at home, in the events of the crisis. I spent every weekend during the five-month period recording the week's events in a diary. Yet, in the 32 years since then, I could not bring myself to read what I had written. Jack Rothman's invitation to contribute to this volume finally provided me with sufficient incentive to revisit the event.

The planets must have been in proper alignment during MFY's development; stated differently and without the astrological metaphor, the formation of the agency was made possible by a favorable confluence of political circumstances. Led by Henry Street Settlement, the social agencies of the Lower East Side of New York City had come together in 1958 out of their concern about gangs that roamed the neighborhood. They proposed to develop a community-wide program that would saturate the neighborhood with services, and thus draw funds for their ongoing programs in a time of fiscal strain. "The problem is not so much how to do it," one of the early documents read, "since the methods are known; the problem is to find sufficient means to meet the whole problem."

The proposal was submitted by the settlement group to the National Institute of Mental Health (NIMH), which suggested it be withdrawn and resubmitted as a request for funds for a planning period. Influenced by the Ford Foundation's Grey Areas community development initiative, NIMH was receptive to a community-oriented approach to reducing delinquency and interested in the possible use of the Lower East Side as a laboratory to test new perspectives. In granting funds for a two-year planning period to begin in June 1960, NIMH posed a number of stipulations. The program had to be innovative, include a significant research and evaluation component, and have a university affiliation. This is the basis for the inclusion of the Columbia University School of Social Work in the group. NIMH also required that the group had to demonstrate community "readiness" by establishing a broad collaborative structure to receive funds—thereby providing the incentive to create a new agency.

A significant element in MFY's development was the creation of the President's Committee on Juvenile Delinquency (PCJD). The Kennedy administration owed its narrow victory in 1960 to the heavy vote in key cities and particularly to the black vote in these cities. Kennedy had to find a way to reward that support without antagonizing other important constituencies.[2] Directly providing funds for community programs to largely Democratic-controlled cities while bypassing largely Republican statehouses was eminently attractive in that regard, and Mobilization was on the scene with a community approach to delinquency, a politically benign and compelling issue. PCJD headed by Robert Kennedy, then the attorney general (and the president's brother), included the secretaries of Health, Education, and Welfare and the Department of Labor, and wielded immense influence in Washington. Its executive director was David Hackett, a close school friend of Robert Kennedy. Lloyd Ohlin, an MFY planner and Columbia professor, was recruited as PCJD's program director, clearly the result of the administration's interest in promoting urban programs like Mobilization for Youth. The President's Committee became MFY's patron, running interference for the program in obtaining sanction and funds from federal departments and the New York City government.

In June 1962, President Kennedy announced at a press conference on the White House lawn that the United States and New York City would support MFY's community demonstration to prevent juvenile delinquency. The agency had been required to include others beyond the original group on its board, and now as reconstituted, the board was composed of roughly one-third of the original social agency members, with the other two-thirds divided between Columbia University and New York City representatives. It was to become painfully clear during the upcoming attack on the agency that, as is typical of coordinating groups, the primary loyalty of MFY board members was to their home organizations.

Winslow Carlton, a patrician philanthropist and former chair of the board of Henry Street Settlement, headed the 60-member group, and a tripartite administrative structure was adopted with three coequal directors, one primarily responsible for administration (Jim McCarthy), one for research (Richard Cloward), and one for program (myself). Approximately 14 other executives headed discrete program areas and were supervised by a deputy program director and myself. Since MFY's directors had primary access to the agency's financial resources through their relationship with its funding sources (NIMH, the Ford Foundation, the President's Committee, and City officials), their influence on agency operations was considerable.

Larger social forces also contributed to shaping Mobilization's actions and reaction before, during, and after the attack on the agency. The early sixties were a time of ferment and change; idealism was stirred and hopes burgeoned that something might be done about poverty in America. Few Americans were untouched in some way by the great social upheavals of the period—the marches and demonstrations launched by the civil rights movement, and the disruption associated with the student revolt and the protests against the war in Vietnam. During the sixties, the pursuit of social change occurred with great immediacy and militancy, and Mobilization inevitably reflected this societal coloration.

On a purely personal note, those were heady days. Mistakenly or not, social workers felt certain that the ways to improve social conditions were known. To be so close to the country's seat of power at Mobilization enhanced for us the meaning and value of our professional contribution. The exhilarating feeling that stemmed from the fact that what we did as social workers could make a significant difference was something I had not felt before, nor have I felt it since.

Although community organizing accounted for only 7 to 10 percent of Mobilization's expenditures, it provided the content for most of the controversy. The project's encouragement of community participation in the 1963 March on Washington generated anonymous complaints to the FBI. Its support of a group of Puerto Rican mothers who questioned a school's program contributed to the antagonism of the educational bureaucracy, and culminated in a public outcry against MFY by the district's principals. Landlords complained to local political leaders about MFY's activities regarding housing violations. Some local political leaders themselves looked askance at attempts to activate the minority community and complained about Mobilization's reformist coloration. Perhaps most antagonistic of all were the police, from whom the *Daily News* derived most of its raw "data" on "subversives" at MFY. Agency lawyers had been aggressively representing neighborhood youth at the station house, and worse still, MFY joined in a public campaign to create a Police Civilian Review Board, an anathema to the police in those days.

Although these activities may be seen as the genesis of the crisis, as important perhaps was the advent of federal funds to combat poverty. Antipoverty money put MFY in the position of competing with the City for federal resources. For example, the U.S. Department of Labor award-ed significant money to Mobilization's youth employment program while it gave short shrift to the City's similar but less professional effort. In addition, a tense internal power struggle over "ownership" of the City's antipoverty efforts took place between the city administrator, to whom MFY was accountable, and the City Council president. The victor was the City Council president who became the City's new Poverty Czar. MFY no longer had a friend in City Hall, and its close association with the city administrator did little to endear it with this now newly powerful official.

It is true, nonetheless, that MFY's activities were perceived as threatening to City Hall and provided sufficient cause for it to go on the offensive. As stated by one high-level City official, "You can't treat the mayor like this; you can't kick him in the ass; after all, he's paying for it." The fact, too, that the attack came during the Johnson-Goldwater presidential campaign provided the political incentive for Republicans to join the agency's other adversaries.

Once an attack takes place, real or imagined grievances can be expected to fan the flames of the conflagration. For example, we had been unwilling to entrust the local neighborhood council of social agencies with implementing the MFY proposal to organize the low-income residents of the Lower East Side, and the council's executives became an active source of false and damaging rumors. Further, MFY had subcontracted about one million dollars to the original social agency group to provide social services, a larger sum than was contained in their original wish list. The lure of the contracts "bought the agencies off," as the planners intended, but an undercurrent of dissatisfaction persisted. Not only had their expectations risen but other programs such as youth employment and education had been accorded greater prominence than their own. As a consequence, although the agency directors were generally supportive, some of them were considerably less so than would otherwise have been the case.

In retrospect, it may be argued that MFY's social action program was overextended. However, there would have been legitimate dilemmas had we wanted to rein it in. (Though, admittedly, reining it in was not on our agenda.) One concern was the need to be seen as standing with the community, to maintain the agency's credibility with its constituency of the poor during those times of minority and civil rights activism. Further, community groups organized by MFY were a source of pressure on the agency to "do the right thing." Our initial contract had provided that community groups would be free to make their own decisions without endangering Mobilization's support as long as they did not break the law. It might, of course, have been possible to persuade participants that an action could seriously compromise the agency and to ask them to desist on that ground. But, then, what is the cost of emphasizing risks to the agency when community action itself entails risks to its low-income participants?

Community agitation brought the issue of subversion in its wake, and early rumblings about the radicalism of some staff began to surface. The red scare spearheaded by Senator Joseph McCarthy had swept the country a decade or so earlier, when legitimate criticism of social injustice was defined by many as serving the ulterior motive of promoting Soviet interests. Thus, a man of Martin Luther King Jr.'s stature was perceived by FBI director J. Edgar Hoover as sufficiently suspect to warrant investigation. While there were, of course, people who joined the Communist movement, their numbers were slim, and the party itself was marginal. Yet, the reputations of members, ex-members, and nonmembers had been ruined and their careers destroyed. These were unsettling times, and those who believed that people should be judged by their behavior rather than their beliefs fought a rear-guard action. By 1954, however, Senator McCarthy had been discredited, and by 1962 the fervor had abated.

One might accuse Mobilization's leadership of political naivete for ignoring the early warnings about "subversives" on staff. But the accusation is easier to make in retrospect, in light of the outcome, than it was at the time. Or perhaps it was hubris on our part, though in view of our civil liberties ideology, we could not have done otherwise. Indeed, we would ourselves have been roundly attacked by important constituencies, including most liberal groups, if we had been publicly perceived as employing a political means test as grounds for hiring or firing. Further, Hackett, the executive director of the President's Committee, had on his own sought the advice of an FBI specialist who indicated that, given the size and scope of the Mobilization program, the evidence in the FBI files was not damaging or of concern. As we analyzed the issue, it did not seem in the interest of any of our major partners to publicly criticize the agency. The City was the only MFY sponsor that we considered to be potentially negative, but it did not seem possible to us that the administration of liberal New York City could gain any benefit from a major replay of a McCarthyite red scare. (The analysis was essentially correct, for the attackers lost a great deal more than they gained as a result of their actions. What the analysis failed to take into account, however, was that behavior may be impelled by impaired judgment and irrationality as well as by self-interest.)

The virulence of the attack shocked all of us. We were accused of printing incendiary leaflets, "fomenting" rent strikes, and encouraging "racial disorders" (the time was one month following riots in Harlem). The story also asserted that "official investigators have found that groups of well-indoctrinated youngsters from the Lower East Side had journeyed up to Harlem to...indoctrinate youngsters of their own age." According to the News, "on high law enforcement official" confirmed the paper's findings, and concluded that this is a "classic example of a takeover procedure by the Communist movement."

We hurriedly called a press conference that Sunday and issued a release denying the accusations. As was true then and later, reporters were a source of rumors, information and opinion. According to a *New York Times* writer, the only truly damaging aspect of the story was a Paul Screvane quotation that gave official sanction to the charges. Screvane was the City Council president, a Democrat, and associate of the Mayor, who had been appointed to head the recently created Anti-Poverty Operations Board. The *News* reported Screvane as saying that "We have heard of the employment of people of this type, and this is why we have been investigating. I would have to consider very carefully the continuance of this kind of program if it is infiltrated with people of leftist leanings." Privately, Screvane denied approximately two-thirds of the quotation to Carlton, which was only Screvane's first falsehood to MFY among many made during the course of the conflict. (One observation culled from reviewing the crisis diary is the discomforting frequency with which people who were engaged in the conflict were fast and loose with the truth, even to nonadversaries and friends. Worse still was the political advantage they gained from their dissembling.)

If the planets (or political circumstances) were well aligned for MFY in its formation, the alignment during the conflict was reversed. The agency's sources of political support had sharply diminished by August 1964. President Kennedy had been assassinated, and Bobby, the agency's godfather, was preparing to leave the Department of Justice to run for the Senate from New York. With the move, Bobby's leverage vanished; he was now the seeker of City support rather than a sought-after Washington power broker. Hackett was leaving, too, and would single-mindedly pursue Bobby's altered political interest, which now conflicted with the agency's. Circumstances couldn't be worse in the City, either. As noted earlier, the acrimonious power struggle within the City had resulted in the loss to the City Administrator's office of the oversight function for poverty and human resources development, leading to the resignation of the official from that office who monitored the MFY program and was its strong advocate. Even the long-time liaison persons to MFY from both the Ford Foundation and NIMH were no longer on the scene. Politically speaking, then, it might be said that MFY was being held together by Scotch tape. The timing for a challenge to the agency's legitimacy was perfect.

Initial reaction to the civil liberties issue was to stand firm. The project directors indicated at an emergency staff meeting on August 17 that they would continue to resist political means testing, as they had in the past. And at the board meeting that afternoon, Carlton surprised and pleased us when he, too, affirmed that the agency's criteria remained performance on the job. Unfortunately, his position was to erode the very next day.

On August 18, Carlton assured Senator Javits, a moderate Republican, that Mobilization would fire any current Communist it discovered on its staff. An old political warrior, Javits felt strongly that it would be damaging for MFY to countenance Communists in its ranks, but he also advised caution to avoid being accused of witchhunting. He suggested that the board acquire a panel of experts who had successfully fought subversives in the past as a cover to legitimate its actions. The political lesson was standard fare: How things were perceived was more important than the actual facts.

The three project directors met with David Hackett from midnight to 2:30 A.M. on August 18 to appeal for a statement from the attorney general. An FBI name check had indicated that there were three lower-level staff who were currently members of extreme leftist groups and about 33 other who had once been members but appeared to be no longer. Among them was the agency's deputy director and my longtime friend, who had joined the Communist party in college. Hackett made, made again, and then further remade the point that if we did not fire the three MFY staff members who were identified by the FBI as current Communists, we were "dead." Further, the niceties of fairness or due process had to be overridden since the three had to be out of the agency by 8:00 P.M. the next day. Kennedy could not defend us by saying that there were only a few Communists on staff, and if he interceded, he risked being "sandbagged" by enemies in the Justice Department once he left to run for the Senate.

Subsequently, Hackett leaned heavily on Carlton, who agreed to firing the three following an immediate appearance without a lawyer at a board committee hearing. This precipitated a series of internal arguments, negotiations, caucuses, and renegotiations during which a position was forged, "cleared" with Washington, and accepted by the board. Mobilization would not maintain current Communists on its payroll; full and complete hearings would be held; past political association would not constitute grounds for dismissal; and a "noted counsel" would be hired by the board with Department of Justice approval to look into the charges leveled against the agency.

I recorded this retreat in my diary as follows: "Cloward seemed almost stunned through all of this, and talking to him, I almost broke down. We were both racked by the moral dilemma. On the one hand, there was the violation of principle and the injustice to the three staff members. On the other, we were convinced that without this agreement the project was doomed. Further, if we made a public fight without Washington's support, the virulence of the conflict could lead to tarnishing the names of numbers of staff."

The risk of hiring a special counsel was clear to all of us. Carlton had agreed to give the Department of Justice prior approval, raising the question of who exactly was the counsel's employer, whether he would be accountable to MFY or to the Department of Justice. A number of safeguards were put forward and adopted by the board. He was, for example, to be responsible to the board alone and would transmit reports only to it. As it turned out, the safeguards were later ignored.

A number of highly respected lawyers declined the position before Carlton found and hired Philip Haberman. We learned with dismay that Haberman had been the associate counsel of the Rapp-Coudert Committee, a forerunner in legislative Red hunting. But, said Carlton, he had a "liberal" civil liberties position. In fact, it became apparent over time that Haberman saw himself as saving MFY but that there was a wide chasm in his and our thinking about how to accomplish that end. He was highly protective of MFY's leadership (particularly Carlton), and hoped to find a few subversives to root out—to demonstrate that his investigation was not a whitewash and that the subversive infiltration had not constituted a "takeover." In a statement Haberman prepared to announce his appointment, he wrote "The leadership of MFY is beyond suspicion, but like many other service organizations, it may have been secretly invaded by Communists and subversives. Such people may always be expected to exploit their positions by promoting civil disorder and anti-social objectives."

Carlton, who was with Haberman and Hackett in Washington, adamantly refused Jim McCarthy's appeal to revise the statement before it was released. "He's wild," said McCarthy. Since Hackett was more likely than Carlton to respond to pressure, I decided to phone him. I argued that the release would further panic the staff. Hackett listened and, I suspected, put Carlton on the extension to hear my argument. He suggested I call Carlton in five minutes; when I did, Carlton was still unwilling to reconsider the release but no longer threatened to fire anyone who refused to issue it. He did, however, put Haberman on the phone, and the latter agreed to delete the offending sentences. Not that it mattered: The *Times* article on Haberman's early background included some quotations from years before that were even more alarming.

At his first meeting with the board, Haberman tried to soften the impression of him conveyed in the *Times* article. While partially successful, he said enough to cause uneasiness. Most disquieting was Haberman's response to one board member's proposal that the group adopt guidelines to reassure staff and others that a rule of law would be followed. Haberman protested vehemently to a simple unequivocal statement that past membership was irrelevant to Mobilization employment, insisting that it could also constitute evidence of current activity. When a civil libertarian lawyer on the board agreed that Haberman was correct, an attempt was made to redraft the proposal. It was abandoned because an equivocal statement appeared more threatening than no statement at all.

Haberman's argument and Carlton's, too, implied that past member-ship could be a significant criterion in the case of higher-level staff. In the first days of the conflict, it was understood that it would take a face-saver for Screvane to achieve a settlement, and there was speculation about what his "price" might be. Hearing Haberman and Carlton, it was a fair presumption that one of 20 top executives might be tagged as the "patsy." I felt an all-consuming gloom, even terror: Not only might the agency be destroyed but the reputation of people about whom I cared a great deal as well.

Haberman's investigation was only one of the probes to which MFY was subjected. The City Department of Investigation entered the fray early, but privately warned that it would not conclude its work until after the Johnson-Goldwater election in November. The City subpoenaed staff and commandeered agency personnel files, raising internal questions and disagreements about how to protect staff from the political juggernaut. Since MFY was formally "cooperating" with the City's investigation, staff was instructed to answer questions regarding their activities at MFY; po-litical affiliations were out of bounds, however. Some of us were critical-ly concerned about maintaining staff anonymity, and had for a time some partial success at preventing unfair exposure. John Marchi, a Republican State Senate committee chairperson, launched still another inquiry, and on October 6, Congressman Adam Clayton Powell, a Democrat and chair of the House Committee on Education and Labor, requested a resume of all personnel, the names of those who had recommended them, and their salaries. This, we were assured, was a probe tactically meant to ward off or counteract unfriendly investigators. In mid-October Haberman called a meeting of all of the investigating parties in order to coordinate their ef-forts. The gathering can best be described as a circus, with the parties scrapping among themselves over who was entitled to which set of papers.

An organization facing a major conflict with elements in its environ-ment will often generate internal conflict as well. This point runs counter to logic and crisis theory; one would expect people who face a common threat to pull together. But solidarity does not occur so neatly in complex organizations in crisis. The different perspectives, stakes, and values of the organization's participants have great force when issues have major sig-nificance for them. The very intensity of the external challenge—the life and death nature of the struggle—is likely to further aggravate potential in-ternal disagreement and erode trust. Such was certainly the case at MFY, most particularly between the board president and special counsel on the one hand and the agency's codirectors and other executives on the other. The tensions mentioned earlier continued throughout the period.

By mid-September Jim McCarthy had resigned as administrative di-rector, ostensibly for health reasons. McCarthy had been a loose admin-istrator and over the years had made enemies of numbers of City officials.

His decision to leave, however, was impelled by personal issues. Soon after McCarthy's departure, the School of Social Work quietly decided that Cloward would eventually be withdrawn as a project director in order to direct the research program independently of MFY. On two different occasions during the period, I composed letters of resignation in the fantasy that my protest would cause some retreat by the City or prevent the implementation of one or another of Carlton or Haberman's positions. The letters may have been cathartic, but they were never submitted. With additional experience, I decided that it would be more effective to refuse to implement policies that violated strongly held values of mine and take the risk of being fired. Thus, when the City investigation began to question staff about their politics and did little to protect their anonymity, I sent a memo to staff with copies to Carlton and the City, indicating that I would no longer direct them to attend the City's interviews. Although Carlton must certainly have viewed my act as insubordinate, he never raised the issue.

There was no shortage of contentious issues. The agency's unwillingness to counterattack was one source of friction. Early in the crisis there was consensus that MFY had to act cautiously in relation to the City since the project would eventually require City support. With time, however, and Screvane's clear and continued enmity, a counterview developed that "cooperation" had failed, and that aggressive resistance or an attempt to inflict political pain was worth trying. Worse, Mobilization was cooperative even when political exigencies did not require it to be. The State did not provide either funds or sanction, and when the Marchi committee launched its investigation, the City Department of Investigation privately but strongly advised that we challenge the legitimacy of its jurisdiction. Carlton's philosophy was to win through wooing, however, and he opted for cooperation.

MFY lobbied influentials, made appeals to elite community associations and social service groups, held rallies, and undertook campaigns such as a petition drive. Some community groups conducted protest activities as well, though this caused mixed feelings on the part of the agency's directors, who were afraid that MFY would be accused of "using" clients (and public funds) to advance agency interests. In all, MFY's defense floundered. It was unduly reactive, responding primarily to the challenge of others, and at no point did it develop a coherent or overarching strategy.

Another major source of contention was Carlton's intention to subcontract the community organization program to another agency, and separate the entire organizing staff from MFY. (The subcontractor could then decide who among the group it wished to hire.) Stiff resistance by the executive staff and others and the obviousness of the ploy resulted in the plan's ultimate demise.

Internal conflict increased with the surfacing of a discussion paper on housing prepared by one of the community organizers for program planning purposes by an agency committee. The paper had come into the hands of the director of the local council of social agencies, and he covertly circulated it locally and in Washington. In enumerating housing problems on the Lower East Side, the paper suggested that the court system was "real estate controlled and a tool of landlords." It proposed a program that concentrated on "direct action, including rent strikes, local political contacts, mass delegations to courts and City agencies, etc.," as well as other ideas and language that were inherently innocent but were volatile in the paranoid climate of the MFY crisis.

Haberman called me to schedule an appointment, but would not tell me what the subject of our meeting was to be. Hardly reassuring was his reason for secrecy: "I don't want you to have time to prepare your defenses," he said. I had forgotten about the existence of the housing paper, but he saw it as a prima facie case of Marxist theory. He paled when I told him that other executives and I had participated in the housing meeting. It would, of course, need to be thoroughly investigated "to stem the damage." (His report ultimately charged us with poor judgment rather than subversive intent.)

The expertise of those who were considered competent to evaluate Mobilization's community program was another issue that festered throughout the crisis. We held that a lawyer was an inappropriate arbiter of the program, and that professionals had the right to be judged by their peers. Eventually, this view prevailed, and a blue ribbon panel of social workers and social scientists was organized to evaluate MFY's community initiative.

Tensions culminated in an executive staff revolt and a highly charged board meeting on October 28. Two days prior to the meeting, a memo from Mobilization's administrative and executive staff was circulated appealing to the board "to reassert its moral and legal responsibility to prevent the devitalization of MFY." The statement listed instances in which the board was ignored or by-passed by Carlton or Haberman. For example, although the board had authorized a special panel to review the community program, "before the panel had held its first meeting, Carlton had advanced plans to contract the entire operation to organizations outside the Lower East Side." Cited, too, was the violation of the board's agreement with the special counsel that his reports would be confidential, to be released only by the board. The statement also decried the fact that, soon after the *News* attack, the board had said it would seek the assistance of politically knowledgeable persons and public relations experts, but had not done so. "Our response to charges, in every instance, has instead been to lend credence to them by promising to investigate."

Some board members from Columbia and the local agencies caucused to review how they might support the executive staff appeal. It is not hyperbole to suggest that MFY was in fact in receivership, at least informal-ly. Carlton and Haberman ignored board directives and made major deci-sions concerning the various investigations and MFY's dealing with the City, following clearance with Washington and in response to its "ad-vice." The executive staff was, of course, less interested in board hege-mony than in protecting MFY's program and personnel, but the issues of board primacy and program integrity were interrelated.

The board caucus was also convinced of the need to assert its policy role and made common cause with the executive staff. It planned to in-troduce a motion reaffirming the initial charge to the special counsel that he would report solely and confidentially to the board. The motion was to be introduced by one of the local board members during the discussion of the issues raised by the executive staff. The motion also included the pro-viso that actions in relation to program and executive and board structure must follow established procedures and be subject to board approval prior to discussion with outside persons.

At the board meeting itself it was clear that out adversaries had also or-ganized. Six or seven of the City board members appeared although no City member had attended since the *News*'s salvo of August 16. Carlton outmaneuvered us as well. The board would meet first in executive session, he declared, to discuss whether it would agree to entertain the staff docu-ment. Haberman and I would make a statement if we wished, but we were to leave the meeting until a decision was reached on recognizing the staff paper. Haberman and Carlton both threatened to resign if the board entertained the paper. In the knowledge that there was a motion to be made later, I said that entertaining the statement was less important than dealing with the issues it raised. It was agreed that they could be discussed subsequently.

Unfortunately, the motion was never offered. An executive committee meeting of the board had been held prior to the full meeting, at which Haberman had apologized for releasing an interim report to Washington and at which he had accepted his accountability to the board. The desig-nated presenter thought, therefore, that the motion was no longer neces-sary, ignoring the other prescriptions it contained. Although 10 to 12 others had attended caucuses, none tried to fill in the breach and offer the motion themselves.

The staff "mutiny" (as Carlton characterized it) was poorly conceived. The conflict should have been spearheaded by board members rather than staff. Further, circulating the document in advance allowed the opposition to mobilize its forces. Nevertheless, the collapse of the board/staff position need not have occurred. I suspect that the motion was not introduced be-cause the members were at that point emotionally spent by the intensity of the conflict over the staff paper. There is probably a limited amount of en-ergy that members without a critical stake in an issue can be expected to expend. In addition, many board members were high-level administrators of organizations that depended on good relations with the City, and they would be cautious about antagonizing it.

The School of Social Work is a case in point. Leadership of the Columbia board contingent rested with the School's associate dean. The associate dean (who was to become a welfare commissioner in a subsequent City administration) expressed principled support for Mobilization's programs and the defense of civil liberties throughout the crisis. Curiously, however, the support rarely translated into action. Proposals for School intervention were met by such comments as "they wouldn't help; they'd only make things worse." Thus did his gloom cast a pall over suggestions for School action. Essentially, his stance provided a prescription for passivity from a moral high ground with no imputation of self-interest. The situation changed following a rally organized by New York's schools of social work at which Columbia was roundly criticized for its notable silence throughout the entire Mobilization attack. The next morning, an emergency meeting of faculty was held to propose that the School speak out in support of Mobilization; otherwise it would be viewed with disappointment by its students and social work constituency. For the first time in three months of the crisis, the associate dean revealed his concern that the School "ran the risk of losing a number of projects sponsored in conjunction with the City."

Although the failure of the October 28 meeting resulted in my feeling a deeply personal sense of loss, a more objective evaluation suggests that the meeting was a standoff. Subsequently, Carlton and Haberman behaved less cavalierly and consulted more frequently than heretofore. A dynamic of the internal discord was that neither side wanted to push the other over the edge; whenever it came close to that, accommodations were sought.

Mobilization's fortunes began to shift in its favor following the national election. Screvane's interim report on November 10 was dismissed even by the Republican press. The *Herald Tribune*, which had supported Goldwater, called it "a report that indicts by implying more than it proves." (A few years later, Screvane ran for mayor. I note with what I hope is pardonable satisfaction that he was vigorously condemned by liberal Reform Democratic clubs in the city for his stance on MFY, and he lost the race.)

Most significant in the changing climate was the November 17 site committee report of the President's Committee. Its panel was headed by Leonard Cottrell, the highly respected director of the Russell Sage Foundation, and consisted of a settlement house director, an educator, a criminologist, two foundation officials, and an attorney. In addition to recommending continued funding of MFY by all of its sponsors, its support of Mobilization's organizing effort was unequivocal. "Of all the projects supported by the President's Committee," it said, "MFY has been outstanding in its efforts to involve local residents in actions to improve their social conditions."

Because of Mobilization's good publicity, Haberman's report was anticlimactic. The report was moderate and supportive, although he told me privately that there was more to the housing business than he had been able to ferret out. He appeared eager to return to his law practice, and was, in part, disconsolate about the agency's current good fortunes, since it damaged his self-conception as the hero who would save MFY.

On the basis of the President Committee's endorsement, it now seemed possible for me to leave MFY without an imputation of guilt. I had decided to do so for personal reasons. The City's endorsement was not yet assured, but a procedure for clearing names with the City's personnel department appeared to be the minimum requirement it would exact. (HARYOU-ACT, a fraternal community action program in Harlem, had agreed to a City name check and was fingerprinting its staff.) Implementing a political means test was not only distasteful to me but might be professionally damaging as well. I was convinced, too, that the vibrancy, idealism, energy, and innovation of Mobilization—its sense of mission—could not survive the battering we had taken. Fortuitously, I was offered a high-level job in the Department of Labor and accepted it. Federal employment had the considerable advantage of demonstrating that I was not "subversive," and certainly not someone skillful enough to forge a coalition of Stalinists, Maoists, Trotskyites, and Castroites, per the whispered accusation of the executive director of the local council of agencies.

On January 15, with the release of Screvane's final report, the crisis may be said to have concluded. The City had retreated from almost all of its accusations, including the misappropriation of funds, a charge that was added during the course of the conflict.[3] No clean bill of health, however, could mitigate the consequences of the bruising experience.

MFY, as do all embattled organizations, sought to maintain stability in a hostile environment through increasing formalization, emphasizing means over ends, the instrumental over the substantive. Rules and procedures served to increase predictability, enhance the control of lower-level staff, and provide a defensive posture in the face of criticism. One example of post-crisis control was the newly "efficient" payroll procedures, causing one executive to state in a memo that the indigenous nonprofessionals employed by the agency were barely able to "stand the blows of the accounting department." One afternoon he found one such staff member "crying in the middle of the street, and another so angry as to be in a state of near-paranoia."

Personnel and training had been combined functions at MFY, led by a social worker. Subsequently, the functions were separated, and a new personnel director was hired. He was an administrator with prior experience in the City Personnel Department whose job application promised that he could help the agency avoid hiring subversive staff.

Staff turnover was considerable. In the eight months prior to the attack, 9 percent of the staff departed; in the eight months following its inception, turnover had grown to almost 25 percent. Particularly hard hit was the community organizing and group services program. Here, there were 16 resignations, and only seven persons hired to replace them. (In a letter to the Ford Foundation, Carlton indicated that by holding unfilled positions vacant, the agency could meet expenses incurred by special studies of personnel and fiscal operations.)

A serendipitous outcome of the Mobilization experience was the pathway into academia that the agency provided. After a six-month stint at the Department of Labor, I was sufficiently "rehabilitated" to gain a position teaching community organization at Columbia. (However painful the MFY experience was, it resulted in enormous learning for me, particularly with regard to the inseparability of policy and politics, as well as the dynamics of organizational stasis and change.) Other staff who gravitated to universities were: Charles Grosser, Harry Specht, Frances Piven, Robert Pruger, Sherman Barr, Gertrude Goldberg, Marilyn Bibb, Pat Purcell, and Phil Kramer. (One might presume they needed the rest!)

Although the organization was severely damaged, its ideas gained increased legitimacy, probably as a result of the program's added visibility, the widespread support it was able to garner, and the commitment of adherents around the country. Nationally, Mobilization may be said to have provided the impetus for lawyers to serve welfare clients and other impoverished citizens, to aid the poor as plaintiffs as well as defendants, and to challenge social policies and laws that were detrimental to low-income people. Mobilization's impact on professional thinking in social work has also been considerable. Among its achievements were (1) initiating the idea of employing local low-income workers in community programs, (2) advancing the concept of the social worker as an advocate of the poor, (3) recognizing the need of the poor for legal assistance in their relationship to agencies administering benefits, (4) reintroducing the notion of subsidized work training for youth, and (5) a dual programmatic focus on both structural change and individual adaptation.

If Mobilization demonstrated that poor people can be organized to deal with the social problems that afflict them, it may also have demonstrated that it can be done only at the cost of seriously risking damage to the parent organization. Indeed, the attack on MFY was subsequently echoed nationally by numbers of community action programs that also came under the gun. In effect, of course, funders call the tune, and while some organizations can develop their own leverage or even insulate themselves from sponsor direction, there are limits to their ability to respond to the requirements for social change in impoverished communities. A political balancing act is necessary to avoid arousing sponsor intercession while remaining true to the needs of the low-income constituency.

The ability of social work agencies to pursue social change on behalf of and with disadvantaged citizens depends on the political climate of the times: how aroused its citizens are and how much political clout they have. Social idealism may burgeon in one period, die in the next, flower again, and subside once more. What grassroots community organizers in social work must strive to do, then, is to push the parameters of the possible and take advantage of opportunities that the times permit.

ENDNOTES

1.   Daniel P. Moynihan, *Maximum Feasible Misunderstanding* (New York: Free Press, 1969), p. 123.

2.   Frances Fox Piven, "Federal Interventions in the Cities," in *Handbook on the Studies of Social Problems*, ed. E. E. Smuggle (New York: Rand McNally, 1969).

3.   Joseph H. Helfgot, *Professional Reforming: Mobilization for Youth and the Failure of Social Science* (Lexington, MA: D. C. Heath & Co., 1981), pp. 94–95.

BIBLIOGRAPHY

Brager, George, and Harry Specht. 1973. *Community Organizing*. 1st ed. New York: Columbia University Press.

A Proposal for the Prevention and Control of Delinquency by Expanding Opportunities, A Demonstration Project Conceived and Developed by Mobilization for Youth, Submitted to the National Institute of Mental Health for a grant, December 9, 1961.

Grosser, Charles F. 1973. *New Directions in Community Organization: From Enabling to Advocacy*. New York: Praeger.

Pearl, Arthur, and Frank Reisman. 1965. *New Careers for the Poor*. New York: Free Press.

Zimbalist, Sidney E. 1970. "Mobilization for Youth: Search for a New Social Work." *Social Work* 15, no. 1 (January):123.

High Hopes,
Hard Realities

Robert Perlman

The original point of departure for these rec-
ollections was this question: What were our expectations of community
organization and how well did they fit with the realities we faced and the
strategies we used to achieve our objectives? I soon found that my
thoughts branched off into other questions and themes.

What attracted us to this kind of work? We came into this field with a
range of expectations as to what CO should and could accomplish—expectations based on our life experiences, ideological commitments, and
personal aspirations. What were our hopes, how realistic were they, and
how did they contribute to our motivation as practitioners?

How are the efforts of a community organization worker legitimated?
Where did we get the franchise for the work we did and the goals we set?
At the end of the day, what was accomplished by "community organization"? As the story unfolded, it became increasingly clear that my experiences, which took place between 1948 and 1968, were profoundly shaped
by the political and social circumstances that prevailed during those years.

It would be foolish indeed to try to respond fully in a few pages to
such a litany of questions. They do, however, provide some useful back-

ground for organizing these recollections. Let me begin with my own expectations.

My ideas and convictions stemmed from a liberal family background: My parents had voted in election after election for Norman Thomas, the perennial Socialist candidate for president, and they talked much about social issues and social justice. In college I was drawn—emotionally and intellectually—to the struggle against fascism in Spain; the beginnings of the industrial labor movement close by in Flint, Michigan; the rape of Czechoslovakia; the status of blacks in America; the issue of inequality. Later, when I was writing public relations materials for a social agency, I was an active member of the Social Service Employees Union in New York.

Fortunately, I never throw anything away, so when I recently asked myself why I went into social work, there, waiting in my file cabinet was the statement I had sent along in 1946 with my application to the school of social work at Western Reserve University. I wanted, I wrote, "to help people work toward a solution of their problems," problems that had "their roots in the inequalities and maladjustments of our social and economic organization."

When I entered social work school in 1946, after four years in the Navy during World War II, I had just spent the summer working with a group of boys in Harlem. It had been a shocking glimpse at the underside of New York; it had also convinced me that I wanted, as I told the Admissions Committee, "to work with groups of young people and adults in such fields as interracial projects, youth clubs, and adult education and recreation programs." In short, I was headed for training in group work in order to work more effectively in "a settlement house or a community center."

I think it was at the point of entering social work school that I first heard about "community organization." It sounded much closer to my interests than group work, since it was about "community" and about "organizing." CO appeared to involve social justice and social change and, although it sounded a bit vague, I was strongly drawn to it and asked to be switched from group work to Community Organization.

I bridled at the school's policy that students could not "go directly" into Community Organization, but had to spend a year in a case work or group work field placement. The unconvincing explanation was that CO was built on the skills and knowledge of "basic" social work. This was not made much clearer beyond some mumbled references to such skills as interviewing. I spent my first year in group work. My second year's field work experience, in a CO placement, was unrewarding. Teaching "civics" to a group of immigrants in a citizenship class was not what I was looking for. Perhaps it was not typical of other placements. Overall, the group work courses at the school under Grace Coyle were magnificent, but the CO curriculum was new, undeveloped, and uninspiring.

What brought CO into much better focus for me was working on a study of the Glenville Area Community Council in Cleveland. David Austin, John Turner, Del Jay Kinney, and I—all of us in school on the GI Bill—collaborated on this group thesis, with Mildred Barry as our faculty advisor. We saw the council as a "test tube for democracy."

The community council had been organized out of concern over the rising social tensions in the Glenville area, where blacks were moving, in increasing numbers, into a community that had been Jewish and "white Gentile." This was the real stuff of organizing a community—helping people to come together to confront their pressing problems: neighbor against neighbor, distrust, discrimination in housing, inadequate recreation, crime, blockbusting, white flight, and the like.

Our main focus was the residents' participation in the council. We did not set out to evaluate the council's accomplishments, probably because we lacked the tools and the time for that kind of assessment. But we did get a good look at the practical side and some of the more theoretical aspects of the work. How could people be brought into the process of achieving change at the neighborhood level? How could the differing priorities of the blacks, Jews, and white Gentiles be reconciled? Was social class more important than race or ethnicity in this context? Should the organization be built on individual memberships, on community leadership, or as a council of professional workers?

In any event, the CO worker, a very able man, found it necessary to build on the existing leadership, especially among professionals, as he sought to attract a broader membership. In an area of about 45,000 people, the council claimed to be a coordinating body of organizations with 8,000 adult members. However, active participation in the work of the council was limited to very small numbers. For example, an ambitious membership drive brought in only 500 new members. Proportionately, people from the black community participated in the council more than the white Gentiles or the Jews; each group concentrated on those issues it considered most important.

Studying the council was a sobering experience. Community organizing on a neighborhood and district basis was hard work: That much was clear. The council had had some concrete accomplishments, such as arranging for 7,000 people to have X rays. Even if we had tried, it would have been difficult to evaluate outcomes. Much of the council's activity consisted of education and political action, such as documenting the area's needs or pressing public officials to improve conditions. These were, in a sense, inputs toward results that might be long in coming. The tangible changes actually achieved seemed limited, certainly in comparison with my hopes—which were, as I look back on it, unrealistic.

I do not recall having any CO job offers when I left social work school. For the next dozen years I supervised group workers in Jewish centers and had only marginal experiences with community organization. In 1959, hearing about a new school of advanced studies in social welfare at Brandeis University reignited my earlier interests in working as a professional interested in addressing social problems. For me, the Heller School opened up new perspectives, new concepts, and new approaches, especially those drawn from political science, economics, and sociology.

The interconnected problems of American cities attracted my attention as a subject for a dissertation, using Boston as a case study. This was an extension of my earlier interest in broad social issues and a later fascination with social history. I learned that, in 1949, a two-year survey of health and welfare resources and needs in metropolitan Boston had been completed. One year later, a general plan for the metropolitan area was drafted as a guide for future planning and development. After some digging, I found "no evidence of collaboration in the drawing of these two plans."

I began to wonder about this fragmentation of social and physical planning and of efforts to deal with the needs of a major American city and so, for the dissertation, I focused on the relationship between the planning of social welfare services and the planning of the physical aspects of the city. At the turn of the century, America's cities were overflowing with millions of new immigrants and were sinking into poverty, exploitation, and corruption.

Settlement house workers, architects, lawyers, sociologists, crusading journalists, "charity" workers, and some political leaders grasped the connections among the cities' problems. They collaborated in a number of ways. It is tempting but idle to wonder whether something like the beginnings of community organization could have emerged from their efforts. It didn't. The dominant trend of the times ran in the opposite direction, toward specialization and professionalism. Social work and urban planning, for instance, were emerging as distinct professions with divergent purposes and technologies.

The reformers of the early 1900s gradually brought about some improvements in labor conditions, tenement house living, public health, and other areas, but these seemed to me, again, to be dwarfed by the underlying problems of inequality and poverty that persisted. By the time of the Depression and World War II, the cities faced serious housing shortages, the spread of slums, the movement of millions of people to the cities, and the flight of others to the suburbs. The federal government's response was "urban renewal," which consisted of slum clearance, then rehabilitation of housing, and ultimately "redevelopment"—especially of the cities' economic cores.

Urban renewal posed some hard questions for community organization. Which social welfare agencies were ready to take an active part in the planning of changes in housing, in recreational areas, in street patterns and highways—changes that would have profound impacts on neighborhoods? And which agencies would promote the involvement of the residents in the politics of urban renewal? Which were prepared to wade into tough, politically charged battles, such as those resulting from the accusation that urban renewal actually amounted to "Negro removal"? My dissertation had explored these issues as they had played out in Boston in the 1950s, and my findings did not encourage much optimism about how they would be handled in the 1960s.

Nevertheless (or perhaps because "social planning" seemed so necessary and so difficult), it was exciting when I left Brandeis to move into the thick of things in Boston. The city was launched on an ambitious urban renewal program, and the mayor had put Edward Logue in charge of the Redevelopment Authority. Logue, a lawyer with an attractive track record in urban development in New Haven, was a dynamic and dominating figure.

Boston's renewal program coincided with the beginnings of a new national consciousness about urban poverty and related social problems. The Ford Foundation was among the first to act by offering to finance new organizations that would address the problems of the "gray areas" in America's cities. To a considerable extent, these were in fact the black areas of American cities. This initiative spawned organizations in a number of cities, among them Action for Boston Community Development (ABCD), which was my employer from 1961 to 1964. The Foundation put much emphasis on involving leaders of the public and private sectors in new relationships and in developing among them an openness to making changes in deeply entrenched programs, especially in the public schools.

As development administrator for the city, Ed Logue hoped ABCD would take on some of the social concerns related to his renewal plans. For instance, the schools in Boston, were in miserable shape, and he wanted improvements in education and in social services that would add luster to "the New Boston." And Logue wanted ABCD to mount a skillful community organizing process, which, combined with improved services, would make his plans for urban renewal more palatable to the residents of Boston's low-income neighborhoods. At the outset and for some time thereafter, Logue controlled the shape and direction of the new organization, though it was to be formally outside of city government and independent of the Redevelopment Authority.

Within a year after ABCD was up and running, President John F. Kennedy's administration took up the growing problem of juvenile delinquency, which was most evident in the same urban areas where the Ford Foundation was focusing its attention. Along with other projects supported by the foundation, ABCD applied for funds from the President's Committee on Juvenile Delinquency.

The President's Committee based its approach on the "opportunity theory" of juvenile delinquency developed by Richard Cloward and Lloyd Ohlin. They called for removing "social, ethnic and economic barriers to opportunities for achieving legitimate goals." The President's Committee encouraged the projects they funded to employ program planners and researchers in a demonstration of "rational planning" and careful evaluation of outcomes. And they wanted the residents of low-income, minority neighborhoods well represented in the planning.

Armed with funding from the Ford Foundation and the President's Committee, ABCD had two levers with which to effect change: money from outside of Boston—which everyone wanted—and some limited influence among community leaders who were rather well represented on its board of directors. It was imperative that ABCD maintain the support (or at least the neutrality) of the major players in Boston: the Irish city hall people, the economically powerful Yankees (who also ran the community welfare council), and the black community that was beginning to find its voice. A few Jews who were active on the social service scene were also important, though most of the Jewish community had already left the inner city for the suburbs.

As ABCD's director of program development, my job was planning, negotiating, and setting new programs in motion, a role that I approached with much relish, for it seemed an opportunity to do something concrete about the very social problems that had troubled me in the years before World War II. As I got down to the daily business of program development, it soon became obvious that a big part of my job was to oversee the writing of grant proposals to bring in funds—not only as inducements to generate changes, but also to keep ABCD afloat.

In practice, my staff and I had to respond to a succession of funding sources, each with its distinct goals, strategies, expectations of ABCD, and time frames for accomplishing its objectives. And it meant keeping track of where the money faucets were. Equally important, we had to maintain almost day-to-day assessments of how far Boston's decision makers—and the bureaucrats who implemented programs—could be pushed or cajoled into making changes.

There was some room—but not much—for the input of professional planners like myself and an expanding staff of specialists in education, employment, welfare, health, legal services, and the like. One of our dilemmas at ABCD was whether to design programs in considerable detail and then try to "sell" them to the appropriate Boston agencies. This was viewed by some as "imposition," but others saw it as legitimate and rational "planning." An alternative was to engage the local agencies in the planning process and risk a watering down of the programs. We tried various combinations of these approaches.

ABCD poked into the public school system to stimulate programs such as prekindergarten and new kinds of guidance services and reading remediation The results, apparently, approved at school headquarters downtown, were frequently undercut as the plans were implemented in the classrooms. We tried unsuccessfully to develop neighborhood-based health centers. In this and other instances we made the judgment that we should work through the community welfare council rather than challenge its planning role. In retrospect, we might have achieved more by striking out boldly and directly with the extremely rich health and hospital resources of Boston.

ABCD sent district "coordinators" to the urban renewal areas to work on the creation of new services and the uneasy relationship between residents and the Redevelopment Authority. Unsure of what their mandate was, the CO workers often got caught in the cross fire inherent in "citizen participation" in urban renewal. Were they representing the citizens in their encounters with the Redevelopment Authority, or were they in reality out on the street as "pushers" for the renewal program?

We were successful in launching several neighborhood-based "multi-service centers," and it is worth pausing to examine that effort for its implications for community organization. The rationale for these centers grew out of widespread criticisms of social services in low-income, predominantly black communities—they were looked upon as inaccessible, inflexible, insensitive to ethnic and cultural differences between consumers and providers, and unresponsive to changing needs.

Some 800 new neighborhood centers, designed to counter these problems, had sprung up around the country in the 1960s; by 1971 there were 2,500. These centers reflected a change in the national political climate. David Jones, then a lecturer at the National Institute for Social Work Training in London, and I studied Neighborhood Service Centers in Boston and five other cities after I left ABCD. We wrote that the Neighborhood Service Centers had "emerged from the Negro Revolution, the civil rights movement, and the rediscovery of poverty."

It is worth noting that somewhat similar developments in community organization were afoot in Britain. In the late 1960s, a national concern over juvenile delinquency led to a government-sponsored study whose purpose was to make locally administered social services more effective. Parallel with this, the Gulbenkian Foundation was supporting a working group that was studying the uses of "community work" and how to improve training for it.

However, as David Jones recently reminded me, there was an important difference in the 1960s between the situation in the United States and in the United Kingdom. In the latter there was a universal acceptance of the welfare state and its social programs; in this country, Jones points out, public social services seemed rudimentary. In both countries, however, attention was now being given to "the participation and community aspects" of the social services.

Typically the new neighborhood centers we studied in the 1960s provided legal aid, day care, employment counseling and job placement, services for families, and the like. Their other main function was to organize groups for collective action on behalf of the residents of the neighborhoods—and there was the rub! The times called for both of these functions at the neighborhood level, but there seemed to be a built-in tension between "service delivery" and "organizing social action."

The neighborhood centers demonstrated "both the difficulty of combining these functions and the difficulty of separating them." The centers found themselves hard-pressed to cope with the conflicts set off by pursuing both these goals simultaneously. They needed cooperative relations with many agencies, public and private, but militant social action tended to antagonize those very agencies. And they needed effective social services to build support for citizen action. The problem seemed to embody the long-standing debate as to the appropriate emphasis on "cause" or "function" as the primary purpose of the activities of social workers.

On another issue, research and evaluation had been firmly incorporated in the planning and execution of ABCD's programs. The researchers and the program staff, who enjoyed generally good rapport, were committed to an "action-research" model whose fundamental objective was the reduction of juvenile delinquency. The discrete programs were expected to contribute—in measurable terms—to this overall goal, which had been set by the President's Committee on Juvenile Delinquency.

In time, tensions developed between researchers and planners at ABCD. As an example, program planners and researchers jointly designed a new reading program for the public schools and developed procedures for its evaluation. Once they were formulated, these evaluation procedures were presumably locked in place. When the programs were implemented, however, practical problems cropped up. Teachers and principals quietly changed certain features of the program or insisted that the record keeping for evaluation purposes was too burdensome. The program staff tried to negotiate compromises in order to salvage the specific program. The research people felt that this undermined their evaluation design. The resulting tensions were, however, manageable.

For four years I had been under continuing pressure at ABCD to "get things done," pressures that left little time or energy to think about the larger implications of *what we were doing*. Moreover, speaking personally, I was so close to events and so invested in achieving "successes" that I could hardly make dispassionate assessments. I now have some thoughts, in retrospect, about the meaning of my experience at ABCD, but first I want to present the views of some outside observers.

Stephan Thernstrom wrote a history of ABCD during its early years (1961–1965), and Peter Marris and Martin Rein conducted a study of the projects, including ABCD, that were funded by the Ford Foundation and the President's Committee on Juvenile Delinquency. In large measure, the analyses and critiques coincided.

When I first read these books I was stung by their conclusions. It appeared to me that they had determined ABCD to be at best a waste and at worst a fraud. However, in time I have come to accept their conclusions as valid for the most part. They were able to see more clearly the forces at work—nationally and locally—than had I, as well as the severe constraints they placed on ABCD's freedom of movement.

Marris and Rein found that ABCD was constantly reacting to a succession of conflicting—and changing—expectations from other actors. Clearly Logue as head of the Redevelopment Authority and the mayor had no interest in a carefully crafted "social experiment" and the attendant research. City Hall and the residents of the urban renewal neighborhoods were impatient with the lengthy planning process and what seemed to them to be a diversion of resources to irrelevant exercises in evaluation. They wanted both immediate action on concrete issues and large-scale programs that would have an impact on the areas of the city that were hurting.

The Ford Foundation was essentially trying to generate new institutional relationships in Boston that would facilitate innovative programs in the "gray areas." On the other hand, ABCD tried more rigorously than most of the urban projects to carry out a "rational social planning model" in accordance with the expectations of the President's Committee on Juvenile Delinquency. It should be noted that the President's Committee at that time was providing most of the financial support for ABCD.

ABCD's strategies were roundly criticized in the books by Thernstrom and Marris and Rein, primarily on the ground that they put too much emphasis on the processes of planning and decision making. Some people couched this in terms of the planners' "social work style" and perceived the ABCD staff, with its concern for process, as "spineless opportunists." Most of the staff people who were in at the beginning of ABCD were in fact social workers who were committed to engaging other actors in inclusive, democratic decision making.

A few critics hungered for new ideas about social problems and their solutions and wanted them to come from ABCD. Thernstrom reports that, at one point, a frustrated Logue told Perlman "I don't want you to talk to anybody. Just write!" He was waiting impatiently for crisp program proposals—like those he got from architects and urban planners at the

Redevelopment Authority—that could be funded and put into action with tangible results in a short time.

Thernstrom noted that the President's committee continued to hope that ABCD would adhere to a rational planning model, but that in fact it was unable to deliver on that expectation. But was the model either feasible or desirable? Could such a planning process work in the real world, where, as Thernstrom noted, "specific programs developed out of a continuing process of bargaining"?

Was it possible, Marris and Rein asked, or even useful to specify a final objective for an action-research project? They suggested that it is much easier (and probably more productive) "to make rational choices if a plan of action is broken down into a series of proximate steps and the plan is open to revision as each step is completed." In their view, incremental and evolutionary planning would have been more practicable.

In addition, Marris and Rein raised the question of "legitimacy" in setting social goals and directing change. Purely "rational planning" as carried out by technicians and bureaucrats might be not only impractical but also undemocratic and untenable from a political perspective. Where does the responsibility for planning lie in a diffuse democracy and "who are the authentic communicators of the people's wishes?" Who had given ABCD a mandate to plan for Boston?

These were the main critical assessments that others made about ABCD as a planning and organizing body. What are my own thoughts today? First, I must agree that among the most compelling realities facing us at ABCD were the expectations and directives coming from its funding sources and local decision makers. As the professional staff we could not—and should not have tried to—ignore the goals set by our sponsors. However inconsistent they were with each other, these expectations represented the desires and the interests of legitimate participants in determining the course of action in Boston. Nevertheless, it was our responsibility as professional workers to voice our own objectives and to defend our strategies and methods, and we could have been more assertive in this respect.

In retrospect, it seems obvious that juvenile delinquency was, for many of the actors on the scene, a code word, a pretext for addressing the pressing problems of poverty, unemployment, and poor education. They were not interested in waiting around to see whether statistics on juvenile crime would show a decline. And so there was pressure on ABCD from several of its constituents to de-emphasize delinquency. Some look back at this as a displacement or derailment of the original policy objective. I see it as a justifiable and inevitable shift in purpose and priorities to bring ABCD's program in line with the political realities of the time.

My own expectations, now appear to me to have been highly unrealistic and even simplistic. It took a lot of chutzpah to think that, within the space of a few years and with the meager financial and political resources at our disposal, we could have a serious effect on the rate of juvenile delinquency or the quality of public education in Boston, not to mention the accomplishment of a host of other laudable objectives we solemnly set forth.

At every level we underestimated the complexity of the social problems we addressed. And we underestimated the kind and amount of resistance that other actors generated to avoid changing their behavior. Time was a crucial factor: We operated as though we had the proverbial 100 days to accomplish our goals!

As for the charge that we had overemphasized process at the expense of product, I think we could have been more skillful in finding ways to engage the other actors so that their interests were taken into account and their resistance diminished. There were many ways of doing this: fuller involvement of the board of directors, inclusion of line workers and not just their executives in program design, smarter use of the media, and open hearings at various stages of the planning, among others.

Perhaps, in the mad rush of those days to capture any piece of funding regardless of the conditions attached, we underestimated our resources to hold out for a more modest—but more coherent and deliverable—set of objectives. Did we make the best use of our lines to power centers in Boston? Could we have joined with projects in other cities in a kind of collective bargaining with the Ford Foundation, the President's Committee, and other funding sources to arrive at more workable guidelines and time frames? Could we even have turned down grants where the conditions were unachievable?

In terms of our strategies, probably it was futile to argue as vehemently as we sometimes did about the choice between "service delivery" and "social action." We might better have sought out the best combination of these and other strategies.

By the end of 1965, what had been accomplished? I cannot give a comprehensive or definitive answer to that, but I can offer some broadstroke impressions. To use Thernstrom's word, the results were "disappointing" when measured against the widely broadcast expectations.

New and effective ideas of what to do about urban social problems proved to be exceedingly hard to come by. I can remember frustrating discussions with our sponsors about whether ABCD had come up with truly "innovative" programs—something they felt we had not achieved and I felt they never adequately defined. We could not point to demonstrated improvements that could be attributed to the juvenile delinquency programs. ABCD had certainly not turned out to be "the human side of urban renewal." Here, again, we might have been both more courageous and more canny in our intermediary role between the Redevelopment Authority and neighborhood people.

In any event, the competing political interests in Boston (and Washington) proved to be more compelling than "new ideas" about social problems. I submit that, far from being a disaster or a distortion of a "proper" process, the thrust and parry of political competition is an essential and potentially healthy element in community organizing, as it is in other expressions of democracy in America.

What had been lacking for decades in the political process was the participation—on anything approaching a level playing field—of the most vulnerable and underrepresented constituencies: blacks and other ethnic minorities; poor people; and consumers of social services. The activities of community organization that I have been describing were, in a broad historical context, attempts in the 1960s by some forces in Boston and in the nation to begin righting this imbalance.

Take the issues of "changing neighborhoods" and urban renewal," which represented problems and opportunities stemming from social and geographic mobility and economic changes. These produced both hope and fear on the part of the minorities, as well as the white working class and middle class. Some people were pushing for change, some for "stability"—which meant freezing the existing conditions. CO workers and planners were called upon, admittedly on a modest scale, to make more manageable certain features of these community strains.

It should not be said that nothing was accomplished. Many individuals and families benefitted from better services. Some lines of communication and action were developed that had not existed before. ABCD produced a meaningful legacy: After 30 years it is still alive and well, with a multimillion dollar budget, a wide range of concrete services to help low-income people in Boston, and a voice on policy issues in the city and state. The neighborhood service center in Roxbury continues to contribute to these same achievements.

One of the worthwhile by-products of ABCD and the neighborhood center has been almost overlooked, perhaps because it took years to become visible. Neighborhood leaders and professionals in the black community gained access and experience that facilitated their movement into positions of more responsibility and influence in Boston and Massachusetts.

How did the surrounding social and political conditions affect the developments I have been describing? A strong case can be made that much progress was made possible by a heightened national awareness of the problem of poverty in America. This was combined with a deeper understanding of the patterns of discrimination in housing, education, and employment that had excluded most black people from access to America's opportunities and resources.

To put this in a broader historical perspective, the early 1960s marked the beginning of a brief period of resurgent liberalism in national policy. The Ford Foundation and the President's Committee on Juvenile Delinquency ushered in a time of ferment, experimentation, and optimism. These two initiatives provided a nurturing context that was critical to the developments we have seen in the preceding pages. They coincided in spirit and in time with the civil rights movement and the political stirrings of black America. It is hard to imagine such a convergence of developments taking place in today's political climate!

The Ford Foundation and the President's Committee on Juvenile Delinquency both reflected and stimulated a readiness to turn away from the conservatism of public policies that had characterized the 1950s. For some of us this seemed to hark back to the unfinished business of Franklin Roosevelt's New Deal. The change in direction, which later included Lyndon Johnson's Great Society programs and the War on Poverty, had three defining characteristics: (1) a renewed emphasis on the needs of the most vulnerable and disadvantaged groups in America; (2) a strong leadership role for the federal government in policy formation and funding; and (3) a legislative mandate to facilitate citizen participation in the planning and implementation of new programs.

These shifts in priorities and roles lasted only about 15 years. While these trends lasted, however, community organization and planning—despite their limitations and our overly optimistic expectations—had a useful and significant role in the advances that were achieved.

Looking back, I've learned that the high hopes with which CO workers approach their task must be tempered by the realization that their efforts are embedded in a much larger social and political context. It takes a clear-eyed analysis to sort out the critical factors as one sets (and resets) goals and selects (and revises) actions.

A CO worker must expect a frustrating gap between his or her ideological commitments and the incremental changes that are possible. A prime reason for this is the fact that each actor in the game exacts a price for political or financial support; the CO worker must decide when the support is worth the price.

In addition, the worker must learn how to manage pressures to achieve visible results in a short time. Some of the most valuable outcomes will come only in the long run. Finally, the worker will be wise to pause in the heat of battle to reflect on what is happening and to make adjustments. It is not necessary to wait 30 years to reflect.

BIBLIOGRAPHY

Gulbenkian Foundation. 1968. *Community Work and Social Change*. London: Longmans.

Marris, Peter, and Martin Rein. 1967. *Dilemmas of Social Reform: Poverty and Community Action in the United States*. London: Routledge & Kegan Paul.

Perlman, Robert. 1975. *Consumers and Social Services*. New York: John Wiley.

Perlman, Robert, and Arnold Gurin. 1972. *Community Organization and Social Planning*. New York: John Wiley.

Perlman, Robert, and David Jones. 1967. *Neighborhood Service Centers*. Washington, DC: U.S. Department of Health, Education and Welfare.

Thernstrom, Stephan. 1969. *Poverty, Planning, and Politics in the New Boston: The Origins of ABCD*. New York: Basic Books.

Neighborhood Work
and Community
Development

MAKING AND SAVORING
SMALL-SCALE GAINS IN
LOCAL COMMUNITIES

Neighborhood Organization: How Well Does It Work?

John B. Turner

Our Sunday guests were taking their seats at the dinner table. I knew that once they began to eat it would become quieter. Later I might have a chance to make my suggestion. Prior to dinner, there was conversation and laughter concerning what went on that morning in church. After the blessing, everyone settled down to Sunday's feast.

Finally, there was a lull in conversation. Now was my chance. In a very confident manner, I blurted out, "There are too many churches on our side of town." I didn't get to say more before being sent out of the room, with my mother and grandmother making disclaimers for what they assumed were anti-Christian remarks.

Several days passed before I had the opportunity to explain that I had made a list of observations of all of the churches, and I noted that many of them had broken steps, broken gutters, window panes in need of repair, and buildings in need of paint. I also observed that most churches had only a few people in attendance on Sunday mornings. I pointed out that if some of them were to merge, members might be able to take better care of their churches.

While the explanation bought back some of my credibility as my mother's son, my first community problem-solving effort stopped right where it began—in the mind of an 11-year-old boy.

That summer, my mother would occasionally put my sister and me under the bed for protection from drive-by gunshots when the Ku Klux Klan came through out neighborhood. I didn't know it then, but that summer, I was having my first encounter with some of the dynamics of community problem-solving, which I would be trying to manipulate for as long as I chose to be involved in work with communities. What is a community problem? Who decides that a situation is a problem, that a situation is sufficiently problematic or ripe to take collective action and how to choose a solution?

If I had been a community organization worker—with my survey results accurate, declining property values cogently predicted, and the need successfully argued for churches to be models for other property owners in maintaining their homes—would the churches have agreed to merge? (I now know that churches are more likely to splinter than merge, especially Baptist churches.)

Should the community organizer drop this initiative or should the worker press on with his belief? And, what priority could church building repairs have in a community where there was palpable fear of violence from the "Klan"?

Twelve years later, standing in line on sick call at Mather Field, California, I discussed with the soldier next to me the status of black Americans as observed in the different cities we had visited while in the Air Corps. He suggested that, if I was interested in work helping blacks help themselves, I should take a job with the Urban League. He spoke about the Cleveland, Ohio, Urban League and a man named Sidney Williams, the executive. Several months later, now stationed in Kentucky, I phoned and made an appointment to meet Sidney Williams.

On August 14, 1945, I was in Cleveland, spending the day with the executive of the Cleveland Urban League. Sidney Williams and I were in the vicinity of 89th Street and Central Avenue attending street rallies organized by the Urban League on employment, health, schools, housing, public safety, and the like. I didn't know that activities like this were taking place in black communities. It was my introduction to citizen participation and to community self-help, and it was most exciting. A few hours later, the end of the war with Japan would be announced. As the full meaning of that event became clearer, I made a decision to forgo a career in engineering.

My first day out of the military and back home, I went to the Atlanta Urban League and declared myself ready to help the black poor of Atlanta.

I was asked what could I do. I had been a mathematics major in college and a pilot in the war. It took less than a millionth of a second to realize that the road to hell was paved with people of good intent.

Later that morning, through the help of the Urban League, I went to work with the local YMCA in one of the disadvantaged areas. After a few months on the job, I also learned that I didn't know enough to work with the poor at the "Y." I thought about entering law, but on the advice of a sociology professor whom I respected, I selected social work.

A few weeks after a memorable preadmissions interview with E. C. Lindeman of Columbia University, I met Henry Ollendorf from Friendly Inn Settlement in Cleveland. Although Henry was a graduate of Columbia, he convinced me that I would always regret it if I did not study with Grace Coyle, an outstanding educator at Western Reserve University (Case Western Reserve). It proved to be advice for which I have always been thankful.

The next year, I turned up at Western Reserve's School of Applied Social Sciences and declared myself a candidate for what I understood to be a course of study in Community Organization. I was told that perhaps I needed a bit more maturity, and that the faculty would appraise that choice later; first, I would need to spend a year studying group work. Although I didn't think so at the time, they were right about both. A bit more maturity did prove helpful, and group work proved to be a very useful foundation for me for the practice of Community Organization. Grace Coyle became my mentor.

During the second year of graduate study, I was permitted to major in Community Organization. The exemplary Katherine Williamson was my field work instructor. She was employed by the Welfare Federation of Cleveland, the social planning agency, and assigned to the Central Areas of Cleveland program unit at the Federation. In addition, she served as the executive director of the Central Areas Community Council (CACC). The CACC was created by a few area leaders and professionals with the support of the Federation to help resolve social problems in the central area.

The Council's membership was representative of social service and health agencies, religious and educational institutions, a handful of small local businesses, and a few indigenous organizations like street clubs and neighborhood organizations. Its core members were socially concerned residents and professionals who resided and/or worked in the area. I was assigned to work with the Council and with Katherine Williamson, which was a significant learning experience for me.

Central Areas had a population of about 110,000, which was predominantly black and low income. At that time it was the historical center of the black community in Cleveland. Much of its housing was substandard. The air was quite polluted. Land use was a mixture of residential, manufacturing, and commercial.

Its residents were the newly arrived poor and the not so new poor. Because of housing discrimination, middle-class blacks, both older and newly arrived, were forced to live in the Central Areas. As additional residential areas opened up for blacks elsewhere in Cleveland, middle- and upper-class blacks moved from the Central Areas. This movement created a leadership drain in the CACC.

Simultaneously, the migration added blacks to leadership pools for community councils in Glenville and In Mount Pleasant, the areas to which many upwardly mobile blacks migrated. Physical mobility of people, often within the same area, has always been a fundamental difficulty in organizing at street, neighborhood, and community levels. Stated differently, when is geographic movement of people to be viewed as a success and when is it a sign of failure?

The Council was the distant equivalent of a "911" number for issues pertaining to community services. Approximately fifty percent of its activity was taken up with proposing, supporting or opposing policies and actions of ward, municipal, county, and state politicians, as well as government and human service agencies. The remaining time was spent in dealing with issues such as crime, housing violations, and youth delinquency. Basic operating funds were provided by the Welfare Federation of Cleveland, which also provided support for approximately a dozen similar locality-based operations in Cleveland.

At the time, most observers gave the Council good marks. However, this was not for bringing about any significant change in the lives of residents. The Council made little or no impact on the group status goals of the poor. Even so, people would rather have the Council than not have it. Its success was based upon a reputation for getting and publicizing the facts about matters having, or threatening to have, a negative impact on the community and its residents. It brought about public scrutiny and occasionally invoked the support of influential members of social agency and civic boards and of the Welfare Federation. Sadly, but understandably, the CACC could not effectively link its more important objectives with sources of power sufficient to accomplish its more fundamental objectives pertaining to such issues as housing, education and employment.

A second important learning experience in graduate school stemmed from collaboration with three other students in writing a group thesis. The three were David Austin, Del Jay Kinney, and Robert Perlman. Our supervisor for this joint enterprise was Mildred Barry. She tutored us like the fine teacher and incomparable practitioner she is. The title of the study was *Community Council: Test Tube for Democracy—A Case Study of the Glenville Area Council.* My colleagues also found this to be an extremely meaningful experience, and David Austin and Robert Perlman comment on it in their reflections in this book.

In contrast with Central Areas, the Glenville Area was populated by mostly lower-middle-, middle-, and upper-middle-class home owners. The population was roughly one-third white and Catholic, one-third black, and one-third Jewish. As previously stated, it was one of the areas to which middle- and upper-class blacks could move. Its schools were considered good. The area contained a senior high school, two junior high schools, six elementary schools, three fire stations, one police district, two branches of the public library, and three political districts.

Located six miles from downtown, Glenville in 1948 was still considered a good community in which to live, a community where people had some sense of belonging and ownership over public and voluntary institutions. Except for strip-mall retail areas, it was residential in character with some exceptionally fine homes and apartments.

The Council focused on protection and promotion of quality living, with interracial collaboration around the business of everyday living as a secondary objective. For these goals and during this period, the Council was generally seen as successful. In particular, it received good marks for securing widespread participation from all three cultural groups. The Council was staffed by an extremely skillful and wise community organizer, Donald Stier. His salary and basic operating costs were provided by the Welfare Federation of Cleveland, similar to the arrangement in Central Areas.

The Glenville case study focused on the eighteen months prior to 1948. It reviewed structure, member participation, and interracial attitudes of members. It did not find the mass participation the Council was reputed to have, nor did it find evidence that the Council positively modified racial attitudes of its members, counter to the popular beliefs held by some.

The study did produce an important finding, the significance of which may not have been fully recognized at the time—namely, that within the middle class, interracial attitudes were not a barrier to collaboration among members of the Council. Even though people had negative attitudes, they could join together to act for the common good in the neighborhood—such as support for traffic lights and crime control. Notwithstanding these findings, the Glenville Area Community Council, led by a creative group of citizen leaders and its very adept community organizer, Don Stier, continued to be highly regarded throughout Cleveland.

Five years later, in 1952, I returned to Cleveland as the Glenville area field worker, and to inherit the legacy of Don Stier. I found in place a core of leaders; integrated Council structures consisting of neighborhood clubs, street clubs, and committees; volunteers; and representation on a citywide Association of Area Councils chaired by the associate editor of the *Cleveland Press* newspaper.

The Glenville area consisted of two and one-half square miles and about 86,000 people. Over time the Glenville area lost some of its middle-class and multiethnic character as nonblack residents and middle-class black residents moved farther east in search of greater class and cultural homogeneity and more distance between themselves and the urban problems syndrome. Taking their place were lower-middle-class and upwardly mobile lower-class families.

Although I would do other things professionally, my work with street, neighborhood, area, and community organizations would be a continuing interest. My reflections about citizen participation and community organization are drawn heavily from these early experiences.

A number of local institutions were early initiators of neighborhood organizations—notably, social settlements, a small number of Urban Leagues, and, in a number of northern cities, local social planning councils. In the 1920s, public health agencies experimented with block clubs as a means of prodding residents to help in solving community health problems. It should be noted that many local churches and citizen groups also independently started organizational efforts. Among other initiators of neighborhood organization at the national level were: The Office of Juvenile Delinquency and Youth Development, The National Association of Social Workers (through its Commission on Community Organization and its Council on Social Work in Community Planning and Development), the War on Poverty, and, more recently, HUD.

Following WWII, a greatly expanded interest in community development occurred on the international scene. A number of U.S. social workers were associated with agencies like The Agency for International Development, which sought to involve local citizens in helping to improve their lives and their communities. For a period of 20 years, I was involved with action and training programs in Egypt, where the American experience could not be applied without modification. There were theoretical similarities but important differences between community problem solving in the United States and in "developing" countries, involving such factors such as differences in government, informal decision making, social culture, technologies, to mention a few.

During the late 1950s and early 1960s, in conjunction with social planning councils and settlements, a few national conferences were held for local area councils. The leaders of these organizations—a diversity of citizens from housewives to politicians—met to exchange experiences and to encourage each other. In the middle 1960s, because of the increasingly prominent role of neighborhood organizations in programs funded by the Office of Juvenile Delinquency and Youth Development, as well as the Office of Economic Opportunity, the National Association of Social Workers sponsored a project to "examine...practice issues involved in motivating people to take group action on their own behalf." The project, called **Neighborhood Organization for Community Action,** "sought to look in an exploratory way at the relevance of selected neighborhood organizations and their programs to the physical, social, and economic problems that beset them." Participant organizations came from a variety of locations across the country, including people from several disciplines. The final report of the project provides a critique of the weaknesses of many neighborhood organizations as well as criteria for improving the effectiveness of their operations.

My interest in community organization originated in concern about issues of racial justice and poverty. After WWII, efforts to organize minorities and the poor for the general purposes of improving their life situations gained public acceptance in some quarters—for example, in minority communities—but enthusiasm in white middle-class communities appeared to decline. It is worth noting that this seemed to occur at the time when organized labor's interest in a broad social policy agenda began to decline. It seems to me that, although it wa not recognized at that time, in urban communities settlements as a progressive force in the lives of the urban poor and dislocated began to lose support.

During these years, the impact of the movement of a largely poor and black migration from the South was making itself felt in big cities of both the North and the South. Also, following the participation of blacks and the poor in WWII in both combat and industrial efforts, dissatisfaction with their housing, jobs, health, environment, and lack of participation in government and community was high. Among blacks and the poor, clearly a restlessness emerged for better treatment, which in turn grew out of the hope they had experienced during the war years.

As diverse as the auspices of grassroots organization with the poor and with blacks have been, there appear to be few, if any, cases where minorities or the poor have embraced goals in conflict with those of our democracy—in spite of the fact that results of most organizing efforts fell short of what the participants hoped would occur. These outcomes may be explained in part by an understanding of the impact of race, class, and power upon organizing efforts.

With regard to organizing in low income communities, it is not always easy to know the social class of residents in a given geographic area. Closed housing in many communities prevented blacks from moving to other areas more consistent with their education and means. Thus, during these years, older areas populated by blacks were likely to be mixed in terms of socioeconomic status. Even specific streets were likely to be mixed in terms of social class.

The lifestyles of the poor are short of some of the personal and social resources needed to survive their environment, which was and still is essentially hostile. As Rainwater shows, the truly poor are much more likely to lack adequate communication skills, find it difficult to postpone immediate gratification for more permanent gains, not own their homes, move their residence frequently, and not belong to groups having instrumental purposes. Without help, they may lack many of the habits, ideas, and resources necessary to engage in and operate citizen self-help organizations effectively.

In spite of these drawbacks, I often came in contact with leaders of almost heroic stature. In many instances, they alone kept the fire of hope alive in the face of interminable odds. I believe that much could be gleaned from a study of such leaders. How and why do they do what they do? How might professionals work more effectively with them?

One difficulty in working with people in lower-income neighborhoods is their tendency to engage in expressive versus instrumental group behavior. Thus, organizational effectiveness in terms of planning and follow-through is often sacrificed. Because of this leaning toward the expressive, people who are oriented instrumentally give up on the organization, preferring individual approaches to group problem solving. In lieu of pinning their hopes on collective action of the neighborhood organization, they choose to move from the neighborhood as soon as they can. If they participate at all, it is often marginal. The worker needs to be able to help the organization maintain a balance between satisfying expressive and instrumental needs of its members. It is a challenge to help people who can contribute to the effectiveness of the organization to remain involved, although they may have selected a more individual course of action for themselves.

To the uninitiated it is important to note that participants in street and neighborhood organizations tend to be overwhelmingly female and often are older, especially in low-income communities. The worker need not be older or female, but he or she must be able to relate to gender and age, that is, must be comfortable with groups that are primarily female and older. The worker should also be sensitive to how both age and gender may determine the approach to problems and the pace with which action is taken in resolving them. Similarly, in the case of race, in working with black or white populations, race of the worker need not be determined by the makeup of the group. The worker, however, must be prepared in matters of age, gender, and race to win the trust and respect of participants.

One implication of this analysis concerns the staffing of work with the poor. The worker must be prepared to provide more than technical assistance regarding the issues. Often he or she must be a coach and role model. Staffing is likely to require more intensive work than with the middle class, where the practitioner is used more as a consultant.

It is not surprising that in Central Areas there were few street and neighborhood organizations. One community organization worker in an area with a population of 100,000 low-income residents could not begin to staff such groups. A large proportion of participants in the CACC were nonresident human service professionals who focused on expanding and improving services, in this case, mainly health and welfare services. It is my impression that, to some extent, an emphasis on services was more attractive to some members, while others gravitated to system change. This situation also offers a challenge to the practitioner's skill in guiding the group. Care needs to be taken to try and focus the group's efforts on both types of objectives. Where possible, the worker should clarify the relationship between system and service objectives.

The extent to which organization goals are buttressed with financial and influence resources that are clearly targeted on the causes and remedies of the status of the poor is a critical factor in the success of community work with the poor. Many initiatives have been undertaken without either financial or influence resources. Initiatives based on partnerships with religious, health, or government organizations that offer jobs and low-cost housing are likely to be more successful than those initiatives lacking these considerations. The more immediate and apparent the possibilities of realizing such benefits, the stronger the attraction to participate in the organization.

Most poor people know that the lack of money is intractably at the center of their dilemmas. They may not know how to find and keep a job. They may not know how to link a job opportunity with a better future. However, they do know that, without money, they are likely to remain poor and disadvantaged. Notwithstanding the initiatives of current welfare reform, the ability to motivate people who have been deeply damaged by oppression, and who view themselves as outside of the system, in my opinion, remains a barometer of the knowledge and skill required in community practice.

A relative lack of social power and influence is at the core of problems for poor black Americans in comparison to white Americans—meaning the lack of options by which to successfully satisfy the basic demands and stresses of living and to pursue life where their talent will take them. The belief that ultimate social power for bringing about social change rests with the people begs the questions: which people and under what circumstance? In the early 1960s, Michael Harrington asserted that the leadership of the country proposes making a social revolution but without the inconvenience of changing any basic institution.

As a master's student, I don't recall formal class discussion about power. I don't recall being taught about the dynamics of ward, city, and county politics or about theories, strategies, and tactics of how to align or defeat the interests of decision makers to achieve the objectives of community action. We learned about how important business leaders were. We were not taught theories and strategies about working with and against power and influence, as described by Banfield, including sit-ins, marches, and reference group theory. We learned that "in order to make an omelet, you first had to break the shell." Later, I would learn about the mobilization of citizen discontent. In thinking back to my early practice days, I certainly knew by that time that some people could make things happen or block them, others could only block things from happening. Some could do neither. It was difficult to teach residents that the ability to block did not translate into the ability to make things happen. Many initiatives needed both but possessed only one or none. I also learned that confronting persons opposed to an objective of the organization could result in political and economic costs to participants.

Over the years, we learned much more about the use of power. Scholars and practitioners began to write about it, and we became more adept as we recognized that, to solve some neighborhood problems, most often decisions had to be made at city, county, state, and/or national levels. We learned about working with coalitions. In low-income communities, most neighborhood organizations are small, with individual memberships of less than a hundred. They are not always well known, or taken seriously by people who make up their potential constituencies. Several years ago, Blum and Turner observed that, as a movement, these organizations have yet to make or sustain effective horizontal (at the community level) and vertical (at the state and national level) linkages with more powerful local, state, and national groups.

In working with black and poor communities, one must assume that their statuses are artificially held in place: Something acts to keep blacks in a position of second-class citizenship; something acts to keep the poor, poor. If community organization is to lessen the poverty of the poor and abolish the second-class citizenship of blacks, some compelling force must be used against those forces artificially restraining the poor and blacks, whether by friendly persuasion or political action. While the restraining forces are located primarily outside of blacks and the poor themselves, some constraints may rest in the behavior of members of the groups, posing other difficulties and calling for concerting influence internal to the organization's constituency.

How does a community organization acquire and use power to persuade those who devise policies and control resources to do what it wants to do, even when they may not wish to do so? The mobilization of the community being served to act and speak with one voice has been widely seen as perhaps the most readily available strategy. It appears to work best when some visible event occurs that clearly offends a majority of the population, and which can be linked emotionally to an underlying issue that has not been satisfactorily resolved.

My experience is that, under our "rules of the game," the organization must wait until such an event occurs and is recognized as such. The organization does not create such events, but the day-to-day work of community building helps to set the stage for reacting effectively. Timing is important. As a rule, the closer to the event, the greater the sense of urgency to act, and the greater the chances of mobilizing significantly large numbers of the affected population. Also, the public visibility of the offending act or event must be sufficient to aid in the mobilization of support and to dissuade opposing decision makers.

There are some difficulties in attempting to use this strategy. Living in close proximity in a neighborhood does not always ensure common communication channels, interests, norms and ordering of values, or readiness to act. The difficulties may be further complicated if the situation of concern may also be attributable in part to persons living in the immediate area. People living in a given geopolitical area or neighborhood do not automatically constitute a community. In such cases, it may be difficult to find consensus around norms and values, common channels of communication, and interests based on religion, business, or family standing. So, the notion of massive participation seems unlikely to occur except in very special circumstances, and cannot be sustained over a long period of time.

Clearly, the community organization practitioner, in working with such an area must be sensitive to the need to assist in building components of a community such as communication channels, decision-making structures, and reinforcement of normative values. Also, the practitioner should have a long-range perspective, while at the same time respecting the need for the organization to show some demonstrable results more immediately.

This situation is nicely illustrated by efforts of a group of public housing mothers who sought to find summer jobs for 40 of their teenagers. They acted as job locators and coaches for the youth, and they found jobs for about a third of the group. However, in their words, the real benefit was that they got to know the youth and vice versa. Youth greeted them by name, and the adults were no longer afraid to walk by them at night. While the larger and more long-range job-finding results were a bit disappointing, the parent group was very pleased at the unanticipated immediate improvement in their relationships with neighborhood youth, and from their sense of greater physical security.

In areas where there is a more developed sense of community, the community organization practitioner may have more success in mobilizing residents to achieve an objective with minimum effort. Glenville was one such area. It was primarily an area of middle- and upper-income home owners. Although the area was experiencing a turnover in population with many newcomers, and while it had a number of long strip-retail areas subdividing the residential areas, it was cohesive and able to function at a relatively high level of community.

For example, when the Glenville Area Community Council discovered that housing values in the area had been grossly overassessed by the office of the county auditor in comparison with assessments in Shaker Heights, one of the wealthiest communities in America, community leaders were galvanized into action. On a night with nearly a foot of snow, almost a thousand people turned out for a meeting with the county auditor. As a result, representatives of the auditor's office were sent to the Council's office to process residents claims for reassessment. It was a hugely successful project. My guess is that two-thirds of those present that night were attending their first—and for many their only—meeting of the Council. Council meetings were usually well-attended, but not anything like what happened on this occasion.

In analyzing this event, three factors were critical to its successful conclusion. First, the people in attendance were home owners who faced the possibility of having to pay a considerable sum of money, out of line with tax assessments in Shaker Heights. This was a highly visible bread and butter issue that evoked much emotion. It seemed to residents that a great injustice was happening. Secondly, effective channels of communication and a highly visible leadership structure were used. The meeting was well-publicized in the daily press. Handbills were distributed door to door on most residential streets. Leaders of street clubs followed up, alerting residents as to what was at stake in terms of people's pocketbooks. Thirdly, residents of the community had a reputation for turning out to vote. It is clear that the presence of a thousand voters who might express their dissatisfaction at the next election made quite an impression on a politically ambitious elected public official.

In areas with large populations and without representative indigenous groups, the community/neighborhood organization needs ways to secure citizen participation on a representative basis. Community/neighborhood organizations need leaders who are known and in whom people have trust. This is especially true of areas undergoing cultural and class transition. It is also true of communities with multiple means of entering and exiting, and that have topographical or other features that divide the area into subparts. Neighborhood and street organizations can play a very important role in bringing people together around common interests (children, property, safety), and these people might never meet otherwise, even if they are next-door neighbors.

Street clubs provide a means for people to collaborate with folk who live on their street as well as with people on other streets, and with other neighborhoods to protect, maintain, and promote the physical and human environment that they share. Glenville at one time had nearly a hundred street and neighborhood organizations. In middle-class communities, street and neighborhood organizations can usually be staffed by local citizens through training programs and staff consultation. Leaders for community councils can be recruited and developed from street and neighborhood groups.

Lower-income streets and neighborhood groups require intensive intervention from the worker himself or herself. Initially, there will be much greater dependence on the worker. Also, it will take much time to develop trust and relationships with indigenous leaders. It takes great skill and some luck to avoid competing with indigenous leaders, to be seen as on the side of the "hood" and to be seen as consistently objective. This practice problem is likely to occur when indigenous leaders disagree over choices among priorities for action or the action strategy to be pursued. When the practitioner's knowledge and wisdom is at odds with the leader's, how is the leader to act?

There was another way in which the Glenville Area, rather successfully empowered itself. During a ten-year period, two people were elected county judges, one to the Court of Appeals; one person was elected to the Cuyahoga County Commission; two people were appointed to the directorship of the Cuyahoga Board of Elections; three people were elected to the Cleveland City Council; and one person was appointed Commissioner on the Ohio Lottery Commission. All of these people were very active in the Glenville Area Community Council at one time. Although the Council played no formal role during their campaigns, the Council provided a platform for their talent and experience, engendering skills that were acted out on a wider stage to the benefit of community whenever possible. It is worth noting that other community councils graduated men and women into public careers, including one person being elected mayor of Cleveland.

Looking to the future and in reflecting on my experience with Community Organization over the last 52 years, the inevitable question is, "How valuable a tool is Community Organization for helping to cure America's social and economic inequities of race and poverty?" We should ask whether it works well enough to remain in our arsenal of social change strategies. And if so, what should be done to make it more effective?

Initially, my expectations of what citizen participation and Community Organization could accomplish were unrealistic. I did not comprehend the difference between group status goals, which involve structural change of a massive magnitude, and micro changes, which are small but hold some significance for many of the people who participate—black, poor, or black and poor. Some battles were won, but to achieve group status goals, a war would have to be won.

Is it important to win battles? Of course it is. Every battle won makes some improvement in some aspect of participants' lives: a safer community; cooperative relationships with their neighbors, be they alike or different; less noise or smoke in their physical environment; job improvements; better schools; personal growth as a result of gaining some greater degree of control over their lives.

At one time, in Cleveland, enough battles were being won to cause some members of the City Council to consider attempting to ban community/area councils. While this endeavor failed, the attempt does suggest the potential power that a coalition of effective community organizations can have. Many battles have been lost as a result of a myriad of factors—such as starting prematurely or lacking the human or economic resources required to be successful.

Resolution of many of the issues confronted by the poor and by blacks require decisions to be made by higher corporate and political decision makers. For more permanent gains, local efforts must be tied in with larger political, economic, and social policies and programs. The challenge is to get the attention of relevant decision makers and to achieve and maintain favorable responses. Neighborhood organizations need to be more skilled in mobilizing power related to particular goals. They also need skill in preventing the misuse of power by members of their groups—for example, when a leader routinely uses his position to pursue personal choices rather than those that represent the best interests of the group.

In work with low-income constituents, there is an especially challenging issue. How can communication be improved with constituents so as to raise better awareness of common interests and mobilize support for targeted priorities? This is a largely untapped source of power. More materially assisting low-income communities will require a larger staff-to-resident ratio and a still greater use of indigenous personnel. To develop more and better trained community workers will require national recognition of the importance of having strong communities as a part of national development.

Clearly, a major factor inhibiting the effectiveness of community organizations is the extremely limited financial resources available to them. Community/neighborhood work is too underfunded to achieve even the modest ends that might legitimately be expected of it. Overdependency on outside resources for staffing and program costs has been a serious handicap. The membership of most organizations has not included powerful individuals with resources to lend support and influence. The staffing needs of these groups is considerable. Greater creativity is needed to improve the funding of neighborhood/community practice and training. Training should be focused on all educational levels, but especially at the baccalaureate level, and should be across disciplines.

Some years ago, a prominent Cleveland community leader of some standing was overheard to privately comment that "there should be a community organization practitioner for every three policemen. Taxpayers would get a better return for their tax dollars." Indeed, community workers should be viewed as necessary as police and housing inspectors. The social policy and power issues are ones that involve human protection and development. These will not come easily. They represent important social battles that must be fought for on the battlefields of economics, justice, and social awareness.

With the increase in mobility of community populations, the increased dependency on technology, diminishing reliance on face-to-face relations, and the increasing polarization by economic status in housing and neighborhood patterns, the concept of community may be in danger of losing its place and utility in society without anyone's having an idea about what will replace it. The time has come and passed for advocating to city, county, and state officials the utility of employing community workers to preserve the viability of communities.

My interest in community problem solving began when I was 11 years old. What advice would I have today for that 11-year-old? (1) Develop a relationship with one or more of the ministers, and get to know their objectives and difficulties (perhaps a bit ambitious for an 11-year-old); (2) Identify the people who exert influence over the minister; (3) Determine ways of linking interests of the ministers with plant improvements; (4) Identify resources inside and external to churches and ways of accessing them; (5) Spread the organizational and geographic base of the effort; (6) Focus public recognition on the efforts to improve the churches and upon the people so engaged; and (7) Don't take yourself too seriously!

BIBLIOGRAPHY

Banfield, Edward C. 1961. *Political Influence*. New York: The Free Press of Glencoe.

Blum, Arthur, and John B. Turner. 1968. "Action and Knowledge Gaps in Neighborhood Organization." Unpublished paper.

Harrington, Michael. 1968. "A Subversive Version of the Great Society." In *Social Theory and Social Intervention*, edited by Herman D. Stein. Cleveland: The Press of Case Western Reserve.

Rainwater, Lee. 1968. "Neighborhood Action and Lower Class Life-Styles." Pp. 25–52 in *Neighborhood Organization for Community Action*. New York: National Association of Social Workers.

Turner, John B, ed. 1968. *Neighborhood Organization for Community Action*. New York: The National Association of Social Workers.

Service and Cause—
Both Sides of the Coin

Margaret E. Berry

In 1965, when President Johnson called for a "neighborhood center in every ghetto," no group was more heartened than the 411 agencies affiliated with the National Federation of Settlements and Neighborhood Centers (NFS). They represented the settlement movement, which for 80 years had been toiling on urban frontiers, often feeling alone and overwhelmed by massive social problems, yet still trying to bring the distant early warning signals to the wider community.

What were these individualistic, occasionally eccentric, agencies? This paper tells the story of their heritage and how they fared in the ferment of the sixties as they were inspired, criticized, or empowered with public funds. It is about the tension between "cause" and "service" that exists for all private welfare agencies, and about the essentially spiritual crisis created by charges of "welfare colonialism." These agencies will be hereafter referred to as "settlements" to distinguish them from other neighborhood centers, although the term is rather dated. I am writing from my perspective as a staff member and then director of Soho Community House in Pittsburgh (1942–51), followed by service as a staff member of NFS

106

(1952–59) and executive director through 1971. I will focus on the time of my personnel involvement and not cover more recent developments.

The settlement movement began with Toynbee Hall in East London in 1884, as a response to the appalling conditions resulting from the Industrial Revolution. The essence of the neighborhood approach was simple. The founders "settled in" to live as friends and neighbors. They offered help, but, even more, they came to learn about the causes of the wretched conditions, to experiment with solutions, and to bring the message to the nation. The founder, Canon Samuel Barnett, was guided by three beliefs: that each person had the capacity to grow and the right to enjoy "the best"; that each had social responsibility and was his "brother's keeper"; and that there was the possibility of evolutionary change. These values have continued to influence settlements' goals and methods.

This rather simple approach was seized on eagerly by many groups dedicated to reform, and it spread immediately to other countries. In the United States, University Settlement opened in 1886 and was followed so rapidly by others that it was considered a "movement." Sponsors included women's colleges, theological seminaries, Catholic and Jewish organizations, and universities; even the Philadelphia Symphony started a music school. By 1911, approximately 400 settlements were established throughout the United States. The movement was partly identified with early feminism, as many of the leaders—such as Jane Addams—were educated, gifted women who found in this endeavor a meaning for their own lives. Also characteristic of the American settlements was their identification with immigrants who found slums their point of entry and who brought color and interest to city life.

Programs were as varied as the neighborhoods served. They pioneered in nursing services, clinics, milk stations. They established camps and playgrounds. They taught citizenship, opened kindergartens and libraries. They studied housing and working conditions and used these studies to support protective legislation. Over the years, many of their demonstrations became accepted public functions, and they moved on to new goals. Graham Taylor, founder of Chicago Commons, defined a settlement as "simply the next most important thing to be done."

Some settlements like Toynbee Hall and Hull House were oriented toward the nation and the reform of society, using neighborhood realities as documentation. Jane Addams, for example, who found a national audience through her writings, could counsel colleagues to "hold their programs lightly." Other agencies—for example, South End House in Boston—focused on the neighborhood itself as giving cohesion and a boundary to reform efforts, finding much in common with city planners. But either way, founders saw an organic link between neighborhood, city, and nation.

This flexible response to neighborhood needs created no dichotomy between providing recreational programs and working for improved sanitation or for federal legislation. Settlements saw "services" to individuals and neighborhood and "cause"—analyzing, mitigating, and helping to eradicate factors that make for suffering and breakdown—as both sides of the same coin.

This period from 1886 to World War I could be considered the golden age of the settlements' social action efforts, as they gave effective leadership to establishing public services, passing protective legislation such as child labor laws, and establishing the Children's Bureau. When in 1912 the Progressive Party included in its platform most of the social action program of the settlements, it was felt that a high point had been reached. And even after the weariness from World War I and the "Roaring Twenties," there came another burst of satisfaction as the New Deal legislation embodied many programs, such as mothers' pensions, that had been settlement goals.

As the pioneers inevitably departed from the scene with their passionate advocacy for social justice, the incoming generation were the technicians, concerned with building the institutional structure. Reflecting the professionalization of the whole private welfare field, they were interested in standards of operation, financing, efficient administration, and staff training. Although some settlements resisted participation in the growing community chest (now United Way) movement, fearing it would inhibit social action, they all inevitably became part of the community welfare planning and financing structure.

This concern with standards and training characterized the thirties to the fifties. Although some proponents of the arts thought that group work was "without content," it became a major method of choice because of its relevancy to both the goals of individual development and training for democracy. During the fifties, a quarter of the group work graduates went into settlements, and in 1965, 42 percent of NFS member agency full-time staff had master's degrees in group work. This interest in relationships as of first importance led to increasing focus on race relationships as a primary commitment.

But most were aware that settlements were not "group work agencies" in spite of being so designated through the welfare councils: Each settlement needed to define a purpose broader than "doing group work." To meet varied neighborhood needs, the skills of many kinds of workers would be needed.

Not to neglect social action, the NFS established its biennial legislative seminars in 1948, with first-hand training and lobbying in Washington for local staff, board, and adult members. (Incidentally, one could measure changes in our nation's capital by where our interracial group could stay. No hotel would take us for the first seminar in 1948. Then we progressed gradually by degrees from low-star status until we eventually made the Willard.)

In 1954, sensing changes at work, the Federation organized an action-research project named *Neighborhood Goals in a Rapidly Changing World*. It was under the leadership of Wilbur Cohen, at that time at the School of Social Work at the University of Michigan, on one of his rare absences from the Washington scene. It brought together 60 settlement leaders, federal officials, and scholars in the fields of economics, population, city planning, housing, education, and health. The objective was to envision what neighborhoods would be like in 1975, with the implications for settlement work. Scholarly papers and lively discussion went into a book designed for discussion in all member agencies, to be followed by relevant case studies in *Neighborhood Centers Today*. It was a wonderful meeting. Papers were of the highest quality. Economist Kenneth Boulding turned out witty verses after every session, and, instead of writing on poverty, produced a most illuminating paper on the religious background of the English settlements, describing the founders as people alienated from their own social class who found some mutuality with the alienated poor, trying together with them to make a better life on Earth. I recall physicist John Weaver, who had just been introduced to settlements at this meeting, saying, "I think of you as a secular church."

Although there was continuing attention to issues like housing, I am struck now by the absence of a sense of *urgency*. The economists assured us that the nation could now afford to end poverty (although the distribution of our wealth would be a political matter). It appeared that we were now free to concentrate on marginal populations—multiproblem families, aging, and hard-to-reach youth. Some wondered if the idea of neighborhoods might not be obsolete, and suggested that settlements might turn their expertise to suburban developments, which were springing up everywhere, without plans or services. After all, from 1951–56 the NFS had been part of United Community Defense Services (UCDS), a consortium of 13 national agencies financed by the "Big Ten" community chests, to give help to 225 small communities overwhelmed by defense-related growth. (I was part of the UCDS team as we experimented with generic services to small communities, and I considered it at that time to be the most exciting recent development in social work.)

But the wake-up calls were beginning in the mid-fifties as the nation rediscovered poverty. Settlements gave increasing weight to the social action part of their heritage with a proliferation of neighborhood improvement efforts—rent strikes and demonstrations, block clubs, and councils. The first federal money came to settlements for juvenile delinquency prevention. Then came the 1954 Housing Act, which mandated citizen participation, and settlements became identified with urban renewal.

It was the conference we held in 1957 at Michigan State University that, in my mind, marked the advent of the community organization workers in force. This lively ten-day meeting produced a useful publication, the *Dynamics of Citizen Participation*. This group of new professionals was full of pride, and perhaps a little arrogant, as they thought of themselves on the cutting edge of practice. They had a mission and found it compatible with settlement goals. They were a bit louder than the group workers had been in their early days, and stayed up later. But they didn't sing! One had brought his bride, considering this conference their honeymoon. It seemed that the "movement" was in for an infusion of new skills and new dedication to meet old tasks.

As the energy of the civil rights movement spilled over into northern cities, and later, as the urgency was explosively demonstrated by 150 significant riots between 1964 and 1968, programs came in a cumulative rush. Everyone's attention was centered on neighborhoods. They were seen as the crucible—both for measuring the well-being of ordinary citizens as well as the significant place for nurturing their capacities and aspirations. The goal, backed with federal funds, was to eliminate poverty, make cities livable, and dampen urban unrest through restructuring service systems and encouraging self-help. The neighborhood was the new frontier.

Edward J. O'Connell captured the kaleidoscopic picture of the different agendas:

> Planners of new towns are proposing neighborhood centers to foster a sense of community; psychiatrists are proposing such centers to cope with racial issues. Some professionals are seeking to strengthen family life, others the democratic fabric of our society. Some advocates want neighborhood town halls for social discussion and debate. Some would like to see centers with clubrooms; others imagine centers with clout. Still others view the neighborhood centers offering a vast potential for more effective delivery of desperately needed services. The neighborhood approach is hailed as a panacea—*the* solution to any number of ills. Not only can it deliver services, but [it can] promote democracy, fight bureaucracy, restore dignity, recapture pride, insure participation, overcome powerlessness and guarantee justice.[1]

In this swirl of activity, settlements were exhilarated to find the national spotlight on local needs, to find themselves in a stimulating marketplace of ideas, and to feel a national will to act, backed by federal funds.

Settlements had a role in this national effort. First of all, they were *there*. In many cases they had roots formed in the late 1800s. They had a building. They had fairly regular—but never enough—financial support. And, like any incumbent, they had a record. People could make judgments about the value of their presence. They had served neighborhood residents sometimes for decades and espoused Community Organization (CO) as a method. They had useful citywide contacts through their boards and the community welfare system. They also had their value system, which influenced their choice of goals and methods.

During this heady period, settlements were active and hopeful. They were there at the March on Washington, at Resurrection City on the Mall. The urban renewal program received their enthusiastic collaboration, for they had struggled for years for slum clearance and increased affordable housing. In helping members to get adequate or appropriate public services, they had brokered many efforts for cooperation or coordination, and were now gratified to hear federal departments (Labor; Housing; and Health, Education, and Welfare; plus the National Institute for Mental Health) acknowledge the imperfection of their vertical delivery systems and seek new collaboration with integrated local models. The demonstration was planned for fourteen Pilot Cities (under the Neighborhood Center Pilot Program, initiated by the secretary of Housing and Urban Development in cooperation with HEW, DOL, OEO, and Bureau of the Budget), and $23 million was appropriated. President Johnson's call for a center in every ghetto nurtured the dream that public financing might establish neighborhood centers as a service available to all urban neighborhoods. I thought we might make a major contribution to the nation, just as the pioneers had won the establishment of parks and recreation departments as public services.

The new neighborhood centers established under the Office of Economic Opportunity (OEO) were at first potentially threatening to established settlements, and were often located in the same area, but as their message of revolutionary change toned down, they ended up with rather familiar services, such as Head Start. Many of them found that the services which they had scoffed at as "Band-Aids" were not so bad when one really needed one. Actually, as OEO began to contract with existing voluntary organizations, settlements were beneficiaries. By 1964, our affiliates were receiving as much from OEO contracts as from local chests (now called United Way).

It was easy for settlements to identify with the goal of citizen participation. It implied the consensus-seeking, enabling leadership style of social work, in which the worker, through self-understanding and discipline, is able to put first the needs of the person or group. At the same time, settlements were not blind to conflict. After all, some had the battle scars from being selected as scapegoats by Alinksy-type organizations.

Boards and staffs of member agencies grew increasingly sophisticated during this period, often in relation to agency policy on the use of the building by autonomous groups, usually for public meetings. We were increasingly serving adult groups, and this required clarity about differences in point of view, dealing with issues of free speech, and acknowledging mutual rights and responsibilities. (Grace Coyle had warned the settlements in 1946 that they must work with self-determining adults or they would be left with only children and the dependent members of society.) I remember only one public fight, when the "Red Squad" of the Cleveland Police Department took exception to an autonomous group's using the auditorium of a settlement.

Such issues were important in clarifying who makes the rules. Was it the board, or staff? If the agency had links to another sponsoring institution, did that help or hinder in a public dispute? The influence of original sponsors might have been strong in the pioneer days when sponsors were raising money, putting up buildings, and participating actively, but these ties tended to diminish over the decades until only a small percentage were in force. What *had* developed was the private welfare bureaucracy—the welfare planning councils and the community chests. New centers were created primarily through the planning and budgeting process. By the forties, New York City was the only "free market" where competition reigned. Agencies, groomed in the habits of cooperative planning and budgeting, willingly conformed. They hesitated to "cause trouble" for their colleagues by challenging the status quo.

I consider myself fortunate to have had an early lesson in the realities of the power structure. This was in the late forties in Pittsburgh, where big industry and big labor were concentrated, and I don't think the dramatic episode has been recorded. Briefly, the Chest-supported agencies had been outraged to hear how the Chest board had capriciously rejected a campaign goal that had been recommended after a summer-long budget process. The agencies, using the power given to them in Chest by-laws, forced a corporation meeting that overrode the chest board's goal. Retaliation was swift. It appeared that the campaign might be aborted. Agency boards were given ultimatums, careers were threatened. We met continuously in strategy sessions, and explored whether we could build an alternative to chest funding that was centered around the Welfare Federation. The issue was finally resolved at a national level between Henry Ford Jr., president of Community Chests and Councils of America, and Dave McDonald, a Pittsburgher who was president of the United Steel Workers of America. When I hear people talk glibly about the power structure, I remember how ruthless and naked the force really was.

The other major constraint against agency social action was the tax-exempt status affecting its financial supporters. Needing money so badly, agencies were afraid to exercise their clear rights to speak out. We were constantly assuring them that they could work within the guidelines of the Internal Revenue Service. The Federation had not been limited, even though it was required to submit to the IRS copies of all its mailings to members and the public. In fact, the only challenge to our lobbying function came from within our membership when, in about 1952, a group of Detroit board members strongly challenged this function. The matter was resolved with the help of New York City board members. We heard somewhat later that this episode had been precipitated when Barry Goldwater had visited a friend or relative in Detroit, had seen a Federation mailing, and had taken great exception to it.

The sharp disagreements arose about two areas of neighborhood organization—confrontational tactics, and a "political" (meaning "personal") style of leadership. Many OEO neighborhood organizations established to experiment with economic concerns attracted entrepreneurial and often charismatic leaders. Saul Kobrin, in a 1967 case report for the Federation, described the general phenomenon astutely, as it was exemplified in a California settlement whose board deliberately elected to become a "change agent" and employ a large CO staff. Dr. Kobrin noted the failure of existing neighborhood leadership to respond to challenges from local constituents and the perceived opportunity for new outside leaders to move in. "This has served," he said, "to give all resident organizing activity something of a political direction. This has meant that community action workers emphasize the development of visible cadres of followers, who may constitute a principle resource in the general competition for attention and influence in an unstable situation."[2] Dr. Kobrin notes that, in this agency, the heavy emphasis on militant block groups resulted in some devaluation of the service aspects of program. The CO workers were fairly independent agents in a free-wheeling mode. Their goals were often hard to operationalize into specific plans and measurable accomplishments. There was little interest in administrative supervision and control—indeed it was considered irrelevant compared to the broad social goals.

There was a related question about the use of paraprofessionals. Traditionally, settlements had always employed local residents and volunteers. But one goal of the antipoverty program was to employ large numbers of young people. There was confusion of roles when aides employed as staff were also members of local groups and foot soldiers in various protests. Were these charismatic leaders building troops of their own for personal political power, or was it for the neighborhood?

Another model was attempted by the East Columbus Citizens Organizations (ECCO) in Ohio, when in 1965 the agency was turned over by its church-sponsored board to become a neighborhood corporation—a "political" experiment in the truest sense of the word. It followed the plan and continuing guidance of Milton Kottler, who hoped to find a way for restructuring municipal government through the decentralization of functions. Major effort went into developing a neighborhood voting structure. (The effort reminded one of an early settlement idea—restructuring the cities around self-determining and self-financing guilds of 100 families each.)

ECCO eventually ran into trouble when outside grants gave out. This was true of other projects, which found that those holding political or economic power would not, in the end, finance threats to that power.

This kind of baring of conflicting interest was maturing for all. It forced consideration of the rather ambiguous position of all "do good" agencies. The Federation had seen this in Warner Robins, Georgia, where we had placed Bernie Shiffman as a "community social worker," financed by UCDS, with the broad assignment to help the town articulate its needs and meet them. We had a pro forma invitation to come. (This was a perfect CO job!) When Bernie was being honored by the town at the close of a successful two-year stint, one of the community leaders confessed to the amused crowd that, at the beginning, he had Bernie investigated by the FBI because "no one works for free except a Communist."[3] "Who pays you," a question that used to seem rather rude, really asks what strings are attached, and is legitimately asked by those to whom you offer help.

These serious efforts brought increased sophistication to the whole field and awareness of the economic factors in the distribution of goods and services.

The National Federation was rather dramatically made aware of the fact that humanitarian aid and nonpartisan helping efforts are viewed as political when there are deep social conflicts. We had been amazed when our worker in a demonstration financed by the Agency for International Development (AID) in a large Caracas barrio was advised to take a different route to work each day, and never to keep the same office hours. We knew for sure that we were considered enemies, however, when a large object fell from a roof onto the spot our worker had passed a second before, and the report was immediately flashed by some observer to the federal department that was our Venezuelan sponsor.

Later, in a domestic political decision, the National Federation declined an invitation to operate a demonstration neighborhood center in Saigon, an undertaking that could be interpreted as an endorsement of the Administration's Vietnam policy, and would have torn apart the Federation.

The Federation's board took a clear political stance when it voted to encourage its Jackson, Mississippi, field-worker to run for a public office on "company time," acknowledging that the main road to change lay in the election of new representatives and that challengers could not afford to give up their jobs while campaigning.

Of course, work in Mississippi had been clearly political from the beginning. I arrived in Jackson in 1966 with enough foundation money to hire a worker, only to discover that the entire Child Development Project (community development based on Head Start) had the second largest payroll in the state. That very week it had been wiped out by the governor, who had fresh legal power to approve or cancel all OEO–funded projects. The workers were desperate to continue their inspiring work. I was able to see some rural centers only because our potential worker had courage enough to drive me around Hinds County, with both of us watching rather anxiously lest a sheriff's car appear. (This was not long after the murder of Michael Schwerner, James Chaney, and Andrew Goodman in rural Mississippi.) I hired one worker on foundation funds, and one on faith. It was heartbreaking to be unable to pick up the whole wonderful effort.

At the fading of this remarkable mobilization period, when national will and federal funds were diminishing, a time of real soul-searching arrived. "Community control" became the popular rallying cry, coupling the drive for local participation with the movement for "Black Power" or "Brown Power." This was a real shock to those who believed in inclusiveness, who tried to "work with" rather than "for," to be accused of "welfare colonialism." Agencies had long subscribed to a goal of participation in decision making: Requirements for membership in the Federation specified neighborhood representation in planing committees and board membership. As of 1968, the percentage of neighborhood residents on boards ranged from zero to 100 percent, with a median of 25 percent. Although most boards could support steps for increasing neighborhood autonomy, their view of society made them wary of a local or separatist approach. And, of course, some were deeply hurt at being pushed out from what they had thought was a mutual endeavor.

(This paper will limit itself to the issue of localism. The consideration of racial separatism, which for a while convulsed the Federation, is a long and complex story impossible to cover here.)

A number of agencies hastened their inclusion of neighborhood board members. In two areas of Rochester, New York, for example, community elections were held for neighborhood representatives. In Stamford, Connecticut, the board voted itself out of existence—to be replaced by one in which half of the membership was to be from the area's housing project. In Philadelphia, the agreed-upon policy was that 51 percent of each board be from the neighborhood served, although numbers were considered less important than effective contribution. In Washington, D.C., Friendship House was physically taken over by a militant group, which invited just one of the "old" board to remain, economist Mary Dublin Keyserling. The centers in San Antonio were met with demands that all board and staff positions be filled immediately which Chicano neighborhood people, and that the community chest guarantee continued funding at the current level. The executive of one excellent settlement resigned to show good faith and clear the way for a Mexican-American successor. As noted above, ECCO was turned over to a neighborhood corporation.

In practice, there was an obvious complication: If only indigenous groups had credentials, which is the most authentic when they compete with each other? Unwilling to argue about credentials, some settlements with a long history of CO backed off from any leadership role and participated only as peers with other neighborhood groups. Of all the issues, this stirred the most debate, going as it did to matters of property and jobs, as well as to the settlements' value system. Board and staff members from outside the area were amazed to find themselves labeled "exploiters." Demands were made to turn over buildings and agency operations to neighborhood groups. Most had not foreseen a situation that might move from the host agency "inviting in" (community participation, fostering autonomous groups) to the host itself being "pushed out." Many staff members had not seen clearly that they were in a "linking" situation, working for an agency that was "in" but not "of" the neighborhood, but which nevertheless was given legitimacy as part of the community-supported private welfare system. Some idealistic staff felt that they should encourage community control even at the expense of their own jobs, that this was a test of sincerity about self-determination.

When the Federation convened a conference for those agencies working on community control, it found a group so genuinely committed to the concept (as variously seen) that the group produced a "manifesto" calling on the Federation to embrace the concept, and require immediately of each member agency that it have an indigenous board and staff. This was considered by a broadly representative group, and then the national board. The resultant statement shows a high degree of open-mindedness and respect for autonomy when it states, in part:

> Member houses should look upon growing interest in agency control as a timely opportunity to realize principles of local democracy which have long been part of the settlement philosophy. We therefore urge settlements to act on their own initiative to transfer control or to share it with local residents in new and creative ways.

Another segment of the national membership, also committed to self-determination, believed from a practical point of view that social change would never be achieved from a local base, and therefore we needed all the allies we could get from all segments of society. But by far the largest segment questioned a strategy that was exclusionary and which failed to see that, in a democracy, all citizens "belong." This viewpoint is reflected in a statement developed by the Executive Committee in 1967 (this issue was pervasive: everybody was writing statements!). It affirmed that "Settlements and Neighborhood Centers are best comprised of people who have vital and deep roots in the neighborhood together with people of the wider community who have a concern for the neighborhood and its importance and who can translate neighborhood needs to the larger community."

Two years later (1969), a statement from the Federation's New Directions Committee (a self-study) indicates that the conflict came to some resolution and that there were clear ways of making it operational:

> The main goal should be community change. This means working to solve community problems, rather than emphasis on neighborhood service. Sometimes the effort will lead out of the neighborhood into the larger city, the state and the nation. Reform will be the measure of success.
>
> This requires a board which is committed and a method by which neighborhood needs are understood. Open community meetings, uses of committees and councils, studies of specific problems, and neighborhood representation both quantitatively and effectively in policy making are essential. A cross-section board should be a prime resource for advocacy of change, for interpretation, and for access to political and economic strength. Such a board with ties in both neighborhood and the larger community can help with communication and personal understandings, bring people of divergent opinions together and make effective assaults on prejudice.

It appeared, from three years of ferment, that settlements were going to act with a deeper awareness of the autonomy of neighborhood residents. But they were not going to give up their own rights to be part of the struggle for a more perfect society, wherever those battles were waged.

As this remarkable mobilization period drifted to a close, with massive problems sill unresolved, what had been the meaning for settlements?

They had participated in an enormous variety of projects in what had seemed like a continuous seminar. Public interest and financial support had led to a remarkable blossoming of long-dormant ideas and experimental approaches. No agency was untouched.

Each agency had learned its own lessons, but there had emerged a consensus in many areas, which can be found in a study titled "Local Community Structure and Civic Participation." This was done for the National Commission on Urban Problems, headed by former Senator Paul H. Douglas. It was directed by Dr. Arthur Hillman, director of the Federation's Training Center, with a research staff of 11. It included field studies in 13 cities and drew on related reports like Pilot Cities and OEO Centers.

As reflected in this report, what had we learned? First, we had seen the scope of the subject—population and economic trends, massive public systems such as health, education, and transportation, as well as institutions like churches and credit unions that impinge on urban neighborhoods. Citizen self-help efforts, seen from this perspective, had limitations. Identified with neighborhoods as settlements were, they did not believe that *massive* social change would come from a neighborhood base.

In considering the neighborhood's potential for initiating social change, it is interesting that settlements seemed to make a link to federal programs or legislation with no difficulty, that communicating with congressional representatives was as natural as breathing. But the city was the missing link. I thought that the charm of the settlement might lie in its individuality, but that might also be its doom. City trends and institutions affected all neighborhoods, but the settlements had no common instrument for research, strategy, and coverage. For a decade we pushed a model for effective city federations with delegated powers, but in the end most of these experiments broke up, as the participating agencies showed conscious or unconscious resistance.

Agencies had grown much more sophisticated in their recognition of economic self-interest and class tensions. They had moved from pleasant projects like street beautification to building low-cost housing, which involved large budgets and hiring staff. Operating on this level required clarity about authority.

Agencies had become aware of the professional aspects of CO methods, and they saw that skills could be learned to analyze neighborhoods and their functions, to select the appropriate leadership style, to choose the best structure and strategy, to use conflict creatively. That neighborhood organizing could be taught instead of being dependent on good intentions or good luck was a source of hope. Certainly the Douglas Commission study affirmed the continuing usefulness of voluntary neighborhood-based agencies performing various roles—service providers, advocates, outreach workers, and brokers, encouraging all degrees of citizen participation in the service of a vital democracy.

The sixties may have produced a new chapter in American life, but the philosophical issues were not new. The question raised in the discussion of community control—how wide are the boundaries of the human "family"—becomes even more problematical as nation-states grow increasingly obsolete in the global economy. In the search for definitions of "brotherhood," the settlements held fast to their founders' principle of inclusiveness.

A second issue was also familiar: Does the end justify the means? This was relevant in respect to the use of tactics that were repellant, particularly those that dehumanized or showed disrespect for opponents. Although settlement workers were often troubled by the awareness that their efforts had not attacked root causes of trouble, and wondered if more militant tactics might have been more effective, the consensus was, in the end, that rancorous conflict was counterproductive and to be avoided. The question of means and ends also related to leadership styles—whether residents were viewed as followers to be mobilized or whether their participation was seen as a developmental opportunity. Was this "enabling" style really paternalistic? The struggle to define purpose was reminiscent of early days in group work and the effort to distinguish between "education" and "character-building" (propaganda?).

During the two-year period of urban riots, many settlement neighborhoods were involved, to the extent that we brought together those with experience to develop a guide on what to do. Although I thought that many workers could share the rage that sparked some of the riots, they were not fanning flames of despair, but were hard at work trying to prevent harm to the frightened neighborhood residents. They were setting up "telephone trees" to spread correct information when wild rumors caused fear; they were keeping buildings open to give a sense of stability. How could they not respond?

Last, in determining whether priority be given to the "service" or "cause" aspect of settlement programs, the choice seemed to be to accept a continuing state of tension. We would work for incremental improvements while waiting for bigger opportunities in the ebb and flow of national life, and provide the mitigating services—two sides of the same coin.

ENDNOTES

1. Edward J. O'Connell, *Welfare in Review* (Washington, DC: Department of Health, Education and Welfare, January-February 1968)

2. Quoted from a case study done by the Federation for the National Commission on Urban Problems. Their report, entitled *Building the American City*, was published in 1969 by Frederick Praeger, New York.

3. The Warner Robins Diary, covering Bernard Shiffman's two years as the community social worker, is available for study at the Social Welfare Archives, University of Minnesota.

BIBLIOGRAPHY

Berry, M. E. 1986. *One Hundred Years on Urban Frontiers. The Settlement Movement 1886-1986*. New York: United Neighborhood Centers of America.

Bond, R. 1990. *Focus on Neighborhoods*. Cleveland, OH: Greater Cleveland Neighborhood Centers Association.

Carson, M. 1990. *Settlement Folk, Social Thought and the American Settlement Movement, 1885-1930*. Chicago: University of Chicago Press.

Chambers, C. 1965. *Seedtime of Reform*. Minneapolis: University of Minnesota Press.

Davis, A. F. 1984. *Spearheads for Reform. The Social Settlements and the Progressive Movement 1890-1914*. New Brunswick, NJ: Rutgers University Press.

Fisher, Robert. 1984. *Let the People Decide: Neighborhood Organizing in America.* Boston: Twayne Publishers.

Hillman, Arthur. 1960. *Neighborhood Centers Today: Action Programs for a Rapidly Changing World.* New York: National Federation of Settlements and Neighborhood Centers.

Hillman, Arthur. 1969. *People, Places and Participation.* Part of a study done for the National Commission on Urban Problems. Mimeographed.

Husock, H. 1992. *Bringing Back the Settlement House. Public Interest* 109:53–72.

National Federation of Settlements and Neighborhood Centers. 1957. *Dynamics of Citizen Participation.*

National Federation of Settlements and Neighborhood Centers. 1958. *Neighborhood Goals in a Rapidly Changing World.*

Rational Planning to Solve Concrete Problems

Gangs and Community Organization

Irving A. Spergel

I started my journey in social work as a group
worker and street gang worker, with special interest in the street gang
problem. My field experience and theoretical interest have lead me from
original consideration of individual personality development and counseling, group process, and street work to community theory, interorganizational relationships, and community organizing. With rapid social and
technological changes in recent decades, and with the increasing severity
and spread of the gang problem—from large urban centers to smaller
cities, suburban and rural areas, and even on Native American reservations—I have come to rely on a complex set of formulations within a theoretical framework of social and personal disorganization to understand
and address the problem.

The youth or street gang (I use the terms interchangeably) has become a major means of youth socialization, a significant component of
community structure, as well, I believe, as an indicator of the failures of interorganizational and community development. The gang problem signi-
fies not only the antisocial behavior of gang youth, but the failure of
various key institutional behaviors of family, school, employment, law

123

enforcement, and social work to understand and effectively address the problem.

The specific missions of a variety of organizations and their lack of interconnection to gang-involved youth or those at high risk may be both response to and aggravation of the problem. The relationships of youth gangs to local institutions and of local organizations to each other are key to understanding the problem and what can be done to ameliorate or control it.

In the analysis of the problem and what to do about it from a community perspective, distinction might be made between the concepts of Community Organization and of community organizing. Community organization, in one descriptive and analytic sense, can refer mainly to the present or proposed structure and processes of organizations, interorganizational, and citizen relationships. The functions of community for purposes of understanding and addressing the gang problem include the interrelated provision of personal social support, social opportunities, social controls, community mobilization, and organizational development to meet the challenges of social change. On the other hand, community organizing in relation to the gang problem emphasizes how structures and institutions are purposefully changed to enhance community functions in order to provide youth—especially gang-prone youth—with the means to develop socially, emotionally, academically, culturally, and economically. The community organizer must contribute in various appropriate ways to increasing the capacity of organizations, community groups, and individual citizens, including gang youth themselves, in the prevention and reduction of the gang problem.

The presence of organized criminal youth gangs indicates a defective community. The street gang must be considered an interstitial component of community structure, sometimes temporary, sometimes of long-term duration, to meet the communal needs of young people. The larger society must be considered only indirectly cause and response to the gang problem. Communities, local institutions and organizations are not simply mirror images of larger societal structures and values. They are not completely shaped by larger cultural, economic, social, and political forces; they must also be viewed as products of internal community characteristics and forces, often in particular space and time.

Youth gangs are often collections of troubled youth whom the community's legitimate institutions have failed. Youth gangs can become part of community structures over time. They interact with family, school, youth agency, police, church, local criminal, and political and economic organizations. Although youth gangs can expand across neighborhoods, cities, and states to perform social, economic, and solidarity functions, they are mainly informal collectivities governed by powerful norms and values. In their more organized and criminal form, they can become "supergangs," "nations," pseudoreligious organizations, even components of major political and economic structures in a society.

Nevertheless, street gangs do not ordinarily serve to integrate their members into mainstream society. They contribute to the defective socialization of their members. They can become quasi-independent structures and forces, partially related to adult criminal organizations—in which case, they further weaken defective legitimate community structure and processes.

My professional transition from group work to community organizing was substantially a product of a particular historical context—the crises, social problems, and challenges and opportunities it provided. During and especially after World War II, American society had to confront the social costs of mass migrations of African Americans, Mexicans, and Puerto Ricans to urban centers, mainly in the North, and their integration into urban life. Drastic social and economic changes and the consequences for socialization weighed heavily, particularly on first-generation male youth from these usually low-income families. In earlier periods, youth agencies and schools had played major roles in facilitating acculturation and socialization of first-generation youth. Once again, in the late 1940s and 1950s, these same types of agencies and (increasingly youth authorities and consortia of youth and social agencies) assumed these tasks.

Clifford Shaw and his colleagues at the Institute for Juvenile Research in Chicago in the 1930s and early 1940s developed the idea of local community committees and curbstone workers to integrate delinquent youth into the ongoing life of the community. The local community committees represented local citizens, organizations, and units of the criminal justice system. The curbstone workers involved with delinquent groups were sometimes ex-convicts concerned about neighborhood and youth welfare and closely connected to the community committees. The later street-worker programs emulated and further developed the notion of curbstone worker, but not the use of community committees. The street-gang-work approach involved professional social work supervision and coordination of social agencies, with little participation or community control by local citizens.

The outreach or street-gang workers of the 1950s and 1960s, when I began my work, employed techniques mainly of recreation, group work, informal or crises counseling, mediation, and some interagency contacts on behalf of the gang members as the means to help and control gang youth and especially to reduce their conflict behavior. Moreover, gangs in this period were not as destructive or omnipresent as they are today. In fact, they were referred to often as delinquent groups or street clubs, rather than gangs. There is little evidence, however, based on social psychological theory and research of the time, that the approach was successful. Malcolm

Klein's research of two projects in Los Angeles in the 1950s and 1960s concluded that such programs resulted in greater group or gang cohesion and in youth commitment to delinquent behavior, at least on a group basis.

In the 1950s, I was a street-gang worker and supervisor of the Council of Social and Athletic Clubs with the New York City Youth Board as well as a director of a gang project, Neighborhoods United, sponsored by the Lenox Hill Neighborhood Association. After a time, I concluded that street-work efforts were of some value, especially when they emphasized individual counseling. Predominant use of group work, that is, mediation of gang conflicts using gang structure and leadership, did not seem effective. In working with or supervising workers with various gangs in different parts of New York City, perhaps the most valuable learning for me in the period was that gang characteristics and problems apparently differed by neighborhood and were probably related to their social and cultural patterns, including the race/ethnic backgrounds of local youth and adults.

My interest in neighborhood and community structure became more focused and systematic after I entered the doctoral program at Columbia University's School of Social Work, then the New York School of Social Work. The writings and research of Richard A. Cloward and Lloyd E. Ohlin were particularly influential. Their theory of delinquent subcultures and subsystems integrated a range of delinquency theories, including social disorganization, cultural transmission, anomie, and especially opportunity theories, to explain the development of delinquent patterns.

Cloward and Ohlin's ideas, which emphasized the integration of the criminal and legitimate opportunities, as well as of norms and values for youth on a neighborhood basis, laid the groundwork for my dissertation. I adapted their analytic framework and joined it with seven years of my experience as a street worker to explain differential systems of gang behavior. The resulting dissertation became my first book and a starting point for my further speculations and research—not only about the influence of delinquent subcultures, but for addressing the gang problem on a comparative community and also organizational basis.

Policy makers and politicians expressed growing concern in the late 1950s and early 1960s about minority youth gangs and their isolation from mainstream American life. This coincided with the beginning of a period of drastic shifts in the economy from manufacturing to service industries. A great many inner-city youth were not attending school, or they were dropouts and could no longer easily find jobs as nonskilled or semiskilled workers. Gangs began to proliferate and develop their own increasingly organized systems of survival and status achievement. Major foundations and the federal government sought to address the problem: The Ford Foundation at first emphasized improved coordination of school, youth-agency, and business efforts to provide better schooling and job opportunities for highly gang-at-risk youth.

Cloward and Ohlin's ideas were the initial basis for a federal shift in support of the development of antidelinquency programs. The U.S. Justice Department's Office of Juvenile Justice and Youth Development favored structural change to increase opportunities for inner-city delinquent youth. This was to replace or at least de-emphasize an approach that favored psychological and individual treatment programs. Federal agencies began to support a variety of social reforms at various government levels. These efforts utilized local social planning and coordination around youth issues, youth manpower, small business development, mental health, housing and urban development, and especially local agency and community involvement. However, those initiatives originally directed to youth development and gangs soon bypassed or no longer focused on youth gang problems but on more general issues of poverty and institutional change. Social work leaders emerged in some cities as champions of planned social change in social service delivery systems, but with decreasing interest in the specific problems of socialization of gang members or control of youth gangs.

Federally inspired criminal justice reforms of the late 1960s also directed state and local government policies and programs away from youth gangs and youth outreach efforts to problems of deinstitutionalization of status offenders and the prevention and treatment of abused children. Federal policy did not at first recognize the changing character of the problem of street gangs. Older youth and young adults no longer graduated from—and instead more strongly influenced—street gangs. Youth gangs became sophisticated and better organized. During this period of increased federal attention to the development of urban opportunities, especially through local citizen and agency empowerment programs, gangs, at times, made illegitimate use of such programs due, in part, to insufficient controls.

After completing my doctoral work at the New York School of Social Work in 1960, I took a position as assistant professor at the School of Social Service Administration, University of Chicago, with primary responsibility for teaching in and developing a social group work concentration. My interests in youth gangs, street work, and delinquent subcultures remained. I continued to modify and test existing small-group program approaches to gangs in Chicago and in other cities even as the gang problem seemed to worsen and change its character. At the same time, I gradually shifted interest to the community and the politicized context in which the gang problem seemed to be occurring.

My teaching responsibilities changed; I was asked to teach a course in Community Organization and to develop a full two-year program in this evolving specialization. Along with other University of Chicago faculty, I became concerned with the problems of population transition and community organization in East Woodlawn, a community just south of the University. It had quickly changed from a white working-class to an all African American lower-class and impoverished community in the 1950s and 1960s. Its local agencies and organizations, particularly its churches, were in ferment about how to address growing poverty and citizen alienation. I placed several of the community organization students in field training at The Woodlawn Organization (TWO), a new and controversial grass-roots community organization. The Woodlawn Organization was in process of coalescing a variety of community groups, agencies, businesses, churches, and residents into a broad community coalition to address social problems. Under the influence of Saul Alinsky and the Industrial Areas Foundation, the organization engaged in social action through deliberate conflict.

The federal Manpower Development and Training Act was passed in 1962. One of Professor Sol Tax's former students who was then in the Labor Department had access to demonstration funds that had to be distributed before the end of the fiscal year. Sol Tax, in the Anthropology Department, convened a small group of professors including myself to formulate a program that would assist unemployed young adults in Woodlawn to prepare for service jobs. We prepared a proposal for the staff of TWO who would conduct the program. A professor in the Education Department agreed to formulate the evaluation, a necessary component of a demonstration grant application.

The University of Chicago administration quickly objected to the development of what originally was designed as a joint proposal. The president and provost called the group of five faculty members to a special meeting in the University administration offices and accused the group of interfering with and trying to influence University in policy in respect to relations with TWO. The University of Chicago was involved in a major imbroglio and also secret negotiations with TWO over the University's intended expansion plans in Woodlawn—of which the small group of faculty were only dimly aware. The Woodlawn Organization, with Alinsky's aid was conducting a major media campaign against the University over the expansion plans, largely to coalesce organizations and citizens in the Woodlawn community. The intent of the faculty group was only to bring in additional resources to the Woodlawn community, and TWO seemed to be the viable local organization to carry out the social development program.

The first meeting by the University administration with the faculty group did not prove fruitful. The president, provost, and also the vice president for community affairs were anxious and did not know how to reconcile the faculty's traditional freedom to conduct research and the

University's institutional interests, which were not the same as those of TWO. In particular, they wanted to avoid attacks by Alinsky and being forced into an unwanted bargaining arrangement. Another meeting was scheduled so that the executive committee of the board of trustees as well as the University administration could jointly meet with the faculty group. The board committee met and quickly resolved the issue. They recommended a simple change in terminology. The faculty group would be permitted to conduct research in the Woodlawn project, but the proposal or proposals would be called "cooperative," rather than "joint." None of the faculty group members objected to this arrangement.

Shortly after the meeting with the committee of the board of trustees, the ongoing conflict between the University and TWO also ended. The University administration began to establish close relationships with TWO, and faculty groups generally became involved in a range of projects—local education improvement, mental health, maternal and child health, housing, day care, and economic development. The new arrangement served the community and the University's training and research interests and needs in a complementary and mutually "beneficial" way. The University also agreed to limit its expansion plans to a single streetwide swath of blocks just south of the campus but in Woodlawn. The University also shortly received the support of TWO during a period of turmoil between students and University during the Vietnam War era. Student efforts to draw TWO into a coalition against the University were not successful.

At about the same time, I was asked by social work students to sponsor a group research project to complete their master's requirements for graduation. The students were interested in interviewing members of block clubs in Woodlawn about housing conditions. The students mainly drew up the proposal and the survey instrument—which I insisted should come to the attention of TWO. The survey instrument raised questions that were largely informational and not potentially embarrassing to TWO. When the student group met with the staff of TWO to let them know what they planned, The Woodlawn Organization, to my surprise, discouraged the students from proceeding. Suspicion of student intentions and TWO's ongoing discussions with the city planning department over issues of housing rehabilitation may have been the reasons.

However, after due consideration, I gave the students permission to proceed. My own view was that no organization should control general community sources of information. The Woodlawn Organization was attempting to control all social and educational projects that took place in the community. The research exercise also appeared to be useful for student learning purposes and could not damage TWO and its efforts at housing rehabilitation. The project was carried out with no difficulty, and a copy of the report was sent to the TWO staff director, who offered no comment or reaction at the time. But the survey came up as an issue two years later in the course of negotiations over my proposed evaluation of TWO's Youth Manpower Project.

My interests in the interaction of gangs, Community Organization, organizing, and research were first joined in the evaluation of the highly controversial TWO's Youth Manpower Project. The middle and late 1960s were a period of political turbulence resulting from not only civil rights, economic change, the antipoverty program, and Vietnam, but also urban rioting, population movements and immigration, and the growth of street gangs in the major urban centers of the country. After the first series of urban riots, staff of the Office of Economic Opportunity (OEO) determined to develop several youth-oriented programs to control the violence of street gangs, to provide training and jobs for these mainly older adolescent minority gang youth, and, in the process, to control the potential for further rioting.

Several incorrect assumptions were behind these programs initiatives: that street gangs had somehow precipitated riots, that gangs represented the interests of community, and that they had the organized power to control riots. In fact, there was no evidence that gangs precipitated riots. Gang members individually joined in the looting and destruction, once riots were underway, as did other youth and young adults not connected to gangs in the urban ghetto. Gangs were obviously part of their communities but did not represent leadership or legitimate community interests. Gangs could be and were used by the police, during the riots in some cities, to patrol and assist in protecting community. In Woodlawn, there was evidence that leaders of the Blackstone Rangers were selling protection to businesses against rioting. Actually little disruption took place in Woodlawn or on the South Side during the mid-1960s urban riots in Chicago. The serious rioting in Chicago was confined to the West Side African American ghetto.

An OEO staff person visited TWO staff and contacted members of the two major warring street gangs, the Blackstone Rangers and the Devils or East Side Disciples. The OEO staff member assisted TWO staff to develop and write a proposal to conduct a youth manpower program to be funded at an annual budget of almost one million dollars. Three or four training centers were to be established with classes and programs for a total of 600 gang youth, aged 16 to 19, from the two gangs. Each of the gangs was to have one or two training centers, and they were to staff and be integrally involved in running the centers, including recruiting members, assisting with instruction, and job referral. The gang hierarchy was deliberately imposed on the staff of the training center structures. Leaders or subleaders of the gangs were to have equivalent positions in the centers. The Woodlawn Organization was also to invite the leaders of the gangs to represent their organizations and to become board members of TWO. Gangs were expected to contribute positively to the community's development, as well as reduce gang fights and crime. The assumption was that street gangs were or could be legitimate, community-minded organizations.

The Woodlawn Organization's organizing staff was to be responsible for the project. Subcontracts were arranged with the Xerox Corporation for General Education Development (GED) training and work orientation, and with the Chicago Urban League for job development and referral. The University of Chicago, particularly Argonne Laboratories, volunteered to place as many of the graduates of the training as possible into a variety of lab assistant or service positions. A total of four professional staff were to be available to implement and monitor a program of 600 gang members at three training centers (the fourth was not established) during a five-day, six-hours-per-day training period. The four staff members were also to be responsible for supervision of job referral, gang mediation, crisis intervention, case management, and interagency and community relationships, among other functions.

The project design was weak, if not unrealistic. The Woodlawn Organization's organizers had no experience in youth work or running gang problems. The YMCA and Boy's Clubs were operating outreach or street gang programs in the area at the time but were ignored by OEO and TWO. Key questions were raised by the Chicago Police Department, the local city anti-poverty authority, and the mayor's office about collaboration by TWO with the gangs. The mayor, himself, would become involved in decision making over the viability and structure of the project and who would control the project.

The Office of Economic Opportunity sought to fund the project by dealing directly with TWO and bypassing the mayor's office. However, TWO was then in conflict with city agencies over issues of school resources and housing rehabilitation. The Woodlawn Organization also saw the project as a means of funding its organizing effort. OEO was in a major reform mode to assist local organizations in dealing with local social problems on community terms, that is, to "shake up" existing urban decision-making processes, especially in disenfranchised minority communities. The Woodlawn Organization's Youth Manpower Project touched off a major political conflict that involved local, state, and national politicians and agencies and contributed to a weakening of a Democratic machine in Chicago.

In the midst of a rapidly gathering political storm, even before the initiation of the project, I received a telephone call from a key research administrator in the Community Action program of OEO requesting me to submit a proposal to evaluate the project. I was selected, in part because of my prior gang research and experience in evaluation of gang programs, and

probably also because of my connection with the University of Chicago—
a fact that could lend legitimacy to the project. Also, OEO could not
fund a demonstration program without a formal evaluation.

While I had reservations about the project idea, the opportunity to
collect gang data and evaluate a gang project run by a militant grassroots
organization seemed too attractive to forego. However, I ran into obstacles in the process of submission of the proposal. The OEO staff member
requested that I attend a meeting with the TWO president, Arthur Bra-
zier, and key community organization staff including the organizer, Anthony Gibbs, who would later become the acting project director. In
response to a challenge about the earlier student block club survey conducted without TWO permission, I indicated that I had no animosity
toward TWO and reminded the president and staff of my earlier support
of various TWO-University projects. I stated that my evaluation would
be professional, objective, and independent. The queries, however, appeared to be pro forma. The Office of Economic Opportunity and TWO,
given the growing attacks on the project, probably had no choice but to
accept me as evaluator.

The University research office also was reluctant for me to evaluate the
project. I was asked by the University of Chicago vice president of community affairs to delay submission of the proposal until a director for the
project was selected and approved by the mayor's office. Mayor Daley had
submitted the names of two candidates for project director acceptable to
him. He also insisted that his director of the local antipoverty program office approve the program's budget and monitor its efforts. The Woodlawn Organization and OEO, on the other hand, wanted to select their
own project director—creating an impasse.

I did not accept the advice of the vice president of community affairs,
although it would prove later to have been good advice. I wanted to study
community organizing as well as gang and program development processes at as early a point as possible. The University of Chicago vice president
relented after a month's delay, and the evaluation proposal was processed
and submitted to the OEO office, as originally designed. The project proceeded with the TWO staff organizer, Anthony Gibbs, as acting director
and with limited budget oversight by the city's antipoverty agency.

Community conflict and politicization of the project grew. A conflict brewed among the organizations supporting TWO. The minister and
staff of the local Presbyterian Church supported the legitimacy of the
Blackstone Rangers in its various activities, including arranging press conferences and storing weaponry in the church vault. The local Catholic
Church expressed public dismay with TWO's project design and conduct
of the project. The Chicago Police Department's gang squad, newly organized, gave special, if not intrusive, attention to the training centers and the
activities of the gang-member staff. A Democratic congressman in the

city opposed the project, while one of the Republican senators from the state supported it. The two major local newspapers also editorialized about the project—one in support, the other in opposition.

In addition, the program had little chance to develop and modify its flawed design. At a minimum, a doubling or tripling of professional staff should have occurred. The leader of the Devil's Disciples agreed to join TWO's board, but the leader of the Blackstone Rangers refused —reportedly stating, "TWO don't run Woodlawn, Blackstone do."

The evaluation was hobbled by lack of cooperation from the Chicago Police Department to provide aggregate and individual-level police data on youth to the project. The Woodlawn Organization limited regular interviews with program staff. Formal interviews of program youth were conducted with some resistance from the Blackstone Rangers. Records of job referrals and placements were obtained with difficulty. However, random but successful observations by evaluation staff of training center activities at different hours and parts of the day were conducted.

The program seemed to be accomplishing little. Instead of a mandated average of 60 youth in training at each center, only 15 youth were regularly present. Little teaching or program-related learning took place. Discussions of gang affairs occurred openly. Few youth were actually placed on jobs or held them. Gang violence did not abate in the area, at least based on aggregate-level police data obtained indirectly from the Commission on Youth Welfare.

The Chicago Police Department complained about the project to the U.S. Senate subcommittee on Government Operations and requested a public investigation about Blackstone Rangers intimidation, as did several local Woodlawn citizens. Full-fledged subcommittee hearings were held and nationally televised, as well as reported in the national and international media. The target gang was the Blackstone Rangers. The subcommittee also issued subpoenas for evaluation records, mainly research field notes. We maintained the confidentiality of approximately 100 formal gang youth interviews that had been placed on tape and did not have identifiers and, in fact, were not requested. However, the Senate investigators did not honor an agreement reached with the University of Chicago's legal office not to release the names of individual youth whose names appeared on field notes. As soon as several names were released to the press, we terminated data collection but continued to analyze data already collected.

The project lasted a year. A second year's funding was agreed to by OEO, but the offer was withdrawn as a condition of the Senate's acceptance of the nomination of the new OEO director. My year-end report of the project was also a source of controversy. It was submitted to OEO as required, but not released to the Senate committee, and one of newspapers accused me of not submitting the report and defrauding the government.

Our report indicated that an insufficient number of program youth were in training—a fact that was probably a serious embarrassment to the OEO. Checks for four times the number of youth in active training were being issued and distributed.

Based in part on our evaluation report, a full-fledged federal Justice Department investigation of the project was initiated. The Blackstone Rangers' leadership was charged with fraud. The investigation revealed that program youth were being lined up by the gang leaders on Friday paydays, and each youth was required to sign over his check. The leaders of the Blackstone Rangers were prosecuted and several received five-year sentences to a federal penitentiary.

Before sentencing, however, the leaders of the Blackstone Rangers—now the P[eace] Stone Nation, and later the El Rukns, were invited to and actually did attend President Nixon's inauguration. The gang had already developed a corporate structure, the "Mains Twenty One." In the course of the project, the gang was able to integrate smaller gangs and street groups into its organization. The gang also supported various candidates for office and even elected two of its members to the local area's Model City council during and immediately after the cessation of the Youth Manpower Project. The Devil's Disciples also added to its reputation and influence, becoming the Gangster Disciples and in due course the largest African American street gang in Illinois and the Midwest. When released from prison, key leaders of the El Rukns became involved in drug distribution activities, locally and nationally.

The Woodlawn Organization's Youth Manpower Project was a watershed in the development of street gangs and precipitated a shift in strategies addressing the gang problem. Population mobility, deindustrialization, weakening of local institutions, a lack of social opportunities, and developing street-level criminal structures were probably the chief elements accounting for the growth of gangs—not simply in Chicago, but in Los Angeles, Detroit, Philadelphia, and other cities in the 1970s. Social disorganization increased as the American economy and government local business and social organizations could not create adequate legitimate means to incorporate minority youth in the larger culture and socioeconomic structure. Projects such as the Youth Manpower program, weak and poorly directed, also failed in various parts of the country.

Vanishing federal interest and funds contributed to the demise of youth agency interest in social outreach programs for gang youth. Urban police departments filled the void in addressing the street-gang problem. A shift in strategy occurred, from treatment and rehabilitation to suppression and incarceration. Deterrence and incarceration replaced social development and opportunity approaches. A critically important element of theory and program development that was also missing was attention to organizational and interorganizational behavior in dealing with, and further contributing to, the gang problem. This was by the lack of coordination of agency and community efforts in the implementation of the various approaches.

My interest in patterns of gang crime or delinquency and their relation to community structures continued after the termination of TWO's Youth Manpower Project. The 1970s and part of the 1980s were less politically turbulent in relation to the problem of gangs. The TWO youth manpower experiment had taught me that the response of organizations and the community to gangs could be a major part of the problem. I became interested in whether and how different patterns of community structure, particularly interorganizational relationships, in different Chicago communities might be linked to different patterns of official deviancy, not only gang crime but also other deviancy problems, for example, status-offending patterns. Factors of race/ethnicity, class, migration, and culture were not the only variables associated with these differences. The way in which organizations related to each other about a particular social problem in a particular community could be part of the problem. This led me to conduct a series of research studies on the issue.

In one set of studies of interorganizational relations on the Near West Side and South Side of Chicago, we looked at how organizations and community groups communicated with each other and exchanged resources around the problem of gangs, delinquency, and crime. Of the four communities selected, three were largely Latino; the fourth was African American. The three Latino communities varied slightly in income or class level and stability. Based on police statistics, the Latino community with the most agencies and community groups and the most contentious interorganizational relationships had the highest level of gang violence. The more settled, mixed Latino and middle-European community, with little interagency conflict, had little in the way of a gang problem. The third Latino community, consisting mainly of newcomer, working-class homeowners, with few local agencies but a relatively large number of Catholic Churches, was experiencing an emerging gang problem. The African American community, comprised mainly of single-parent families and long-term residents in high-rise public housing, where public agencies were dominant and in close cooperative relations, had low rates of gang violence but very high rates of juvenile delinquency and other serious social problems.

In a second research, a statewide evaluation—part of a national test of the status offender deinstitutionalization strategy of the federal government in the middle and late 1970s—we examined issues of diversion and incarceration of juveniles who run away from home, are ungovernable, who violate curfew, are truants, or abuse alcohol. An aspect of the research was to look at patterns of relationship and exchanges among organizations concerned with the problem in three communities. Two of the Chicago communities were African American, one middle class, the other low income. The third was a mixed, mainly white, ethnic working class.

The worst status offender problem existed in the poorest community, but this community also had the largest number of public voluntary agencies as well as a large number of block clubs. The agencies were highly sectorialized, that is, organizations were mainly in contact with other similar organizations about the same types of problems—juvenile justice agencies, schools, churches, housing, family welfare, child welfare, and youth agencies. Runaways or ungovernable youth were almost exclusively processed by official agencies, police, decentralized units of the court, residential programs, or a special unit of the State Department of Children and Family Services. A great deal of official labeling occurred, and the highest rate of status offending was in this community.

The other two communities had fewer public agencies and relatively more voluntary agencies and churches. These two communities had few specialized service or community development sectors. Communication and exchanges took place among different types of organizations around the problem of runaways or ungovernable youth. Fewer official exchanges about status-offender youth occurred and fewer youth were officially labeled as status offenders. Lower prevalence rates of status offending characterized these two communities. Social problems and family crises, including youth problems, were dealt with mainly at an informal interagency and grassroots organizational level. We interpreted this to mean that there was a greater sense of community, and that specialized agency responsibility for the problem of status offending was minimized.

In a third research conducted in the late seventies and eighties, we examined community characteristics—as indicated by a combination of demographic, socioeconomic factors, and mobility rates—in relation to gang homicide and delinquency in the highest gang violence and crime areas of Chicago, using police statistics. The highest gang homicide rates were in inner-city, low-income, recently settled Latino communities, mainly Mexican, Mexican American, and Puerto Rican. Rates of juvenile delinquency and those of other social problems were moderate. The highest general crime and delinquency rates were in inner-city, very low-income, less mobile African American communities. These were communities with the highest poverty and unemployment and lowest mortgage investment rates. Again, there was a relationship between type of community and its patterns of deviance. The specific way organizations were related to each other in these communities was not that clear, but there appeared to be some congruence with our earlier findings.

It was clear to me from these three studies and the earlier TWO Youth Manpower experience that the pattern of local organizations and their interrelationships—as well as the socioeconomic and political context in which these relationships developed—was critical for explaining a social problem such as gang crime. Casework or group work, alone, with targeted youth would not be sufficient to effectively intervene. Organizing the community meaningfully to address the problem would be essential.

I subsequently organized a set of pilot demonstration efforts within a theoretical framework drawn from these studies. The gang problem worsened in Chicago, as it did in other large cities. Gangs began to emerge in smaller cities and suburban areas in the late 1980s and early 1990s. I was granted funds by the Illinois Criminal Justice Information Authority to conduct a pilot gang violence control program in the Humboldt Park area, one of the two highest gang violence areas in Chicago in the middle 1980s. Based on the poor—if not negative—results of TWO's Youth Manpower Project, I sought to involve a variety of organizations, including the Chicago Police Department, and street or youth outreach workers in a cooperative arrangement targeted to several violent gangs at war with each other. An assumption of the pilot effort, which only endured nine months (based on available funds), was that the gang problem consisted of both what gang youth did and the fragmentation of agency or community response to gang activity. The intervention implication was to strengthen bonds among organizations and community groups as a deterent to negative gang activity.

The Chicago Police Department was friendlier to me in the 1980s than it had been in the 1960s, partially because the Gang Crime Unit's commander was now interested in a nonpoliticized cooperation with some form of human service approach in dealing with the gang crime problem. The unit also collected gang crime data that it agreed to make available to the project for evaluation purposes. The Gang Crime Unit became closely associated with the outreach program, the Gang Crisis Intervention Service (CRISP) project. I conducted the project with the aid of two graduate students and three local outreach workers. A key objective of the project design was to broaden the involvement of churches, the network of youth agencies, the schools, block clubs, and the police in the project, which was only partially achieved. Monthly meetings were held with various churches, agencies and community groups, and local residents, as well as police representatives to assess the ongoing gang situation, to participate jointly in the development of services and facilities for gang youth, and to protect the community from criminal gang activities. A community consortium to support the project was not achieved, however.

There were some project accomplishments. Former leaders of gangs did work together to mediate and reduce violence, to assist youth with school problems, and even to hold occasional staff meetings in the local district police station. Police statistics indicated that gang-related arrests for the nine-month period for younger youth in Humboldt Park declined, compared to a prior similar nine-month period in a similar community.

There was little effect on patterns of gang violence of youth 17 and over—
the more serious offenders.

Shortly after the termination of the Humboldt Park gang project
(CRISP), a tragic event galvanized the African American community and
city government to address the gang problem more extensively. A gradu-
ating star basketball player, the best in the nation according to the media,
was killed in a robbery committed by two gang members near his high
school. Civil rights groups and local community organizations demanded
action from the recently elected first African American mayor of Chicago,
Harold Washington. I was telephoned shortly afterwards by two of the
mayor's close advisors, his chief political organizer, who was a graduate social work community organizer, and Anthony Gibbs, now the director of
the Mayor's Citizen Advisory agency. Both had been staff organizers of
The Woodlawn Organization in earlier years; as in most endeavors, contacts and relationships over time build on one another in political ways.
The director of the Mayor's Citizen Advisory agency had been the former
acting director of TWO's Youth Manpower Project. The two advisors
and I met at a local pub, near the University of Chicago. Because the
mayor's advisors were not clear as to what to do, I suggested that the
CRISP and the Philadelphia Crisis Intervention (a youth gang intervention
project that emphasized collaboration with probation and neighborhood
groups) models might be useful. Both advisors were interested. The
mayor's chief political advisor saw, in addition, the potential of the gang
crisis as a basis for organizing community social agencies and neighborhood groups in support of the mayor's reelection campaign.

The plan that evolved was the formation of a series of nine or ten
local youth coordinating councils throughout the city to address youth
and gang problems. Local youth and neighborhood groups and agency
representatives who supported the mayor were to be given key positions
on the councils. A citywide crisis intervention network (CIN) unit was
also to be formed. Both components were to be under the control of the
Chicago Department of Human Services. A struggle for resources ensued. The established youth agencies pressured the City Council to allocate most of the $3 million project for gang prevention, essentially to beef
up existing programs in these agencies. I testified before the City Council,
urging a greater portion of funds to the Outreach Crisis Intervention Project (CIN), which would also be related to the local councils. The established agencies were requested to better target and provide services to
hardcore youth. The City Council allocated more funds to the crisis intervention project.

I was then appointed to the central coordinating committee of the
new set of initiatives, which was located in the Department of Human
Services. I resigned after a year's service, after it became clear that local
human service agencies were not prepared to reach out to the streets or to

other agencies to target the gang problem, but only to obtain funds to support existing programs, and to some extent to keep gang youth out of these programs. Also, the CIN program focused its efforts on recreation and not a broad range of services or the development of social and economic opportunities for gang youth. The CIN outreach staff were poorly or laxly supervised, and the police did not work closely with them, as intended. After two years, charges of corruption were levied against the CIN outreach worker program. Several workers were arrested for drug possession; others were viewed as failing to contact or serve youth on the street as they were supposed to. There was little evidence of interagency collaboration. The objectives of the program were not met. The gang problem continued to increase in severity, and the CIN program was abandoned after about four years.

At the termination of the Humboldt Park CRISP project, and while CIN was still in progress, I undertook a study of the gang problem in Chicago Public Schools for the Illinois State Education Department. At the completion of the study, I advised the state and local Chicago boards of education to pay more attention to the growing gang problem, provide extra services, and especially to involve police, youth agencies, as well as families in collaborative efforts to target problem gang youth. While the state and Chicago took no action on any of these recommendations, I was able, with grant funds from The U.S. Department of Education, to develop a special short-term demonstration and to set up a research program at four Chicago middle schools that had serious gang problems. Two of the schools were assigned to be program and two were control or nonservice schools. Only a year's funding was obtained from the U.S. Department of Education, however.

The objective of the project was for the school's staff to reach out to gang youth who were causing trouble in the school and community, involve parents and local school councils, and provide them with extra contacts, service, and social controls in some interrelated fashion. Youth were to be suspended but remain in the school building and at the same time receive extra support with remedial service. School staff would also reach out to homes to make sure gang youth attended class. The school council would also focus on involving parents of gang youth in school affairs. Youth from different gangs at war with each other were to be jointly involved in additional community-centered program activities. The two experimental schools received funds from the grant for these extra activities.

Even though the program had promising results, further funding could not be obtained. Student violence was reduced. Attendance of the target youth improved. Everyone seemed pleased with the progress made. Also, surveys of several hundred sixth- and eighth-graders—African American and Latino youth—in the four schools were conducted and indicated that different community and cultural factors were associated with different patterns of delinquency and gang involvement. African American students were more pervasively associated with drug and crime subcultures and criminal systems. The Latino youth experienced more problematic situations at home and at school. Prior delinquency was a better indicator of gang involvement of students from the African American but not from the Latino communities. Different social, family, and community processes seemed to be operating for youth. Again, in this project as in earlier and later ones, we integrated research and intervention design in order to better understand and address a complex social problem.

Our most systematic and broad-scale research and development program on the gang problem was initiated through a major grant by the Office of Juvenile Justice and Delinquency Prevention (OJJDP) between 1987 and 1991. The project, more research than demonstration in its earlier phases, permitted us to formulate a systematic and comprehensive community approach to the gang problem. In the course of the first phase of the project—literature survey, national surveys, conferences, focus groups, and field visits to five cities with apparent successful gang programs—we identified a number of conceptual and organizational relationship problems. (1) The terms *gang, gang member,* and *gang incident* were not clearly defined; (2) various types of organizations were addressing the problem, but often in sharply different and inconsistent ways; (3) there was little coordination or collaboration of efforts; and (4) sharp conflict occasionally existed among organizations over ideology and/or resources. We discovered that the gang problem varied in scope and seriousness across cities and within cities and across time, depending on certain factors: distributions and concentrations of population by age, gender, race/ethnicity; socioeconomics, for example, family/household income, education level, population mobility; and the nature of organizational/interorganizational response to the problem.

In our search of the literature and a survey of organizations of over 50 cities, we were able to conceptualize key interrelated strategies for dealing with the problem: suppression, social intervention, community mobilization and provision of social opportunities directed to target youth, as well as innovative organizational and interorganizational arrangements. Community mobilization and the provision of social opportunities were the least common strategies used, yet, based on survey responses of executives and community leaders, they were perceived as most successful.

We developed a series of models and manuals of policy and practice addressed to specific types of organizations and their interrelationships. The organizations we addressed included police, probation, parole/aftercare, prosecution, judges, youth and human services agencies, schools, business and employment agencies, grassroots organizations or neighborhood groups, churches, city officials, and planning agencies. Essentially, we advised that different community structure and organizational as well as programming arrangements had to be developed. Community mobilization at various levels was the key strategy to be employed in the reduction of gang crime. Improved data gathering techniques and systems, communication, planning, and teamwork activities across agencies and community groups were to be encouraged and induced. Community organizing would have to be interrelated with direct services and social opportunities, as well as with controls for gangs and gang youth.

The models and manuals did not immediately become the basis for OJJDP policy and program implementation. A delay of three years occurred before the final national implementation and testing phase of R & D effort took place. Meanwhile, we were offered an opportunity through Criminal Justice block grant funds to the State of Illinois, to test the outcome of the basic notions. We were asked to draw up a concept paper for the Chicago Police Department. Only law enforcement agencies could receive grant funds. Our project design could only contain some elements of the model. It was to include a team of four police officers (two full-time tactical and two neighborhood relations officers), three full-time adult probation officers, four youth outreach workers, and one community organizer. Originally, the Department of Human Services was expected to participate and supply youth workers; the Chicago Police Department, particularly the Gang Crimes Unit, was to coordinate or manage the project. The Cook County Adult Probation Department, under the sponsorship of the Chicago Police Department, agreed to be part of the demonstration.

The Chicago Police Department showed some resistance to taking full responsibility for the project, and the Department of Human Services refused to participate. As it turned out, I became responsible for coordination of the project and for the development of the outreach or community youth worker unit through the School of Social Service Administration. The project operated in the Little Village community, an area of extremely high gang violence southwest of the Loop, Chicago's central business district.

The goal was the reduction of gang crime, especially gang violence for those youth targeted and for the test area generally. In the course of the five-year project period, approximately 200 hardcore gang youth, aged mainly 17 to 24, and an additional 100 peripheral or associated gang youth in two major gang constellations were targeted and served through the interrelated suppression/service/opportunity provision strategies.

A number of successes were achieved. The norms and practices of police, probation, community youth workers, and community activists were modified in the course of collaboration. An unusual and diverse team of workers was developed and operated cohesively. Our analysis suggested that, as a result of the program, gang crime for target youth declined—based on self-report and official individual-level police data and using comparison groups. Area rates of gang violence rose less than they did in the six comparison high-gang-crime community areas selected at the start of the demonstration and research, at least during the first four years of the project. Community residents perceived statistically significant positive police changes and gang crime reduction, comparing Little Village with an almost identical nearby community—Pilsen—between the first and third project years.

However, out community efforts were not entirely successful. We are not able to sustain the organization of a coalition of agencies and community groups. The key sponsoring agency, the police, was not prepared to integrate the approach into its community policing program citywide, we advised at various times during the course of the demonstration, or even to continue the project in Little Village, although funding was available for an additional three years. I had decided earlier to slowly withdraw from the project as its coordinator. I was not an agency administrator, and we expected the Chicago Police Department and a cluster of local community agencies to take over. But the fragmentation and weakness of local private and public agencies and community groups could not be overcome. The demonstration project could not succeed against both entrenched community agency inertia and competition and a strong police suppression tradition. Pieces of the Little Village Gang Violence Reduction Project, however, were to be sustained. The Chicago Police Department would begin a systematic citywide collaboration with the Cook County Adult Probation Department around the gang problem. The integration of a human service and community involvement component was left vaguely to the future. My concern was that such a partial continuation of the model would lead only to enhanced suppression.

Although the idea of a comprehensive community-wide model to address the gang problem was not immediately supported by Chicago's governmental or institutional leadership, the concept has been adopted and is currently being elaborated and tested by the Office of Juvenile Justice and Delinquency Prevention. Two major national programs are in progress one of which is "The Comprehensive Community-wide Approach to Gang Prevention, Intervention, and Suppression Program," initiated in 1994 in five cities (Bloomington, Illinois; Tucson and Mesa, Arizona; San Antonio, Texas; and Riverside, California). The model is also being tested as part of the "Safe Futures" program initiated in 1995 in five other locations (Boston, St. Louis, Seattle, and Contra Costa and Imperial Valley Counties in California). The author is presently evaluating the process, outcome, and impact of the first of these two long-term programs. The Urban Institute is evaluating the development of the model in the latter five locations.

There are certain things I have learned about community organization and community organizing in trying to understand and address the gang problem over several decades. These observations and principles, I believe, are common to organizing across a variety of types of social problems:

1. A community and the problems to be addressed are a combination of reality and construct.

2. Communities are a complex of organizations, neighborhood groups and individuals with variable interest and capacity for effective policy and program development.

3. Community organizing requires attention to the attitudes and interests of leadership and local citizens in resolving particular social problems and the availability of resources—economic, moral, organizational, local community, and authoritatively based—to support these efforts.

4. The community organizer can effectively address the community's problems only through a network of organizations, community groups, individuals, and government at both policy/administrative and street levels involving team efforts in relation to specific problems.

5. The many inducements, constraints, and conditions available to the organizer include not only professional social work commitments; social, moral, and economic resources; and skills of individual persuasion and facilitation of group interaction planning and evaluation; but also use of timing, good luck, persistence, and continuity of effort over time.

6. The community organizer is a leader and an enabler, who does not have to seek or precipitate conflict. Conflict at different levels is inevitable in any effective organizing process, but it must be contained.

7. Theory, analysis, and research must guide the organizer at all times in the determination of effective approaches. The integration of research, program, and evaluation activity is essential to any significant organizing effort.

8. Finally, the organizer must recognize that governmental policy both affects and is affected by good local community or neighborhood problem-solving capacity and institution building efforts in a democratic society.

BIBLIOGRAPHY

Brager, George, Harry Specht, and James L. Torczyner. 1987. *Community Organizing.* 3rd ed. New York: Columbia University Press.

Cloward, Richard A., and Lloyd E. Ohlin. 1960. *Delinquency and Opportunity: A Theory of Delinquent Gangs.* Glencoe, IL: The Free Press.

Gold, Martin, and Hans W. Mattick. 1974. *Experiment in the Streets: The Chicago Youth Development Project.* Ann Arbor, MI: Institute for Social Research, University of Michigan.

Hardcastle, David A., Stanley Wenocur, and Patricia R. Bowers. 1997. *Community Practice Theories and Skills for Social Workers.* New York: Oxford University Press.

Klein, Malcolm W. 1971. *Street Gangs and Street Workers.* Englewood Cliffs, NJ: Prentice-Hall.

Miller, Walter B. 1962. "The Impact of a 'Total-Community' Delinquency Control Project." *Social Problems* 19(2):168–191.

Moynihan, Daniel P. 1969. *Maximum Feasible Misunderstanding: Community Action in the War on Poverty.* New York: The Free Press.

Rothman, Jack. 1995. "Approaches to Community Intervention." Pp. 26–63 in *Strategies of Community Intervention*, 5th ed., edited by Jack Rothman, John L. Erlich, and John E. Tropman with Fred M. Cox. Itasca, IL: F. E. Peacock Publishers.

Schlossman, Steven, Gail Zellman, and Richard Shavelson. 1984 (May). *Delinquency Prevention in South Chicago.* A Fifty-Year Assessment of the Chicago Area Project. Santa Monica, CA: Rand.

Shaw, Clifford, and Henry D. McKay. 1943. *Juvenile Delinquency and Urban Areas.* Chicago: University of Chicago Press.

Spergel, Irving A. 1995. *The Youth Gang Problem: A Community Approach.* New York: Oxford University Press.

Thrasher, Frederic M. 1927. *The Gang.* Chicago: University of Chicago Press.

CHANGING AND UPGRADING
PLANNING METHODS:
THE HEALTH FIELD

My Community
Organization Journey

Mildred C. Barry

In the fall of 1933, in the midst of the Great
Depression, I enrolled as a group work student in a two-year program to
earn my master's degree in social work. My knowledge about social work
and the fledgling group work specialty was limited. I had no career goals.
College mates told me about this opportunity: to earn a master's degree in
a program that provided a stipend to cover my expenses while I taught activities to groups of underprivileged kids. It seemed like a good deal, and
it proved to be so. It started me on the route to community organization
so that, when I retired at the compulsory age of 65 in 1977, I could look
back on a career full of challenging experiences, one that was fun and had
contributed, in some measure, to the development of community organization and to the profession I love.

My profession is social work. My specialty is Community Organization. My jobs have been in Cleveland, Ohio, in both academic and practice
settings and have carried various titles, the last one being: director, Health
Planning and Development Commission, Federation for Community
Planning, Cleveland, Ohio. Health planning will be at the center of this
narrative, but let me get to that in good time.

As I reflect on a career that spanned almost half a century, I strip away lots of the chaff. I focus on what has seemed central—or key—to what I believe and to how I have tried to operate.

First. What is central to social work? It is to help persons live more productively, or as some say, to fulfill their potential. This includes helping them understand and deal with their problems. And this, in turn, means helping them find and use resources available to them, their own and those outside themselves. And to do these things—to help persons— we must open our ears and eyes to listen and hear and see them. This simple but fundamental principle applies whether these "persons" are seen as individuals or in groups or in communities. And we must understand ourselves.

Second. What is important in looking at ourselves? What makes one a professional? It is, of course, everything about us. And it is about how we feel and treat other persons. It is the skills and knowledge we've learned and how we apply these.

Third. What is important about the world around us? The environment we live in, the events that happen. Everything that impinges on us affects what we are and what we do and also affects those we work with as colleagues or as recipients of service.

I mention these plain truths because, when persons ask me what I do in various situations, these simple principles underlie what has become natural to me. How, then, do I answer when people ask me what I was doing in the many different settings and situations from settlement house worker to community health planner that spanned 40 years?

Let me put it this way: It was as if I were paddling a canoe down a river through shoals and rapids, sometimes pausing to join with people on one shore sometimes being carried rapidly down the swift river to another landing where the people and their problems were more complex. My role was my extension of what I believed social work as related to communities was all about. Communities, however defined.

There were always the big historical upheavals—depression, war, uprisings—that affected all our lives. There were events that shaped the national movements and organizations to which our work was related. There were local events—the politics, the power plays, the big guys versus the little guys, the racial and ethnic tensions, the heroes and the villains—that impacted how we operated.

An example comes to mind. When I was on the staff of University Settlement during the alphabet years of FDR following the Depression, we had an active program with young adults who were unemployed, who couldn't find jobs. Our settlement director, who knew the director of the Cleveland Metropolitan Park District, worked out an arrangement with him and the local head of WPA (Works Progress Administration) for our young adults to build a camp in a nearby metropolitan park. Under WPA, it didn't cost much and our members raised the extra money needed. The WPA lodge and other buildings were rustic in style and well constructed, and the camp (which I directed for a few summers) proved a good addition to the settlement house program. Under the tutelage of a student in training, this same group of young people wrote a "labor musical," which helped raise the money. It also attracted local and national acclaim. I arranged to have them perform at a National Federation of Settlements conference. But that musical got us, and me in particular, in trouble. The closing act ended with the whole chorus shouting, with arms and fists raised, "Unite Labor Unite." The settlement director and I were called down to Community Chest headquarters, where I was admonished for encouraging such a production. I explained that the raised fists were not in support of subversive labor movements, but expressions of young adults seeking jobs. This took some explaining, but neither my director nor I backed down and the threatened cut in our Chest support was forgotten.

But I digress. I pick up my story at my entrance to the school of social work in the fall of 1933. Social work was struggling to become a profession and an acceptable partner to other helping professions, and "group work" was a stepchild in the social work profession. I didn't know enough to realize I was part of this emerging discipline.

Group Work was started by W.I. Newstetter ("Noodles") and colleagues in Cleveland at the School of Applied Social Sciences, Western Reserve University.[1] Field practice was located in settlement houses and other group service agencies in the city, but, in addition and in order to have a controlled, research-oriented setting, a new settlement was started, financed by an anonymous donor. This, eventually called University Settlement, was where I had my field practice and later returned to the staff as a program director and then acting director at the start of World War II.

When I first came to Cleveland as a graduate student, I faced culture shock. I was born and grew up in China as the eldest child of Presbyterian missionaries. I attended Wooster College, where "mish kids" were no oddities. But field placement at University Settlement in the Polish-Slovenian section of southeast Cleveland meant living with four other women above Kasprezak's Furniture Store in a predominantly Roman Catholic community—a community where first- and second-generation ethnics centered their lives in their parish churches and families took great pride in owning their own homes on gardened plots. The Depression hit these people hard. Job seekers had difficulties because, in spite of looking white, they had unpronounceable names.

My field placement included working at St. Stanislaus, the largest Polish Catholic Parish in Cleveland. I loved it. I became fascinated by the people, their lives, their organizations, their culture, and the beautiful gothic church central to their lives. My master's thesis, with Newstetter as my adviser, was on "community organization" and drew mostly upon my experiences at St. Stanislaus. Understanding groups and communities was as important as understanding individuals and families, and we thought, integral to social work as a helping profession.

After getting my master's degree I worked at the YWCA in Hartford, Connecticut, for a year, then returned to University Settlement as girls' worker, then program director, where I also had an appointment as a field instructor at the School of Applied Social Sciences. I was named acting director of the settlement when the director was called to war, but I faced obstacles that made me dissatisfied and so I was glad to accept an offer from the Junior League of Cleveland to be their placement secretary, a position requiring a social work degree. I was employed by the League but loaned part time to the City of Cleveland to serve as co-director of the Civilian Defense Volunteer Bureau. This double-duty job meant finding volunteers to meet all kinds of requests, public and private, war-related and not. A wonderful experience. I learned about Cleveland's organizations, its political, corporate, and social structures, the "big-wheels," and the decision makers and leaders who got things done.

After a year, I was asked by the executive director of The Welfare Federation[2] to become secretary of its Group Work council, a position I held for two years, 1944–46. The Welfare Federation was the social planning agency in Cleveland distinct from the Community Chest. In those days, the Chest raised the money through a united appeal, but the Federation did the budgeting and allocation of funds. Also at that time, if I recall correctly, most of the Federation's own funding was from the Community Chest. As Group Work Council secretary I worked with all the group service agencies in Cleveland that received any degree of support from the Community Chest (later called the United Way). My job with the agencies related to their function and program development, community relevance, and standards. The Federation's finance director was my colleague in working with the agencies on budget and fiscal accountability.

The experience with the Group Work Council, which was a professional executive position, afforded me the opportunity to know all the group service agencies, their programs and operations, and the budgeting and allocation procedures. The Council and its budget committee were comprised of a board member and the executive of each member agency. I kept the minutes of the meetings, recording key issues and discussions, not just formal actions. I played a role in facilitating the analysis of a problem or situation and identifying possible alternative solutions. I learned much about group process—the problem-solving, decision-making process. I drew on these experiences when I prepared fictional case studies later for teaching.

In 1946, I resigned my job to start a family. When World War II ended, my surgeon husband was able to enter private practice and we put a down payment on a home. Our baby daughter was born. It was a happy time. I had no plans to continue my career, satisfying though it had been. But when Leonard Mayo, dean of the school of Applied Social Sciences, asked me to be a thesis adviser—the students could come to my house for conferences—I accepted. It was refreshing to intersperse diaper changing and back-fence gossiping with visits from my thesis advisees. Many post-World War II students were able to get an education due to the GI Bill of Rights, and the earnestness and dedication of these aspiring professionals was stimulating.

Later, when Dean Mayo moved to administrative office at the University and asked me to replace him as instructor of two classes in Community Organization, I accepted. That is when I had to conceptualize what I had been practicing as well as study the literature and course outlines he had developed.

Replacing Leonard Mayo as the teacher of Community Organization was more than a challenge. It was awesome. Leonard was a charismatic speaker and leader, nationally known and recognized in our field, admired and like by us all. Perhaps to my advantage was my available time and eagerness to explore what this "thing called Community Organization" was all about. (There was no major in CO offered by the school at that time.)

"Community Org. I" was a required course for all first-year social work students, and an elective for other graduate students such as those in medicine and nursing interested in public health. The CO I course outline bequeathed to me was primarily a listing of community organizations in Cleveland, with names of their representatives who would describe the organization and respond to questions. All types of social organizations or systems were included, as well as the courts and government bodies. This was, in effect, a survey course. I had no trouble organizing it and scheduling lecturers because I knew most of them, thanks to my Civilian Defense and Group Work Council experiences.

After a couple of years, I changed the focus of this first-year course from concentration on "community organization" as a noun, to "community organization" as an active concept—the how-to or method. I convened a group of practitioners from the community as advisors. Under the new format, which focused on the "community," its situation or problems, and the potential role of the CO worker, an early assignment to CO I students was: "Write about your hometown or community." Students weren't clear about what was meant at first but came to realize that it was what each thought his or her hometown or community was. This varied, I recall, from a single block in the Bronx to a large rural ranch in Texas and to other communities large and small. I asked them to describe "my hometown" in all kinds of ways they thought significant, or that would make the place alive: geography, political organization, decision makers, social and intercultural structures, major problems, major strengths, and so forth.

The papers were read in class (as many as could be scheduled in several sessions) and evoked fruitful discussions about how to look at and begin to understand a community. This led to how one would explore the community's resources necessary to researching problems and potentials for solutions, and to approaches that a CO worker might take when, for example, entering a new job or a new town or addressing a new kind of community problem.

The other CO class I taught was a second-year elective seminar. Enrollment was about 20 students with concentrations in both casework and group work. We used case materials as the basis for analysis, including several fictional cases that I prepared. We also drew upon the students' experiences: For example, a student from India, who was preparing to deal with severe life-threatening situations there, sought to learn how to apply American "theory." We dealt with issues and how to address them. For example: CONFLICT. Some think "conflict" should be introduced into a community situation, others, including me, do not favor this. I know of no situation where there is no inherent conflict, so why introduce it? It may need to be articulated—brought to the surface to be dealt with. One way to ensure this is for the CO worker to see that all significant points of view are represented. This is one rationale for inclusion of volunteers with professionals—for interracial and intercultural mix, for inclusion of the sophisticated agency and the unsophisticated grassroots one. The CO II seminar discussions enabled us to introduce, elaborate, and debate such matters.

During my tenure as a CO instructor at SASS I developed associations with faculty in other institutions who, like I, were formulating theories about community organization. I remember, in particular, Arthur Dunham at the University of Michigan who was an advocate of "community development" and the preparation of workers for overseas, and C.F. "Mac" McNeil of Ohio State whose experience with Community Chest and Councils led him to direct his teaching to preparing workers to staff such positions. I think in Cleveland we were influenced by the "area council movement," developed by W.T. "Tom" McCullough under the Welfare Federation banner, and Tom's focus—then and later—on the importance of community planning.

I felt a real commitment to expanding and evaluating community organization concepts. I prepared a paper on community organization process for presentation at a Council on Social Work Education conference. I tried hard to get Community Organization firmly established at SASS but was unsuccessful. I believed that Community Organization was a specialty in its own right, or at least deserved more attention than two courses given by a part-time instructor. I recommended to the Dean and Faculty that SASS employ a full-time faculty member (not I) to establish a sequence (whatever called) in Community Organization. This was not approved, possibly due to lack of funds, possibly to lack of real commitment.

I was offered opportunities to return to practice and, in 1954, accepted a part-time position back at the Welfare Federation to staff the "Committee on Older Persons" called COOP. COOP had been formed by a charming elderly lady and was comprised of board representatives of philanthropic homes for the aged. COOP meetings were like a tea party, minus the tea and crumpets. But over time I was able to help them relate the problems they were facing in their particular homes to broader social issues, and we were able to augment membership of COOP with persons from the greater Cleveland community with special expertise such as law, housing, social security. We enlarged COOP's concern beyond the philanthropic homes for the aged per se to include more community and national issues facing the elderly.

The Federation had a parallel committee, the Committee on Chronically Ill, staffed by a medical social worker whose major thrust was to establish an information and referral service for the chronically ill and disabled. When this was accomplished and she moved to direct that service, I assumed responsibility for staffing that committee as well as COOP. The two committees worked closely together, although with different agendas.

This was the era when concerns for the elderly and chronically ill were gaining public recognition. We worked on improving nursing home standards and housing for the elderly, as well as promotion of local programs and activities such as the "Golden Age Hobby Show." I, with volunteer lay leaders, prepared and presented testimony locally and before the Ohio Legislature. I was included in the Ohio delegation to the White House Conference on Aging, and in other ways participated at local, state, and national levels. We played roles in the National Council on Aging and the Joint Commission on Chronic Illness (joint endeavor of American Hospital Association and the U.S. Public Health Service).

I staffed COOP and the Committee on Chronically Ill from 1954 to 1960, at which time my career took a shift. Tom McCullough, who had been in Philadelphia for a time, returned to Cleveland to replace the retiring director of the Welfare Federation. Tom believed that the historical Cleveland tradition of separating fund-raising and the budgeting/allocation process should be changed; that the Federation should divest itself of the budgeting-allocation function, turning it over to the Chest (United Way), and that the Federation should expand its social-planning role to be inclusive of all health and welfare agencies, public as well as voluntary, plus professional and citizen organizations concerned about the community's welfare. The situation in the Cleveland Health Council afforded opportunity to start these changes, and I became a part of this.

The structure of the Welfare Federation in those days consisted of several major Councils (as well as committees, departments, and services), namely: Group Work, Case Work and Children's, and Health. (There was also an indirectly related Hospital Council.) The Health Council had been formed years earlier by a highly esteemed Clevelander, Howard Whipple Green, known for starting the Real Property Inventory, who was a leader in public health but formed the Cleveland Health Council for the voluntary sector in order to allocate community Chest funds to participating voluntary health agencies. When Howard Green died, Tom McCullough was asked by the Health Council lay leadership to help it redefine its purpose and select a replacement for Mr. Green.

It should be noted parenthetically that these events occurred during the time from about 1950 to 1975 that was a pivotal historical period in America for social welfare councils and the community chests with which they were associated. As Professor Jack Rothman later commented:

> Community welfare planning in the United States in this century took place in large measure by way of the Community Chest and welfare planning council field through the fifties, with councils raising and allocating funds and councils engaging in a limited form of social planning. Council planning typically pertained to Chest-supported agencies on such matters as: (a) priority studies of need for particular services, (b) coordinating activities, and (c) (in some cases) the allocations of funds. The emphasis throughout was on "voluntarism," minimizing the duplication of social services, and avoiding multiple appeals. A key objective was to discourage government involvement.[3]

Tom McCullough took a broader view than was typical in many parts of the country. He was in the vanguard, nationally as well as locally, seeking to refocus welfare councils from "councils of social agencies" and their internal parochial views, to "welfare planning" organizations that would address the whole gamut of health and welfare concerns in the public as well as the private sector. As Rothman commented further:

> In the sixties, the pattern became destabilized. There was a great deal of urban unrest and a rising public awareness of unresolved social problems, mainly brought about through the actions of the civil rights movement and similar organizations. Also, the government mounted extensive community programs through "War on Poverty" type initiatives. To keep themselves relevant, councils and Chests (now called the United Way) needed to broaden their sights and do a higher level of planning—planning that was more competent and complex and relied more on careful research and community expertise. Such planning would have to branch out beyond the narrow domain of social agencies and be less concerned with coordinating and programs of private, Chest-supported organizations. The planning process would have to take into account and join in with the massive community programs that were being established under public auspices. The Chest/council field re-

sponded in various ways. A bibliography relevant to changes in local community planning through councils and funds is attached. [It follows the endnotes at the conclusion of this article. Ed.][4]

In Cleveland the changes were progressive and significant. They came to fruition when the Welfare Federation changed its name, and enlarged its function, to become the Federation for Community Planning. And these changes were propelled by what happened in the Cleveland Health Council and the role that I was to play from 1960 on.

In 1960, I was offered the job of replacing Mr. Green as executive secretary of the Health Council. There was some opposition to my appointment. I was a woman. I was a social worker. Some wanted a man. Some wanted a medical doctor. What turned the tide for me, apparently, was the fact that my husband was a successful, highly regarded surgeon, and that I had a creditable record staffing the Committee on Chronically Ill. The job description included the understanding that the Health Council would shift its membership and function to become inclusive of a wide range and variety of health organizations in the metropolitan Cleveland area and would direct its energies to community health planning. This would prove to be more easily said than done, but resulted in an exciting decade ahead.

To accomplish its objectives, the Health Council needed additional staff. An able young African American man with an MPH from Pittsburgh was employed as my associate. This white female with a master's in social work and black male with a master's in public health balanced the equation and made a good team. The Council also needed outstanding lay leadership. The president of the Federation, who was completing his term and had been involved in the restructuring, agreed to accept the chairmanship, willing to be "downgraded" because of his commitment to this effort.

The new Health Council divided its task into two parts—the council of health agencies, staffed by my associate, and the community health planning unit, which I staffed. Also, to direct the health planning effort, a health planning board was formed comprised of carefully selected professional and lay leaders. Its first task was to review the local health picture, from data collected by my associate, noting the existence of about 150 health and related organizations, and the findings of previous local studies and surveys. The board concluded that, in spite of many organizations and sizeable expenditures for health, and evidences of progress, the community continued to have significant health problems. What should be done? Finally one member spoke up: "Our trouble is we don't know where we want to go. We need goals. Health goals for Cleveland. Then we can decide what needs to be done." Thus the Cleveland Health Goals Project was born—a project that lasted over six years, 1960–66, and cost over half a million dollars, financed by local foundations and the U.S. Public Health Service. It included a nationally recognized team of consultants and 29 position paper writers who were experts in their respective fields of health, plus hundreds of local lay and professional persons and a staff of a medical doctor, a doctor of social work, and me as project director.

Initially the Health Council chairman and I searched for a person with the desired leadership qualities to become chairman of this Health Goals project. We agreed on a man we both knew and had confidence in who had been successful in business and on boards of the university and United Appeal and other organizations, and who had demonstrated the qualities of interest and commitment that we needed. We invited him to lunch in a well-known eating establishment known for hosting important campaign dinners, Chamber of Commerce events, luncheon meetings of the Federation, and the like. We presented our carefully planned appeal. He agreed, with the proviso that he could delay his involvement for a year because of other commitments. So it was arranged, and together we worked out the scheduling that would make this interval productive: getting seed money, searching for likely consultants, selecting a top-quality Health Goals committee, and hiring or arranging for staffing. These tasks the chairman of the Health Council and I undertook. He provided the seed money as an account that made it possible to finance the search for consultants. We formed a steering committee to help us, particularly with the selection of potential consultants. Among those on the steering committee were the dean of the medical school, the founder of Blue Cross of Ohio, a former president of the American Medical Association, the president of Western Reserve University, and the deans of the schools of dentistry, nursing, and social work. We explored funding potentials. Except for my salary (which was part time) and office expenses, all the costs of the Health Goals project were to be funded by special monies. We were able to get grants from local foundations.

The Steering Committee developed a list of potential consultants. The consensus was that an innovative approach was needed. After evaluating the potential list, three physicians with varied experiences in the public health arena were selected. These three met separately with the steering committee. Each presented an exciting, innovative approach to the task: how to set health goals for a large metropolitan community. The steering committee (including me as staff) could not choose among the approaches of the three so agreed to their suggestion that the three meet together with me to see what might work out. At that meeting, a full day affair, the air was full of excitement as we all discussed the project potentials and problems. Finally one asked me: "Would you take all three of us as a team?" They suggested a fee of $100 per day per consultant, plus expenses. I reported back, recommending excitedly that we accept their offer, which we did.

The consultant team constructed the framework, or parameters, and selected the health subjects, which came to total of thirty. They chose out-of-town, nationally recognized consultants to be invited to write position papers on each subject, which would then be reviewed by local panels. A member of the consultant team issued the invitation to the writer; our local staff selected the panel members. The position paper writer was asked to prepare a paper that would apply the best-known professional knowledge pertaining to the particular health condition of his concern to a large metropolitan community. The idea was to make the recommendations applicable to a typical American city and not be skewed by the existing conditions of Cleveland. The applicability for Cleveland would be developed locally.

The findings of the Health Goals Project were reported in 1966 in six volumes. In the first and major volume, titled "Health Goals Model for Greater Cleveland," the Preface states: "This study differed from usual community health studies which focus on an aspect of health, or on an examination of existing agencies, or upon a study of health needs. In contrast, its aim was to set goals which would elevate the level of community health, basing its conclusion upon predictable results from the application of knowledge and experience. This meant a striving for new ways to categorize health components as well as development of a methodology designed to accomplish this unusual objective."

The conceptual framework of the project contains these phrases: "Health is both an individual and a public responsibility.... This highest of hopes—optimal health for all people in our society—is beyond the ability of any community to achieve, but not beyond the ability of a community to seek. It was this aspiration...that led to the development of the 'continuum concept' as the framework from which the goals emerged.... Four levels along this continuum were identified as: Positive Health; Prevention of the Onset of Disease or Injury; Early Recognition and Treatment of Disease or Injury; Prevention of Severe Disability, Social Isolation and Untimely Death."

The Health Goals Model report is divided into two parts. Part One lists health goals and the key elements for their achievement; Part Two reviews systems for the preparation, development, and delivery of health services. There are nine health goals, listed by subject, namely, reproduction, nutrition, dental and oral health, infectious and communicable diseases, trauma and safety, chronic diseases, handicapping conditions, mobility, and mental disorders. Subgoals are listed under each with key elements for achievement.

In Part Two the systems are divided into two sections: functional systems and structural systems. Functional systems include information/ intelligence, professional and technical education, community health education, and systems for regulations/controls/standards. The structural systems are: hospital system, voluntary health agency system, system for the effective development and administration of public health, the health professions, the school system, the welfare system, governmental responsibilities, and community-wide planning and development.

To quote further form the Health Goals Model's review of the process and the roles of participants and staff: "The Committee carefully considered how best to take full advantage of expertise from 'home and abroad.' It found what may be a unique answer in the conduct of community studies. The 30 health areas were covered by 29 position papers, written by 29 out-of-town experts, reviewed by 29 panels with a total of 564 different individuals invited and 339 different individuals in attendance. This produced a wealth of material for the use of Committee, consultants, and staff. The Project also called upon local committees to review survey findings as reported to the Profile (the research volume reporting Cleveland status, etc.). The involvement of so many lay and professional local experts should be a good omen for the usefulness of the Model in the Cleveland scene."

Great credit is due to our advisors and consultants. Personnel from the U.S. Public Health Service were helpful advisors in the early stages. Later we got the consultant team of three, whose names and positions at that time were: Cecil G. Sheps, M.D. M.P.H., general director, Beth Israel Medical Center, New York; Irvin J. Cohen, M.D., executive vice president, Maimonides Hospital of Brooklyn; and Conrad Seipp, Ph.D., Graduate School of Public Health, University of Pittsburgh (replacing William H. Stewart, M.D., former chief, Division of Community Health Services, U.S. Public Health Service, who became U.S. surgeon general during the formative stages of the project).

We three members of the Health Goals project staff participated in all the meetings of the large representative Health Goals Committee and the panel sessions. One or more members of the consultant team were usually present also. I, as project director, was part of the steering committee and met regularly with the consultant team. There were several lengthy conferences of the three consultants and three project staff in which we assessed progress and charted our future course. Staff kept careful records.

In October 1967, after completion of the project, the chief consultant Dr. Cecil Sheps and I presented a paper to the Medical Care Section of the American Public Health Association. We noted: "The interaction and fusion of thought which occurred between the continuing consultants and staff undoubtedly played a significant part in helping the Health Goals Committee, itself, synthesize contributions from various disciplines. Twenty-seven consultant staff meetings, some of two-day duration, were held over a four-and-one-half-year period. The consultants brought to these conferences technical knowledge of high professional quality and breadth of scope, and information about national developments and trends. Staff brought a perception of the community generally, information about individuals and events specifically, and special skills in community organization. The interaction in this group resulted not only in a fusion of knowledge but the formulation of concepts and procedures important for committee work. The committee…recognized this as a sophisticated and stimulating form of consultation."[5]

The Health Goals Committee, under the continued enthusiastic leadership of its chairman, was committed to implementation of findings and recommendations of its report and programmed a variety of undertakings for this purpose. One such was aimed to change and strengthen the community's health planning structure. It was prepared to do so within the aegis of the Welfare Federation by restructuring the Health Council in fulfillment of the original objective of its mandate. However, it had to adapt to changes made in Washington.

Congress enacted the National Health Planning and Resources Development Act (PL 93-641, 1974), providing for establishment of new agencies for health planning and a nationwide network of Health Systems Agencies, usually to cover a sizeable area of several counties. (I recall these described as comprehensive health planning or CHP agencies.) Guidelines for submitting grant applications were distributed. Endorsement by the public health department of the largest city in the area was mandatory. The Welfare Federation, as part of the Health Goals implementation endeavor, received grant application directives and used its resources (Health Council, Research Department, and so forth) to prepare the grant application.

I spent a large portion of my time overseeing these matters and soliciting endorsements from relevant organizations. Endorsements were obtained from health agencies and others, including the several county public health departments in the area. The holdout was the Cleveland Health Department, key to approval. Initially the Cleveland Health Department encouraged the Federation to apply to be the CHP agency, as a follow-up of Health Goals. However, the physician member of the Health Goals staff team, who was employed as Health Director of Cleveland when the HG project terminated, preferred to have the City apply to be the CHP agency for the area. Consequently, the Federation gave its backing to the City of Cleveland, and we provided the City with all the basic health and other data required. The City's plan called for establishing a new CHP agency, and many members of the Health Goals project participated in designing the agency, selecting the members and board, and helping it become established once it was approved and funded. The new CHP agency was named the Metropolitan Health Planning Corporation (MHPC), and a hospital planner from New York City, Lee Podolin, was employed as director. He, in turn, hired staff and got the operation underway in refurbished offices in a downtown office building. MHPC operated successfully for a number of years until federal funding terminated and there were insufficient local funds to maintain operations.

During MHPC's lifetime, I worked closely with it. Lee contracted with me to direct several projects slated for us to implement under Health Goals that were also included in MHPS's agenda for comprehensive health planning. One of these was dental health, another alcoholism. The latter is a good example of how we operated.

The final report dated August 1973 was titled "A Comprehensive Plan for Alcoholism Services in the Four County Region Submitted by the Alcoholism Planning Project of the Metropolitan Health Planning Corporation with the Cooperation of the Federation for Community Planning." Ohio had a mandate and money to develop a comprehensive plan of alcoholism services for the state and regions. It contracted with MHPC for our region, and Lee, in turn, contracted with the Federation. I was project director, and we employed two planning associates on MHPC staff, housed in Federation offices. As Podolin stated in the foreword to the report: "The arrangement enabled both organizations to coordinate Project activities closely and allowed each to draw easily on the resources of the other. Without this arrangement, it is highly unlikely that an undertaking of this magnitude could have been conducted so successfully in such a short period of time."

This alcoholism project was started in July 1972. An advisory committee was formed. (Here our knowledge of persons and organizations was important in forming a balanced and effective committee—for example, assuring that Alcoholics Anonymous [AA] was represented, as well as the social-work oriented Center on Alcoholism.) A guidelines paper was drafted by staff after study of the literature, the Health Goals position paper on the subject, and federal and state laws and directives, and after consultation with many informed sources. This was reviewed and approved by the advisory committee in February 1973. The model was then designed. As the report explains: "This Model, while designed specifically for the four-county Region, is based on provisions of the law and the State Plan and particularly on requirements for a Regional Council and for Treatment and Control Centers."

There were other collaborative undertakings between MHPC and the Federation. Of significance was the fact that, with the establishment of this federally mandated CHP agency, there was no role for a voluntary community-wide health planning agency, and we had to adjust accordingly. We became project oriented rather than community-wide health planning oriented, and we focused on areas where the social aspects were of equal or more importance than "health" aspects. One project we undertook was directed to the frail and impaired elderly. We were able to get local funding to employ an MPH graduate to staff this. We also helped other organizations implement Health Goals recommendations, and engaged in community and state initiatives related to health. One example: I assembled an interracial team of physicians and other health professionals to help a local community center in the inner-city, riot-struck Hough Area plan for heath services. Meanwhile my black associate was doing a special project with the Junior League.

During this period from the mid-sixties to the mid-seventies, the Federation and its councils were changing. These changes were partially the result of upheavals in the national chest and council movement and partly the result of the Health Goals project, which recommended that the Health Council and its planning board be reconstituted as the Health Planning and Development Commission, whose priority mandate was implementation of Health Goals. As noted earlier, the Federation's director, Tom McCullough, was an influential leader locally and nationally in the effort to shift the purpose of councils of social agencies so that they would become effective community planning agencies. In Cleveland, the shift was successful, and the name and purpose of the Federation was changed to Federation for Community Planning. The Health Planning and Development Commission replaced the Health Council but was updated later to become the "Commission on Health Concerns" and a parallel "Commission on Social Concerns" replaced the Case Work and Children's Councils.[6]

Throughout these various enterprises the significance of able and committed leadership deserves special recognition. We could not have undertaken a project of the magnitude and complexity of Health Goals without a chairman who gave time, energy, direction, and financial resources over almost a decade during and following the actual project. He and I had regular conferences in his office (the company headquarters building where he hosted all the Health Goals Committee dinner meetings, at his expense). He taught me modern business practices, including "management by objective," and we conducted the Health Goals project that way, as well as subsequent projects that my associate and I directed. This chairman was also very receptive to my sharing with him my philosophy and manner of operations.

This mutual sharing also occurred between me and the chief consultant of the Health Goals consultant team and the director of MHPC. At that time I would not have phrased it as "how I operated as a CO worker." Rather I used the term "community health planner." And simply put, this term meant not to plan FOR but to plan WITH. In the partnership each brought his or her expertise, and we learned from each other. In the conduct of a project, all participants were part of the "planning with." During these final years of my career, from 1960 on, much of my job was administrative—the designing, structuring, organizing, and administering of the operation. Again, in cooperation with others, but my responsibility. As an example: In order to implement Health Goals we needed additional funding, so the chairman and I approached local foundations. He made the contacts, scheduled the conferences, and opened each interview with an explanation of the general purpose and the nature of our request. I then followed with the substantive outline of the undertaking that we were proposing. As another earlier example: In selecting the panels for review of position papers in the Health Goals project, at first the consultant team of doctors tended to discount the value of input by nonphysician professionals and lay persons. My job was to be sure that there was this participation, that staff's selection of these persons was creditable, and that the consultant team's perceptions were changed. At the close of the project the chief consultant told our staff member who was writing the process analysis report that he had learned how valuable input from nonphysicians could be.

We all took pride in the Health Goals project. It was directed toward goals, and therefore dealt with how to solve problems whose solutions would help us achieve goals. It was multidisciplinary in concept and in execution. It based its findings and recommendations on sound professional knowledge, tempered by the realities of the community's institutions and people. It involved a large cross section of those providing and those receiving a great variety of health and health-related services. Its leaders were able, skillful, and caring. Such experiences are exciting.

Not long ago, someone asked me how it was possible to get any consensus on the subject of "health," considering all the issues raised in this country. References were made in particular to the controversies surrounding proposals for a national health program that were developing under Hillary Rodham Clinton's leadership. I am reminded of an attempt we made some years ago under the Health Council to have an acceptable policy on "health rights," namely to answer the questions: "Is health a right?" or "Is health care a right?" We convened a large cross section of Cleveland physicians who argued for several sessions. Finally the group agreed: "Health IS a RIGHT" "Health CARE is NOT a RIGHT." Reactions to this conclusion were mixed! But most felt the opportunity for dialogue had been productive. This subject remains on the national agenda.

When asked about my role as project director for Health Goals and subsequent implementation projects, I respond: I was there, I was the director, the facilitator, the enabler. I listened; I kept careful notes and helped formulate points of potential consensus and dissension; I was able to communicate with professionals and laity, and to interact fairly and objectively. It was NOT my role to be an advocate for a particular program or doctrine. My advocacy was for the best possible means to achieve the HEALTH GOALS formulated by our collective effort.

I have been extremely fortunate in my career. My husband was a highly respected surgeon in private practice and on the faculty of the medical school. My various jobs put me in contact with many professional and lay leaders in the Greater Cleveland area and gave me a deep respect for volunteers. During the time my daughter was living at home I worked part time and was able to be an active parent at school, church, and social events. My jobs allowed me this flexible, part-time schedule; my home life provided me the support and nourishment that I have always cherished. Social work, and particularly Community Organization, have offered an ever-changing, challenging, dynamic career. A fulfilling life! I am indeed grateful!

ENDNOTES

1. Currently, Mandel School of Applied Social Services (MSASS), Case Western Reserve University, Cleveland, Ohio 44106.

2. The Welfare Federation, a council of social agencies in Cleveland, Ohio, was a nonprofit corporation that was directed and operated separately from the Community Chest. It functioned primarily through councils, initially of voluntary agencies: Case Work and Children's Councils, Group Work Council, Health Council, Hospital Council. It was reconstituted in the late sixties and early seventies, changing function and name, and is located on Huron Rd., Cleveland, Ohio.

3. Personal correspondence.

4. Personal correspondence.

5. Mildred C. Barry, "A New Model for Community Health Planning," with coauthor Cecil G. Sheps, M.D., *American Journal of Public Health*, February 1969.

6. The organizations changed functions and membership to focus on community planning, and to be inclusive of all bona fide health and welfare agencies, public and voluntary, and citizens' organizations. The Health Council changed to Health Planning and Development Commission, later to the Commission on Health Concerns. A parallel council was the Commission on Social Concerns.

BIBLIOGRAPHY

Akana, Paul. 1977. "Some Thoughts on Planning." Washington, DC: United Way of America, Research, Development and Program Evaluation Division.

Brandwein, Ruth. 1977. *A Working Framework for Approaching Organizational Change: The Community Chest-Council System from 1946 to 1971*. Ph.D. Diss., Brandeis University, Florence Heller Graduate School for Advanced Studies in Social Welfare.

Brilliant, Eleanor L. 1990. *The United Way: Dilemmas of Organized Charity*. New York: Columbia University Press.

Demone, Harold W., and Herbert C. Schulberg. 1974. "Planning for Human Services: The Role of the Community Council." In *A Handbook of Human Service Organizations*, edited by Harold W. Demone and Dwight Harshbarger. New York: Behavioral Publications.

Tropman, John E. 1971. "Community Welfare Councils." Pp. 150–156 in *Encyclopedia of Social Work*. 16th ed. New York: National Association of Social Workers.

United Way of America. 1984. *Revitalizing Community Problem Solving Within the United Way System*. Alexandria, VA: United Way of America.

Wenocur, S. (1976). "A Pluralistic Planning Model for United Way Organizations." *Social Service Review*, 50(4):586–600.

THE CONTEXT OF
INTERVENTION

Disruptive Dissensus: People and Power in the Industrial Age

Richard A. Cloward and Frances Fox Piven

To say that we have been preoccupied with questions of when and how lower-strata people can win something from their rulers, and how organizers and intellectuals can help them win it, would not be an overstatement. We've thought of little else during our careers. And we think we've learned some lessons about power from below.

We begin this reflection by looking back at the twentieth century, in search of answers to four key questions. What did people from below win during the industrial era? When did they win it—incrementally, or in great bursts? How did they win it—by forming poor people's organizations, or by disruptive protest and electoral dissensus? And did organizers employ strategies consistent with these historical experiences?

What is striking to us is how little attention is paid to these questions in the field of community organizing, perhaps because the answers are too painful to face. What the history of this century reveals is that poor people won little as a result of countless community organization ventures.

Saul Alinsky was the preeminent leader and teacher of community organizers in the post–World War II period. To his mind, "Power and organization are one and the same."[1] Organization yields influence; the larger the membership, the more the influence. Once formed, the poor people's mass membership organization makes sustained political action possible. According to Fisher's history and analysis of grassroots organizing in the United States, Alinsky, after a brief involvement in the formation of the Congress of Industrial Organizations (CIO), "blended 1930s union-style organizing and politics with a focus on the citizen rather than class, and on the community rather than the factory," and he wanted to "apply the techniques he had mastered while working with the CIO to the worst slums and ghettos," in the hope of establishing people's organizations throughout the country.[2] In the late 1930s, Alinsky first applied the union model to organizing in a depressed, white ethnic working-class Chicago neighborhood that was "back of the meat-packing yards" (the locale of Upton Sinclair's muckraking book, *The Jungle*). And due in no small part to Alinsky's influence, successive generations of organizers in the post–World War II period adopted his slogan, "Organization is power," and went forth to "Build organization"—organizations of tenants, organizations of welfare recipients; organizations in neighborhoods, and to unite them citywide, then statewide, and ultimately in national federations. But the evidence shows that this theory of power from below does not work in practice.

Our most serious fallacy is that organization, as such, does not compensate for the fact that lower-strata people lack conventional political resources. The idea that formal membership organizations are the key to power from below is impervious to evidence; it has become a catechism. And what gives it such durability is the legitimacy it receives from dominant beliefs about how influence is exercised in the electoral-representative system. Most of the craft of organizing is about building membership organizations of dues-paying voters by identifying felt grievances and mounting "actions" or demonstrations to secure positive responses from local authorities, thus giving people incentives to join. Some organizers emphasize the way these experiences can politicize members. Others emphasize the psychological empowerment that political engagement generates. But the core assumption is that what poorer people lack in other resources they can make up for with organized votes. A mass of disciplined voters will presumably give the organization influence with political authorities. Horwitt, one of Alinsky's biographers, says that "Alinsky's influence, relevance, and legacy live on in no small part because he effectively advanced the great American radical ideal that democracy is for ordinary people." Horwitt also quoted Ernie Cortes, one of the nation's best-known, Alinsky-style organizers, who defines the essence of the poor people's organization as "teaching people about what politics is really about—public discourse, negotiations, how to argue, when to compromise, not just the quadrennial plebiscite we usually call politics."[3] It all adds up to normal politics; poorer people can win if they organize electorally. To our minds, it's Jeffersonian romanticism.

The fact is that poor people's organizations do not achieve electoral power because they do not develop mass membership. Tenant organizations, which first emerged in the late nineteenth century, never boasted many members, and even those not for long. At its short-lived peak in the 1930s, the Workers Alliance of America, the largest organization of the unemployed in American history, claimed several hundred thousand members, but this at a time when there were millions of unemployed. Fisher reports that Alinsky's organizations had limited membership.[4] In the 1960s, the National Welfare Rights Organization never claimed more than 25,000 dues-paying members. After years of organizing, beginning in welfare rights in the 1960s and then as a senior staff member with Associated Community Organizations for Reform Now (ACORN) in the 1970s, Gary Delgado reported that ACORN's national network was composed of groups of little size. The arithmetic of mass-based organizing is easily calculated: thousands organized, millions unorganized.

Nor are poor people's organizations permanent. They are plagued by constant membership turnover and other instabilities. Alinsky's organizations had "a life span of six years at most," according to Fisher.[5] Most poor people's groups dissolve within a few years of forming, forcing organizers to develop new ones, endlessly.

We frequently asked organizers to cite historical examples of poor people's protest organizations that succeeded in attracting a mass base and that lasted a reasonable length of time—networks of rent strike organizations, for example. None could be given. Nor does Alinsky cite any in his two influential books. That poses a serious problem of credibility for this mode of thought about lower-strata people and power. It's true that poor people's organizations sometimes form, but they do not last, or they are mainly shells to legitimate leaders.

Just before his death in 1972, after a lifetime spent inspiring and leading several generations of valiant grassroots organizers, Alinsky concluded that organizing poorer people had failed, and it wouldn't have mattered much if it had succeeded because the lower-strata people were not sufficiently numerous to have electoral influence. "Even if all the low-income parts of our population were organized—all the blacks, Mexican-Americans, Puerto Ricans, Appalachian whites—if through some genius of organization, they were all united in a coalition, it would not be powerful enough to get significant, basic, needed changes."[6] To gain much larger numbers of voters, he advocated organizing the white middle class. George A. Wiley, leader of the national welfare rights movement, had the same idea shortly before his death a year later, in 1973: "Only a broad-based movement aimed at the economic interests of a majority of Americans will ever succeed in bringing about the changes we desire."[7] In a word, the failure to organize lower-class numbers can presumably be overcome with middle-class numbers—cross-class voting blocs. But it's hard to see why those higher in the class structure would privilege the interests of those below, or even treat them equally. Nor is there any reason to believe that large numbers of people of either class would join up. Nor have they.

Alinsky, Wiley, and other organizers were discouraged in part because they had succeeded in organizing only a few tens of thousands of people who then dropped out and had to be replaced with people who also dropped out who had to be replaced, and so on. Organizers were also discouraged because grassroots organizations had not succeeded in winning national concessions. Given their localistic character, these organizations won whatever they won from county or municipal governments. But the great victories of lower-strata and minority people in the industrial era (collective bargaining rights, voting rights, income-transfer programs) were won through the federal government. The victories were national, the legislation covered whole categories of people: the New Deal and workers, the Great Society and minorities. However, efforts to construct enduring national federations of local poor people's groups so as to gain influence with the federal government have not succeeded: The National Welfare Rights Organization, the National Tenants Union, and other organizations disappeared after the 1960s. Alinsky himself was never able to form a national umbrella organization. Poor people's organizations have always lacked the scale and stability to influence national politics.

There is no mystery why. To be poor means to command none of the resources ordinarily considered requisite for organization and influence: money, skills, and professional expertise, access to the media, and personal relationships with officials. It is certainly true that an organization such as the National Association of Manufacturers has influence. Its members have money, control of the media, and a host of other resources, and they have more or less bought up key figures in the electoral system. By aggregating and coordinating these resources, the industrial association has a high probability of winning what its members want. Lower-strata people have little to aggregate and coordinate. To be sure, an organization of a million poor people sustained by dues of a dollar a month might have some influence it they were concentrated geographically. But reaching and persuading the million people requires resources that poor people's organizations do not have. Start-up costs are high; organizing is labor intensive. Not enough dues come in to finance maintenance, even when organizers are paid only subsistence wages. Resourceless individuals make for resourceless—and small—organizations that cannot win victories. Organizations that win no victories cannot build a membership, and they will not last. Powerless people have nothing to aggregate and coordinate, which is why they're powerless. Power is determined by the class distribution of conventional political resources: Those on the bottom are there because they have no resources for power. Our deepest objection to the pluralistic/organizational theory of power from below is the widely accepted belief that organization, as such, can substitute for political resource deficits.

Organizing theory suffers from too much analogizing to unions. Neighborhoods have no source of power that even begins to be comparable to worker strike power. Only riots, which Alinsky deplored, would measure up.

Equally important, unions developed by exploiting features distinctive to the factory structure that are not present in community settings. Before they unionized, factory workers were already assembled and they regularly related to one another in the plants. The mass-production factory consolidated the industrial proletariat, producing a sociological substructure on which to build union superstructure.

But poor people's organizations could not be built on similar substructures. Poorer people had no community patterns of interaction equivalent to those among workers in factories. In the post–World War II period, the urban slums and ghettos were continually being destablized: by out-migration of the working and middle classes and in-migration of the minority poor; by vast urban renewal projects and gentrification that uprooted poor communities. Meanwhile, ethnic and racial heterogeneity stirred raging animosities. The social bases of poor people's organizations were riddled by instability and cleavage. Confronted by growing numbers of blacks from the South in the post–World War II period, Alinsky's Back of the Yards Neighborhood Council devoted itself to keeping blacks out. Without substructures of solidarities and a sense of common interests, organizers had little chance of forming organizations of any scale or durability.

Unions also developed stable membership owing to the accommodations by employers. These accommodations went far toward solving union problems of organizational maintenance. It was apparent to key industrialists in the 1930s, plagued as they were by spontaneous strikes and shutdowns by unorganized workers, that unions could (and eventually did) help regulate this undisciplined and sometimes rebellious workforce. Consequently, employers agreed to require employees to join unions and to authorize the factory payroll department to withhold dues from their paychecks. This accommodation between labor and capital, prompted by the disruptive power of the strike, provided unions with large memberships and treasuries, and durability. The power of these external supports is shown by the low union rolls in "right-to-work" states that prohibit such coerced union membership; if workers don't have to join unions and pay dues, most don't.

Needless to add, poorer people in other institutional contexts cannot force accommodations with their opponents that would provide similar external organizational-maintenance support. Organizers sometimes talk of trying to force landlords to make participation in tenant organizations a condition of tenancy, including deducting dues from rent checks, but we do not know of any important successes. Compulsory union membership and check-off arrangements were won in mass-production industries, but not much at all in small businesses. Most slum and ghetto landlords are small operators, and the proprieties they own are usually scattered. The point is that organizers in varied community settings cannot depend on external structures to support organizational maintenance, and they are therefore forced to devote an inordinate proportion of their time to trying to enlist new dues payers, or to collect from existing members. It is extremely labor-intensive work.

Overall, it seemed to us that the capacity to create mass formal organizations that can exert conventional political influence in a regular way varies with location in the social structure, both in the sense that social cohesion varies from one setting to another (such as factory and community), and in the sense that resources for conventional political influence vary by social class. Lower-class communities are least favored by either structural criterion. We concluded that the lower-strata people have to be drawn together by sheer organizer grit, and that any resulting formal organization could be sustained only by enormous investments of organizing effort.

To sum up so far, poor people's organizations fail as vehicles of power from below because they cannot attract a mass base, they rarely surmount their localistic character, and they do not last. The dominant theory of power held by organizers is about political organizations that don't exist in poorer communities.

In 1993, Karen Paget published the results of a survey she conducted on the success of grassroots organizing during and after the 1960s—including groups sponsored by Alinsky's Industrial Areas Foundation, Citizen Action, and ACORN—and reached this overall conclusion: "Citizen organizing, by neighborhood and issue, is now entering its fourth decade...but has not done as much to empower the poor, revive democratic citizenship, or create new political majorities as its adherents had hoped."[8] Put plainly, mass-based permanent organization is not a source of power from below.

But if grassroots organizing cannot empower the poor or create political majorities, it nevertheless does something else that is important. The achievement of grassroots organizers is that they nurture subcultures of poorer people, however few and unstable, where the ideal of justice is kept alive. If the ideal of justice were suffocated and extinguished by ruling-class propaganda, there might be no times of turmoil, and no victories.

We have argued since the early 1960s that lower-strata groups, confronted as they are by an elite that controls the wealth and power of major institutions ("the command posts," C. Wright Mills called them[9]), can win victories, not when they organize, but when they employ disruptive protest: incendiarism, riots, and strike waves, sit-ins and other forms of civil disobedience, great surges in claims for relief benefits, rent strikes, and sabotaging the workplace, such as disabling mining machinery or assembly lines. In our judgment, events in the twentieth-century United States substantiate this argument.

What people won is clear. They won the National Labor Relations Act in 1935, which for the first time in American history made collective bargaining and strikes legal. And they won legislation governing wages and hours and benefits and working and safety conditions. Blacks won the Civil Rights Act of 1964 and the Voting Rights Act of 1965, which toppled the southern caste system and opened the electoral system to them. Economic entitlements to protect people from raw market forces were won in both periods and largely eliminated hunger—for example, the old age pensions and unemployment benefits of the Social Security Act of 1935, and the Food Stamp Act of 1964. Medicaid and Medicare were enacted in the mid-1960s, providing medical care for the poor and elderly.

The dates of these and other federal measures tell us when victories occurred. Labor rights and social welfare legislation were won in the 1930s; civil rights and more social welfare legislation were won during the 1960s. Indeed, all of the labor, civil rights, and social welfare legislation of consequence in the industrial era was enacted in just two five-year periods: 1933–1937 and 1963–1967 (with the exception of the Supplemental Security Income legislation in 1972, which was a delayed congressional reaction to the state and local fiscal burdens resulting from the great rise in the relief rolls that began in the early 1960s). Such clustering of legislative concessions is a datum of singular importance. Lower-strata groups made important gains only twice in the industrial period. This is a key lesson about power from below in the industrial era: What was won was won all at once, not gradually.

Victories were preceded by disruptive protest on a mass scale. Industrial strike waves and unemployed marches, as well as rioting and looting, came to a head in the mid-1930s: Fifteen strikers were known to have been killed in 1933, and 40 more in 1934, and in a period of 18 months, troops were called out to cope with strikers in 16 states.[10] Civil disobedience and civil disorder also came to a head in the mid-1960s—for example, the civil disobedience campaigns in Birmingham, Alabama, during the spring of 1963, which were met by police who unleashed teeth-snapping guard dogs and rib-crushing, high-pressure water hoses against voting rights demonstrators, and made mass arrests. Then, as police violence worsened, rioting broke out. Four years of rioting and looting followed in northern cities. Twentieth-century history shows a strong correlation between political conflagrations at the bottom and concessions from the top.

We attribute a causal role to this correlation because the rise and fall of disruptive protest defined the beginning and ending of times when people won something. Other forms of protest, lawful protest—such as lobbying, litigating, demonstrating, and union-sponsored striking—go on all of the time. But unlawful protest—unorganized strike waves, looting, rioting, mass civil disobedience—goes on little of the time. In sum, we took the position in 1977, in *Poor People's Movements*, that moments of mass defiance fired the most important episodes of class and racial reform in the twentieth century.

How then does disruptive protest develop, in contrast to poor people's organizations? One thing is clear: It is not initiated by existing organizations, either established unions or preexisting grassroots community organizations. To the oligarchs of the craft-based American Federation of Labor (AFL), the industrial worker uprisings in the 1930s spelled trouble. These leaders had been elected by constituencies they knew and understood; they had a long-established rapprochement with employers. Insurgency by workers outside of their control put it all in jeopardy. More generally, the historical record shows that unions often played a very ambiguous role at peak moments of labor strife.[11] In the 1930s, the craft unions did not organize the industrial workforce. Unorganized workers shut down the factories, and then organized the CIO. Civil rights organizations obviously did not start or support the riots; they would have lost legitimacy, resources, and access to centers of power. If it had been left to established organizations to promote disruptive protest, there would have been little or none.

Riots and other forms of popular protest are "mobilized" by institutional forces of great scale; they are not "organized" by activists. The relationship runs in the other direction: Mobilization from the bottom swells the ranks of activists. Most of the time, poorer people feel hopeless—a hopelessness based on their assessment of the realities of power in their lives. This sense of hopelessness gives way only under exceptional conditions, as in the 1930s and 1960s. It is surely because huge social changes are at work—perhaps it is the precursors of upheaval that Tocqueville, Marx, Durkheim, Weber, and other analysts have identified: intensified grievances; weakened societal controls; new socioeconomic structures that aggregate people, giving them new collective capacities for political action; or divisions in a ruling class that may lead an elite fraction, either tacitly or explicitly, to encourage insurgency from below. The question of the conditions under which people become ready to mobilize in disruptive protest is far from settled, and we take no position on the matter here except to suggest that it probably takes a concantenation of these and still other forces before masses of people decide that resistance is possible.

Whether protestors win or lose depends on the interaction between institutional disruptions and the state, and that relationship is mediated by the electoral system. The institutional conditions that lead to disorder in the streets generally lead first to volatility at the polls. In democracies, people generally make their discontent known initially at the polls, since voting is the normative method of seeking political change. Elections are like thermometers; they register the temperature of the electorate, or of sections of it. But if discontent is extreme, it can break out of the electoral system and take form in the streets. The two go together, and also reinforce one another. Electoral volatility encourages protest, and protest encourages electoral volatility.

To us, disruptive protest is one key to understanding the power of voting in these periods. A successful disruption produces crisis and breakdown in a significant institution: specifically, strike waves shut down the mass-production industries, and civil disobedience disrupted southern caste arrangements and threatened the low-wage labor system it protected. Such disruptions have widespread political repercussions, intensifying volatility among electoral groups—some hostile, some sympathetic, but all aroused, and thus worsening electional cleavages. Although a small poor people's lobby can be ignored with impunity by political leaders, institutional breakdowns that contribute to discontent among large and variegated segments of the electoral cannot be.

Disruptive protests have communicative power, the capacity—through the drama of defiant actions and the conflicts they provoke—to project a vision of the world different from that in ruling-class propaganda, and to politicize millions of voters. Industrial workers projected a vision of worker rights as the alternative to untrammeled property rights, and blacks projected a vision of civil equality as the alternative to white supremacy. Protest movements draw the attention of wide audiences to these visions, including the attention of latent participants and sympathizers, and of opponents. It is mass protest (the worker strike waves that shut down industrial production in the 1930s in the face of militia, Pinkertons, and company thugs, or the black boycotts and civil disobedience campaigns followed by mass arrests that kept the South in chaos and its jails filled during the late 1950s and 1960s) that galvanize public attention, that force people to ask themselves how they stand on the issues in contention, and that polarize opinion in support or in opposition, including polarizing the opinions expressed by millions in the voting booths. In other words, the reverberations of protest on the electoral system go far toward explaining why protest sometimes succeeds. Concessions are won, in short, not so much because people can be depended upon to vote their interests in the course of conventional political action, but because mass protest has the power to politicize them on great scale.

Put another way, disruptive protest does what the political parties do not do. For reasons that are deeply rooted in our history and governmental structures (not least mass disenfranchisement of the poorer classes by voter registration procedures during most of the twentieth century), the political parties in the United States are not sharply class-based. This distinguishes the United States from Europe, where labor-based parties formed late in the nineteenth century. In the absence of programmatic political parties to enunciate issues and draw the lines of electoral conflict, it is difficult for people to define their interests in a way that is consistent with their class position. Thus movements generate the conflicts that politicize voters, and that make votes count. To avoid worsening polarization and to restore institutional stability, political leaders must either promulgate concessions or institute repression. This capacity to create political crises through disrupting institutions is, we have always thought, the chief resource for political influence possessed by the poorer classes.

If the twentieth-century United State is any guide, poor people make advances when a dominant coalition is either forming or fracturing, as in the 1930s and 1960s. Northern industrial workers left the Republican party for the democrats in the class realignment of 1932. Then, in the post–World War II decades, disaffected white southerners deserted the Democratic party, mainly because they thought the Democratic party was responsible for the race, gender, and sexual revolutions. It was during these two electorally unstable periods that poorer people made gains through government.

In the 1930s, the interplay of electoral instability and protest posed a great threat to Roosevelt. He could not know, during his first term, whether the flood of working-class defectors from the Republican party who brought him to power would reelect him in 1936. Had a democratic realignment occurred in 1932, or hadn't it? Unemployed marches, riots, and later strikes kept that question in doubt. A million and a half workers were on strike in 1934, and the political threat they represented was magnified by their threat to economic recovery. If the coal mines shut down, so did the steel mills and then the automobile factories. In order to shore up his majority, Roosevelt had to fear not only how workers would vote, but whether he could get them back into the plants. It was this interaction of economic disruption and political disruption that put pressure on Roosevelt to support labor's demands, which he eventually and reluctantly did (mainly by endorsing the National Labor Relations Act of 1935).

In the 1960s, we were struck by the divisive electoral dynamics by which civil rights legislation was being won. The southern civil rights movement was succeeding, we thought, because it did not try to form mass-based permanent organizations among the southern black poor (as some organizers preferred). Instead, the movement mobilized mass civil disobedience to challenge historic caste arrangements. Confrontation by confrontation, southern whites got angrier, more of them began voting third party or Republican, and as the Democratic party's regional base collapsed, blacks gained political influence. The way we put it at the time is that "By activating support among northern liberals and the growing concentrations of black voters in the cities, *and especially by enlarging the tide of southern white defections*—civil rights protests changed the political calculus."[12] The only recourse left to the Democrats was to replace some of the white defectors with new black voters, and so the party passed civil rights and voting rights acts to dismantle the caste system and enfranchise blacks, all of this at the exact peak of northern rioting and southern civil disobedience.

Tactics to provoke dissensus are effective only at times when large-scale social or economic change has already undetermined a majority coalition, making it vulnerable to attack. Since the leaders of the coalition will resist realignments of power and policy as long as possible, it is essential that electoral divisions, which are already being worsened by changing institutional conditions, be worsened all the more by disruptions. In a memorable saying, Alinsky admonished organizers to "Rub raw the sores of discontent"; we add, "Rub raw the sores of dissensus." It is then that political leaders will attempt to stabilize a new realignment, or attempt to staunch defections from an existing realignment, and concessions to the bottom may become possible.

In the 1960s, we called this mode of analysis "dissensus politics" to differentiate it from the received wisdom about consensus politics and coalition-building as the key to power. If the liberation of blacks from southern serfdom had depended on coalition with whites, they would be in bondage still. Dissensus politics is the politics of exacerbating divisions. Lower-strata people win when they threaten to cleave dominant electoral coalitions by exposing and worsening fractures in party systems, as we said in the 1960s:

> A cadre, acting on behalf of a minority within a coalition, engages in actions which are designed to dislodge (or which threaten to dislodge) not only the minority, but, more important, *other significant constituent groups in that same alliance*. Through the cadre's ability to generate defections among other groups in a coalition, its impact becomes far greater than the voting power of the minority. If the strategist of consensus looks for issues to bring groups together, then the strategist of dissensus looks for issues and actions that will drive groups apart.[13]

In sum, since disruption and dissensus depend on each other, the term "disruptive dissensus" best describes what we mean when we speak of a mobilizing model, as contrasted to an organizing model. It is to the interaction of disruptive protest and electoral dissensus that we owe the two great moments of reform in the American industrial past.

When disruptive dissensus emerges, do organizers develop strategies consistent with it? Most do not. During quiescent periods, it is reasonable for organizers to emphasize organization-building. But turbulent times present new possibilities and require new strategies of action to maximize them. At such moments, we thought organizers should shift from building organizations to mobilizing disruptive dissensus. Alinsky's error, we would say, is that he didn't make that shift when the turbulence of the 1960s began. Instead, he kept building organizations. So did most other organizers. What they did was try to convert disruptive protest into poor people's organizations. This is the way we summed up the role of many organizers during times of turbulence:

> In the 1930s, when millions of mass production workers broke out in strike waves, union organizers passed out dues-cards; when tenants refused to pay rent and stood off marshals, housing organizers formed building committees. In the 1960s, when people were burning and looting, organizers used those "moments of madness" to draft constitutions and recruit members to a host of grassroots organizations.[14]

To put the point another way, history shows that two theories of power were at work during turbulent periods. Lower-strata people had their theory of power, but most organizers had another. One was a theory of power through mass disruption, and the other was a theory of power through mass organization.

There is an often unacknowledged reason for the ubiquity of the organizing credo. In the 1960s, for example, expanded grassroots organizing campaigns were spurred because politicians and philanthropists didn't know how to cope with riots and other apparently leaderless street actions; they couldn't figure out with whom to negotiate. Consequently, elites supply resources to groups that might help cool things down and restore civil order. At these moments, old organizations can gain resources, and new organizations can be funded. These incentives are difficult to resist. The temptation is for organizers and poor people's organizations to garner legitimacy and support by defining themselves to elites as the alternative to rioting, by claiming that they can redirect civil disorder into constructive political channels. In a word, many organizers play the elite game of trying to channel unrest into organization-building. But when unrest subsides, the poor people's organizations that were formed or expanded during times of turmoil are abandoned—first by their patrons and members, and then by most organizers.

Consistently, when mass unrest surged, it was generally condemned by existing organizations and leaders. In the 1960s, for example, mayors and governors, as well as religious, civic, and academic notables, all joined to warn that trouble in the streets was a serious setback to racial progress in the 1960s, and business leaders formed "urban coalitions," offering thousands of jobs for middle-class black and white professionals, and with grants to grassroots organizations, to see whether spreading some money around could help restore order. (Utility executives were especially active in these ad hoc coalitions; it had become all too clear that Molotov cocktails dropped down utility manholes onto masses of color-coded wires produced an awful melted mess.)

Civil rights and grassroots organizers often added their voices in denunciation. They thought that rioting was counterproductive, that it interfered with the constructive processes of bargaining, negotiating, lobbying, and running political candidates. Grassroots organizers, many of them tutored by Alinsky, told people to stop rioting and start organizing. With Alinsky's approval, FIGHT, one of his typical membership organizations located in the ghetto of Rochester, New York, sent leaders and organizers into the street when rioting broke out in 1964 to tell people to cool it. FIGHT even appealed for help from Martin Luther King's Southern Christian Leadership Conference (SCLC), and it was a measure of SCLC's concern about the spread of riots that Andrew Young and James Bevel, both key staff members, were deployed to Rochester to help calm things down. As one of Alinsky's biographers approvingly says, FIGHT "mediated between the edgy police and angry street people," and "When the Watts district of Los Angeles blew up a year later, in August 1965, Rochester's FIGHT was busy organizing and training its members to exercise…black community power."[15] Indeed, Bayard Rustin, the most senior civil rights organizer after Martin Luther King, wrote an article in the September 1995 pages of *Commentary Magazine*, just as the Voting Rights Act was passed, urging the movement to shift "from Protest to Politics" (as if protest were not politics), and went into the Harlem streets to beg people to turn from burning and pillaging to electoral mobilization. But is it conceivable that there would have been New Deal legislation without strike waves, or Great Society legislation without urban riots?

However, not all organizers emphasized organization-building during these periods. Some organizers were swept along on the tidal wave of spontaneous defiance, and employed disruptive strategies with a minimum of organizational superstructure. One illustration is the role of organizers in rent riots and mass resistance to evictions in the 1930s. As unemployment rose, large numbers of families in many places could not pay their rents, and evictions increased daily. In 1930 and 1931, small cadres of organizers, often led by Communists, began to use strong-arm tactics to prevent marshals from putting furniture on the street. Or if the furniture was already on the street, they put it back, even when families were not at home. Roving neighborhood squads helped people turn utilities back on. These tactics frequently resulted in beatings, arrests, and even killings, but historians estimate that these tactics succeeded in restoring 77,000 evicted families to their homes in New York City, and comparable numbers in other cities such as Detroit and Chicago.[16]

The same point can be made for the direct-action phase of the civil rights movement. Martin Luther King's Southern Christian Leadership Conference was a loose coalition of black activist clergy; the Student Nonviolent Coordinating Committee (SNCC) was a loose coalition of student activists; and the loosely coordinated activists in the Congress of Racial Equality (CORE) did what SCLC and SNCC did: They did not so much try to organize members as to mobilize mass demonstrations and civil disobedience that provoked white mob violence and mass arrests of demonstrators. These extraordinary activists disrupted the southern caste system, and produced widespread and deepening political dissensus. And they did it with a minimum of organizational superstructure.

Even events that looked organized were not, at least not in the sense of formal membership organizations. In 1955, a small group of prominent black, middle-class leaders in Montgomery, Alabama, decided to call for a bus boycott after Rosa Parks was arrested for sitting in a white-only section. These leaders did everything they could to get the word out: Thousands of leaflets were distributed throughout the community, and ministers preached boycott from the pulpits. Still, organizers and activists are always passing out leaflets and preaching protest, year after year, decade after decade. Except for rare moments, however, few people respond.

Montgomery was different. The startling historical datum is that on Monday morning, four days after Parks was arrested, the buses were empty, and this in a community of 50,000 blacks who depended heavily on buses as their only means of transportation. It was one of those infrequent moments when masses of poorer people were ready to mobilize to defy the authorities. What leadership cadres did was suggest a simply way that people could vent their anger and express their hope—Walk, don't ride!

These activist strategies, by mobilizing disruptive acts rather than organizing members, work *with* the tides of popular defiance rather than against them. Mass disruptions by lower groups display no formal systems of authority, division of labor, or formal membership. Rent riots have no bureaucratic structures, no constitutions, no officers, no committees. Ghetto residents don't need an organization to protest; riots erupt from webs of everyday relations. In other words, spontaneous mobilizations characterize these periods. A study of the 1960s riots, using a stringent definition of riot (more than 30 persons involved, blacks only, and not growing out of civil rights demonstrations, school settings, or other planned activities that might provoke conflict), found that there were "341 disorders" of "spontaneous origin."[17]

In the early 1960s, we began to formulate specific disruptive dissensus strategies that could be mounted by cadres of organizers. We were at the time at Mobilization for Youth (MFY) on New York City's Lower East Side, which is generally credited with being the flagship of the antipoverty program. (Richard A. Cloward and George A. Brager founded MFY. Richard was director of research, and Frances Fox Piven was a senior research associate; the two of us began a career-long collaboration while at MFY, and married years later. For a further discussion of MFY, see the article in this volume by Brager.)

In considering strategies, it is important that organizers keep in mind that disruptive protest does not consist of just civil disorder. To be sure, much of what people do in these periods (striking, rioting, looting) risks severe repression. Elites suppress disruptive protest with laws and sanctions, criminalizing power from below. And, of course, organizers who promote civil disorder are also criminalized. But mass disruption is a many-splendored thing; it takes many forms simultaneously. Strike waves, riots, and looting are the more obvious means, and they provide cover for less visible forms. Moreover, defiant actions that are repressed during quiescent times may be tolerated during tumultuous ones. When there is rioting in the streets, people may stop paying rent regularly to the landlord, their ancient enemy, with less risk of eviction. Or people may start demanding subsistence from the relief commissioner, another ancient enemy, with less risk of rejection. Much to the point of this analysis, these less obvious modes of defiance may have enormous potential for mobilizing disruptive dissensus.

We first made this argument when ferment broke out over dilapidated ghetto housing in the 1960s. In the climate of rising discontent, a maverick radical named Jesse Grey announced a Harlem rent strike. On November 1, 1963, Grey led 16 buildings on strike. A month later the number had risen to 50. Volunteers from the Northern Student Movement then joined forces with Grey and another 50 Harlem buildings went on strike. On the Lower East Side, a CORE chapter took six buildings out, and its efforts were augmented when Mobilization for Youth helped a variety of community groups form "The Lower East Side Rent Strike," bringing about 50 more buildings into the movement. In East Harlem, another group of buildings struck, some organized by the East Harlem Tenants Council and others by two CORE chapters. A union of low-paid blacks and Puerto Ricans, Local 1199 of the Drug and Hospital Workers, helped put 30 more buildings on strike by working with tenants who were union members. Meanwhile, an especially effective CORE chapter in Brooklyn organized 200 buildings. With Grey at its head, a massive protest seemed about to burst forth from the black slum.

The question was the strategy the strike should follow. On the one hand, the law already allowed rent withholding as a strategy to obtain housing repairs, provisions that had in fact been won in response to earlier strikes. But the steps laid out in the law were elaborately bureaucratic, and the courts interpreted the law rigidly. Judges admitted only the inspection records of the Department of Buildings as evidence of hazardous violations. To obtain those records, organizers had to fill out forms and arrange and follow up appointments for inspections; check agency files to make sure that hazardous violations had been posted; and meanwhile see that rents withheld by tenants were being collected and deposited in a private escrow account. (If the tenants lost in court, these funds were turned over to the landlord; if they won, the money was turned over to the clerk of the court, to be given to the landlord after repairs were made.) Finally, organizers had to shepherd tenants through the courts.

We argued that tenant organizations would become mired down in these elaborate procedures, that legal rent strikes would fail. "In playing by institutional rules," we said, "activists take on the full complement of inhibiting requirements imposed by powerful groups who make the rules. Unable to meet these requirements, they can only lose."[18]

On the other hand, we thought tenants had a way of disrupting the slum housing system, one that would not meet undue repression by the authorities, given the temper of the times, and that might possibly win major housing concessions from government. That power depended on preventing landlords from recovering the rents. "The key to a disruptive rent strike," we said at the time, "is for tenants to pocket the rent, not place it in escrow in the courts," as prescribed by law. Widespread action of this kind would throw the slum housing economy into chaos, since many landlords would be forced to abandon their properties, to default on mortgages and taxes, and to leave thousands of tenants in buildings without services or even minimal maintenance. To our minds, "spend the rent" campaigns were the only way the disruptive power of tenants could be unleashed. The fact that many tenants were already defaulting on rent payments suggested that organizers could mobilize many more to do the same.

Of course, "spend the rent" campaigns could succeed only if most evictions were forestalled, and that would require some planning, coordination, and communication. They key problem would be to develop a neighborhood communications system for reporting evictions. Organizers could leaflet a neighborhood, asking tenants threatened by eviction to call a central telephone number so that organizers could be dispatched to watch the apartment. Another approach would be for organizers to hang out in the neighborhoods, watching for the marshals, poised to call on people to resist them. In addition, reserve forces—perhaps sympathetic students (quite a few were active in housing organizing in this period)—could be available for quick mobilization to protect a particular block if public officials decided to try to break the strike by a dramatic show of force. If furniture was already on the street, organizers could put it back; if marshals had not yet come, organizers could crowd the tenement stoops and stairways, forcing mass arrests in order to carry out an eviction (something marshals would be loath to do for fear of setting off rioting). But these are tactical details. The overall strategy was to bankrupt the slum housing system by denying landlords rent. And had that strategy been followed, and had it spread to other cities, large subsidies might have been won from Congress to begin rehabilitating the slums. As strategy, it was the difference between organizing mass membership organizations and mobilizing disruptive actions on a mass scale.

As for the organization question, we said the less superstructure, the better; the less membership building, officers, committees, and constitutions, the better. Times of turbulence call for looser and more flexible organization forms. We thought the main job of housing organizers should be to expand the strike by encouraging tenants to spend their rent money for other family needs, and by inciting them to join in resisting evictions.

Was there reason to think poor blacks and Hispanics would join in? At the same moment in the South, blacks engaged in civil disobedience were facing down mob and police violence.

Finally, we said mass unrest would not last, and that mobilizing strategies should be implemented quickly. We said constantly in these debates with organizers, "Turbulence will not last. Get people what you can, while you can." Above all, we opposed any effort to build tenant organizations. We argued that such organizations as might be formed on the crest of unrest would collapse and disappear when unrest ebbed; energy and resources devoted to organization-building would be wasted.

But housing organizers saw it differently. They set for themselves the goal of building mass-based tenants' organizations. At the outset, they were not dismayed by the elaborate procedures they had to follow. Indeed, they defined them as a means of educating tenants and building tenant associations. Canvassing door-to-door for housing violations was a way of making contact with tenants; filing "multiple form" complaints with the housing agencies was a way of stimulating building meetings; assigning tenants the responsibility for collecting rents and managing escrow accounts was a way of strengthening building committees and developing leadership. And through the resulting tenant groups, organizers believed the poor could be educated to the larger political issues underlying slum housing. The goal was mass organization capable of exerting regular influence on government; each arduous bureaucratic task would contribute to the creation of a permanent people's organization.

However, the bureaucratic rites by which repairs were to be exacted, and tenants educated, exhausted organizers and bewildered tenants. Meanwhile, landlords exploited bureaucratic intricacies and corrupted housing officials in order to evade or overcome the challenge. Even occasional tenant victories in the courts yielded only minor and temporary repairs. Unable to produce repairs quickly and to multiply them widely, tenant affiliation did not expand, and the strike developed little political force. As tenants and organizers were increasingly overwhelmed and worn down by procedures, the strike faltered and then collapsed, only a few months after it began, and landlords simply recovered their rents in court. There was not much of a strike, and no disruptions, because the rules of the public agencies had dictated activist tactics.

As for slum and ghetto housing, it was increasingly abandoned. But the process of abandonment was on the landlords' terms. Without a national crisis created by disruptive rent strikes in the northern central cities, landlords could dump their buildings on municipalities and take tax write-offs, or torch them for insurance, and ultimately rehabilitate some of them for the new urban gentry.

To us, as before, the political moral was clear: no disruption, no dissensus, no victories. The organizing moral was also clear: Organizers repeatedly try to do what they cannot do, instead of doing what they can do. They can't create mass-based permanent organizations, but they can, if only rarely, exacerbate institutional disruptions and worsen electoral dissensus.

In 1965, a year after the failed rent strike in New York City, we proposed another disruptive dissensus strategy—this time to "flood the welfare rolls" and "bankrupt the cities." We predicted that the resulting crisis of urban finances, and the accompanying outcry by the white working class and other Democratic constituencies, would pressure national Democratic administrations to federalize welfare, thus relieving the fiscal and political crisis in its urban strongholds.

In formulating this strategy, we were very much influenced by the failed rent strike. It did not produce electoral dissensus. It did not generate dissensus because it did not disrupt the slum housing system. Without the clamor of landlords, mortgage lenders, and insurance companies faced with the dire financial implications of a massive breakdown of compliance with the rules of rent paying, and without health and fire officials warning of threats to public safety of tenants in buildings without services, the rent strikers put themselves at the mercy of the courts, and the courts were not disposed to discomfit landlords, much less disrupt the slum housing system. By contrast, we thought a welfare explosion would generate dissensus (as indeed it did).

Again, what had caught our eye is that people were already beginning to flood the rolls. Unled and unorganized, people were applying for relief in greater and greater numbers. Like rioting, the rise in applications was another expression of the institutional heavings and rumblings that contributed to the political earthquake of the 1960s. Thousands of black families migrating from the South remained marginalized from urban labor markets during the 1940s and 1950s. Times were especially hard during the recessions in the late 1950s. Labor department officials began using a new term in 1966, subemployment, a concept combining substandard wages and unsteady work. The national nonwhite rate was three times as high as the 8 percent white rate, and in central cities it averaged around 35 percent. A huge pool of impoverished women and children built up.

The relief system depended on powerful norms sanctioning self-sufficiency at any cost (any job at any wage) to deter people from seeking public aid. The rolls rose by a mere 110,000 net between 1950 and 1960 (from 635,000 families to 745,000), and this at the height of southern agricultural displacement and migration to the cities. However, beginning in the 1960s, applications began to rise, nearly doubling nationally from 588,000 in calendar 1960 to 1.1 million in 1968. What rising applications signaled to us was that people were ready to defy norms, to fight the welfare system, just as they had been ready to fight the bus system in Montgomery.

There were even spontaneous crowd actions. In the mid-1960s, beginning on Friday of a Memorial Day weekend, the Melrose welfare center in the South Bronx suddenly began filling with Puerto Rican mothers and children who refused to leave because they heard a rumor that a rich patron had left $50 million to be distributed by the welfare department to the poor. It would not be quite right to say they staged a sit-in; it was standing-room only. It was a crowd of kids whining, fighting, and playing, as mothers shoved and maneuvered baby carriages to the restrooms.

The same rumor in the 1950s or in the 1970s would not have provoked this response. It was one of the occasional moments when people are ready to resist the authorities. Mayors in big cities in the 1960s suspended eviction proceedings between June and September, since confrontations between people on the streets and marshals carrying furniture to the curbs were full of danger. Two major urban riots had been set off by incidents between the police and welfare recipients. At the Melrose center, the welfare guards and city cops were instructed merely to keep more people from getting in the building.

When we learned of this event, we went to see it, and heard messages of fear and reassurance, futility and hope, being passed back and forth between kin and neighbors at the ground-floor windows. Food parcels were packaged to fit through the two-inch wire mesh. On Tuesday morning, four days later, the word came down from on high to start the check-writing machines, and tens of thousands of dollars poured out for clothing and furniture grants to which people were entitled but rarely given.

Furthermore, in a climate of actual and threatened riot, political authorities were admitting more families to the rolls; as application rates shot up, so did approval rates, from 55 percent nationally in 1960 to more than 70 percent by 1968. And the rolls doubled from 745,000 families in 1960, to 1.5 million in 1968; by the early 1970s, they had quadrupled, to 3 million. Unorganized and unled, a major disruption of the poor relief system was underway.

We had noticed the rise in welfare applications in the early 1960s. Mobilization for Youth had a series of neighborhood service centers—storefronts, actually, that provided a range of concrete services to people who walked in (for example, people who had been burned out of their apartments). Many people had no money, especially victims of the southern agricultural revolution who had come north. Workers in the neighborhood service centers reported incident after incident of desperate families who had been denied welfare benefits, some of whom had been given bus tickets to return south instead. We decided to estimate the number of single-headed families with incomes below welfare levels who were not receiving assistance to see whether what was happening represented an unnoticed mobilizing possibility. Rough estimates were not difficult to make: Welfare eligibility levels were known from state to state, family structure and income data were readily available from the census. We concluded that only one-third of eligible families were on the rolls (although publicly we said half were, just to be on the conservative side).

The implication was obvious: A welfare explosion was potentially in the making. We thought organizers could make the welfare explosion even larger by mobilizing additional eligible but unaided families to get on the rolls. And the payoff could be enormous. Millions of poor families would get income, together with medical care and nutritional supplements. Extreme poverty would be greatly reduced.

But we saw a further possible gain. We thought disrupting the welfare system by "flooding the rolls" would create fiscal crises and worsen dissensus politics in the northern big-city strongholds of the Democratic party (just as the civil rights movement was disrupting the caste system and worsening the dissensus in the Democratic party's regional base in the South). White ethnics would be angered by rising welfare costs (they were already aroused over competition for jobs, housings, schools, and local political power). On the other hand, the black poor would find allies among white liberals (as indeed they did), and the fight would be on. It seemed to us that national party officials would have to pay attention and find a remedy for the widening conflict in Democratic urban strongholds. The remedy, we thought would be a federal takeover of welfare, thus relieving local fiscal and political pressures. A federal system would mean a national minimum income standard in all states, which would sharply reduce poverty in the South, where low AFDC payments kept families below subsistence. To mobilize a welfare explosion, we advocated

> ...a national network of cadre organizations rather than a national federation of welfare groups. This organization of organizers—composed of students, churchmen, civil rights activists, anti-poverty workers and militant AFDC recipients—would in turn seek to energize a broad, loosely coordinated movement of variegated groups to arouse hundreds of thousands of poor people to demand aid. Rather than build organization membership rolls, the purpose would be to build the welfare rolls. The main tactics should include large-scale "welfare rights" information campaigns; the enlisting of influential people in the slums and ghettos, especially clergymen, to exhort potential recipients to seek the aid that was rightfully theirs; and the mobilization of marches and demonstrations to build indignation and militancy among the poor.[19]

Not unexpectedly, organizers saw it differently, and we again debated the question of organizing mass members or mobilizing mass disruptive acts. In this case, applying for welfare was the disruptive act. To us, flooding the rolls, bankrupting the system, and provoking white-working-class outrage were the potential sources of power. To organizers, however, the source of power was a national network of welfare rights organizations with sufficient members that its leaders could lobby Congress successfully to enact guaranteed income legislation. We said few people would join, and that even they would fade away once mass unrest subsided. We said organizers should mobilize millions of families to go on the rolls. They said that the National Welfare Rights Organization (NWRO) which they began forming in late 1966, would grow, and persist and become powerful (it went bankrupt several years later). We again said "Get people what you can, while you can."

To be sure, NWRO promoted some disruptive action, too. Although fervent believers in the organizational catechism, the organizers were nevertheless caught up in the political tides of the moment. Wiley, who headed NWRO, and some of the other organizers were also veterans of the loosely structured disruptive protests of the civil rights movement. So they marched around crowded welfare waiting rooms exhorting mothers to demand their lawful entitlements, to come to meetings, picket, sit in, go to jail, pay dues, and be part of a new welfare organization. Flare-ups between recipient demonstrators and the police even provoked riots—in 1966 in Cleveland's Hough area, and in 1967 in Boston's Roxbury area. As tensions grew more heated, welfare offices lost control over eligibility and termination decisions, the methods and procedures of fending off applicants collapsed, the rolls exploded, and a fiscal and political crisis erupted that greatly exacerbated cleavages in the big-city Democratic coalitions, as we had predicted.

However, the remedy was not quite what we had anticipated. Instead of nationalizing AFDC, the federal government nationalized the relief systems for the indigent elderly and disabled by absorbing them into a new federally financed Supplemental Security Income (SSI) program in 1972 under the Social Security Administration, thus helping to relieve state and local fiscal and political problems.

Nevertheless, the poor got several trillion dollars in means-tested benefits between the late 1960s and the present, including nutritional, housing, and medical subsidies. They won what they won by mobilizing an institutional disruption that generated political dissensus. And what they won was not negligible.

But these periods end. Turmoil does not last, whether in the streets or voting booths. It subsided by 1938, and again by 1968. Nothing is so striking about disruptive dissensus as its rare and fleeting character. It erupts, flowers, and withers, all in a moment. Even so, disruptive dissensus enabled people to win concessions from their rulers during the twentieth century, as nothing else did. No theory of power from below that does not begin with these historical facts can be adequate.

Twentieth-century history thus provides little support for the evolutionary perspectives that pervade European and American theories of welfare state origins, development, and growth. What the twentieth century reveals is contraction, as well as expansion. The struggle to institutionalize civil and labor rights and the right to social provision did not follow a simple linear progression; victories were followed by defeats. To our minds, periods of expansion and contraction expressed shifts in the balance of power between people and their rulers. A social contract won by the poorer strata, and broken at first chance by their rulers; a class compromise won, and betrayed. What we saw were accommodations between the rich and poor forged and reforged in a continuing process of conflict, as we first said in 1971 in *Regulating the Poor*.

Turmoil subsides partly because institutional dislocations moderate. With the emergence of a wartime economy in the late 1930s, members of the unemployed organizations dropped out and went back to work. People can also be placated, as were workers when they won the right to organize and blacks when they won the right to vote. At the same time, the concessions that are won redirect protest—industrial workers were channeled from strikes and sabotage to regularized collective bargaining procedures, and blacks from civil disobedience and civil disorder to electoral politics. As part of this process, earlier mobilizing cadres are co-opted; many civil rights leaders took high posts in the Great Society programs which their protests won, or they ran for office in the South, where protests had made it possible for blacks to vote.

Shifts in public opinion also help bring tumultuous periods to an end by freeing dominant groups to safely and decisively repress protest. Elections register such shifts. In 1938, Roosevelt's effort to overcome conservative Democrats who were blocking the New Deal program was resoundingly defeated. Nixon's election in 1968 transferred national power from liberal to conservative elites, and the rhetoric of law and order replaced the rhetoric of rights and entitlements.

Of great importance, capital remobilized to discipline labor in the aftermath of both periods of turmoil. As challenges from the bottom subsided, elites moved to take back some of the concessions that they had made. In the 1940s, business reined labor in under the banner of anticommunism by pushing through anti-communist legislation that drove radical leaders out of the union movement (the corporation-financed witch-hunts of the McCarthy period). Business also pushed through anti-labor legislation that encapsulated strike power—by imposing limits on the times and circumstances that workers can legally strike, such as the prohibitions on secondary boycotts of the Taft-Hartley Act of 1947, and the requirement for 120-day cooling off periods.

Beginning in the 1970s, business went on the attack again, this time under the banner of globalization. Welfare state programs, especially for those at the bottom, are being restructured or abolished so as to enforce work discipline throughout the society at the same time that wages, benefits, job security, and unionization are under assault. Union membership is down from a peak of 35 percent of the labor force in the late 1950s to less than 15 percent currently. In the United States, the industrial age is ending virtually without a labor movement.

The consequences are awesome. Income and wealth concentration have reached historic extreme. The United States resembles a Third World economic and political oligarchy. Or it could be said that we are in the Second Gilded Age.

When tumultuous periods end, the cadres and organizations that formed on their crests also wither or disappear. The Worker's Alliance of America, the largest movement of the unemployed in American history, collapsed in the late 1930s, even though there were still millions of unemployed. Naison's account of tenant organizing in New York City during the 1930s ends by noting that the citywide structure that coordinated local tenant organizations "proved fragile":

> Never did City-Wide's fund-raising produce over one thousand dollars per year.... The slum tenants...lacked the resources to subsidize it, or the political skills and inclinations to build the kind of stable organizations that could give City-Wide real permanence. City-Wide survived on the

politically-motivated idealism and skills of underemployed professionals, both of which were vulnerable to shifts in political climate and improvements in the economy.[20]

We watched the same thing begin to happen in the mid-1960s. Rent
strikes flared up, sputtered, and died out. The National Welfare Rights Organization lasted for six years, going bankrupt in 1973, but it had been
clear in 1968 that it was disintegrating. Local welfare rights groups
throughout the country could not sustain themselves once external resources from the antipoverty program, such as the many organizers from
the ranks of Vista Volunteers, began to contract. A mere handful of local
welfare recipient groups survived into the 1970s, but they found that
maintaining even a minimum membership had become all-consuming.
The more middle-class civil rights and students organizations met the
same fate. SCLC persisted largely in name only after rioting stopped;
CORE collapsed when unrest died down. SNCC formed in the 1960s
and dissolved before the decade was out, as did the few poor peoples' organizing projects sponsored by Students for a Democratic Society. The
1973 recession was the knockout blow, what with Ph.D.s driving taxi-
cabs. Student activists went back to college, and many rioters no doubt
went on the welfare rolls. A few activists carried on past the mid-1970s,
but they had little by way of resources or constituencies. When the conditions that stimulate disruptive protest recede, and the conditions that
subdue it advance, the change to build poor people's organizations of any
scale is over.

As for unions, the stellar case of mass-based permanent organization,
they had become so hobbled by oligarchy that they scarcely resisted the
business assault. Perhaps labor will be revitalized as a result of the election
in 1995 of John Sweeney and other insurgent leaders to head the AFL-
CIO. Shortly after his election, Sweeney called a small meeting with sympathetic academics in which we participated. The union leaders were blunt
and to the point. To recover their lost strength, and reverse their ongoing
net losses of 300,000 members a year, the unions would have to organize a
net of more than a million new members a year for 20 years. They asserted that the goal is unachievable by the usual union organizing strategies,
even greatly expanded. The only hope, they said, is a larger movement to
reawaken hope and change the political calculus. To our minds, a new period of disruptive dissensus is the only hope.

In any event, whether because of repression, co-optation, concessions,
channeling, or their combination—or because of other demobilizing
forces—the plain fact is that periods of mass protest come to a close. What
is probably most critical is that poorer people themselves conclude that the
political tides have turned, that their moment of power has passed.

There is an irony here. Disruption nourishes organization, but organization does not nourish disruption. Organizations flourish only in the

climate created by mass disruption; when mass disruption declines, so do the organized grass roots. The historical evidence thus shows that poor people's organizations have a dependent, even parasitical relation to the very disruptive protest that they disparage; they form and thrive during periods when there is a surge of political energy from the bottom, only to wither or disappear when the energy subsides. In a word, poor people's organizations are not alternatives to disruptive protest; they are the creatures of it.

What should organizers do during periods of reaction? We said earlier that these were the times when organization-building makes sense, if only to keep the idea of resistance alive. But other strategies can also be pursued. This question preoccupied us greatly, especially after Reagan's election in 1980 and the intensified class war against the working class and the poor that his victory foretold. We hit on an idea that we thought might eliminate class and racial bias in the voter registration system, a venture that resulted in the National Voter Registration Act of 1993, commonly called "motor voter." The Act also provides for voter registration in AFDC, Food Stamps, Medicaid, and WIC agencies.

The reason we undertook this rather conventional electoral reform project is that the success of disruptive protest depends, as we said earlier, on the ability of the protestors to galvanize and polarize electoral blocs, to fragment or threaten to fragment electoral coalitions. But protestors obviously need supportive voter blocs if this process of dissensus is to benefit them. This means, for one thing, that the social base from which protestors are drawn must be fully able to vote.

What drew our attention to voter registration, as we wrote in 1988 in *Why Americans Don't Vote*, is that the American electoral system was much less open during the industrial age than it was in other capitalist democracies, and the restrictions imposed by spreading voter registration methods were an important reason why. At the turn of the century, northern industrialists, usually in coalition with state Republican parties based in rural and small-town areas, used their power in the state capitols to establish restrictive voter registration procedures, including literacy tests, to keep voting down in urban working-class precincts. As Walter Dean Burnham has shown, northern presidential turnout averaged more than 80 percent in the elections between 1848 and 1896, but then dropped to 55 percent by World War II. Southern Democrats and their planter allies used similar strategies to drive turnout down to 19 percent in 1924, from an average of more than 60 percent during the last half of the nineteenth century; they disenfranchised not only blacks, but most poor whites, leaving few to vote besides the planters and their allies. With so much of the industrial and agricultural working class excluded from politics, a labor-based political party, which might otherwise have developed in the

Great Depression, was precluded. As a result, the electoral path to reform was not as open to the American working classes as to the working classes in Europe. Here they had to go into the streets.

The Voting Rights Act of 1965 (and subsequent amendments) did much to lower barriers to registration and the ballot. Literacy tests were prohibited, for example. But huge disparities in registration rates favoring well-off whites remained. In the 1980s, two out of three of the 50 million unregistered citizens lived in households with income below the median. Since many of the unregistered were poor and probably social program beneficiaries, we thought the persisting upward class skew in registration rates could be reduced if people were permitted to register to vote when they applied for AFDC, food stamps, Medicaid, and WIC benefits. With that idea, we formed a small reform organization in 1983 called the Human Service Employees Registration and Voter Education Campaign, or Human SERVE. We squatted in two offices at the Columbia University School of Social Work, courtesy of then dean George A. Brager. From there, with six telephone lines, a liberal travel budget, and a small staff financed with roughly $5 million in foundation grants over the next ten years, we importuned governors, state legislatures, and the Congress to enact the necessary legislation. Congress did respond a decade later (when the National League of Women Voters and all of the major national civil rights and voting rights organizations joined us, giving our effort some political muscle). The National Voter Registration Act was signed by Clinton in May 1993 (a year after Bush had vetoed it).

The Federal Election Commission's report on the first two years of implementation—1995–96—shows that millions are in fact registering. As many as 50 million could register by the end of the first four-year driver's license renewal cycle in 1999 (90 percent of eligible voters drive), leaving the reservoir of unregistered almost dry, and potentially reducing class and racial inequalities in registration rates to the vanishing point.

However, only 30 percent of those who signed up in public assistance agencies during the first two years went to the polls in the 1996 Clinton/Dole presidential election (considering that both parties were attacking them, who were they to vote for?), compared to 60 percent of all others who registered during the same period. We did not expect anything much different. Voter turnout from the bottom rises and becomes politicized during times of turmoil, not during the times between.

What we do hope is that full voter registration will contribute to greater political dissensus when a new period of turmoil erupts. Defiance will emerge again; it always has. People have always shown the capacity to resist. At some juncture, they will decide they've had enough, and disruptive dissensus will follow. The question then is what activists will do. Will they organize, or mobilize?

Rules for Mobilizing Disruptive Dissensus

Disruptive dissensus is mass action that is (1) unlawful or maginally lawful, (2) institutionally disruptive, (3) electorally divisive, and (4) sometimes spurred and guided by cadre organizations.

RULE 1: Cadres should organize during times of quiescence, in the hope of keeping ideas of social justice alive.

RULE 2: Cadres should keep testing for disruptive protest possibilities. Watch for indications that people are ready for defiant challenges, and do not denigrate spontaneous disruptions when they begin to occur. Adopt a stance that points toward political possibilities, that gives hope, and that encourages people to act on their grievances. Remember that no one, not academics nor pollsters nor pundits, predicted the great outbreaks of protest in the past.

RULE 3: Cadres should use mobilizing tactics to expand disruptive dissensus during times of turmoil. They should not play the elite game of trying to convert mass unrest into poor people's organizations. If a particular form of mobilization breaks out, organizers should consider whether to try to escalate it. Organizers should also scour social contexts for unnoticed opportunities for disruptive action. Every social context has latent power possibilities, but some may not be readily observable, and thus go unexploited. Given their concrete historically specific social circumstances, what can people from below do that might disrupt significant institutions? What can they do as particular categories of workers, as unemployed, as single mothers, or as neighborhood residents, tenants, consumers?

RULE 4: Cadres should assess the likely political impact of the disruptive actions underway, or of the actions they identify. In other words, cadres should do power analysis. If people are mobilizing in a particular way (or if they might as a result of organizer intervention), what are likely to be the reverberations on key institutions and on electoral coalitions?

RULE 5: Cadres should try to identify mobilizing strategies that are marginally lawful so as to minimize the risk of repression.

RULE 6: Cadres should lead. They should engage in "exemplary actions" (e.g., leading mass arrests) in order to exacerbate institutional disruptions and worsen dissensus politics. Traditional organizing doctrine says organizers should stay in the background and encourage the emergence of permanent indigenous leadership. Some indigenous leaders will always be present or will emerge. But when mass unrest breaks out, there is no time for the typical emphasis on leadership training; it is a more appropriate activity during the long periods of quiescence between times of turmoil.

RULE 7: Cadres should mobilize rapidly during times of turmoil. Periods of disruptive dissensus do not last. They key political question is whether people will get as much as they can, while they can.

A final word. We wish to say, to future generations of organizers, that being identified with popular struggles has mattered to us. To participate in them, and to think and write about them, has given our lives meaning. May it do so for you.

ENDNOTES

1. Saul Alinsky, *Rules for Radicals* (New York: Vintage, 1972), p. 113.

2. Robert Fisher, *Let the People Decide*, updated edition (New York: Twayne Publishers, 1994), p. 58.

3. Sanford D. Horwitt, *Let Them Call Me Rebel: Saul Alinsky, His Life and Legacy* (New York: Alfred A. Knopf, 1989), pp. XVI and 548.

4. Fisher, *Let the People Decide*, p. 143.

5. Ibid.

6. Cited in Karen Paget, "Citizen Organizing: Many Movements, No Majority," *The American Prospect*, Summer 1990, p. 120.

7. Ibid., 121.

8. Ibid., 115–116.

9. C. Wright Mills, *The Power Elite* (New York: Oxford University Press, 1956), p. 9.

10. Frances Fox Piven and Richard A. Cloward, *Poor People's Movements* (New York: Pantheon, 1977), p. 126.

11. See, generally, Jeremy Brecher, *Strike!* (Greenwich, CT: Fawcett Publications, 1974).

12. Richard A. Cloward, "Dissensus Politics: A Strategy for Winning Economic Rights," *New Republic*, April 20, 1968. Reprinted in Richard A. Cloward and Frances Fox Piven, *The Politics of Turmoil: Essays on Poverty Race and the Urban Crisis* (New York: Pantheon, 1974), p. 167.

13. Ibid., 166.

14. Piven and Cloward, *Poor People's Movements,* p. xxii.

15. Horwitt, *Let Them Call Me Rebel*, pp. 197–98.

16. See Piven and Cloward, *Poor People's Movements*, p. 261.

17. Seymour Spilerman, "The Causes of Racial Disturbances: A Comparison of Alternative Explanations," *American Sociological Review* 35, 4(1970):630–631.

18. Frances Fox Piven and Richard A. Cloward, "Rent Strike: Disrupting the Slum System," *New Republic*, December 2, 1967. Reprinted in Cloward and Piven, *The Politics of Turmoil*, p. 160.

19. Piven and Cloward, *Poor People's Movements*, p. 284. For the original statement of the strategy, see Richard A. Cloward and Frances Fox Piven, "A Strategy to End Poverty," *Nation Magazine*, May 2, 1966, which is reprinted in Cloward and Piven, *The Politics of Turmoil*.

20. Mark Naison, "From Eviction Resistance to Rent Control: Tenant Activism in the Great Depression." In *The Tenant Movement in New York City, 1904–1984*, ed., Ronald Lawson, with the assistance of Mark Naison (New Brunswick, NJ: Rutgers University Press, 1986), p. 127.

The Impact of Politics, Economics, and Race* on Social Work Community Organization

David M. Austin

As I look back some 50 years, I am struck by the way in which both particular individuals and particular events have been important in the evolution of my personal understanding of social work Community Organization (CO) and its relation to the larger sets of political, economic, and cultural forces shaping this society. The year 1946 was very significant—and a good departure point for this narrative. It is framed by a series of personal transitions that largely coincide with the pattern of national developments—the late forties in Cleveland as a student and social worker; the fifties in Boston and again in Cleveland

*I recognize that "race," "ethnicity," and "minorities" are all inexact, and essentially inappropriate, terms to refer to the dynamics of cultural transformation in the United States that began to occur during the last half of the twentieth century. The image of "race" was, however, the most powerful representation of these changes in both popular and academic writings.

as a CO-planner practitioner during the Eisenhower years; in Cleveland and again in Boston during the sixties as a project director and victim of political confrontation and then a student and community action researcher—the Kennedy-Johnson years; and then in Austin, Texas, as a teacher during the seventies and the years since.

I arrived at the School of Applied Social Sciences (SASS), Western Reserve University, in 1946, knowing very little about social work as a profession or about CO. But I was aware of the issues with which social work was concerned, in particular the issues of discrimination and segregation and poverty. My minister father came out of WWI experiences as a committed pacifist, and experienced the intensity of racial prejudice and hatred as a young minister in Indianapolis at the height of the Indiana Ku Klux Klan movement in the 1920s. In the depth of the Depression, he pushed for local action to help destitute families in a small town dominated by traditional conservative economic philosophies. I went to high school in a city with only one Jewish family and one black family. I attended college in a city (Appleton, Wisconsin) in which no hotel would provide accommodations for Marian Anderson when she came to the Lawrence College campus. And in the U.S. Army in Panama, I saw sharply defined patterns of segregation in both the military and civilian society.

I was also a member of the first WWII/GI Bill generation of social work students at SASS. The SASS faculty, in their wisdom, had just added CO as a curriculum concentration. Social work practice was defined as the triumvirate of "casework," "group work," and "community organization."

The 1946 SASS faculty included Dr. Grace Coyle, who, coming from a national leadership position in the YWCA, had been the person who introduced social group work and the analysis of group dynamics to the national social work curriculum. Dean Leonard Mayo, in teaching community organization, drew on his experiences as the director of a children's institution in New York and as a social welfare leader with the Cleveland Community Chest and the Welfare Federation.

Following the end of the war in the mid-1940s, Cleveland faced a period of extensive neighborhood transition, often with racial conflict. There were existing elements of neighborhood associations, some of them continuing from the civil defense block organizations of the early 1940s. The Welfare Federation funded a staff of full-time CO practitioners to work with individual neighborhood associations in critical areas. This included the Glenville community, which was undergoing a transition from a predominantly Jewish homeowner population to a predominately African American one. Florence Ray, executive secretary of the Welfare Federation Group Work Council, who was responsible for overseeing this community organization initiative, served as a role model for those of us who thought of ourselves as potential "community organizers."

Bob Perlman, John Turner, and Del Jay Kinney also entered SASS in 1946. Bob Perlman provided access for the four of us to do a group master's thesis dealing with the history of the Glenville Area Community Council. Mildred Berry, executive secretary of the Welfare Federation Health Council, who taught community organization at SASS in our second year, was our faculty thesis advisor.

The CO curriculum made little conceptual distinction between CO at the neighborhood level, represented in Cleveland by the community councils, and CO as agency coordination and planning at the city leadership level, represented by the Welfare Federation. What was clear was that CO practice, like group work and casework, was primarily focused on interpersonal processes—that is, how inclusive self-help groups were organized and how democratic decisions were made, not with specific outcomes impacting poverty, racial segregation, or general patterns of discrimination. The neighborhood organizing process was primarily focused on community involvement in neighborhood improvement, neighborhood by neighborhood. In many neighborhoods that also meant dealing with local patterns of discrimination in housing, employment, education, and politics—but without any vision of a community-wide strategy.

The general philosophy appeared to be that if the processes of neighborhood community organization were open and orderly, then the democratically determined outcomes could be expected to be beneficial for neighborhood residents and the city as a whole. A similar focus on the group decision-making process characterized the social planning efforts at a city wide level. The process support role of the CO staff person was reflected in job titles—executive secretary of the Group Work Council and executive secretary of the Case Work Council.

Almost as significant as the lessons learned about CO during my SASS years, including a brief introduction to *Reveille for Radicals* and the Saul Alinsky model of community empowerment and confrontation, was the lack of attention in the curriculum to the relationships between politics and social planning, on the one hand, and economics and economic policy issues. The curriculum approach to understanding social policy—learning the titles of the Social Security system—and to neighborhood community organizing included no attention to employment patterns, patterns of property ownership, issues of public finance, or other relevant issues of applied economics.

Zuria Farmer, a casework student and resident of Friendly Inn Settlement, and I were married at the end of our first year as students. After graduation, I began work as program director at University Settlement in Cleveland, while Zuria began work at the Youth Bureau, a specialized adolescent counseling service. I also put my "group work" skills to work as a unit director and then camp director at a city-funded summer resident camp. With girls and boys coming from each of four settlement houses, there was first-hand experience with the impact of racial and cultural differences among children coming together from very separate, and segregated, neighborhoods.

I learned some important extracurricular lessons while a student and a beginning social worker. Foremost was understanding the powerful impact that racial discrimination, poverty, and living conditions in inner city neighborhoods had on the lives of people; and how bitterly efforts to change those conditions were resisted by persons with the power to make changes, as well as by residents of traditional European immigrant neighborhoods. As students, we became aware of the experiences of friends and colleagues who were denied service in restaurants and excluded from the local amusement park, the segregated pattern of public housing developments, the discriminatory employment patterns, and the tensions in changing neighborhoods.

Cleveland had experienced a very rapid increase in the number of black families moving from the South in response to the wartime labor needs of steel mills, the machine tool industry, and the auto industry. Neighborhoods were identified with the settlement patterns of European immigrants and the earliest African American families. These divisions were reflected in the segregated membership patterns of neighborhood settlement houses and the enrollment patterns in the school system. These patterns of segregation and discrimination were barely beginning to crack under pressure from the black community.

In 1951, Zuria and I moved to Boston. I began work at the United Community Services of Boston (combined fund-raising and community planning structure) as the executive secretary for the Boston Federation of Settlements. In 1953, the mysterious midnight death of an immigrant Jewish rabbi in Roxbury, a death that the media blamed on teen gangs, led to a citywide demand for action. I was assigned to staff the planning initiative, which resulted in a proposal for a three-year comprehensive demonstration project. The proposal was influenced by the newly established New York City Youth Project under Jim McCarthy with its street-corner gang workers.[1] The Roxbury proposal incorporated the tripartite model of social work with alienated youth—street-corner gang workers; a casework project—interagency collaboration focusing on chronic-problem families; and a community organization project—developing a Roxbury interagency council.

When funding appeared, I was selected to become project director. The street corner worker project became operational—five full-time street-corner social workers, women and men. The chronic-problem family agency collaboration never got beyond the point of attempting to deal with the idea of a single "case manager" who might coordinate the involvement of separate agencies in households that included an adolescent gang member. The interagency council came into existence but had little effect on the real events taking place in Roxbury. The entire project had positive impacts on some particular adolescent gang members. But there were very few long-term consequences for a neighborhood undergoing a rapid process of ethnic transformation in a city with a long, and continuing, history of intense and bitter conflicts among ethnic populations.

I began to develop some understanding of the complex political and economic environment within which such a project operates—a project that operated smoothly at the direct-service level—and the resistances to a new initiative in a community in which there were already well-established power structures and turf boundaries. The operational environment included the state youth corrections agency, the Boston Police Department, the United Community Services with its attention focused on its fundraising strategies, public housing administrators, and the several neighborhood settlements. Working with urban anthropologist, Dr. Walter Miller, who served as research director, also gave me an appreciation of the complexity of attempting to evaluate the impact of a diffuse, multipurpose social intervention.

My professional activities during these Boston years included membership in the American Association of Group Workers and serving as the first chairperson of the Boston chapter of the newly created National Association of Social Workers. And it was in Boston that I taught my first class, an evening class in CO at the Boston University School of Social Work.

A decision by the United Community Services not to fund the Roxbury Youth Project beyond the original three-year plan coincided with an invitation from the Cleveland Welfare Federation to return to Cleveland as the executive secretary of the Group Work Council. Florence Ray was leaving Cleveland to staff the Group Work Section of the new National Association of Social Workers.

Back in Cleveland again in early 1957, I was the CO practitioner serving the Group Work Council, composed of board and staff representatives of group work and recreation agencies including settlements, the scouts, and the Ys. The Cleveland Welfare Federation had not yet been affected by the new Pittsburgh model of the community organization specialist as a planning technician, accountable to the community-wide civic leadership power structure, rather than to a council of agency delegates.[2] It was clear that the Welfare Federation planning process, based on the several interagency councils, was controlled by the nonprofit voluntary service organizations that were members of the Community Chest, although the public human services sector was already much larger.

The most urgent social planning issue in Cleveland was the transformation of the Hough district, a community in which, in 1950, black households included some 10 percent of population. A decade later this 10 percent had increased to nearly 80 percent. This was a part of the pattern of massive cultural transformation taking place in the industrial centers of the North and West. These changes were a result of the pull factors of employment in war/defense-related industries, including the Korean War years, and the growing push factors resulting from the mechanization of cotton-picking in the South. Moreover, urban renewal was pushing black families from older residential neighborhoods into adjacent areas, such as the Hough Area, that had previously been occupied by Caucasian families. And then the heavy industry recession at the end of 1950s—which was a key factor in the Kennedy election—destroyed much of the household income base of black neighborhoods: last hired, first fired.

At the request of the Cleveland Foundation, the Group Work Council initiated a needs assessment that included active collaboration with the Hough Area Community Council, one of the neighborhood councils that had had Welfare Federation support since the mid-1940s. As the staff person assigned to this needs assessment effort, I became involved in some of the national developments dealing with the problems of rapidly changing inner city areas. This included participation in a congressional hearing during the later Eisenhower years dealing with proposed "juvenile delinquency prevention" legislation. The draft legislation, which was not enacted, included the concept of federal funding for intensive, multi-intervention demonstration projects directed at youth problems, similar to the plans being developed for Mobilization for Youth in New York City.

Among those interested in such a multi-program—or "saturation"—approach were Paul Ylvisaker and David Hunter of the Ford Foundation, which was initiating what became known as the "grey areas" projects in Boston, Philadelphia, New Haven, and Oakland. The "grey areas" projects were distinctive because they included the concept of an independent, inner-city, community-based agency with local neighborhood participation. The Ford Foundation leadership rejected the idea of working through social welfare planning councils, convinced that they were controlled by establishment civic leaders who were unresponsive to the concerns of the black community. I met in New York with Ford Foundation staff at their invitation but there was no Ford funding for a Hough Area project.

But early in the administration of President Kennedy, Congress passed legislation, largely at the initiative of Attorney General Robert Kennedy, creating the President's Committee on Juvenile Delinquency and Youth crime. This legislation incorporated the concept of comprehensive community-based initiatives that was embodied in the Ford Foundation projects and Mobilization for Youth.[3] With the legislation in hand, the President's Committee, headed by the attorney general, invented the concept of "planning grants," a concept that was not included in the legislative language. The first round of planning grant allocations included Houston, Texas; New Haven, Connecticut; and the Hough district in Cleveland. My role shifted from that of a Welfare Federation staff person to planning director of the Hough Area Project under the sponsorship of an Advisory Council, which included representatives of the city, county, city school board, Welfare Federation, and juvenile court.

With a combination of grant-funded and loaned planning staff, and with great intentions, but no research-based information to learn from, we plunged into the preparation of an elaborate, multiprogram proposal, ranging from early childhood education to youth job training. Formal neighborhood participation was minimal, given the time constraints on the planning grant (one year) and the high visibility of the desperate problems affecting young people in the area. Neighborhood deterioration was increasing rapidly, in part as a consequence of two rounds of state-initiated cuts in the level of AFDC benefits, and of red-lining by banks, which made it impossible to get loans to maintain properties in Hough. Unemployment, nonpayment of rent, weekend move-outs and vandalized empty apartments resulted in the widespread abandonment of properties by bankrupt property speculators.

Planning went forward in the context of increasingly angry racial confrontations involving, in particular, the Cleveland Board of Education, which was dominated by members who were sympathetic to the concerns of the traditional European-ethnic neighborhoods on the west and south sides of Cleveland. These community leaders viewed their neighborhoods, and their public services, as being under attack both by black citizens, who were rapidly increasing in numbers and becoming increasingly vocal about their grievances, and by the social and religious "liberals" who supported them. The Martin Luther King marches in the South were on daily television, and the 1963 March on Washington included Clevelanders. As I continued to work with the leaders of the Hough Area Council, who became highly visible advocates for the black residents of the Hough Area, I became publicly identified by members of the school board with such advocacy. I had done little to develop a political support base for the project at the city level, which might have protected the central purpose of the project, and also saved my hide.

I approached this project as a technical social planning initiative—which is what the federal planning grant required—rather than as a political exercise, which is what the local community setting actually required. And support building at the larger community level would have been more important than building neighborhood support through more local participation in the planning process.

Project developments moved quickly with the goal of mobilizing all-out action in the community. In the spring of 1963, *Community Action for*

Youth, became the first completed proposal to be submitted to the President's Committee. After an internal battle in the federal Professional Review Panel over the weakness of the evaluation research design in the proposal—but with an imminent congressional decision on renewing and extending the legislation authorizing the President's Committee—funding was awarded to Cleveland for program implementation.

The announcement of a multi-million-dollar federal grant changed the local dynamics dramatically. The president of the school board, who had been elected to that office on a platform of hostile opposition to the increasing demands from black families for better schools, declared that only if the School Board could designate the project director would there be any cooperation from the school system. My appointment as acting director for the implementation of the project made it possible for the flow of federal dollars to begin. That it was designated as a temporary appointment also allowed time for city-level organizational opposition to my appointment as permanent director to solidify. The central issue was to assert that the white citywide leadership, including the school board, was firmly in control of the money, and therefore of what was to happen in the Hough Area.

In the summer of 1963, a deputy school superintendent was appointed to be the project director; I was appointed to be associate director for programs and research. In November, President Kennedy was killed, Lyndon Johnson became president, and Robert Kennedy's influence in the federal government changed dramatically. By the end of 1963, I had been forced out of Community Action for Youth and had landed in a temporary position at SASS in a Ford Foundation funded research project for which Dr. John Turner was the principal investigator.

The Community Action for Youth project soon merged into the Cleveland Community Action Program under the Johnson War on Poverty, a program that was firmly controlled by the existing authorities. However, faced with what had been more than two decades of promises and special projects, while actual living conditions continued to deteriorate, Hough Area residents rioted in the summer of 1966. There was widespread torching of empty houses and buildings, mobilization of the Ohio National Guard, and a declaration of martial law. Many of the scars from those events are still present in Hough, although today there are also new houses being built.

My experience in the Hough Area painfully dramatized for me the connections between a formal community organization planning process and the political economy of the larger arena, including presidential policies, political struggles around race and the control of education at the city level, the influence of national foundations like the Ford Foundation, the impact of the south-to-north migration of black families, the impact of urban renewal within cities, and the pervasive impact of economies on neighborhood reality. Indeed, it was primarily the politics of race and ethnic conflict that derailed most of the systematically planned, large-scale, social science/social research/social planning urban initiatives of the early 1960s from Boston and New York to Oakland, and from Mobilization for Youth to Model Cities.

None of those initiatives really addressed the underlying economic dynamics of household income and home ownership and the connections between those dynamics and the economic forces of the larger city. It was as though the problems of youth could be addressed apart from the economic problems of their parents and the neighborhood commercial and real estate infrastructure, and without regard to the exploiting and controlling forces in the larger urban community. This experience also impressed on me that it was impossible to fit multidimensional social interventions in a turbulent society into a neat experimental social science evaluation research model, regardless of the mandates of the funding body.

My part of the Priority Determination for Services to the Aged project at SASS, supported by the Ford Foundation, involved nine community decision-making case studies, cutting across social welfare, education, and urban development. The most critical finding was a distinction between (1) *uncontested incremental* community change initiatives, which represented changes within an existing social and political consensus, changes that could be systematically planned and implemented; and (2) *contested "step-changes,"* which "pushed the envelope" in terms of the existing consensus, such as the racial integration of a high school in Indianapolis.

Contested step-change initiatives precipitated a struggle among formal and informal political forces, and any "planners" or "organizers" in the middle were usually among the casualties. It was the outcome of that struggle, not systematic analysis and plan development, that shaped the final outcome. For social work the problem was that, while there existed an intellectual commitment to models of systematic planning and change, many of the issues that social workers became involved with at a planning level were, in reality, issues of contested step-change that were beyond the power of social workers alone to change. Political power analysis was more relevant to the potential for change than were needs assessment surveys.

In the fall of 1964, Dr. Herman Stein, shortly after his installation as dean, succeeding Dean Nathan Cohen, said to members of the SASS faculty, "If you are under 45 and do not have a doctorate, go get one..." A little later, Dean Charles Schottland called from Brandeis to say that there was a National Institute for Mental Health mid-career pre-doctoral fellowship that could make it possible for me to enter the Florence Heller School doctoral program. In the summer of 1965, we (Zuria, Clayton, Judith, Paul, and I) returned to Boston, and I joined the new Ph.D. class at the Heller School.

During the sixties and early seventies the Heller School was the largest social work Ph.D. program in the country. Many of its graduates later became senior faculty and deans in schools of social work, as well as social researchers and policy analysts. During the sixties the Heller Ph.D. students were nearly all men—many of them, like me, part of the original GI Bill generation. Only at the end of the decade did the student body include significant numbers of women as well as men, including Ruth Brandwein, who had served as dean at SUNY Stony Brook; Mary Davidson, dean at Rutgers; June Hopps, dean at Boston College; Anita Harbert, director at San Diego; and Eunice Shatz, who has served as CSWE executive director and dean at Tennessee.

The central focus of my experience as a Ph.D. student at Heller was serving as research director, and then project director, for "Patterns of Participation: A Study of Community Representation in Community Action Programs" under Dr. Arnold Gurin as faculty principal investigator. This research was an effort to determine the actual consequences of the Community Action requirements for "citizen participation." Twenty cities were selected, and full-time researchers were employed to gather information on the community action program in these cities.

In the analysis of the programs it became evident that the concept of citizen participation meant very different things in different communities. In the smallest communities—50,000 population or less—the community action program was absorbed by the existing social and political consensus. There were service programs but little evidence of consequential changes in the basic social and economic dynamics of the community.

In some larger cities the citywide community action board, which included representatives from several poverty areas, spent their time deciding how to divide up the dollars so that every neighborhood got a portion. The dollars earmarked for particular programs were important primarily because they represented jobs in high-unemployment neighborhoods, not because they represented high-impact service programs.

There were three cities in which citizens participation did have consequences. In those cities, a central community action staff person, who, it happened, was a social worker, conceived of citizen participation as being the creation of a citywide political action coalition. This initiative to build a coalition was undertaken covertly without approval by the citywide governing board. In these cities, which were caught up in racial conflict, the coalition became a force for changes in the social and political consensus. In each case, when the central board, primarily representing traditional business and civic leadership, finally realized what was happening, the key staff person was fired. But the coalitions survived and continued to be a force for change.

What became evident from this study was that only when developments within particular urban neighborhoods were viewed within the larger political economy context could their real significance be assessed. Unless such an inclusive perspective was used, an analysis limited to the community action agency and to the machinery of citizen participation, had little significance. But one strength of these community action programs was the opportunity for the development of community leaders from black and Hispanic backgrounds. Many of them went on to local, state, and national political leadership positions. But the impact of the War on Poverty on individual urban target areas was minimal, like the Model Cities programs—in part because of the more powerful economic, social, and political forces at work during the sixties and seventies.

By the time the community action research was completed in 1969, Richard Nixon was president. Community action programs were being dismantled. No one in Washington was really interested in the conclusions that we had arrived at. Patrick Moynihan and Edward Banfield rushed into print to proclaim that citizen participation and, indeed, the entire war on poverty were failures.

One of their charges was that citizen participation had been translated to mean confrontation between the residents of poverty areas and the establishment, rather than "bootstrap" neighborhood improvement and cooperation with existing authorities. Our research suggested that only where such confrontations took place was citizen participation likely to be linked to any important changes in the local pattern of discrimination and poverty. Where the exchanges between the leadership of poverty neighborhoods and the establishment were manipulated, or stifled, neighborhood residents in many cities continued to be frustrated and angry. It was also clear that, as a white, educated male, I and many of the other individuals involved in staff leadership positions in the 1960s community change projects had the particular advantage that we could ultimately escape personal involvement in these community conflicts, and the violence, and move on to new opportunities, as these projects were being disbanded.

With my doctoral dissertation, which examined differences in action tactics among the neighborhood associations in the community action study cities, nearly complete, I was invited to join the Heller faculty. While a faculty member at the Heller School I had another experience with the politics of social welfare. When Governor Francis Sargent initiated a search for a new commissioner of public welfare, I submitted the name of Steven Minter, a graduate of SASS, then in county welfare administration in Cleveland. When Minter was appointed, he asked me to chair the statewide Citizens Advisory Board required by Massachusetts law. That legislation required that a client "representative" from each of the public assistance categories be included. The AFDC recipient representative, who was very angry, and outspoken, had no hesitation in telling off— in the spirit of the Welfare Rights Movement—the more traditional members of the Advisory Board. Their response of resigning, or resorting to silence, was similar to what had taken place in several of the community action boards when rough-tongued neighborhood residents found easy targets for their anger and frustrations.

This experience provided an interesting lesson in the role of advisory bodies. In being advisory, with very limited official authority, we had none of the authority of an official *board*. I had a good personal relationship with the commissioner, and with a very capable staff person assigned to support the work of the Advisory Board. However, we were able to discuss and advise on only the very smallest part of the agenda of a multi-million dollar operation in which there were continuous negotiations with a primarily hostile state legislature, confrontational negotiations with a state employees' union, and running arguments with federal administrators over federal regulations. However, the Advisory Board did serve as a symbolic, publicly visible, element in legitimating the agency to the general public, regardless of any impact we might actually have on policy decisions made by the commissioner, the legislature, or the governor.

I also learned about the politics of state government and state administration from Zuria's experiences as a social worker at Walter Fernald State School, with responsibility for the family care placement program. She, and her supervisor, Doris Rodman, director of social services, expanded the family care program by proposing and establishing an innovative collaboration between the Department of Public Welfare and the Department of Mental Health and Mental Retardation for the community placement of residents of the state school. Public Welfare dollars paid the costs of foster care and community medical care while the Fernald State School provided for supervision of the family care placements. This was a forerunner of future initiatives made possible by SSI and Title XX to create alternatives to lifelong residential care in the state schools.

As messy, and frequently corrupt, as the Massachusetts governance and administrative processes could be, I came to understand that governance in a culturally diverse and divided, contentious, rapidly changing multilevel society entailed a continuous process of give and take, involving legislators and administrators, with negotiations and trade-offs, and informal as well as formal decision making. This is the price for avoiding the polarization and confrontational violence that occurred in the Hough Area, and, later, in Boston over school desegregation.

While at Heller I had the opportunity to be a member of the faculty team that taught an introductory course in social planning to a combination of Heller students and MIT city planning students. Other members of the team were Professor Robert Morris from Heller and Professor Bernard Frieden from MIT. This was in the days of urban renewal and the Model Cities program when there were dreams of community-based advocacy planning uniting urban planners and social planners. The disappearance of federal funding for comprehensive social and physical redevelopment, however, resulted in the drifting apart of the two processional fields in the 1970s.

I was also caught up in two examples of how a small, focused leadership group can mobilize a dramatic confrontation in polarized environments. In the early 1970s a small group of black students at Brandeis seized a central administration building, demanding more substantial attention by the university administration to the recruitment and support of black students. Some Heller School students played important supportive roles for the black students, though not as building occupiers. This was a part of a continuing struggle about how much of a priority should be given to broadening the inclusiveness of the Brandeis community, including the Heller School. Within the Heller School, this event precipitated an intensive argument about the relationship of social work to such confrontational tactics, while in the University confrontational rhetoric escalated among faculty, administration, and students. The resolution of this event was a dramatic case example of the politics of communication—that is, the ability of a person in a position of power, in this case the president of the University, to control the definition of reality for the media so that victory could be declared regardless of the specifics of the actual outcome.

Brandeis students became an active part of the nationwide leadership network in the confrontation with the Nixon administration over the Kent State/Cambodia events. The entire Brandeis campus, including the Heller School, was shut down, and for a few days I was a participant in an active discussion among faculty and students of methods for mobilizing a nationwide demonstration among schools of social work. The end of the academic year and the impact of more far-reaching developments affecting the Nixon administration and the war in Southeast Asia brought an inconclusive end to this episode.

I was a part of the Heller community, as student and faculty, for some two-thirds of the Dean Charles Schottland era, when the school was a major mid-career advanced training center for social work and social work education. In the 1970s, with the departure of most of the faculty with social work backgrounds, the Heller School became a multidiscipline, applied social science, policy research center that also included graduate students. Today, the Heller School is much more similar to schools of public policy such as the Kennedy School at Harvard and the LBJ School at the University of Texas at Austin, than to graduate schools of social work.

In the fall of 1973, I joined the faculty at the School of Social Work at the University of Texas in Austin, as the school began a new program of doctoral studies. My arrival also marked a curriculum shift within the master's program. I followed a faculty member who had taught locality-based CO against a background of personal experience in a neighborhood settlement house. I suggested a shift in the "macro" curriculum to a focus on administration, as being more consistent with the nature of the actual employment market for those master of science in social work (MSSW) graduates interested in macro practice. That curriculum pattern has persisted for nearly 25 years with Administration and Planning being one of three second-year concentrations currently available to MSSW students.

After I came to Texas, I continued to be involved in professional affairs, serving a term on the board of NASW, and as a member of the Council on Social Work Education (CSWE) House of Delegates. In 1983, at the CSWE Annual Program Meeting (APM) in Los Angeles, University of Michigan Professor Armand Lauffer, a Brandeis classmate, convened a meeting of persons teaching CO to protest the lack of program content on CO in the APM program. An ad hoc planning committee, of which I was a member, organized independent symposium meetings ahead of the APM during the next two years, in Louisville and New York, before the APM began including such symposiums in the official program.

At the Louisville session it was agreed to broaden the scope of the symposium to include Administration as well as Community Organization, and to add women faculty members to the initial all-male planning committee. The final outcome was the creation of the Association for Community Organization and Social Administration (ACOSA) as a membership organization of faculty members who teach in CO and Administration.

My continuing interest and involvement in CO have largely been reflected in attention to developments in the Austin community. One important element in the evolution of my own understanding of CO has been the Industrial Areas Foundation (IAF) movement (also known as the Interfaith Movement) in Austin and in Texas. The IAF movement is an outgrowth of the Industrial Areas Foundation—the institutionalization of the concepts of Saul Alinsky. The IAF community mobilization movement has expanded in Texas to the major urban areas and the Lower Rio Grande Valley. Significant elements in the IAF approach include: a comprehensive strategy that is based on, but moves beyond, individual neighborhoods; the use of church congregations, and other existing organizations, as the building blocks for membership recruitment rather than organizing new block associations; the deliberate selection of action issues that unify neighborhoods, not divide them; systematic empowerment training; development of spokespersons and leaders from within the membership; and staff organizers who belong to the organization, not to an outside service agency. Today, IAF is recognized as a significant participant in political/governmental decision processes at both city and state levels in Texas.

The other major CO activity that I watched, and participated in from time to time, was the development of a community-wide social planning council in Austin—the Social Planning Advisory Council (SPAC)—based in the public sector, rather than in the voluntary nonprofit sector. Initiated by future governor Ann Richards when she was a Travis County Commissioner, a coalition of city, county, school board, and United Way organizations was created, primarily to provide guidance on the allocation of funding from city and county governments to local nonprofit organizations. This funding began by using federal revenue-sharing money in the 1970s, but was continued after those funds disappeared. SPAC—now named the Community Action Network (CAN)—has survived more than 20 years, first with part-time staff support from city and county governments, and recently with a full-time staff director of its own and an expanded social planning mission.

The experience of SPAC-CAN again reflects the interface between social planning and politics. While the budget analyses and recommendations to the city council and county commissioners have often included critical comments about the financial requests from some organizations, the elected council members and county commissioners are also aware that the network of nonprofit staff members and board members, and potentially service users, is a significant political constituency. This is a constituency that can provide support in local elections, and can also attract media attention any time there are proposals to cut the level of funding support for these service organizations. Indeed, the majority of the members of both governing bodies have throughout all of the these years been persons favorable to continuing the funding for nonprofit service organizations.

My most recent experience in CO practice came with my appointment in 1988, as chair of the Task Force on Social Work Research, by the director of the National Institute for Mental Health. Dr. Juan Ramos, a classmate from the Heller School, was the NIMH project officer, without whose assistance nothing could have happened. As it turned out, my role as chair and project director was that of a CO practitioner, rather than a research specialist. Central to the outcome was an early decision by Task Force members that their assignment was not simply to collect information and write a report, but to use the Task Force process to make something happen that would improve research-based knowledge resources for social work practice.

The three-year term of the Task Force included a national "needs assessment" that depended largely on the cooperation of schools of social work and individual faculty members, and an outreach process to locate and communicate with a broad range of special interest groups within social work. This was followed by an intensive process of negotiation with leaders in the five national professional associations in social work and social work education as well as with successive NIMH directors, to establish a consensus on next steps to expand research resources within social work.

Using the framework from the earlier study of community decision making this was an "uncontested step-change," that is an important and substantive new development both for the profession and for NIMH, but one that did not mobilize substantial divisive political forces either within the profession or within NIMH. It did not involve a political battle, but it did require constant attention to political relationships among social work constituencies, within NIMH, and between NIMH and members of Congress.

As I look back over some 50 years there are some impressions that dominate. In all of the local community practice activities that I have been involved in, or observed, the dynamics of race and ethnic relationships have been the single most powerful factor in shaping actual outcomes. Societal developments involving system-level conflicts and competitions, implicit and explicit, among traditional white/Anglo community populations, African American community populations and Latino community populations have overrun most local community development/community planning initiatives, even when these conflicts were not central to the issues being addressed. I expect that these conflict will be central to developments at the local community level during the next 50 years. *What is, is what will be*, until there are far-reaching changes in American society.

It will be the combination of economic forces and political forces, shaped by issues of race and ethnicity, that will determine the nature of such changes. I am more certain than ever that the teaching of community practice in social work requires a great deal more attention to the "political economy" of social welfare, that is the politics of the economy and the economic dynamics of politics, if we are to understand real community processes in today's society. Moreover, any substantial approach to community "development" requires a strategic vision that takes into account both economic and political forces and goes beyond a "one neighborhood at a time" example. With the destruction of the Marxist model of radical transformation of society from the bottom up, and the emergence of a large, culturally diverse middle class, a new view of the "good society" is needed to provide a strategic framework for community practice. The IAF example suggests that that strategic framework needs to include a much more thorough examination of the use of confrontation as part of the process of "neighborhood empowerment." Such a framework also needs to include serious attention to the fundamental, and powerful, sources of resistance to real change in the position of those persons who are exploited and "oppressed" in this society.

In the early days of social work, one issue was whether social case workers should focus on proper moral behavior or on understanding the actual dynamics of behavior, good and bad, of real people. At the macro level there has been a strong tendency to teach moral principles—what the good community should be like, what a socially just society should be like, what the responsive human service agency should be like, with only limited attention to the very real human processes that shape real communities, real organizations, and real societies.

For example, historically, community practice in social work has given priority attention to the concept of organizing "block clubs" and "neighborhoods" within an idealized model of relatively self-contained, stable residential districts that might be helped to develop a form of decentralized, informal self-government, with an assumption that such processes would always have positive results for all local residents. Indeed, there is a general assumption that "lower class" residents in low-income and exploited communities will, if they become an organized constituency rather than remaining an unorganized constituency, come up with collective decisions that fit a "liberal" view of values in American society, and vote for "liberal" political figures. However, the voters in many of these communities have been a major part of the support for socially conservative legislators. Indeed, it is the "special interest" nongeographic "communities," such as the communities of persons with disability conditions, that have often had the most strategic influence in local, state, and even national political/governmental decision making on targeted issues that have directly affected the lives of disadvantaged and oppressed persons.

I had an opportunity to observe this issue when Zuria was a legislative advocate with the Texas Association for Retarded Citizens when that organization proposed and was successful in passing state legislation protecting group homes for persons with handicapping conditions from restrictive zoning controls. This legislation, passed in 1985, was one piece of a larger coalition initiative among disability "special interest" groups in Texas that, in turn, was directly connected to the passage of the American with Disabilities Act and the signing of the legislation by President George Bush.

Finally, I continue to be struck by the degree of intellectual isolation that exists within social work. We began with social work practitioners drawing on their own experiences to teach the next generation of social workers. We have progressed to having students read textbooks written by faculty members with social work practice experience. We insist that only social workers can teach practice, or supervise students in field placements, or be deans and directors of social work education programs. We listen to social work speakers at social work conferences. We generally avoid dealing directly with persons who might be intellectually critical of social work practice: If someone is critical we know that he or she really doesn't understand what social workers are trying to do. It is much more comfortable for us to talk only with others who are part of our conceptual community.

One advantage of being a teacher is that it requires you to reexamine old ideas and understandings every time you meet with a group of students—influenced by your own experiences, their experiences, and by what others have written. My ideas continue to evolve, as I examine CO, or community practice, in the larger context of the conflicting forces shaping this society.

ENDNOTES

1. See the article by Irving Spergel for a description of the New York City Youth Project.

2. See the article by Mildred Barry for a description of how the Federation moved toward a community-based planning model.

3. See the articles by George Brager and Robert Perlman for fuller accounts of the development of the President's Committee on Juvenile Delinquency and Youth Crime and Mobilization for Youth.

BIBLIOGRAPHY

Alinsky, Saul D. 1969 *Reveille for Radicals*. New York: Vintage Books.

Austin, David M. 1972. "Resident Participation, Political Mobilization, or Organizational Cooptation." *Public Administrative Review* 32 (September, Special Issue): 409–420.

Austin David M. 1997. "The Profession of Social Work in the Second Century." In *Social Work in the 21st Century*, edited by Michael Reisch and Eileen Gambrill. Thousand Oaks, CA: Pine Forge.

Hamilton, Dona. 1997. *The Dual Agenda: Race and Social Welfare Policies of Civil Rights*. New York: Columbia University Press.

Knapp, Daniel, and Kenneth Polck. 1971. *Scouting the War on Poverty: Social Reform Policies in the Kennedy Administration*. Lexington, MA: D. C. Heath.

Matusow, Allen J. 1984. *The Unraveling of America: A History of Liberalism in the 1960s*. New York: Harper & Row.

Schwartz, John E. 1983. *American's Hidden Success: A Reassessment of Twenty Years of Public Policy*. New York: W. W. Norton and Sons.

Shirley, Dennis. 1997. *Community Organizing for Urban School Reform*. Austin, TX: University of Texas Press (Industrial Areas Foundation Mobilization for School Reform in Houston).

INTELLECTUAL
AND
PROFESSIONAL
ARENAS

A Very Personal Account of the Intellectual History of Community Organization

Jack Rothman

Most people in our field find the battles and vicissitudes of community organizing the most exciting aspect. The organizational and political maneuvers and the interpersonal involvements are endlessly intriguing and enriching, and those elusive hard-won victories are exhilarating. I have shared in all this, but for some curious reason the most interesting element for me has been grappling with the idea of what Community Organization is and how to conceptualize strategies and tactics that work. So I decided to write about the intellectual history of Community Organization, and more particularly, about my personal encounter with that stream of thought. I'll start my story at the point of my college years.

Like many other people, I stumbled into my professional field by happenstance. I was in my last year, last semester of undergraduate work at the City College of New York, majoring in psychology. C.C.N.Y. was an academic hothouse in 1949, filled with children of the poor and of immigrants from many nations, but largely Jewish and from Eastern Europe. Everyone at City was essentially on a scholarship because students had to attain a substantial high school GPA for admission and then could attend tuition-free (except for a five-dollar library card fee, as I recall). The place, a Gothic architectural enclave in Harlem, had the reputation of being the Harvard of the economically downtrodden. The student body, primarily seasoned veterans of World War II, was deadly serious, intensely intellectual, acutely political, and stridently competitive: For the majority this was their one ticket into the middle class and into mainstream American society.

The psych department was first rate, and as I went along I began to take an interest in the social psychology area (taught then by Kenneth Clark), leaning more and more toward the sociological side of things. That's why I was registered in a sociology course on community research during that last semester, and had already applied and been accepted for doctoral work in the sociology department at the University of Chicago. During a break in that course, I began to chat in the corridor with another student, who made a friendly inquiry about my future plans. I told him about my graduate school status and my interests in research, social reform, community action, and improving race relations.

He asked me whether I knew that I could do much the same thing in social work, through a specialization called Community Organization. The truth of the matter was that I had never heard of social work and didn't realize it was an established professional field. (That was by no means unusual back then.) He told me that I could earn a master's degree in two years, much less than the four years or so it would take to get the Ph.D. That caught my attention! I only had two years of the GI Bill left, and I was worried about what would happen in Chicago after that support ran out. Nobody in my family had ever done postgraduate work, so I had no idea that departments try to hold on to you and move you ahead after you've completed your foundation work, rather then let you drop off an academic cliff.

"Can you get a job with that degree?" I asked and learned that, indeed, you can. I decided after that casual conversation to consider a shift and looked into going for the social work master's, thinking that with an income-producing credential in hand I could continue on toward the Ph.D. on a part-time basis, using my earnings to support my further studies. This might be a necessary detour on the road I had chosen.

I soon found out that there were only two universities in the country, at that time, that offered Community Organization (also call CO) as a full two-year specialization (which was the only option that interested me): Ohio State and Boston College. I later learned that both programs were promoted and subsidized by Community Chests and Councils of America (now the United Way) as a means of training fund-raising and welfare-planning executives for work in that field.

It was now very near the end of the academic year, so (attracted by the idea of experiencing living in the heartland of the country) I hastily applied to Ohio State and was promptly accepted as a graduate student. I went packing for the Midwest.

It turned out that Ohio State and social work both were a letdown from City College. Cold War anti-Red hysteria was raging full blast in Columbus, and the University president thought it necessary to set up an outpost of Senator Joe McCarthy's loyalty brigade on campus. The conservative atmosphere in the town of Columbus, with both of the major newspapers in the Republican camp, was a sharp contrast to the progressive/radical mode I was accustomed to. The Community Organization curriculum at school also had a narrow and, it seemed to me, shallow quality. It struck me as more a trade school for training fund and council executives than a broad academic program.

My first-year placement was in the Akron Council of Social Agencies, a stodgy place dominated by the status quo point of view of the city's economic and professional elites, who were in charge. They directed a lot of their effort toward promoting "voluntarism" and minimizing the government's role in human services. Chests and councils, it was obvious, were in the business of maintenance rather than social change, but they raised funds and planned services that had benefits for some (while making sure to keep philanthropic appeals and spending levels under control). I supposed this was necessary work, but I didn't want to do it.

When I asked for a second-year placement in an organization dealing with race and ethnic issues, I was told that the school didn't offer those kinds of opportunities. Persisting, I was informed that I could have the placement if I identified such an agency and set it up—which I proceeded to do after some fumbling around.

My thesis experience shows how far we have come since then. I wanted to do my thesis on race matters and decided to study municipal human relations councils, which had begun to emerge after an ugly race riot in Detroit during the war. My advisor let me know that he wasn't at all sure that this topic belonged in social work, but if I made a convincing case for it in the thesis, I could proceed. So, much to my astonishment, I had to start my thesis off with a whole section that justified the involvement of social work in problems of racism.

Course work in Community Organization was at an early level of development. At that time, there were two readings that were considered cornerstone statements: one by Kenneth Pray,[1] and the other by Wilbur Newstetter,[2] who became my dean when I later joined the faculty at the

University of Pittsburgh. The thrust of the Pray piece was to define community organization as a practice within social work. In his view, if you do CO in social work you must use a nondirective approach and give full sway to client self-determination (this, my instructors indicated, was a "process" orientation or goal). In other words, Community Organization is valid only when it's mental set is molded after casework's. Pray focused exclusively on social relationships and social adjustments in the community, with the people themselves finding satisfactory solutions to whatever problems they decided to tackle.

Substantive problems, goals, and outcomes were far less important. I was familiar with nondirective theory through my previous study of the work of psychologist Carl Rogers, and considered it only one of various alternatives to helping. Pray made me uneasy because I was interested in tangible results—like better housing and a more equitable distribution of resources.

Newstetter had been a group worker and pioneered in establishing outstanding group work programs at Case Western Reserve and the University of Pittsburgh. What I saw was that he was applying group work concepts to community organization, referring to it as "Social InterGroup Work." Thus, group work became writ large on a community canvas, with the main emphasis on adjustments among groups to achieve mutually satisfying relationships with one another and among the members of the groups. The "from-and-to" relationship between representatives of groups and the "intergroup" entity received a great deal of attention. The practitioner was largely an enabler for an interactive process, with attaining that process goal apparently the primary intention. But Newstetter conceived of the worker sharing some level of responsibility with the group for outcomes: thus, you could see some light between him and Pray on that issue. Both he and Pray focused on "adjustments" and "process"—not such substantive aims as social change, problem resolution, and social justice.

We students were also directed to an earlier landmark publication, the Lane Report,[3] which was another fundamental document. Sponsored by the National Conference on Social Work and issued in 1939, it attempted to conceptualize Community Organization for the profession. Under the leadership of Robert P. Lane, discussion groups in six different locations were set up to explore the subject and try to generate an official definition of CO as a subspecialty within social work. The final report reflected a diverse range of views among the deliberators but settled, ultimately, on the core function of achieving an adjustment between social welfare resources and social welfare needs.

The focus here was on social services: planning and coordinating them efficiently, doing program development, and carrying out necessary administrative tasks. Adjustment came into play again, but in a more material context. Lane had been a chest/council executive, and the statement reflected the outlook of that field. There was a "task goal" orientation here, and it was apparent that the Lane Report and the Pray/Newstetter position were not in harmonious alignment.

One thing that was emphasized in all my classes was that, as social workers in the community, we should avoid involving ourselves in politics. Politics was a dirty, abrasive business and out of step with professionalism. It required taking sides, and we needed to be impartial so that we could embrace all interests and not antagonize anyone. A leading publication on neighborhood councils from around that time, which I managed to pull out of a musty folder, put it this way: "The district council fails in its potential value, however, if it is regarded only as a pressure group...without due regard for the needs and interests of other elements in the community...Council action should be undertaken on a non-partisan basis, with approach (sic) made to leaders in both political parties to interpret the problem and the recommendations...and not on the basis of political sponsorship."[4]

I thought that this was nonsense. I reasoned that if we always leave the political arena to people whose interests are counter to those of our clients and hostile to our professional values, we lose out, and so do our clients. This was a big question in my mind; my disagreement with the prevailing professional ideology was a sore spot that would need to be worked through.

In reading older, more historical materials, two appealing writings came to the fore. One was a book from the twenties by Eduard Lindeman on the community[5] that emphasized democratic fellowship: the banding together of citizens to achieve such things as economic security, effective public health agencies, and free education. Lindeman was an adult educator and social philosopher, which accounts for his emphasis on small groups working and learning together and pursuing goals that embodied solid humanistic values.

In 1930, Jesse Steiner wrote a pioneering book with the title *Community Organization*.[6] He was a sociologist and appropriately brought the perspective of that discipline into his work. I liked how he emphasized rigorous social analysis and acknowledged the complexity of social problems. He saw the community as a distinct social unit, delineated separate conceptions (models?) of Community Organization, and laid out an array of assessment and intervention techniques for planning. Lindeman seemed to lean somewhat in the process direction and Steiner toward task goals, but both had a kind of scholarly demeanor that I had come to admire, and expect, in my undergrad studies.

Other readings that fascinated and excited me were even older. These were the writings, practical and action-oriented rather than theoretical, of Jane Addams and others associated with the settlement house movement and with Progressive Period reform, like Florence Kelley, Lillian

Wald, and Mary Simkovitch. No enablers they, but aggressive social advocates who campaigned to eliminate child labor abuses, aid trade unions, improve housing conditions for the poor, and promote peace. That was more like what had attracted me to the field but which, apparently, had gone into decline.

Ohio State had provided some benefits. I had been given an orientation to social work and learned some practice skills, both in the field and in class. I also met my future wife there! But the curriculum and program seemed weak, with little theory, particularly theory supported by social research. My advisor had given me leeway to elect courses in sociology, psychology, and economics, and that filled some gaps. In retrospect, I can understand that, at that time, social work was a profession in transition from agency-based training to university-based education. Academic norms hadn't yet penetrated very deeply. For example, the New York School of Social Work hadn't even come around to changing its name to include an attachment to Columbia University.

Most of the teachers had been selected because they had had long years of experience in the field (the faculty was, overall, considerably older than faculties now), and few had advanced degrees. There was an enormous amount of regard for having been a "doer" in the world of practice and also some distrust for what was called the "purely academic." If truth be told, there was a streak of anti-intellectualism running through the profession, both in the schools and in the agencies.

Students who challenged teachers and debated ideas vigorously were viewed not as serious or innovative thinkers, but as immature rebels who were rejecting legitimate knowledge. In keeping with the psychoanalytic dogma that infused clinical thinking at that time, these students were manifesting "resistance" because they had not worked out adolescent-level authority problems with their parents, and they were too often "counseled out" of the school. A friend of mine who fought against this form of scholastic indoctrination barely escaped being expelled, and has gone on since to become a preeminent policy theorist. I remember thinking around the time I graduated that, if I ever was given the chance, I would try to come up with a better curriculum than what I had experienced.

With my new degree in hand, I set off for New York to get a job and sign up for Ph.D. studies at Columbia University. It was fairly easy to register part-time for a customized cross-disciplinary social science program that I put together under my advisor, Goodwin Watson, a well-known social psychologist. But I ran into a blank wall on the employment front. While my school and I, too, believed you could go to work in CO by specializing in that field during your training, word of that concept had not reached New York, or almost anywhere else in the country.

The au courant view in social work at the time was that you had to work a good eight to ten years in casework or group work before you could possibly go into CO. You needed that foundation to move up to some kind of higher calling. I began to think of it as the second-story theory of social work. The notion seemed utterly bizarre to me. For example, only when a person was fully imbued with a clinical perspective, thought like a caseworker, had skills that honed in on the inner psychic working of individuals in a one-on-one format, and had no real grasp of social forces or community politics and how to impact them—indeed had been socialized to think and work in a contrary way (was thoroughly mistrained, you might say), only then was the person considered ready to practice CO.

But this mumbo jumbo was widely believed, and I couldn't get a job. I wound up taking a summer stint as a camp counselor with a group work agency to garner some income, and was lucky enough to impress my supervisor, who hired me for a full-time position there. I went on to hold a number of positions while I proceeded incrementally with my doctoral studies over a nine-year period (I had to support my wife and a child with a regular job). Tuition support was much more rare then than it became in the next decade.

I did group work in neighborhood centers in Brooklyn and the Bronx, directed a two-county decentralized youth program (BBYO) that involved a combination of group work and CO skills, and then joined the planning and neighborhood development department of the New York City Youth Board, probably the most innovative agency in the city at that time.

At the Youth Board I headed a program to stabilize a racially changing neighborhood, an area that was being stampeded into disarray and social turmoil by the panic-selling techniques of greedy real estate brokers. I organized an interracial neighborhood action council that put concerted citizen pressure on the brokers—directly by personal advocacy and picketing at realtors' offices, and indirectly by working through the state attorney general. (Later I wrote an account of the project that, incongruously, was published as an article in The Nation and by the Council on Social Work Education as an extensive case record.) I also organized a youth council in the Brownsville section of Brooklyn that gave adolescents a voice in community affairs and a channel into the political and professional leaders who influenced programs for young people. I was glad, finally, to be doing the kinds of things I set out to do and which met my concept of CO. (Irv Spergel, who appears elsewhere in this volume, concurrently was a colleague in the Street Gang division of the Youth Board.) While at the Youth Board I became active in the staff union and served as the vice president. Our local, District 37 of AFSCME (American

Federation of State, County and Municipal Employees), was one of the most progressive units of organized labor nationally.

Though I wasn't in a social work school during this time, I tried to keep up with substantive thinking in the field. Two developments seemed especially important to me. In 1955, Murray Ross published what I consider the first contemporary textbook in the field of community organization.[7] It embodied a systematic theoretical approach drawing heavily on broad social science thinking and research findings. Ross, like Lindeman, had an adult education background and was interested in the small group for learning citizenship, developing collaborative attitudes, and taking communal action. Thus, he leaned very heavily on social psychology as the undergirding discipline to inform his formulation.

Ross identified a sequenced set of phases that he postulated described all community intervention, and he put forth a series of intriguing ideas, such as the distinction between the geographic community and the function community (community of interest), the community therapist notion, and a set of different practice role categories. Although he covered a range of tendencies, he ultimately came down on the side of process and enabling, viewing social action as falling outside of social work.

This book seemed to have come out of nowhere. Ross was largely unknown among social work CO people, although he had a position at the School of Social Work at Toronto University. But his book caught on immediately and in a big way, and it became the leading textbook in the field for a good ten years.

The other major development, a few years earlier, involved Bradley Buell and his Community Research Associates, who conducted their original work in the Twin Cities area. In 1952, they published *Community Planning for Human Services*, which prompted widespread discussion in the field.[8] Buell and his group used controlled research methods to carefully assess community problems and plan well-defined service delivery strategies. Their work showed that a relatively small number of multiproblem families disproportionately swallowed up the resources of multiple agencies who served them in an uncoordinated and wasteful way.

The Buell team charted ways of identifying these families and their characteristics. From this, it derived methods of planning for service integration and coordination focused on the given families and involving techniques of "reaching out": decentralizing services to be in closer proximity to potential users, using "aggressive" casework, and assigning "detached workers" to engage street gangs on their own turf. Community welfare councils had been using social surveys and other research tools for years, but not in this kind of disciplined and technically sophisticated way. The Buell approaches were well received, and their service plans were replicated in locations across the country including, in a major way, by the New York City Youth Board.

Around the same time, Floyd Hunter published *Community Power Structure*,[9] a book that inspired a spate of studies of power and influence in American communities. Hunter introduced a methodology and mode of thinking about community decision making that energized numerous sociologists and political scientists and eventually impacted community organization practice literature substantially.

I should also mention the establishment of the Florence Heller School for Advanced Studies of Social Welfare at Brandeis University. This was to be an exclusively doctoral-level institution focusing on macro intervention. The founders viewed it as a major instrumentality for producing scholars and researchers to enrich knowledge as well as top-quality administrators for community, administrative, and policy positions. It was a unique and heartening development but one that did not reach its full promise from a social work standpoint. (Other authors in this book [Austin, Perlman] give additional commentary.)

I finished my doctoral work in 1960, on the threshold of a new (and as yet unforseen) notorious decade. Already things were beginning to stir. A liberal-talking John Kennedy had been elected president, ending the quiescent Eisenhower regime that bred the "Silent Generation." A dynamic President's Committee on Juvenile Delinquency and Youth Crime was established in Washington, and it promoted Mobilization for Youth in New York, to whose community action arm I saw many talented former group workers begin to stream. George Brager was one of them, and he tells the Mobilization story in another article.

Turning the usual procedure on its head, I took my residency in the last year of my studies, conducting and writing my dissertation at a frantic pace. I had been intensely immersed in both social science studies and community organization practice for a protracted period of time, and the result was that I came out a hybrid, fusing the two in an inseparable way.

I identified substantially with both camps, but discovered that the admixture made me a marginal figure, often not fully accepted or trusted by either side, yet sometimes able to link one to the other. In his book, *The Marginal Man*,[10] Stonequist makes the point that bifurcated people, such as minorities, who stand between two cultures, one foot in each and both feet in neither, struggle within themselves to achieve a measure of integration. Through their ability to combine disparate elements in creative ways, they often develop innovative ideas and solutions. I think that happened to some degree in my case, as my story will later suggest.

I wanted to enter university teaching in my next job, but in what direction should I go? The answer soon became obvious. In social work, I would receive full credit for nine years of professional practice in my appointment. In a social science department, I would have to start at year one, probably in a lecturer category. Pragmatics carried the day, but a problem still remained. Community Organization was a peripheral area of study in social work and was established in only a handful of schools around the country. The year I graduated there were two openings in CO nationwide. Only the University of Pittsburgh offered me a position, and that settled that.

It was a lucky break. In the late fifties the University of Pittsburgh, under the leadership of Meyer Schwartz, had started what many consider the first contemporary educational concentration in community organization. It was a full-fledged two-year program, which substituted a broad and forward-thinking approach for the old, narrowly focused United Way framework I had studied under, and was heavily influenced by social science literature and the literature of allied professional fields, such as public health and urban planning. It made extensive use of the constructs of the "planned change" theoretical school, in particular Ronald Lippitt's *The Dynamics of Planned Change.*[11] It was an open-minded and innovative operation. (Details are in the Meyer Schwartz article.)

Considerable thought went into formulating a systematic intervention sequence or study-diagnosis-action progression, using the planned-change knowledge base. The program opened up field placements in what were then nonconventional settings, such as the mayor's office, city council, militant neighborhood advocacy groups, and urban planning departments, legitimizing new roles and auspices for practice. As one of the two faculty members on board, I had an opportunity to take part in every facet of the program, from teaching, to field work administration, to curriculum development.

Also, Pittsburgh was in the throes of a vigorous and broadly based metropolitan redevelopment and facelift that energized and involved every element of the community. That made it a great laboratory for field placements and research. At the same time, Mike Schwartz was spearheading an effort within NASW to construct a "Working Definition of Community Organization" aimed largely at gaining recognition from the profession for this practice subspecialty. He documents his extensive endeavors to garner legitimatization from both NASW and the Council on Social Work Education elsewhere in this book. With all of this buzzing around me, Pittsburgh was a stunning place to be at that historical moment.

But it was a relatively short stay. After two years, in 1962, I moved on, having received an invitation from the University of Michigan to join the faculty there. Arthur Dunham, who was hailed as "the dean of community organization faculty" nationally, was retiring. Arthur had by far the most longevity in the field, having begun at Michigan in 1936. He was an assiduous compiler and chronicler of CO literature, always pushing for greater professionalization and analytic clarity. His singular contribution, from an intellectual standpoint, was bringing international community development into the social work realm and creating its early literature base for the profession. Arthur also had a delightful sense of humor. It was he who taught me that a committee could be defined as a form of human organization that takes hours to produce minutes.

Michigan had a powerful appeal for me because, in my view, it had the strongest social science capability, across departments, of any university in the country, including the presence of Ronald Lippitt and other pioneers of the planned-change school. In addition, the School of Social Work had initiated a serious, high-caliber joint doctoral program in social work and social science, which went on to become the premiere program of its kind in the world.

My assignment was to develop and expand the CO program, instituting a two-year course of study. Up until then, students had to take a first year in casework or group work before they were allowed into a second-year concentration, which was the pattern in the vast majority of schools. It was informally known among faculty that, in many instances, students were shunted toward CO only when they showed themselves inept in the more fundamental area of casework, because they lacked necessary interpersonal skills. This was an exclusionary rather than inclusionary process.

As I went about building the program, the sixties began to move into high gear. There was the civil rights movement, student activism with its embrace of the counterculture, anti-Vietnam protests, and a budding feminist consciousness. On the professional level, there were the Community Action Program of the War on Poverty, the Peace Corps, and a variety of Ford Foundation–sponsored community-based ventures, to mention a few.

In Chicago, and then fanning out across the country, Saul Alinsky swung into action with a melange of neighborhood projects, conducted under the auspices of the Industrial Areas Foundation. This initiative involved an improbable combination of grassroots militancy, derived from trade union activism, under the financial sponsorship of the Catholic Church. Alinsky was a master of creative, dramatic tactics, and I believe his tactical ingenuity comprised his major intellectual contribution.[12] For example, he would get participants to throw dead rats on the city hall lawn to highlight slum housing sanitation abuses, or set up a raucous picket line around they mayor's sedate home in the suburbs. Alinsky had a vitriolic animosity toward social workers, which he expressed frequently and publicly, and this thwarted possible interconnections and mutual influence between his team and the community organization arm of social work. [Irving Spergel tells more about this in his reflection.]

About this time, Roland Warren published his seminal *Community in America*.[13] This volume had an enormous impact, in that it provided a cogent, embracing social system analysis of communities. Since the community was the target of intervention and the arena in which it took place, it was important for practitioners to have a firm theoretical and analytic grasp of this consequential social entity. Warren provided this grasp in a way that was in advance of anything that preceded it. Warren was a sociologist who had conducted surveys and other research in social work agencies and served as a faculty member at the Florence Heller School at Brandeis.

Other sociologists, such as Mayer Zald and Eugene Litwak, colleagues of mine at Michigan, injected highly significant perspectives from organizational theory and interorganizational analysis into the intellectual stew that was simmering. And then there was the influence of Michael Harrington, author in 1962 of *The Other America*,[14] which more than anything else alerted policy makers and the public to the condition of the have-nots and set the War On Poverty in motion. Harrington was a gifted social critic and prolific writer and also a political organizer who established the Democratic Socialists of America, which I was moved to join as a founding member.

The writings of a talented group of former GIs and other postwar social work professionals were also beginning to make their mark. This included "hard" analysis people like Harry Specht, Robert Morris, and George Brager, as well as such breaking-the-waves thinkers as Martin Rein and Richard Cloward, to note just a few.

As a result of all this ferment, the number of community organization concentrations and students began to multiply. There was strong interest among young people and there were jobs aplenty. At Michigan we rode the tide and soon had the largest community organization student body in the country at one time, with 40 enrolled in the program over both years. (To indicate the scope of what was happening, there were but three students when I arrived.)

Events were overrunning our academic know-how. The student body was expanding much faster than was our theoretical and conceptual equipment. At the national level, growth and enthusiasm surrounded CO curriculum development, but also confusion and a lack of coherence. I was confronted with the dilemma of what to teach a burgeoning group of mostly young people, who were often confrontational and distrustful of entrenched lackeys of the system, such as university professors.

I struggled to compose a unitary and inclusive conception of Community Organization, in keeping with the dominant clinical wing of the profession. There, a fairly unidimensional practice paradigm prevailed, the Freudian/diagnostic/ego psychology frame that had been articulated by writers such as Florence Hollis and Gordon Hamilton. But it was proving vexing to bring the various elements with which I was wrestling into alignment: process goals and task goals, directive and nondirective practice, conflict and cooperative tactics, planning and community development, enabling and advocacy.

It was as though I was trying to pack a large and assorted pile of conceptual clothing into a cognitive suitcase, and every time I pressed it closed there was a sock or the end of a tie sticking out. Inside the suitcase, incongruent articles were positioned together, like hiking boots on top of a freshly pressed shirt. No matter how I labored, there were always contradictions and rough edges.

Around this time, during a very cold winter, I attended a Council on Social Work Education annual meeting in Canada. Between sessions I found myself taking a brisk walk with Martin Rein, whose second-year student placement had been at the Brooklyn agency where I had a beginning job. Since it was very much on my mind, I told Marty about my frustration in trying to construct a conceptual model of community organization. Marty, constitutionally an iconoclast and skeptic, muttered, "Why does it have to be a single model?" For me, that was one of those aha/eureka! experiences that we often hear about but seldom have. Indeed, why does it have to be a single model? But where do I go from there?

It happens that my students gave me the answer. As they presented themselves in class they themselves didn't compose a unitary group. They seemed to break, roughly, into three clusters who were expecting different things from the school and from me. One group was identified with the social movements then in force (SNCC, Alinsky/IAF, SDS) and had a strong social action bent. Their aim was to aid the oppressed, promote social justice, and change society.

A second group had the Peace Corps or VISTA in mind, with the intention of working closely with people at the local level. They were motivated to bring people together to discuss their problems cooperatively and engage in collaborative self-help. I came to call this approach locality development.

A third group was interested in improving the delivery of service to people who need them, and in bettering coordination and effectiveness among service agencies. They were looking toward jobs that involved social planning in agencies like the United Way and health-planning bodies.

It became presciently clear to me that these different sets of interests and motivations could not be encompassed comfortably by one practice conception, and that it would be useful to formulate three models or approaches as represented by my students. I staked out these three modes in analytic detail, weaving the different untidy conceptual components in among them as appropriate. I then went beyond that to show patterned variations among the intervention modes. Taking a set of about a dozen "practice variables" (like goals, practitioner roles, tactics, and beneficiaries), I illustrated how intervention differed in predictable ways across the models. The different approaches, I noted in a precautionary alert, were ideal types that did not exist in pure form in the real world, but rather typically were implemented in mixed configurations and often phased sequentially over time.

I specifically included social action in this conceptual triad, and analyzed it using the identical practice variables that I applied to the other modes. This was my way of trying to bring academic legitimacy and parity to robust political and social advocacy, which in the past, and even at that time, was an activity that was considered crude, unacceptable, and unprofessional by the majority of social workers. I believe this analysis helped to turn things around.

I presented a paper embodying this framework at a meeting of the National Conference on Social Work in San Francisco in 1968. At the end of the session, I announced that I had copies for those who were interested. Almost the entire audience rose and came forward. That had never happened to me before, nor has it happened since. The paper came out at a time of great expansion and excitement in the field, but also of tumult and perplexity about the nature of Community Organization. In trying to clarify the conundrum for myself, I had apparently clarified it for others. The formulation later became the organizing frame for a textbook, *Strategies of Community Organization*, which I edited with colleagues at Michigan.[15]

This trinitarian framework is consistent with earlier currents in CO intellectual history. Locality development was reflected in the process writings of Pray, Newstetter, Lindeman, Ross, and others. The social planning approach was seen in the Lane Report, in Steiner's work, in the writings of chest/council/United Way professionals, and in the charity organization societies that came before. Social action can be located historically in the settlement house movement, the reform period of the Theodore Roosevelt administration, and intermittently in *Proceedings of The National Conference on Social Work* over the years.

In those years it was a bit risky to depart from the established casework formula of a single-practice modality. But, in time, clinical practice also diversified and began to include variations such as behavior modification, cognitive therapy, and an ecological framework. I believe intellectual development in CO has been retarded by misguided efforts to conform to a social work paradigm that is shaped, overridingly, by a clinical perspective.

The framework developed provided for me a usable mapping of the terrain of community intervention. It gave me a platform from which to apply social science to the community area. The immediate task, it seemed to me, was not to tinker with and refine the niceties of a grand theory, but to use research to develop specific empirically based intervention strategies and tools for practice.

My first venture was a research utilization project involving the retrieval and synthesis of a massive pool of published research studies from diverse disciplines and professions. This emergent meta-analysis resulted in a book, *Planning and Organizing for Social Change: Action Guidelines from Social Science Research*, which was published in 1974 by Columbia University Press and presented several hundred empirical generalizations and action guidelines (really hypotheses) to inform practice within the framework.

From this I moved on to construct an intervention research methodology that sought to use empirical methods to design concrete, user-ready tools and techniques of intervention.[16] To be trite and encapsulating, I was reaching to discover a systematic, research-based way to put social science to use, calculatingly, to improve the human condition, or, more precisely, to provide the equipment to those who were engaged in that project on the ground. Over a 25-year period (most recently at UCLA), I applied this social R&D/design and development methodology in various contexts. Initially, my colleagues and I field-tested, developed, and evaluated techniques for promoting innovations, fostering participation, and changing organizational goals. We proceeded, in keeping with the methodology, to present our findings in handbooks and manuals that practitioners could easily follow[17] and then to explore ways of diffusing the materials widely to relevant agencies and practitioners.[18] The strongest influence on my work, I think, has been Kurt Lewin, who was inextricably committed to the union of theory and action, and he is the one person I would want to consider myself following as a disciple.

I used intervention research over time to develop, among other things, a case management intervention mode—a combination of individual and community practice,[19] policies and programs for runaway and homeless youth, [20] and culturally relevant program approaches for Latino populations.[21] My colleague at Michigan, Edwin Thomas, was engaged in similar work, and the interaction between us was very valuable. I think this design and development activity integrates, in almost pure form, the social science/social practice dichotomy that was propelling me. I also believe it is the most relevant and powerful research approach currently available for our practice-centered field and for the other applied social professions to create intervention technology.

The review of these activities diverts us from important concurrent endeavors. Since the sixties there has been an accelerating pace of intellectual development in the field as scholars have attacked a wide range of problems and theoretical issues. I condense ruthlessly, because to do full justice to this more recent period could take more space than is available here. Broad theoretical treatments have appeared in textbooks by Brager and Specht,[23] Rubin and Rubin,[24] Perlman and Gurin,[25] Taylor and Roberts,[26] Lauffer,[27] and Mondros and Wilson,[28] just to single out a small number. The Perlman and Gurin book, issued in 1972, was part of a national Community Organization Curriculum Development Project based at Brandeis. The authors formulated intervention in terms of analytical and interactional tasks and saw the organizational setting as crucial in shaping the parameters of practice.

Substantive theoretical work has been done in narrower topical realms such as coalitions,[29] race and ethnic organizing,[30] feminist organizing,[31] social action,[32] and neighborhood work.[33] Policy practice, which overlaps in part with social planning, emerged rapidly and made important progress.[34] Significant contributions have been made in sister professions, such as community psychology, public health, urban political science, and urban planning. Comments from reactors to the reflections, who represent some of these fields, elaborate on this.

A portentous event was the appearance of the *Journal of Community Practice* in 1994, under the editorship of Marie Weil. This is the first scholarly journal in social work that is dedicated expressly to propagating knowledge in the community intervention area. The formation of ACOSA, Association for Community Organization and Social Administration, in the 1980s is another event with high potential for furthering community organization intellectual development (for example, it is ACOSA that sponsors *Community Practice*).

This has been a personal and subjective excursion through CO intellectual history. Others doing a more comprehensive and objective review would include different works and other participants: That is the cost of subjectivity. Other reflections in this book, fortunately, bring out what I have overlooked.

The intellectual status of CO has made an enormous, immeasurable leap over the 50-year period that I've recounted here. But in the realm of research and theory, we are not up to the level of our colleagues in the clinical area, and in such fields of practice as child welfare, mental health, and gerontology. Let me ponder briefly about why this might be so.

CO people are passionately dedicated to improving conditions of life in communities. By temperament, many of us are action-oriented and pragmatic—acutely predisposed to immerse ourselves in the dynamics of "doing." This predisposes against the solitary and detached reflection in the university setting that research and theory-building require. It also leaves insufficient time to engage in that kind of reflection. A strong commitment to being in the thick of the fight for social change even engenders, sometimes, a negative view of research and scholarship. Our admirable ideological bent has a counterproductive underside.

Another possible and important explanation relates to our situation in the social work profession. Since the twenties, when psychotherapy made its indelible imprint on the profession, CO has been in a marginal position relative to casework. We have been a small minority (even during the highpoint of the sixties) and have been looked on by our clinically minded colleagues as some combination of Peck's Bad Boy and the stepchild. In a recent survey, Steve Soifer reports that only 15 schools of social work currently have a CO concentration.[35] Oh, yes, the Jane Addams legend and the commitment to social justice are trotted out for public meetings and ceremonial occasions, and then put back in the closet. Over the years, we constantly have had to fight a rear-guard battle for recognition and resources. That wasted energy and that lack of resources may be part of the explanation for academic shortfalls.

As I write these words, the *NASW News* (January 1997) contains a report on a meeting of macro practitioners that urged NASW to include a community organization track in its 1997 conference. It is dismaying, to say the least, that such a reminder about a community organization *presence* at its national gathering was necessary at this late date. The group also spoke to the need to set up, at last, a CO specialty section within the organization (subsequent action steps were taken), and to exert more energy toward attracting additional social work students to the specialty. The article also contains a refutation of the myth that there are not enough jobs for CO graduates, an old saw that for long has offered justification to our clinical compatriots not to direct students to the specialty, or to actively steer them in other directions.

We have a tough intellectual agenda to carry into the next century. We have to find ways to strengthen our theory-building capacities and to expand the amount, type, and quality of research we produce. That inward-looking activity is critical. But another intellectual challenge is to consider whether the social work profession is willing to provide the status and resources necessary to swell our numbers and enable us to achieve the highest level of academic excellence. In their historical overview, *From Charity to Enterprise*, Wenocur and Reisch[36] make the point that community organization did not receive recognition as a method of specialization from the Council on Social Work Education until very late in the game. The reasons for this, they state, involved, "insufficient political power to open the doors of the professional enterprise to another specialty, and insufficient conformity to the dominant casework model." They add also that within the CO ranks there was a low level of "collective self-identity and organization" (p. 233). If social work is reluctant to or incapable of offering a compatible home, then what organizational and academic actions and options present themselves? The Federation of Clinical Social Work Societies certainly has not been hesitant to go its own independent way when it thought its interests were not best served by NASW.

A long time ago, when I was just starting out with him, Mike Schwartz posed these kinds of questions to me (he may not even remember). But I was young and didn't want to risk having such disconcerting thoughts about that to which I was about to dedicate my productive years. After a long string of battles with tone-deaf colleagues, which only led to fighting the same battles over again, I am ready to put these issues on the table. Further intellectual advance, it seems to me, requires a consideration of substantive as well as professional-organizational quandaries and strategies.

ENDNOTES

1. K. L. M. Pray, *Social Work in a Revolutionary Age* (Philadelphia: University of Pennsylvania Press, 1949).

2. W. I. Newstetter, "The Social Intergroup Work Process," in *Proceedings of the National Conference of Social Work* (New York: Columbia University Press, 1947), pp. 205–217.

3. R. P. Lane, "The Field of Community Organization—Report of Discussions," *The Proceedings of the National Conference of Social Work: Selected Papers from Sixty-Sixth Annual Conference, Buffalo, New York June 18–24, 1939, Vol. 66,* Howard R. Knight, ed. (New York: Columbia University Press, 1939), pp. 495–511.

4. *Neighbors United for Better Communities: A Handbook on District Community Councils* (New York: Community Chests and Councils of America, Inc., 1956), p. 21.

5. E. C. Lindeman, *The Community: An Introduction to the Study of Community Leadership and Organization* (New York: Association Press, 1921).

6. Jesse Steiner, *Community Organization: A Study of Its Theory and Current Practice*, rev. ed. (New York: Century Co., 1930).

7. M. G. Ross, *Community Organization: Theory and Principles* (New York: Harper & Brothers, 1955).

8. Beull, Bradley, and Associates, *Community Planning for Human Services* (New York: Columbia University Press, 1952).

9. Floyd Hunter, *Community Power Structure* (Chapel Hill: University of North Carolina Press, 1953).

10. Everett V. Stonequist, *The Marginal Man* (New York: Russell and Russell, 1961).

11. Ronald Lippitt, Jeanne Watson, and Bruce Westley, *The Dynamics of Planned Change* (New York: Harcourt, Brace and Company, 1958).

12. S. Alinsky, *Rules for Radicals* (New York: Random House, 1971).

13. R. L. Warren, *The Community in America.* (Chicago: Rand McNally, 1963).

14. Michael Harrington, *The Other America* (New York: Macmillan, 1962).

15. Fred M. Cox, John L. Erlich, Jack Rothman, and John E. Tropman, eds., *Strategies of Community Organization* (Itasca, IL: F. E. Peacock Publishers, 1970).

16. J. Rothman, *Social R&D: Research and Development in the Human Services* (Englewood Cliffs, NJ: Prentice-Hall, 1980).

17. J. Rothman, J. L. Erlich, and J. G. Teresa, *Promoting Innovation and Change in Organizations and Communities: A Planning Manual* (New York: John Wiley and Sons, 1976).

18. J. Rothman, J. G. Teresa, T. L. Kay, and G. C. Morningstar, *Marketing Human Service Innovations* (Beverly Hills, CA: Sage Publications, 1983).

19. J. Rothman, *Guidelines for Case Management: Putting Research to Professional Use* (Itasca, IL: F. E. Peacock Publishers, 1992); J. Rothman and J. S. Sager, *Case Management: Integrating Individual and Community Practice* (Boston: Allyn & Bacon, 1998).

20. J. Rothman, *Runaway and Homeless Youth: Strengthening Services to Families and Children* (White Plains, NY: Longman, 1991).

21. Jack Rothman et al., "Mexican-American Family Culture," *Social Service Review*, 52:2, 1985.

22. J. Rothman and E. J. Thomas, eds., *Intervention Research: Design and Development of Human Services* (Binghamton, NY: The Haworth Press, Inc., 1994).

23. G. Brager and H. Specht, *Community Organizing* (New York: Columbia University Press, 1973).

24. H. J. Rubin and I. S. Rubin, *Community Organization & Development*, 2nd ed. (New York: Macmillan, 1992).

25. Robert Perlman and Arnold Gurin, *Community Organization and Social Planning* (New York: John Wiley, 1972).

26. S. H. Taylor and R. W. Roberts, *Theory and Practice of Community Social Work* (New York: Columbia University Press, 1985).

27. A. Lauffer, *Social Planning at the Community Level* (Englewood Cliffs, NJ: Prentice-Hall, 1978).

28. J. B. Mondros and Scott M. Wilson, *Organizing for Power and Empowerment* (New York: Columbia University Press, 1994).

29. T. Mizrahi and B. Rosenthal, "Managing Dynamic Tensions in Social Change Coalitions," in T. Mizrahi and J. D. Morrison, eds., *Community Organization and Social Administration* (New York: The Haworth Press, Inc., 1993), pp. 11–40.

30. R. G. Rivera and J. L. Erlich, eds., *Community Organization in a Diverse Society* (Boston: Allyn & Bacon, 1995).

31. C. Hyde, "A Feminist Model for Macro-Practice: Promises and Problems," *Administration in Social Work* 13:145–181.

32. R. Fisher and J. Kling, *Mobilizing the Community* (Newbury Park, CA: Sage, 1993).

33. B. Checkoway and J. Van Til, "What Do We Know About Citizen Participation? A Selective Review of Research," in S. Langton, ed., *Citizen Participation in America* (Lexington, MA: D. C. Heath, 1978).

34. John E. Tropman, *Policy Management in the Human Services* (New York: Columbia University Press, 1984).

35. Steve Soifer, "Social Work '96 Sessions," *NASW News*, January 1997.

36. S. Wenocur and M. Reisch, *From Charity to Enterprise: The Development of American Social Work in a Market Economy* (Urbana: University of Illinois Press).

Organizing the Professional Social Work Community

Chauncey A. Alexander

...Atlantic City, New Jersey, NASW Delegate Assembly, April 18, 1969

Delegates from 172 Chapters, colorfully clad Californians and more austere-appearing New Englanders, with all combinations in between, milled around the lobby of the Atlantic City Convention Center. "Why don't they open the Assembly Hall so we can get started?" "It's way past time!"

Doors were finally opened. Delegates filed in, at first startled, then dismayed, at the yells and slogans from students, young and old, who occupied the long rostrum. Holding the Assembly captive for more than an hour, they pressed their Coalition for Action Now (CAN) demands for changes in NASW's role in society.

Typifying the frustrations, antiestablishment challenges, and organizational enigmas of the 1960s, they proclaimed that NASW "has yet to demonstrate its right to represent the organized concerns of social work practitioners, young social workers, and students, in responding to the per-

235

sonal suffering and environmental chaos which characterize contemporary American society."[1]

In a call for a <u>national social action system</u>, ten actions were demanded for organizing, funding, and staffing from NASW resources. After a mixed reception and heated arguments from an anxious Assembly, the students' demands were rejected. But some calm was restored with the intervention of President-elect Whitney Young to establish a committee to deal with the issues. The committee later reported back to the Assembly.

The students started a tumult. Black caucus delegates demanded 75 percent use of Association's resources for combating racism; delegates from chapters and regional coalitions called for better services and more resources; caucuses and affinity groups proposed their special-interest programs. Virulent criticism fell on the national leadership with complaints of inadequate programs, heightened by revelation of severe financial debt. A "Fire Executive Director Joe Anderson" cabal was underway until cooler heads of the Western Chapters Coalition intervened.

As the organizer and one of the leaders of the Western Chapters Coalition, I had helped build a positive program proposal that we were taking to the Assembly. We were ready to exercise our past experience at "working the floor" with organized debate assignments, timely microphone appearances, and constant contact with other chapters and coalitions.

As a longtime Los Angeles representative on national bodies—the "Bartlett" Practice Commission, 1960 Reorganization Task Force, Division of Social Policy, and others, I was an ardent volunteer and enthused at NASW's advances. However, diverse pressures in the latter 1960s created erratic leadership responses in spite of the efforts of some of us to support a steady progressive course.

It was another of those watershed periods, another of those "crossroads" times for social work about which leaders expound. But, in spite of significant social welfare advances, the issues were deeper and more critical than prior disruptions since the Depression years.

The American society was in crisis—trembling from internal conflict over social justice and the Vietnam War. The drive of corporate reaction against World War II–inspired social and racial equity programs was weakening the resistance of labor and liberal organizations to attacks on working conditions and social programs.

The social work profession was reeling, in turn, from external attacks and blame from politicians, as well as community and client groups, for not "ending poverty." Social workers had not solved the social problems of crime, health care, and other social dysfunctions, they said. Others accused social workers of being "establishment lackeys."

Internally, the profession was wracked with dissension. The increased effort to respond by "social action" had garnered reactions from conservative community and agency leaders. Those reactions were often reflected in NASW leadership ambivalence over the risks and demands of any such aggressive course. The social work profession's defensive posture from the antiestablishment attacks of the sixties, and the bitter struggles of clinical versus social action advocates for control of program and resources in NASW meant that most of the 172 chapters were split, or captured and dominated, by ideologues of that battle.

The ancient ideological conflict over the basic role of the social work profession between "clinical" versus "social action" advocates had flared into open conflagration over competition for Association resources. Nationally, the "social action" caucus of the NASW Board had captured control of resources in their futile attempt to respond to the "ills of the Big Cities." All other units were made nonoperative, heightening the frustration and anger of their leadership. Social and personal frustrations were demonstrated by both legitimate and opportunistic attacks on NASW by social workers, members or not.

Simultaneously, the rank and filers were calling for effective action against attacks on social programs and their agencies, each field of practice and each modality specialty, demanding attention to their special problems.

National and chapters were on the defensive from criticisms by ethnic minorities, "indigenous" workers, and the active Welfare Rights Organization. The new Clinical Social Workers Society was making the most of membership recruitment opportunities in several states inasmuch as the NASW 1963 reorganization, six years earlier, had provided no special structure for private practitioners. Before long, the Nixon administration directly attacked social workers, finally topped by John Ehrlichman's infamous derision, "Social workers should get honest jobs." We derived super-satisfaction later when, as NASW's Executive Director, I could issue a press release saying "When Ehrlichman gets out of prison, social workers will help him find an honest job."

In the Assembly, with a turbulent display of "Democracy will prevail," delegates from various chapter and specialty group coalitions worked the floor microphones to achieve agreement on priorities for:

- Affirmative action and antiracism efforts in the profession by adoption of a seven-point program of the Black Caucus
- Personnel standards emphasizing professional competence
- Revision of public assistance programs and adoption of a universal benefit system for Americans
- Action program for a universal, comprehensive social service system
- Humane immigration laws
- Integration of ACSW as an integral unit of NASW
- New standards for local units and creation of state units

- Combining NASW and the National Conference of Social Work
- Approval of holders of BSW degrees as professional members
- Establishing of uniform dues rates

And most important, a final "balanced" program for NASW was adopted. It was written on-the-spot by Lorenzo "Gip" Traylor (later elected NASW national president) from the Assembly actions and the program analysis successfully championed by the Western States Coalition.

That Assembly brought radical changes in program, structure, financing, and leadership, as well as a future, to NASW, the organizational representative of the social work profession. Coincidentally, it furthered changes in the concepts of community organization in social work that were taking place in that same period.

Four months after that 1969 Delegate Assembly, I was asked to apply for the executive director position at NASW. My selection brought new dimensions to my life, with the awesome obligation of organizing the entire professional community of social workers.

Three converging paths led to that exceptional challenge and my acceptance: (1) 30 years of volunteer service in professional associations—AAPSW, AASW, ASCO, and NASW[2] (I had worked as a volunteer in most positions and at all organizational levels); (2) experience in most types of social work practice, including casework and psychotherapy, group work, research, community organization, administration, and management; and (3) parallel education, all this while working, through a master's degree and all doctorate education, except the dissertation.

That 30 years was coincidentally the main period of analysis of community organization development in social work practice and in education, misconstrued as it was as one of the three basic "methods" in social work.

Community Organization is a field of practice to which the social work profession was learning to apply its own methodology. But, by 1970, Community Organization as an operating concept also was being supplanted by intellectual partialization of its practice activities, for example: (1) the emphasis on "social action" priorities (principally legislation); (2) the less activist and safer "social planning" and "social policy" emphasis; (3) definition by size of client components, "micro-mezzo-macro" divisions; (4) research utilization as a process; and (5) the citation of community organization as a subset of management/administration. This phenomenon is demonstrated currently in many schools of social work where one or more of the above have been substituted for the original community organization courses.

The effect of this search for "meaning by fragmentation" is also demonstrated by the fact that Community Organization is not listed in the 1971 or 1977 *Encyclopedia of Social Work* but linked with four aspects of social planning. Ten years later the 1987 *Encyclopedia* had further fragmented the concept under titles of: Community-Based Social Action, Community Development, Community Theory and Research, and Social Planning *and* Community Organization. Three separate articles appeared on Social Planning, and Social Planning in the Voluntary and Public Sectors.

Fortunately for me, from Wayne McMillen's two components of the community organization process, I read and practiced each theoretical development. Excited by Kenneth Pray's landmark question and answer in 1949, "When Is Community Organization Social Work Practice?" I had read, discussed, and worked through hundreds of hours of delineation of "community," "goals," "planning," and so forth, and finally to "process" and "application."

By 1970, the utilization of social work methodology in all types of organizational communities was clear to me. All in all, my 30 years had been Community Organization 600, a progressive education.

When Sally and I arrived in New York on December 1, 1969, a fresh snowfall and stereotypical New Yorkers' indifference chilled us thoroughly. But, inside, people are much the same and our California commitment to greet every person we were near brought, first, shock, and later many enjoyable interactions. In contrast, the reception from the professional community was "Welcome, and good luck!"

When I entered the 33rd and Park Avenue offices of NASW in New York, I had a mission in mind. The NASW must mobilize the professional social work community toward common membership goals, most of which were already defined by NASW's policies, created since its origin in 1955, 14 years prior. To do so meant defining and implementing the responsibility of all professional social workers, utilizing the highest ethical and practice standards, often different from their responsibilities as agency-based employees or private practitioners.

It was my experience and conviction that the professional association, the NASW, was the embodiment of the social work profession—its representative, rather than some abstraction of all possible social work activities. Other organizations represented components of the social welfare field: CSWE (Council on Social Work Education) represented educational systems and educators; NCSW (National Conference of Social Welfare) represented primarily social agencies; and the "affinity groups" of ethnic minority and small practice specialties represented their special interests.

But only in NASW, that combination of seven professional groups, was there responsibility for the totality of practice advancement, professional standards, and community service of the profession, all drawn from broad membership consensus, with requisite benefits of organizational collaboration.

I also had plans to correct specific organizational problems impacting the professional community that had hindered the execution of those responsibilities, viewpoints garnered from 30 years of Association volunteer work. It was embodied in a ten-page analysis of NASW I had given in Seattle on March 17, 1967, at the invitation of the Washington State Chapter. It had been distributed to the 1969 Delegate Assembly by George Nishinaka, our Los Angeles Chapter president.

By that time I had long-held convictions and written about applying social work principles and practices to Community Organization.[3] The cooperative self-determinative social work process as applied to a community (a defined situation) for me was the utilization of the pioneering work of the "Bartlett Commission" of the 1960s. It defined the essential elements of social work practice as the application of social work values, purpose, sanction (authority), knowledge, and method, to which later I had added a sixth, "techniques." The resultant use by the practitioner demonstrates "skill." Utilizing those categories helped me clarify the components of each crisis I encountered, while a problem-solving process helped me know where to start with finding solutions.

Naturally, reorganization of the national professional community through NASW was more formidable than its symptoms proclaimed, as is usual in social work with clients, groups, or communities. Theoretically, personal experience, conviction, and plans—combined with Delegate Assembly priorities—would develop into an orderly organizational process.

Not so! The Assembly battles were reflected in the board of directors, where certain acting-out minority, liberal, and conservative members attempted to extend or retract the Delegate Assembly mandates. More sophisticated educators and agency executives exercised their own agendas, while meeker directors complained later.

Most directors, in good conscience, brought their own vision of what was important, under pressure from their constituents or from local or national staff members with whom they had worked in committees. Many felt stampeded by demands of the Assembly and wanted national action on their own special interests.

Fortunately, several factors combined to bring eventual focus and direction to the group. First was the prestige and leadership acumen of President Whitney Young. A national figure, successful leader of the National Urban League, and under consideration for the nation's vice presidency, Whitney did not need the NASW presidency. But he accepted the post because of his commitment to social work even though he knew the desperate condition of the Association. Given an agenda, with our prior discussion of objectives, he mobilized additional objective board members to make realistic policy decisions. After about one and one-half years of NASW service, Whitney's untimely accidental death was a personal and organizational tragedy, but the course we had collaborated on was in place.

Second was the technique of constantly bringing the board back to the "balanced program" and priorities of the Delegate Assembly. That meant placing all the necessities and demands in an understandable functional framework of (1) practice advancement, (2) professional standards, (3) community service (legislation, social action), (4) membership services, and (5) administration. This required reactivation of a limited number of selected organizational units, initiating discussions regarding reorganization, and stimulating board members to lead the parade in their regions.

Third, we reminded board, chapters, and members of the profession's historical role by an analysis of the general organizational trends reflected in NASW. The social work profession, tattered as its organization was from without and within, needed to relearn its purpose and have a sense of its own development. So, it was necessary to use the "influence of history" to remind of past achievements, to stipulate the necessity for "professional leadership" to designate the mission, and to advocate "balanced program" as the means.

My editorials and speeches constantly reminded leadership and members how in its beginnings—the 1950s and early 1960s—NASW was trying to achieve *professional unity* through administrative amalgamation of the seven prior organizations.

The period primarily for developing *professional consensus* began in 1959, as demonstrated by consecutive Delegate Assemblies' production of a Code of Ethics, Goals of Public Social Policy, Standards for Personnel Practices, and many other policy positions.

The turbulent social scene of the middle sixties brought the next emphasis on *professional action*, burning hot in 1965 and gaining momentum. This delineation of differential growth patterns seemed to give national and chapter leadership some sense of depth regarding past growth and a new motivation for future tasks.

Certainly, the most compelling crisis task was the impending financial disaster. I am not ashamed to say that Joe Hoffer, NASW treasurer and longtime National Conference executive, and I used that misfortune fully to obtain much-needed discipline in the organization.

The evenings of my first month were spent going through the financial records, which revealed that the Association was more than $750,000 in debt and could operate only another two months without collapsing. A chart of the differential flow of income and expenditures by the month showed that fact conclusively. Using Delegate Assembly priorities, I designed a radically reduced budget of $1,120,000, including a financial catchup plan to move from cash to accrual accounting, negotiated a future line of credit with the bank, and obtained board approval.

Eventually, every Association operation had to be analyzed for its benefit to the members and the profession, as well as its efficiency and cost-benefit. Simultaneously, each program had to be considered for its draw on expenditures and its fundraising potential. It took four lean years, a very competent and workaholic comptroller, John Cabot, and tough finance committees to put the Association in a sound fiscal position with accrual accounting in place. Eventually, John Cabot established and implemented an accounting system for chapters, one designed to move them from cash to accrual accounting.

A second crisis existed in that NASW was overwhelmed by its own structure—the chapters that had multiplied to 172 by 1970, of variable sizes, jurisdictions, programs, and dues rates. Betty Adams, a truly competent and longtime AASW/NASW associate director, was trying to survive in the tide of demand for chapter and membership services. She and I divided assignments to meet with key chapter leaders, members, and schools of social work.

To encourage greater organizational unity and strengthen chapter participation in national decision making, we initiated annual chapter and staff leadership meetings, in addition to the required policy-making biennial Delegate Assemblies. They were opportune for learning about dissatisfactions and leadership priorities, but it was evident that we had to provide a stable financial base for the Association.

In desperation, and despite the acrimony, the Delegate Assembly had approved a radical increase in dues subject to a membership referendum. We were committed to implementing it, although I was convinced it could not succeed because of member disillusionment and the low dues levels in the many chapters. The dues increase lost!

Two more years of membership education, new and better service to members, and the proposal of a $55 standard rate paid off, set as it was at a level slightly higher than the dues required in a few major chapters that contained a majority of membership. The second referendum won, initiating a stable financial base for national and chapter programming, which in turn required new fiduciary responsibility from the leadership. Later, a raise in the ACSW fee strengthened the Association for the increasing work required by an activated membership.

Part of the educational process required membership involvement in understanding the dysfunctional structure of 172 disparate chapter units. National and some local committees engaged in analyses, with the few chapter staff aiding and Association publications publicizing the findings. *Consolidation of chapters to 50 state and five special geographic units was achieved.* This combination of organizational, financial and leadership restructuring enabled the eventual staffing of all 55 units, providing the necessary personnel underpinning for more unified and effective volunteer operations.

Community Organization means obtaining participation through involvement, so in the five functional areas, we had to initiate crisis-focused programs and stimulate membership response to the need they expressed. Each move meant program design, approval from a particular committee, checking with chapters, finding finances and often clearance through the finance committee, then on to the board for approval, a process-heavy activity. Fortunately, we had the advantage of a year's participation of volunteer public relations specialist Sally Alexander, who designed and produced numerous interpretive and membership service materials, such as priority program guides, until we could afford another professional.

The fundamental organizational tasks were to unify and mobilize our professional community, involving (1) our board and chapter leaders; (2) the members, directly and through their chapters; (3) our staffing and specialty-interest issues; and (4) the establishment of new relationships with external organizations.

The following illustrations relative to the five Association functions—administration, membership service, practice advancement, professional standards, and community service—are offered as a sampling of the issues and responses in this challenge of organizing the professional community.

Administration   In all social community organization work, two select affinity groups—(1) the policy makers, the board of directors, and (2) the community of employed staff—have their own special relationships. In a professional association, those components of the larger community have unique powers and special pressures that can make them readily cohesive or chaotic. As in hi-tech organizations, caste differentiation and culture confusion come easy. Therefore, NASW's mission, the profession's ethical principles, policy clarity, and practice examples must mix in the right proportions. The following sample from each group is illustrative.

Board of Directors   The implementation of Delegate Assembly priorities and Association revitalization required what was essentially a community organization process—problem solving, from issue identification and analysis through all the steps to eventual evaluation. The overriding Delegate Assembly issue of racism brings strong "recollections" since it occupied so much time and energy of NASW personnel and volunteers.

The final affirmative action position accepted by the Assembly Black Caucus was a goal of 30 percent NASW ethnic minority staff, with the same goal for students and faculty in schools of social work. This represented a compromise over the demands of the caucus for higher percentages. Yet, the goal was twice the ratio of minorities in the population and five times the ratio in social work, so it represented a formidable challenge.

It was necessary to educate staff and volunteers to the goals, and eventually to replace the business manager, who had recruitment responsibility. In three years, with staff cooperation, we were able to move from 8 percent to 21 percent minority staff. We broadened the recruitment goal to all minorities of color and for women.

The move of the national office to Washington, D.C., in December 1972, provided opportunity for greater changes, and by 1975 we had 42 percent minority staff and nearly 70 percent female staff, which reflected gender distribution in the membership. Implementation of policy revealed more practical difficulties of implementing affirmative action. The most significant problem was to deal with the staff tendency to identify job possession with a particular gender or minority. The board of directors was highly pleased with the success of this program!

The next logical step with affirmative action was application to the member leadership structure, which was approved by the Delegate Assembly. This precipitated virulent debate, ambivalence, and conflict in the board of directors. Amidst this discussion, a small group of members convinced the board, despite our success with the staff program, that the member affirmative action program should be operated by an independent operator, reporting to a board committee. When such a motion passed barely, I immediately submitted my resignation on the principle of integrated functional integrity—that implementation of affirmative action was my responsibility, which should not be administratively divided with members.

Considerable furor erupted the following few days, which coincided with the Annual National Symposium and gave opportunity for much gossip and speculation. A week or two later, I was asked to rescind my resignation and given full authority for the program. I appointed my associate, Len Stern, as the affirmative action officer, and he did his usual outstanding job. We implemented the program, first with national units and then chapter membership structures—even in Montana where there was only one minority member. The disparities in chapter leadership led to the recognition of the need for special membership recruitment programs of minorities into NASW membership. Generally, chapter leadership demonstrated exceptional commitment to the program.

At the end of three years, NASW was the second national organization, following the precedent of the YWCA, to implement a national member affirmative action program. We had placed minorities in at least 30 percent of leadership positions, along with 70 percent female leaders. That implementation experience has provided valuable case material for my Social Policy and Management classes for these last 12 years at California State University, Long Beach.

A major management and administrative challenge was the community organization milieu. It is the external environment in which NASW must operate, nationally and locally, and tries to play a significant role in the acceptance and progression of the social work profession. Two examples may suffice.

Despite the golden years of the sixties with attempts to "conquer poverty" and ameliorate social problems, I found that the NASW had not made a power niche for itself on the national scene. The Department of Health, Education and Welfare (HEW), in its most halcyon days, used the NASW as a rubber stamp for its selected programs, but had not provided a quid pro quo that advanced the membership interests or helped build social work organization or power. Interorganization relationships were mostly the personal property of a few governmental and individual NASW leaders. They were built upon a personalized basis rather than furthering leadership negotiating positions on program and legislation that would build relationships and structures for continuous political clout.

Only the inside work of the late Corinne Wolfe and a few other faithful governmental professionals within HEW provided us with the information to make a few gains on social work issues over the years and slow the Nixon program to reduce federal social welfare programs.

A last situation, from another standpoint, illustrates the problems of external factors affecting NASW and its ambivalent position between bureaucracies and consumers. Interestingly, it is curiously relevant in view of the current changes in public welfare.

Shortly after arriving at NASW, I received a demand letter from George Wiley, national Welfare Rights Organization (WRO) Director for the $40,000 "promised" to that organization. As NASW chapter chair in Los Angeles, working with Johnnie Mae Tillman, one of the original WRO organizers, I was knowledgeable about the development of WRO. Our chapter had provided $4,000 to help them start their organization.

I checked all available records and found that the NASW leadership had, in ambivalent fashion, expressed favorable responses to WRO's earlier request but was vague as to when they might contribute. I answered Wiley with a request for a meeting with him and his leadership.

Joe Hoffer, our treasurer, and I met with Wiley, two of his staff, and about ten of his executive committee, who were all welfare mothers. Wiley said previous meetings had generated promises of support, while his staff took a harder line about our commitments. His WRO leadership made their case for why social workers had a greater obligation to them.

I responded regarding the importance of their mission and stated that I understood how they had experienced favorable impressions from the previous responses they had received. However, I explained NASW's financial position, pledged our cooperation nationally and locally on their campaigns, but said I was sorry that it was not possible to allocate any money.

Wiley was silent, but his staff became verbally abusive while the executive committee members began horror stories of mistreatment by "social workers," which meant the profession *owed them financial support*. My response was to recognize their feelings, apologize for any past actions, and propose a bargain.

I explained that if they would provide me identification of any of our members who were abusive, I would see that they were disciplined. We could not provide any funds, but I reiterated that we would obtain chapter cooperation throughout the country to support them with organization and legislative work and, I hoped, in joint efforts. Despite their disappointment, they finally seemed to find definitive responses satisfactory.

Later, on a national TV show with Wiley, I tackled him regarding his generalized attacks on "social workers." After that, surprisingly, we had fine working relationships. Later, I was fortunate to work with James Evans and Tim Sampson, social workers not involved in the previous incident, as top WRO staff, while following up on our cooperation pledge. Collaboration advanced after that. After George Wiley's untimely death, Jim Evans became a highly valued NASW staff member.

National Staff   On the afternoon of my beginning day, December 1, 1969, after briefing department heads, I held a staff meeting of all personnel. I recognized the tension under which staff had been operating and said that, with their help, any necessary changes would come only after a five-month analysis. I emphasized NASW's responsibility to its members and nonmembers, and to our clients and communities. Later, it was astounding to have so many employees thank me, some with tears in their eyes, saying this was their first meeting in two years. There was no question of the reservoir of hope and desire to be part of a successful enterprise.

Three months later, I was participating in the official personnel committee, where I watched my six social work board colleagues in an exercise of domination and well-intended "p/maternalism" with the three professional staff members who were on this traditionally joint committee. That combination encouraged inordinate requests from the staff representatives, principally for professional staff benefits with little attention to secretarial/clerical and maintenance positions. The additional benefits proposed were those that the beleaguered Association could not possibly meet and would be unfairly distributed.

After three such meetings in six months, and analyzing the personnel policies and benefit structure. I found significant disparities in the employee program. I proposed committee restructuring to make it a board personnel committee exclusively, without employee representation, and an altered benefit structure that would provide greater equity among employees. This was to be presented for full staff consideration with reasons for the changes.

It was fought in the beginning by the three staff representatives, but eventually, after much discussion, the staff collectively approved the proposal. Suggesting that they elect a permanent staff committee, I offered to meet with them whenever they felt the need, and did so.

After moving the national office to Washington, D.C., in December, 1972, it was not long before the staff committee provided the basis for union organization. There was a period of inordinate demands, staff ambivalence, and some high emotion in which my experience as a union organizer many years ago proved helpful. We eventually held an NLRB election and negotiated a contract. After that, except at contract renewal times, staff relations ran smoother, because most personnel problems could be settled by checking the contract for the responsibilities of management and employees.

I was never successful, though I tried, to bring the chapter staff into the contract for a unification of staff organization throughout the country. Staffing is the only component of NASW that is not part of the unified professional structure and organization. By design, the Delegate Assembly establishes policy, and the board of directors and national staff implements it, in concert with the chapter board's and staff, each within the limits of their jurisdiction. Only in the personnel area is there not unification, which creates inequities in staff policies, practices, recruitment, training, and so forth from chapter to chapter, as well as often building local staff territorial domains.

Membership Services   Each of the Association functions have the goal of providing services to the members. However, there are collective advantages to be obtained for members by virtue of their numbers—insurances, consumer purchase services, information, and effective response. The Association was under heavy criticism for its deficiencies with this function.

NASW had not entered the technological age—having, as it did, a hand-processed membership records system that was out of control. Because of the financial situation, it took three years to introduce a computer system into that area, and then an arduous period of perfecting it.

However, one historical service incident will be of interest to many readers—that of the creation of malpractice insurance protection for members. It was brought to my attention that many inquiries and requests were being received regarding insurance coverage for social work practitioners, especially in private practice.

Upon investigation, I was amazed at the interest and demand. Working with Richard Imbert, agency for the psychologists, we designed a program for social workers. We presented a proposal for the service to the existing Insurance Committee, which for many years had monitored the NASW program for retirement, disability, and life insurance. Surprisingly, they voted against the plan, first because "social workers don't get sued and there is no need for it," and a second time because it "served only a small private practice group."

Having been a party to the growth of private and part-time practice in California, and with the assent of the executive committee, I established malpractice protection as an administrative function and responsibility with negotiated controls for low-cost insurance. Rick Imbert took the economic chance. Now the American Professional Agency is the standard for social work practice insurance, an integral membership service.

Practice Advancement Jump-starting chapter programs was essential to demonstrate positive movement in the Association. So, as emergencies were met, we scraped together four $2,000 seed-money grants for continuing education projects for which chapters competed. The grants program was expanded rapidly as it demonstrated results. Another start-up service was the provision of national speakers to stimulate chapter programs. PIP (Professional Information Program) and SPICE (Special Projects in Continuing Education) recruited well-known social workers, such as Virginia Satir, to become part of a jointly operated package program for a chapter-planned event.

A necessary reorganization of the NASW Annual National Conference was undertaken through the conference committee. It became more efficient and effective with special staff training obtained from the National Education Association, creating staff who could properly service the operational requirements of educational leaders. A new sense of self-esteem seemed to surge through the Association.

Not enough praise can be given to Beatrice Saunders, NASW's veteran publications editor, who had insulated the publications department so that it was the most intact operative unit in the national office. *Social Work* was, and is, the flagship journal of the profession. We expanded it from quarterly to bimonthly as soon as possible, a tangible increase of direct service to individual members.

By 1972, our editorial committees agreed to needed specialty journals, *Health and Social Work, Education and Social Work*, and *Practice Digest. Social Work Abstracts*, operated under contract with the National Institute of Mental Health, was a key reference and research tool. We ended the contract with NIMH and created *Social Work Research and Abstracts* by adding research articles to the *Social Work Abstracts* journal, making a more valuable tool for researchers. The *Encyclopedia of Social Work* was the basic intellectual source for the profession, so we produced it as often as financially feasible.

Unfortunately, our clinically oriented committees did not see the necessity for an "Administration" journal. It was badly needed to rerecruit and serve social workers (supervisors to executives) who had resigned NASW membership feeling abused by the 1960s attacks on the "establishment" and the emphasis on "clinical" practice.

Although we tried to serve our social work manager members through annual National Conference programs, we could not meet their needs. This "clinical" dominance and the dogged commitment of Robert Maslyn eventually led to the separate organization, National Network for Social Work Managers. Bill Cohen, too, of Haworth Press had the vision to launch a successful *Administration in Social Work* journal that has been valuable to the field.

To help move away from the clinical/social action dichotomy standoff, in 1972 I commissioned Paul Kurzman of Hunter College to research and write a definitive article on "Third-Party Reimbursement" for *Social Work*. He clarified current status, cost, utilization, standards, training, opposition, and precedents and set forth an 11-point program for the profession. We papered all chapters and sister organizations with the article to bring some rationality to current arguments. It helped reduce the "separatist" advocacy and jump-started implementation efforts, particularly negotiations with insurance carriers and licensing drives by state chapter.

An early incident illustrates a typical problem of unifying the profession. I negotiated recognition of social workers for insurance payments to ACSW-qualified practitioners with Aetna Insurance in 1973. However, Aetna withdrew a few months later, as a result of objections and interference by the national president of the Clinical Social Workers' Society. As Aetna said, "until the profession gets itself together...."

Professional Standards   Another challenge for professional unification was to obtain community recognition of the profession through certification and licensing. Only eight states had some form of loose regulation of social work practice. In the absence of practice standards, a professional standard had been established in 1961 via the Academy of Certified Social Workers (ACSW), brainchild of Bert Beck, the innovative NASW associate director from 1955 until 1965.

It was another front-burner item for me to move ACSW qualification from experience-rating to an objective examination in order to put practice standards into effect. Negotiations, trial testing, and establishing national test sites inaugurated ACSW as the standard for professional practice throughout the country. It also served to stimulate licensing interest at the state level.

Not satisfied with the first testing company, we changed to Educational Testing Service at Princeton, New Jersey, which gave us an advantage in technical test construction. However, the ACSW tests soon revealed two disparate problems in testing social workers: (1) a bimodal result—a few high, but mostly lower results on objective examination of ethnic minority social workers; and (2) obvious disparity of test performance among the graduates of different schools of social work.

Heated internal debates ensued, with honest differences and biases showing and hidden. The Association spent at least a million dollars over several years on test analysis, reconstruction, and alteration, but the pattern held. It seemed apparent to me that deficiencies in the general education system available to minorities accounted for most of the differences, but committee leadership continued the search in test construction. Schools of social work obviously had different qualities of education.

To partially correct those ethnic minority inequities, adjustments were made in scoring qualification levels, while research continued. Simultaneously, score results and ranges of each ACSW applicant were transmitted to his or her alma mater in order for the school to evaluate its graduate's performance. However, NASW Board leadership was never willing to investigate causation in curricula or to apply standard setting to the schools.

Simultaneously, early work was concentrated on developing the *Standards for Social Work Manpower* (now the politically correct "Labor Force") with the dedicated leadership of Fr. Bernard Coughlin, Dean, St. Louis University School of Social Service. The Committee defined six levels of differential practice. They were promulgated to combat the confusion regarding preprofesional, professional, and advanced practice designations. Those definitions were utilized to design a three-level model statute for licensing and certification. A national licensing campaign was promoted, combined with special visits to chapters for planning licensing efforts with state legislatures.

The ACSW and Manpower documents, with program guides, launched the combined national/chapter campaigns for standards and licensing, which in 13 years obtained regulation of social work practice in most of the states. Those efforts advanced insurance coverage and also helped validate the creation of other standard-setting documents on major practice areas of the profession.

Community Service   Variously titled "social policy," "planning," "social action," "legislative action," "community organization," and the like, this Association function was essentially the transfer of professional social work knowledge into policy and programs to benefit the community and advance social services.

However, it was a whirlpool of contending views and vested interests fed by external predators and internal competitors, and mostly limited to legislative concerns. Utilizing policies adopted by the Delegate Assemblies over the years, we tried to establish unifying and advanced positions on issues via leadership commissions and task forces. We then moved into concerted action via chapter and coalition efforts.

To obtain policy impact, we first created the Educational Legislative Action Network (ELAN—borrowed from "elan vital") to build a national action network based on local units. Members were recruited directly and through chapters in congressional districts to work with members of Congress as combined consultants and advocates. That structure was serviced by our exceptional organizer and lobbyist, Glenn Allison, and an ELAN newsletter. Later, Glenn was also responsible for the Social Service Coalition, which resulted in Title XX of the Social Security Act.

The ELAN experience overcame general membership reticence, and some vocal opposition, to aggressive legislative action by the profession. It also educated membership to the necessity to be active participants in the political process. It led to the acceptance of Political Action for Candidate Election (PACE), conceived and promoted in the 1974 Delegate Assembly by Charles Knox, then an aide to Congressman Augustus Hawkins of Los Angeles.

It is often hard to remember the elementary community organization technique to educate first, then call for action, in the heat of desire for results. But I purposely held PACE's activation in abeyance until 1976 to allow time for the ELAN program to fully educate the membership. PACE then became opportune for obtaining social work influence, beginning with the Carter/Mondale presidential election.

In Puerto Rico for the International Federation of Social Workers meetings, immediate Past-President Maryann Mahaffey, President Arthur Katz, and I mapped out the PACE campaign to mobilize the social work profession. NASW was the first endorser, worker organizer, and benefactor from that successful presidential campaign.

As the balanced-program approach, the financial recovery, and the structural change to 55 state chapters began to take hold, the legislative program became a centerpiece activity with significant membership support. It increasingly demonstrated the need for additional research and policy development in each of the functions at the national level. Despite several years of negotiation with foundations, the National Institute of Mental Health and other governmental agencies for financing, I was unsuccessful. We were able to initiate a library and information service, but

252 THE REFLECTIONS: DOMAINS AND THEMES

it took Bob Stewart, in his presidency years later, to found the National Research Center.

"Recollections" lead to rejuvenation, and to regrets. They fan the flames of self-esteem and the embers of failures, while conjuring what might or should have been. The crises of NASW taught many lessons regarding the organization of the professional social work community.

For the first four years, the tasks of organization were driven by the financial, programmatic, and leadership crises that demanded immediate attention, while at the same time I was trying to initiate beginnings of organizational activities that would produce longer-range results.

This peek into the past has had to limit details regarding participants and process in the exciting mission of organizing the social work profession from 1970 to 1974. Not included are the up-and-down relationships with our sister organizations—the Council on Social Work Education, the individual schools of social work, the National Social Work Assembly, and the National and International Conferences of Social Work. Necessarily absent are the teamwork stories of health, economic, and civil rights coalitions; the legislative struggles with the U.S. Congress and state legislatures; international organizational efforts; and many other failures and accomplishments. Nor are noted the nine more challenging years that established a critical mass base in the United States of some 100,000 professional social workers.

The practical lessons of the first four years of my NASW experience solidified my opinions—ones related to community organization theory, to principles, to method and techniques, and, specifically to the organization of professional social workers.

My work with the professional social work community validated for me that community organization is an "area of practice to which various organizations and individuals apply their own sets of values, purposes, authority, knowledge, method, and techniques to the extent of their own individual and collective skills." We in social work apply our own particular set and process to community organization.

As an NASW staff member, I experienced increased psychological comfort from application of what was a constant problem-solving process, somewhat different from social agency responsibilities. Every day involved demands for solutions to personnel, program, financing, and leadership issues in which I felt the understanding of the "process" was a saving feature. What was the problem and in what stage was it? Was the true problem identifiable? Was a policy formulation needed? What implementation would be correct, and how should it be accomplished?

The endemic operating problem was the conflict created by the clash between social work principles and the individualistic power principles of the general society that infected organizational deliberations and decisions. Chamelion-like, opportunism was colored as "realistic" and "necessary," but fortunately, given enough time for debate among staff and leadership, professionalism usually would prevail.

Second is the "seeing the whole picture" problem. Although this is the goal and is typical of community organization challenges in most organizations, it has special features in a professional membership organization. Each member, and more so for leaders, begins with a baseline of values and knowledge that provides technical expertise and conditions his or her approach to problems and issues. In a professional organization, that baseline establishes a certificated credibility for each person.

However, the scope of the social work profession, encompassing as it does work in all the societal institutions (family, health, religion, education, etc.) is complicated enough. Add to that the fragmentation by activity areas such as fields of practice, practice techniques, and multiple operational sites and jurisdictions. Then, also consider the multiplicity of agency structures and variable policies in which they work. As a result, each individual comes to Association activity with the strength of his or her own professional conditioning, which must become part of a group process in work and decision making. The result is the necessity for continual educational experience, hopefully from local unit to state chapter to national units.

The values, or principles, that worked for me were those I incorporated in writing the *International Code of Ethics for Professional Social Workers*.[4] In brief, they included two principles on the unique value of every human and the right of self-fulfillment; one on the goal for each society to provide maximum benefits to its members; and two others on the professional responsibility to devote disciplined knowledge and skill to resolution of personal-societal conflicts and the primary obligation of service over self-interest.

Of all the techniques required, the three key tasks were (1) constant focus on goals and their key objectives in a melange of cross-cutting demands and issues, (2) continual fact-finding and research for analyzing problems, and (3) futures-thinking to counter the driving force to immediate issues.

Appropriate history and research of social work organization and policies proved their worth again and again in dealing with partialized observations or biases. This was noted previously with the use of the historical role of NASW, the balanced program and priorities policies, and organized agendae.

What seemed to work best was engaging the necessary participants (board and chapter leadership, personnel, allied organization leaders) in problem/issue identification and analysis. That provided testing of viewpoints and the introduction of data or information, along with some tentative "what if" formulations. This inherently was a joint educational process among member and staff leadership, some of whom usually had strong views and often used "power" tactics to get their way if they could. But strong views evoked strong reactions among strong leadership, which usually brought a compromise. It may have represented a balance of views, but it was not always the most operable solution.

Fortunately, with a ready resource of technical experts on a variety of subjects in NASW membership, it was often possible to start at the policy formulation stage in dealing with a subject or issue. In that sense, a stage of education, of deliberation and testing, was bypassed, so that when it reached the decision-making group (members, boards, or delegate assemblies) there was often a reworking process that had to take place.

Much could be said regarding the political and cultural factors that play such an intense role in a professional organization. However, there must be an end to each task. This ending must recognize the egocentric nature of a "recollections" effort. Paramount in my memory is the fact that all of these retrospections were possible only because of the efforts and accomplishments of dedicated NASW staff, officers, and membership.

For my memories, grateful thanks goes to each and every one of them.

ENDNOTES

1. *Summary of Proceedings 1969 Delegate Assembly*, NASW, Atlantic City, April 20–24, 1969, pp. 17–18.

2. American Association of Psychiatric Social Workers, American Association of Social Workers, Association for the Study of Community Organization, and the National Association of Social Workers.

3. Chauncey A. Alexander, "The Psychiatric Social Worker in the Community: Effective Programming and Planning," *Journal of Psychiatric Social Work*, XXII, no. 2 (January 1953): 91–95; "The Concept of Representativeness in Community Organization," *Social Work* 1, no. 1 (January 1956):48–52; "Fundraising As Social Community Organization Work," *Social Work Papers* 6 (December 1958):43–53; and five additional related articles prior to 1969.

4. International Code of Ethics for the Professional Social Worker, adopted by the International Federation of Social Workers General Meeting, San Juan, Puerto Rico, July 10, 1976.

BIBLIOGRAPHY

Alexander, Chauncey A. 1982. "An Overview of Administration, Policy and Planning as Specialization in Social Welfare Practice." *Administration in Social Work* 6, no. 2/3, pp. 7–18.

Kurzman, Paul A. 1973. "Third-Party Reimbursement." *Social Work* 18, no. 6 (November):11–23.

McMillen, Wayne. 1945. *Community Organization for Social Welfare*. Chicago: The University of Chicago Press, p. 25.

Pray, Kenneth L. M. 1949. "When Is Community Organization Social Work Practice?" *Social Work in a Revolutionary Age*. Philadelphia: University of Pennsylvania Press, pp. 274–287. Delivered at the National Conference of Social Work, April 1947.

ACADEMIC PROGRAMS AND PROFESSIONAL TRAINING

Development of a Specialized Curriculum in Community Organization

Meyer Schwartz

By way of explaining how I found myself as a social worker with special interest in the community and community organization, it is necessary to start with a short personal history. I believe this is relevant to the development of my professional career.

My father came from Poland, my mother from the Ukraine. I had two siblings, an older brother and a younger sister. Born in 1913 into a home where the language was Yiddish, I was the only one in the family who completed high school, who graduated from college as well as graduate school. Contrary to the norm in Jewish immigrant families, my family did not encourage me or my siblings to seek higher education. My home was devoid of books. Originally, I had no desire to attend college, but I was unsuccessful in finding employment in the midst of the depression. In 1931, I was accepted for enrollment in the College of the City of New York (CCNY). My family resided in a low-income area in the South Bronx and remained in that community during their entire life. I believe that my outlook on life, my identification with the poor, was a direct result of my home and community environment.

As a youngster I suffered a bout of appendicitis. I was treated at Lincoln Hospital, where I was not only cured, but was also "deloused." After recovery, I was sent to a summer camp for two weeks, which was my first experience with a social welfare agency. I was healed and sent away to recuperate, which at the time was all free of charge.

While attending CCNY I worked the night shift in a factory for $16 per week. This job lasted only a few months—until the union called a strike, and the factory moved from New York to New Jersey. This was my first lesson about unions, and the response of business to a strike.

After I graduated from CCNY with a major in sociology, I decided to leave home, but in order to survive I had to "go on relief." Roosevelt and Hopkins literally saved my life. Immediately, I informed the caseworker that I wanted to work for the WPA (Works Progress Administration). At that time, "caseworkers" in both public and private social agencies were truly "all-purpose" workers. After evaluating a situation, the caseworker not only was able to counsel the client, but was in a position to issue financial assistance, hand out vouchers for clothing and furniture, make arrangements for medical services, and the like. In other words, the caseworker performed multiple tasks and was a "generalist."

In 1936, the caseworker arranged for my assignment to a WPA project called the "Youth Service Bureau," a program servicing detached youth groups in poverty neighborhoods. Actually, we served street gangs. I was sent to the South Bronx, where I was assigned to a youth group that was sponsoring dances in a renovated neighborhood loft. The program was successful and earned the members quite a bit of money. My professional capacity was to attend these dances and supervise. (This group had also rented space in a tenement cellar, but members refused my visits to that locale.) The group was composed of adolescents—high school graduates or drop-outs—who had organized a lucrative business for themselves by charging an entrance fee of approximately 25 cents to participate at the dances.

Everything went well until a gang of about 15 youths from another neighborhood arrived to shake down my group for money. My efforts at intervention resulted in my being beaten up by one of the intruders. They threatened to return, and did so a number of times, continuing to threaten us. But eventually, police intervention succeeded in driving this gang from our "turf."

This experience from 1936 to 1939, working for the Youth Service Bureau, awakened my desire to learn more how to cope, how to deal with, how to negotiate with groups and gangs of all types. While on this project, I learned how to develop programs that were both attractive and useful for this type of population. One of the most successful programs—and well attended by these adolescent boys and girls—was a film and lecture on sexuality and the prevention of venereal diseases. This program was arranged with the cooperation of the local public health clinic. In retrospect, I can't say whether the audience actually carried out the recommendations of this lecture.

The youth project was disbanded in 1939, which left me in a quandary. How I was to earn a living in the future? While working on this project, I met a number of social workers and became friends with Norman Lourie, who was writing his thesis for the New York School of Social work. At his suggestion that I contribute a chapter about my experience with street gangs, I gladly participated. Norman Lourie later held a number of prestigious positions, as director of Hawthorne Cedar Knolls, one of the earliest therapeutic schools for emotionally disturbed youths, and later as commissioner of public welfare in Pennsylvania.

At the recommendation of Norman Lourie, I was hired as a counselor at the Hebrew Orphan Asylum by the executive director, Maurice Bernstein. I am extremely grateful to Maurice, who, without questions, gave me a job that I sorely needed. He has become a lifelong friend. He took a chance and became my mentor during this period of change—the closing of the Hebrew Orphan Asylum, which was accomplished by placing all remaining children into foster homes.

Maurice encouraged me to apply to a graduate school of social work; this created difficulty, as I had been paid only a small salary plus room and board and had no funds. I cobbled together money saved from a summer job as a waiter and busboy in various hotels in the Catskills, loans from Maurice and friends, as well as a loan from CCNY. This enabled me to attend Western Reserve University School of Applied Social Sciences, where I had been accepted as a student. I chose Western Reserve because of the excellent reputation of its Group Work Department and its department head, Grace Coyle.

In 1941, I enrolled as a group work student. My field work placement was in a settlement house in an Italian Catholic neighborhood. Despite my being Jewish, I had no difficulty during this first-year field experience. Both having lived in a poor New York neighborhood with a mixed ethnic population and my experience with street gangs had prepared me well for my first professional experience.

After graduation, I returned to New York City and accepted employment as director of activities in a local settlement house. Then I took a position at the Irene Kaufman Settlement House, a Jewish-sponsored multipurpose agency located in the Hill District of Pittsburgh. This was a rapidly changing neighborhood, from predominantly Jewish to African American. At that time, the board of directors was contemplating a change: to turn the agency over to the black community. This proposed change interested me very much, and my experience with the People's Forum, the neighborhood council composed of Jewish residents remaining in the Hill District, as well as with leaders of the newly established African American community, including local politicians and clergy, sparked my interest in community organization. Our task was to consider unified approaches to community problems, and to smooth relationships between two disparate population groups.

I held a variety of positions at the Irene Kaufman Settlement House, starting as director of activities, and rising to acting director, but found most rewarding my activities involving the resolution of community problems. I followed my major interest, which consisted of developing relationships with various groups in the African American community, with the goal of integrating this agency and eventually turning over the building and all the programs to them. This process was slow and painful. (I wrote my master's dissertation for Western Reserve based on my experience with the proposed change process within the settlement house and the local community.) I received my master's degree in 1946 after acceptance of this thesis, which was used for teaching purposes for a period of ten years by Western Reserve University.

Although the board of directors was moving slowly in the direction of this change, long-entrenched staff, especially in the physical education department, was adamantly opposed to the proposal. This department drew the largest number of members and thus was very influential in delaying change from Jewish to black membership. Integration proceeded slowly by age groups, from nursery school to older members, with the cooperation and careful intervention of the local elementary school and community groups.

I was much involved with influential persons and groups in this growing African American community. I met with the local black newspaper editor, clergy, school personnel, and local politicians. I arranged public forums and made speeches; I developed committees of the board of directors to further the goal of disinvesting the Jewish community from this large and highly visible social agency located in a rapidly changing neighborhood. I supervised a student who staffed the People's Forum.

At about that time I found an article by Wilbur I. Newstetter, dean of the Graduate School of Social Work, describing community work, which he called "intergroup work." I realized that, in fact, I was participating in "community work." This had not been my actual job description, and it was an exciting discovery for me.

When I advised the board of directors that I believed the time had come to finally turn over the settlement house to the African American community, and that the new executive director should be an African American, the board was not ready to accept my assessment of the situation. I therefore rejected the offer of appointment as executive director.

Two years later, the Irene Kaufman Settlement House was turned over to the African American community.

I accepted employment as administrative assistant at the Jewish Federation, the Jewish equivalent of the United Way or the Community Chest. This agency sponsored and/or partially funded a variety of Jewish agencies, from the Jewish hospital to the Family and Children Service, to educational services, to group and recreational agencies, refugee integration, services for the aged, and so forth. This position would add significantly to my experience in the field of community organization, in part because a major role had just been added to the Federation: to raise funds for the newly established State of Israel.

My position consisted of supervising and participating in studies of various problems faced by the community, such as Jewish education and population studies, and the agencies serving the community, for example, the hospital and the Home for the Aged. The Federation not only raised funds for the various affiliated agencies, but sought to improve services to meet current needs. The actual studies were performed by both professional staff and consultants hired for specific tasks. My responsibility was to brief and fully prepare the chairperson of each specific committee of the board of directors regarding progress and recommendations for action, based on our work. The chairperson needed a full understanding of the problems in order to implement programs based on the results of studies. As the professional responsible for a number of board committees, I rarely spoke at meetings, and answered questions only when the chair requested that I do so. At that time, this was the protocol for the person staffing board committees.

I realized that I was servicing as a "community work professional," as outlined by Newstetter, without the formal training that might have enabled me to work more effectively and with less "trial and error." Following the CO model suggested by Newstetter, I supervised a social work student whose "intergroup work" assignment was to improve the community's approaches to recently arrived refugees, most of them Holocaust survivors, and to assist in determining which agencies might best effect their integration into the American Jewish community.

While at the Jewish Federation, I published and presented a number of papers dealing with Community Organization including "Our Voluntary Committee Life," "Urban Renewal and Social Work," "Groupwork and Community Organization," and others. During this period I also started teaching on a part-time basis at the Graduate School of Social Work, University of Pittsburgh.

Eventually this led to my appointment in 1957 to the full-time faculty as associate professor, with the goal of developing a formal curriculum of Community Organization. It was anticipated that CO would become another specialization in the field of social work, which had always been a major interest of Dean Newstetter. Until this period, Community Organization, then called "intergroup work" at Pitt, was not considered a major specialization, such as group work or casework. However, at least one course in "intergroup work" had been required of all social work students. Only a few second-year fieldwork placements in CO had been available. These students, interning in community work agencies, were required to take additional courses in "intergroup work." Prior to the initiation of the two-year sequence in CO, all students had a first-year placement in either casework or group work. Because of the dearth of field placements and a probable lack of student interest, only a handful of students per year graduated with a major in "intergroup work" (or CO). Moreover, the employment prospects of graduates with a major in CO were uncertain; I speculate that this may have contributed to the lack of emphasis in the field.

There was no opposition to the development of a two-year curriculum in Community Organization at the School of Social Work in Pittsburgh. As noted above, for many years all student's had been required to take at least one course in "intergroup work" taught by the dean and other faculty. I preferred to call it Community Organization or community work.

My prior work experience caused me to realize that CO is a "real specialization"; that professional staff needs not only a longer and more intensive period of study in theory, but also longer and more varied field experiences before gradation and entry into the job market. This is how the four-semester specialization was spawned.

Beginning in 1947, there was significant progress in exploring professional concepts to guide professional social work practice in the field of CO. Papers by Pray, Newstetter, Barry, Sieder, and Carter and books by Green, Murphy, and Dunham opened the possibility of arriving at a "conceptual framework" for social work practice in the field of community work. An essential ingredient for professional education was at hand in the form of concepts from the social sciences. The two-year program was initiated at Pitt in the fall of 1958.

While there was no expressed opposition to a new two-year CO concentration within the school at Pittsburgh (Wilbur Newstetter favored the program and as a "strong dean" was able to influence the faculty in that direction), there was considerable resistance and disfavor in the profession at large. For this reason, I had to present a substantial rationale for the program. I have been able to uncover unpublished papers from the time that show the approach I took and arguments I used to gain support in the profession for a two-year concentration. Let me draw from a paper I delivered at the Council on Social Work Education annual program meeting in 1959 to illustrate.

First of all, I had to offer clear reasons for establishing this kind of program at that time:

- There is a need and a demand for more trained community workers.
- Our school, as well as other schools, has been turning out a very small number of trained community professionals.
- We think that a more intensive curriculum will attract more students to enter the field, particularly if they know that they do not have to take casework or group work before they can be eligible for community work. We reasoned, on this score, that with intensive training in community work they would be qualified to take beginning positions in community work and would be more readily employed by the community work field because they had intensive training—that is, the employing agencies would not insist to these graduates that first they had to be employed in a casework or group work agency. In short, agencies would have more confidence in them.
- Further, our previous curriculum for community work, which comprised two courses concentrating on the social intergroup work process and one year of field placement in a community work agency, simply did not allow the student enough time to acquire the range of knowledge, understanding, and skill for community work, neither in the practice of social intergroup work [community organization] nor in the practice of administration, promotion, and research.
- In addition, our previous curriculum for community work had another defect—namely, the relatively short time the student had in this concentration, the small number of students (not more than two or three at one time), and the consequent limited variety of field placement. All combined to place a damper on creative development of theory and practice in community work. The previous way of training did not give us, in the school in Pittsburgh, the opportunity to develop further theoretical formulations for the field of community work, based, as it was, on the limitation referred to.

In addition, I had to show that this was a professional role, equivalent in professionalism to the established social work areas of casework and group work.

A *graduate* school of social work seeks to turn out professional practitioners who are objective, impartial, and motivated by a service ideal. This service ideal embodies the essential values of social work. The school aims to produce professional practitioners who have such characteristics as, for example:

- They are able to initiate and sustain a professional relationship while dealing with the intimate facts of individual and community living.
- They are able to refrain from discriminating on a personal basis and to keep personal interests subordinated to clients and community needs.
- They are able to continue self-education throughout their professional career in order to keep pace with new social work knowledge, while at the

same time making maximum time available for the function of helping people in the here and now.

- They are able to maintain a self-critical attitude and be disciplined in the scientific appraisal of evidence, while at the same time they are able to be decisive (in the face of uncertainty) and not postpone decisions beyond what the situation requires, even when the scientific evidence is inadequate.

- They are able to have and hold detailed knowledge of a specialization, while at the same time being well-rounded and broadly educated. These characteristics of the professional social worker, gained in *professional* education, culminates in a "professional self-image." These characteristics become part of the professional self. In short, attitudinal learning is as important as theory, relevant knowledge, understanding, and technical competence in the acquisition of a professional education.

It was important to indicate that these are knowledge areas relevant to community organization, and to spell these out. Students, I stated, needed to:

- Understand the individual and community.
- Understand social work organizations and problems.
- Understand the nature of research in social work and have beginning skills in it.
- Understand the fundamentals of social work methodology—the generic concepts in casework, group work and community work.
- Understand study-diagnosis and plan of action process and have skill in its uses.
- Understand and have skill in educational/promotional methods.

While recognizing knowledge lapses in CO, I contended that it was important to move forward:

True enough, there is no unified theory at hand as yet in the social sciences in the form of a proven comprehensive scheme that would explain the cause and effect relationship in the whole of society. What we do have in the social sciences is a movement toward hypothesis and social theory, which seek to or do explain relatively limited segments of social life. The progress made in conceptual thinking in the field, in particular in drawing upon relevant "sensitizing" concepts from the social sciences, allows us to proceed with a fair degree of confidence in proposing a further development of our curriculum. We can draw on concepts as embodied in the terms social status, role, social stratification, and the so-called "power structure" and manifest and latent functions of organizations.

It is our conviction that unless we try to expand and intensify our training for community work to meet the need and demand, we will not gain the momentum to develop our theory, and consequently to practice. If I do not misread the history of the development of casework and group work, I think it was the need and demand from the field for better trained workers that lead to better theory building [and] training....

Beyond substantive knowledge, I wanted to emphasize that the student in his training, has to acquire pertinent skills and attitudes relevant to the work. This I addressed as follows (with apologies for the gender-slanted language of the time):

- He needs to be able to carry himself with ease in public, in an appropriate fashion in diction, dress, and manners *while at the same time* expressing his individuality.

- He needs to be able to view the participants with whom he works as partners with himself in a common enterprise serving a community, and see himself as enabling his partners to serve their community via his particular expert competence. He views himself as sharing with them and receiving from them knowledge, understanding and skill and responsibility, *while at the same time* exercising a professional vision of the What, When, Where, Why, and How community work should be performed.

- He needs to be particularly sensitive to the occupational and social outlook of business (large and small), labor, farmer, and professional participants in community work; that is, he needs knowledge and understanding of their changing status and role in the social structure, *while at the same time* not being a captive of any of the outlooks of these social groups.

- He needs to be able to view the services and progress of a community work agency, not as ends in themselves, but as part and parcel of larger entities (communities) *while at the same time* visualizing people's needs as those of unique individuals, not amorphous masses, and not necessarily restricted to the "disadvantaged," and always endeavoring to perfect the services fo this community work agency.

- He needs to be able to exercise, in executive fashion, appropriate authority and control vested in his position *while at the same time* using such authority and control in a responsible, sanctioned manner, without coercion and being beholden to any one social group.

- He needs to be able to bring to his community a philosophy grounded in a basic commitment and support of a democratic way of life, to be able to expound and uphold his particular view of "people, places, and things," in a democracy, *while at the same time* holding to a respect for different viewpoints as to the best possible relationship of "people, places, and things" in a democracy.

I pointed to the challenge in trying to integrate this multifaceted and complex set of skills:

At first blush, all of the above, which we think a community worker needs to *be*, strikes one as contradictory. And indeed it is in a fashion, but Robert Merton, writing on the sociology of medical education, noted that professional work educators can be conceived as facing the task of enabling students to learn how to *blend* compatible or potentially incompatible norms into a fundamentally consistent whole. Indeed, the process of learning to be a social worker can be conceived as largely learning to blend seeming or actual incompatibilities into consistent and stable patterns of professional behavior!

When that is done, we have a mature professional community worker—never completely realized, but always striven for—in class, in field instruction, in practice.

I also emphasized the broad professional and intellectual dimensions of the work as contrasted with the task-specific technical aspects of the role of the community worker:

> The pressure from the field is to introduce skills, e.g., for example preparing minutes, agendas, notices, promotional devices, reports, and so forth. We do include these skill areas, but only in light of their use as illustrative of basic concepts. For example, if I am presenting in a practice course the uses of the "agenda" in community work, I bring to the forefront the relationship of the worker to the ubiquitous chair, the enabling help of the worker to the chair, and the variations that follow in agenda construction dependent upon analysis of the chair's role, the nature of the subject matter under consideration, and the developmental stage of the problem under discussion by a community group, and the nature of the community group. From these considerations, the agenda then becomes not a superficial mechanical gimmick, but rather an integral part of helping a community group move toward constructive change.

The dean and faculty were receptive to the two-year curriculum. Students were asked to take the same basic core courses required of all social work students. From the first day they were enrolled in a two-year CO specialization; there were field placements as well as a sequence of four semesters of theoretical practice courses.

In 1958, I discovered a book by Ronald Lippitt, Jeanne Watson, and Bruce Westley, entitled *The Dynamics of Planned Change*, which I found relevant to the practice of community work. I adapted the authors' ideas and prepared a curriculum outline entitled "Study-Diagnosis–Plan of Action, Outline for Community Work Practice." It appeared to me that Lippit's study characterized the CO worker as an "agent of change," helping an organization to alter its way of working, when engaged with other organizations. My summary of the essence of the book became a 13-page outline, which was distributed to all CO students. I wrote to Ronald Lippit with a copy of this summary to advise him how I was using this material in my courses in community organization. His response was very favorable, as he approved not only of the summary outline, but how I was applying his material in the field.

All students used the 13-page outline in their field placement for many years. It made a fundamental change in the nature of the community organization curriculum. Following is a summary of the course work I planned for the four semesters for students entering the specialization.

The first course (year one) dealt with the concept of community and the nature of community problems. The problem-solving concept of study-diagnosis-plan of action was described, with reference to the involvement of citizens and the appropriate professional role of the worker. The dynamics of planned change as presented by Ronald Lippit and his associates were examined and applied to a variety of problem situations. Relevant social science concepts were studied, including social status, social stratification, power structure, and the manifest and latent functions of organizations. There was also coverage of methods of community analysis, including community surveys, priority studies, need assessment, resource identification, and the setting of standards.

The second course (year one) focused on community participation and the distinctive norms of the profession of social work regarding the worker's relationships with community groups. The intergroup process was scrutinized from the standpoint of the role of representatives of groups in a problem-solving multigroup entity; the relationship of representatives to their own groups; and the balance between seeking substantive objectives determined by the intergroup and maintaining harmonious relations among groups within the community. The enabling role and function of the worker received special emphasis.

The third course (year two) attended to administrative methods and techniques associated with community work. Areas covered included the maintenance of standards and of program and financial accountability; financing, budgeting, and allocations; the relationship of financing to social planning; and appropriate community participation in administrative processes. Field experiences and records were drawn upon extensively, and the role of the worker in exercising administrative functions was highlighted.

The fourth course (year two) gave emphasis to educational and promotional processes. The relationship of public relations and propaganda to educational and promotional activities in community work was examined in light of social work values. Students examined public attitudes toward social welfare and the formal and informal network of communications in the community. Topics included institutes, workshops, conferences, forums, and conventions, as well as the various forms of mass media, including press, television, and radio. Written communication also was covered, including letters, memos, reports, minutes, and notices. Effort was made to teach specific skills and delineate professional roles in their application.

The courses were updated yearly to meet the needs of the students and the agencies and included such administrative issues as budgeting, staffing, policy, records, personnel policies, emerging issues, and problems in specific local communities. The effects of newly passed legislation were included: course content was updated from year to year to reflect these changes.

Pressure from the field to introduce the teaching of specific skills—such as preparing an agenda, writing minutes, preparing notices, writing reports, preparing publicity releases, budgeting, and the like—was also addressed during the practice courses. Examples of committee work and the worker's relationship to the chair and to boards of directors were used to illustrate some of the tools utilized by community workers to help community groups move toward constructive change.

I felt confident that there would be no difficulty in finding appropriate field work placements for the four-semester sequence. That proved to be true. In retrospect, our students were welcomed by a variety of agencies. Currently I can't recall all the names of the agencies involved in the student placements, but various categories—social planning agencies, community chests, agencies in low-income areas, neighborhood councils, fund-raising agencies, urban renewal programs, and housing programs—were represented. Also included were neighborhoods where a community worker might be helpful in organizing the residents to address pressing community problems. Additional type of agencies were planning commissions, as well as organizations serving new immigrants and various ethnic groups. Pitt students could also be found in local governmental or quasigovernmental agencies. To sum up, a wide variety of experiences allowed our students to practice with complex community problems, to interact with diverse population groups, and to gain professional competence by applying theories and principles learned in the classroom.

At the start of the two-year program, all students were male; no women applied, and I made no effort to recruit them. Women did not appear to be attracted to CO and remained in more traditional social work roles. In 1958 and 1959, the new program was small; all applicants to this department who had been accepted to the School of Social Work were admitted to the CO sequence. If memory serves, there were six or eight students in each class during the first two years. And as our reputation spread, and our graduates found excellent positions, the program expanded rapidly, and more students were accommodated. In 1960, Jack Rothman joined the faculty to assist with teaching and the counseling of the enlarged student body.

A few students who requested the CO program had fathers who held positions in community chests. I suppose they expected to secure equally well-paid and prestigious positions upon graduation.

Each agency assigned a field supervisor of its choice. Incidentally, some community work students were not identified as "social workers" by agency personnel; I wonder if there was a built-in bias, both in more deprived neighborhoods and in planning and fund-raising agencies.

Immediately upon the initiation of the two-year program, I started promoting this new curriculum by speaking at the local chapter and national meetings of the National Association of Social Workers (NASW),

United Community Funds and Councils of America, and the Council on Social Work Education (CSWE), where I presented the full two-year curriculum at the annual program meeting in January 1959. I delivered papers at the National Conference of Social Work, the Council of Jewish Federations and Welfare Funds, the Department of Public Welfare, and in other venues.

During the first three years at Pitt, I participated in endless discussions and programs regarding the need to treat Community Organization as a distinct specialization. Why was all this promotion necessary? I believed that CO deserved accreditation as a social work specialty. The Council on Social Work Education held a favorable position, but social work clinicians—especially in the casework field—were less inclined to recognize community work as a legitimate social work discipline. I served as a consultant to four schools of social work. To summarize, I spoke and/or presented papers on 33 separate occasions; 14 of those contacts were with the CSWE.

On the whole, this new curriculum was well received, though I vividly recall an incident at a curriculum committee meeting of the Council on Social Work Education. It was suggested by one of the participants, a caseworker, that CO Students were not sufficiently mature to tackle complex community problems. I responded that there appeared to be no difference in the maturity of CO students and those in casework—who were required to address serious family problems of clients who were older, more mature, and had a multitude of experiences that young casework students might not understand or appreciate. I believe that settled this criticism.

During this period, I was appointed to a number of agency boards and served on many committees—on the national committee on curriculum development of the CSWE, and committees of the NASW regarding community organization. I publicized CO up and down the country and circulated our curriculum material to every school of social work that requested it. I published a few articles in a variety of journals. I believe that my efforts may have been influential in the certification of the two-year CO curriculum by the CSWE.

A few words about some of our students: One day the chair of a neighborhood council telephoned in some distress; it had been noted that one of my students was carrying a gun. Of course, I was alarmed as well. I requested that this young man see me in my office, and inquired if the report was accurate. Yes, he admitted that he carried a weapon. His explanation: He had testified against someone in his hometown, not far from Pittsburgh. Because he was fearful that some friends of this person would come "after him," he was carrying the gun for his protection. This student was advised that carrying a gun to his assignment was unacceptable. He was removed from his field placement, and allowed to take a one-on-one tutorial with me to fulfill his requirement for graduation.

Another instance comes to mind: A board member complained to the executive director of a prestigious agency that a student had attended a board committee meeting smoking a cigar. He considered this inappropriate behavior on the student's part (it was acceptable for committee members, all successful businessmen, to light up cigars). I reviewed this with my student and suggested that he smoke cigars on his own time.

For young persons to act in a professional manner requires not only expertise and specific knowledge, but also the knowledge of how to dress appropriately. I believe this may have been more important 40 years ago. Nonetheless, when one student arrived in class and at the placement agency in dirty, disreputable clothing, I spent an hour or so lecturing the class on proper dress, appearance, and demeanor. At the end of the period, I suggested that "If you can't be the smartest, at least be the best dressed." I can't recall how often some of my ex-students reminded me of that statement.

To illustrate an example of what it means to be a "professional," and to enliven a class, I sometimes played a brief recording from *Brecht on Brecht*, entitled "The Old Hat." (This episode, a play within a play, describes how an actor—in preparing for a part—goes into extensive and excruciating deliberation with himself just to decide what type of hat to wear to best portray a particular character.) Basically, it is not relevant to the profession of social work, but it is illustrative of "professionalism" in general, how thoughtful, studious, and totally prepared a professional in any discipline should be.

I had a few outstanding students. One wrote a complex research paper on economics and economic theory. Since I was not then, and am not now, expert in this field, I forwarded his report to the chair of the Economics Department, requesting that he critique the paper and advise me. To my dismay he returned it, unread, with a note that, as a faculty member in the School of Social Work, I had no business permitting students to study and write on economic theory. My first experience in the turf battles at institutions of higher learning. I graded the paper "A." This young man became a professor and subsequently dean at a prestigious school of social work.

I gave individual tutorials to a few of the more outstanding students during their two years. This did not appear to cause resentment by other students, though in retrospect I cannot be certain.

When I started teaching full time at Pitt and initiated the two-year sequence in CO, I was quite sure that the CSWE would accept CO as another specialization in social work. This led me to the opinion that we ought to turn to the "art" of teaching CO practice. I state categorically that CO teachers should practice from time to time what they teach, and thereby refresh the course work of CO with a sense of its diversity.

Herewith is a short selection of a few of the many assignments I undertook in this field while teaching.

- After my investigations within the Department of Community Mental Health Services, Commonwealth of Pennsylvania, I wrote a paper "Mobilizing Community Resources for Mental Health" (mimeographed).

This experience served as an illustration for my students of the necessity for CO staff participation in community studies prior to the development of a plan of action in any community. I outlined the various principles and made suggestions how such studies should be performed.

- Action Housing is an organization devoted to renewing housing in poor neighborhoods. I recall that while at that agency I was asked to assess a neighborhood that action Housing was considering for service. One technique that I invented was to walk in all directions—north, east, south, and west—and to accost local residents, inquiring if this was the designated neighborhood. In this manner, I determined the actual natural neighborhood boundary as specified by its residents. In this pursuit, I learned that this particular neighborhood did not need the services of anyone to improve the housing stock. I verified this by interviewing realtors in the area, as well as visiting homes of residents and of the principal of the elementary school. In addition, when I approached the parish priest, identifying the agency I represented, he showed me the door and suggested that this agency's service was neither needed nor wanted.

I cite this example to illustrate how an imaginative method, not found in current texts, can be utilized in the classroom.

- I was invited by Dean Newstetter to undertake a study for the Packer Foundation of Tioga County, Pennsylvania, regarding how this foundation's money should be distributed to improve all types of community services in this rural community.

The leader in Tioga County was the county judge. He welcomed me and assured me of his support in this study. In order to better understand him, I listened to some of his court hearings, where I found him to be dogmatic and apt to deliver quick decisions. He invited me to attend weekly meetings in a backroom of the local hotel, where he met with five other "big shots." The judge introduced me and my reason for observing. After my attending a series of such meetings, a statement was made in my presence that this community was not ready to see "lunch pails" on Main Street. This meant to me that they were not ready to invite new industry into the town at that time.

In exploring this small town, I noted a proliferation of auto repair shops on each street. I asked the economist participating in this study to interpret this phenomenon. He had learned that residents of this community had to travel for employment to the nearest industrial city in the State of New York, a distance of approximately 40 to 50 miles. This suggested to me that the power structure of this community was not looking to serve the interests of the town's population by soliciting new industries to settle there.

The economist, on his own, made an appointment with the manager of the local bank, and learned more than he probably should have regarding the financial standing of its wealthiest residents. He wanted to convene a meeting with these individuals for discussions, but was stymied by the judge, who suggested that such a meeting be held in another county and not in "his" town.

I recounted this aspect of my study to the students to illustrate the power structure in Tioga County, and how a few persons can determine the course of action, or inaction, without considering the needs, wishes, or involvement of a greater number of residents.

Another insight into this community dealt with adolescents who were in trouble with the law. In an effort to rid the community of troublemakers, the judge referred these youngsters to the military recruiters. Just another example of the uses of power, which, in 1960, was not an unusual solution.

- Under the U.S. Senate Committee on Manpower and Poverty, I was assigned to assess poverty in Appalachia, in an effort to determine how best to assist these communities, and to prepare a report for this committee. From my general reading I was aware of the economic conditions in this area. My first effort was to visit a family on welfare and what I observed disturbed me a great deal. The family—husband, wife, and two small children—lived in a shabby wooden structure. I introduced myself; they were in poor condition, awaiting their relief check. The children had bloated stomachs, suggesting lack of proper nutrition. I did not spend much time with them, but I left some money with the family. I was angry and upset with the welfare department and visited their office. I confronted them for failure to send the family's check. It was one of the few times in my professional career that I lost control.

Despite this, I continued my efforts to study these communities and learned to my disgust that the example of my first visit was not at all uncommon. When I reported my findings in writing to the Senate Committee, I concluded that it would be more humane to "shoot the starving people" than to continue to allow them to live in such deplorable conditions. In reality, I omitted this last angry sentence from my report.

The experience in Appalachia was one example of how a professional can get caught up in his own feelings, and thus lose effectiveness as a practitioner. The irony was that the Senate Committee, without my knowledge, sent a group of physicians to different areas of Appalachia. When they filed their report it was clear that they found the same miserable conditions as I had.

I used this experience in a classroom session and explained to the students that there are some situations in CO practice that can arouse very strong emotions, may be difficult to control, and that one should guard against.

• In a Ford Foundation study with a colleague from the School of Social Work, the charge was to determine the best use for land to be released by the army and returned to civilian use. The Department of the Army contracted with the Ford Foundation for this study. The location was a rural area in the South.

The banker, lawyers involved in the transaction, and the local newspaper editor were contacted. Most of the residents in this community were African American.

My colleague and I, as well as the banker, the lawyers, and the newspaper editor, were all white. The lawyers suggested that this land be used to build a processing plant for locally grown produce. The banker avoided all serious discussion and offered drinks all around. The newspaper editor was not particularly interested in the disposition of this parcel of land, but queried us regarding the personnel of the Department of Health and Human Services.

One African American visited us at night. He told us that the community was not involved in the decision making, but that he himself was unwilling to participate because his medical education was being paid by a wealthy local resident.

I also met with a well-known African American woman community activist. She stated without equivocation that the Ford Foundation was mistaken by sending our team to study this plan, as we did not know—nor could we understand—her community, its population, and its problems.

When we submitted our report, we suggested that the banker, the lawyers, and a group of local citizens, including the lady mentioned above, should be brought together in a "locked room" until a decision regarding the disposition of the land could be reached.

This example illustrated to the class that sometimes CO workers are unable to find a solution acceptable to all because of vested interests and divisions in the community.

The lesson of these examples is that teaching community work or Community Organization is dynamic and changing all the time; it must be adapted to current problems. Faculty need to keep abreast of current legislation as it affects the communities and local population.

Now we are faced with new challenges: welfare reform at the expense of the poorest and most vulnerable populations. Cuts in food stamps, the elimination of federally mandated assistance to families with dependent children, time limits, cuts in housing subsidies, cuts in supplemental security income (SSI) for legal immigrants, and the like are only some of the current issues to be addressed by community organizing staff and students. Schools of social work must implement new curricula to train workers to address the problems that will result from these legislative nightmares.

BIBLIOGRAPHY

Greenwood, Ernest. 1956–57. "Theory Building in a Profession." University of California School of Social Welfare, Faculty Colloquium.

Hunter, Floyd. 1953. "Community Structure." *A Study of Community Power Structure.* Chapel Hill: University of North Carolina Press.

Lippitt, Ronald, Jeanne Watson, and Bruce Westley. 1958. *The Dynamics of Planned Change.* New York: Harcourt, Brace and Co.

Ross, Murray. 1955. *Community Organization, Theory and Principles.* New York: Harper Bros.

Schwartz, Meyer. 1959. "Professional Training for Community Work." Annual Program Meeting, CSWE, January. Mimeograph.

Schwartz, Meyer. 1962. "Defining Community Organization Practice." New York: NASW. Pamphlet.

Schwartz, Meyer. 1965. "Community Organization." Pp. 177–189 in *Encyclopedia of Social Work,* edited by Harry L. Lurie. New York: NASW.

The Rise and Decline of CO at Berkeley

Ralph M. Kramer

"...and between them with impunity,
they proceeded to mess up the community."
—Dr. Seuss

Perhaps it was to reduce the likelihood of such a mess that an MSW program for CO (Community Organization) was first established in the School of Social Welfare at the University of California at Berkeley (UCB) in 1964. The name Berkeley can evoke two contrasting images. The first is associated with one of the great research multiversities of the world, filled with Nobel Laureates and a legendary history in the struggle for academic freedom. The other, a more recent image, is Berkeley as theatre, as the scene—at least since the sixties—of countless student protests, sit-ins, strikes, picketing, and demonstrations: opposing the war in Vietnam, fighting against racial and ethnic discrimination, and for gender equality and countless other causes.

While the first conception of Berkeley attracted me as an undergraduate in the late 1930s, there was already a long-standing tradition of student activism opposing ROTC, war, and imperialism, and defending civil liberties and the struggling farm workers union. At the time, I could not foresee how these two faces of Berkeley—as a premier educational institution and as an arena for social action—would become intertwined in my personal and professional life for over 50 years. That story is embedded in the larger epic of Berkeley and the School of Social Welfare, and I begin with my entry on this stage as a participant-observer. Because of the turbulent character of those early years, the narrative cannot be strictly chronological.

After obtaining my degree from the newly launched two-year MSW program at Berkeley in 1946, and a subsequent career as a family agency executive and director of a social planning council in the San Francisco Bay Area (SFBA), I was invited in the mid-fifties to teach the first CO course required of all MSW students. This was also the period when Dean Milton Chernin made four new appointments to the School's faculty—a sociologist, an economist, a cultural anthropologist, and a historian—to strengthen the new doctoral program that started in 1960 and in which I was enrolled. While these appointments added to the growing nonclinical component of the Berkeley faculty, which ultimately consisted of almost two-thirds of the professional staff, at least 80 percent of the MSW students continued to specialize in direct services to individuals and families. This mismatch, except for the first period of five years has, with slight variations, continued since then.

At the beginning, however, in the midst of the gathering storm of the sixties, the Council on Social Work Education (CSWE) had approved the establishment of new two-year master's programs in CO. After receiving the first doctorate in social welfare at Berkeley in 1964, I was appointed to the faculty to establish a new CO methods concentration in the MSW program. Soon after, as one turbulent year followed another, I ruefully concluded that it was the wrong time, the wrong era to have started my somewhat postponed academic career as a somewhat over-aged assistant professor, but, as the proverb says, we do not choose the time of our birth or death.

Today there are probably few persons who have not heard about the Berkeley scene during those years, or seen images of it on TV, in newspapers or books. Todd Gitlin's *The Sixties: Years of Hope, Days of Rage* is one of the best of the books—a vivid, masterful account of the "cyclone in a wind tunnel,"[1] which was in full strength when the first group of nine students enrolled in the new MSW program in CO.

The year 1964 also marked the inception of the Free Speech Movement (FSM) and the emergence of Mario Savio as its rather reluctant leader of several sit-ins in support of students' rights. At the beginning of the fall semester, FSM students set up a few card tables to distribute leaflets and posters, and to organize for political action on campus. Taken by surprise, a nervous University administration overreacted, and called for strict enforcement of the University's regulations on the distribution of political literature. Following a dramatic march of deputy sheriffs led by the Alameda County district attorney, the campus was shut down for two days to prevent further violence, and the world was never the same. From then on, in retrospect, it seems as if the air was periodically filled with shouts and sirens, helicopters and tear gas, the campus swarming with police from Berkeley and Oakland in gas masks, with National Guardsmen, or the California Highway Patrol, all armed and facing masses of students in an escalating series of confrontations. There were unscheduled demonstrations almost daily in Sproul Plaza, an enormous open space at the entrance of the campus between the Administrative Building and the Student Union on behalf of Vietnam, a Third World College, People's Park, and many other campus issues. Facing famed Telegraph Avenue with its counterculture icons and havens on the south side of the campus, Sproul Plaza has continued for 30 years to be the primary rallying stage for student political and social action.

Because of the unpredictable nature of these events and the recurrent calls to strike or boycott classes as a way of showing support of or opposition to various causes, faculty often had no way of knowing if any students would ever appear in class, whether one could even get into the room or be able to leave the campus. To reduce this uncertainty, many classes frequently met in churches, restaurants, and homes. One aspect of this "protest heard round the world" is epitomized in the following incident. One day when I was conducting a class, a group of pickets assembled outside our building, Haviland Hall, and began a rhythmic chant that I barely heard. Later, a student who was watching outside told me that they were shouting repeatedly, "Shut it down. Down with Kramer!" Curious, he went up to one of the pickets and asked him, "Who's Kramer?" The student shrugged his shoulders and said, "Kramer? I dunno," and resumed his chant.

True, Berkeley was more than an episodic theatre of the absurd; faculty and student groups throughout the United States were mobilizing to fight poverty and discrimination, to defend civil rights, and to loosen some of the rigidities in university education. This was the context for the launching of the first "macro" or nonclinical specialization in the School of Social Welfare after a decade of faculty discussion. The story of its stormy takeoff, and subsequent more conventional development over three decades, is an example of the ways in which the conditions present at its birth can continue to influence an institution.

A new program of professional education in CO at Berkeley was established in the same tumultuous year that the Civil Rights Act was passed, and it continued beyond its formative period to be influenced by political forces inside the University and in the world. For example, a continuing source of tension and cleavage among faculty members and students, particularly in the first decade, was related to efforts to increase the proportion of ethnic minorities among future MSWs. The new CO program, which implied social action in a Berkeley setting, was naturally attractive to some of the minority graduate students who had been recruited by a faculty committee recently appointed for this purpose. Most of these new students also qualified for stipends available as part of an initial fivefold increase in the total number of governmental grants to the School during the mid-sixties. A threefold increase in the number of minority students resulted, and to this day they continue to comprise over a third of the MSW students, the highest proportion of any graduate school on the Berkeley campus.

This initial takeoff period during the sixties was also accompanied by growth in total MSW enrollment, peaking at 387, but dropping rapidly afterwards to an average of 278 in 1971, when federal funds were sharply reduced and University enrollment ceilings lowered. The timing of this earlier expansion had its demographic roots in the arrival of the postwar baby boomers on college campuses through the United States during this era, and was reflected in the extraordinary increase in the number of graduate students within a very short period of time. For example, starting in 1944 with the first two-year MSW program, it took 17 years—to 1961—for the first cohort of 1,000 students to graduate from Berkeley, but only 8 years for the next 1,000 in 1969, and 9 and 10 years, respectively, for the subsequent cohorts of 1,000.

The increased number of CO students starting in 1964–65 accounted for a significant part of this growth, amounting to 66 students—over half of whom were black (the preferred term at the time rather than the later African-American) or Chicano—during the period ending in 1971–72 when a total of 150 students had completed one to two years of CO methods. This number gradually declined to an average of about 40 students in the School—20 in each year, which represented about 15 percent of the MSW students at Berkeley. The pattern of this growth in student enrollment—initial rapid takeoff and expansion shortly after launch, particularly in CO—may have contributed to the volatile climate in the School during those years.

Some sense of the ambiance in the School during the fall of 1968 may be conveyed by the following incident. One of the new black fieldwork supervisors, angered by the presence of only 66 minority students out of the 387 in the School at that time, recruited 15 additional black students literally "off the street," marched them into the acting dean's office, and demanded that they be admitted with full scholarships to the MSW program with no questions asked. Shocked and intimidated, the School's admissions staff complied, but after a few months most of these new students dropped out and their sponsor-supervisor was also subsequently terminated.

Ironically, even though over a five-year period the School almost doubled the percentage of minority students (1964–1969) from 18 percent to

34 percent, Chicano and later Asian students filed complaints with CSWE, NIMH, and the San Francisco Civil Rights Commission alleging discrimination in the admissions process. At about the same time, Haviland Hall became the center for students who organized the Third World Strike on campus in 1969 demanding their own college, a larger share of financial aid, the admission of at least 30 percent minorities as students, and more ethnic faculty. Similar demands were presented separately to the School of Social Welfare, backed by personal threats to the dean. These were taken seriously and important School files were moved off-campus as a safeguard against their destruction or misuse, but this and other similar incidents gradually lost their potential to frighten School staff members.

In addition to the strains in the School stemming from the changing ethnic composition of the student body, there were also the first rumblings of the sharp divisions within and between the class and field faulty and students in the two major MSW tracks in the School—Indirect Services, which included CO and enrolled about 15 percent of the students, and Direct Services, which prepared students for social work with families and individuals. From the beginning, the basic class and field structure of their educational experience was markedly different. Because many of the CO field placements involved learning techniques of neighborhood organizing, block placements of four days a week were arranged for the second-year students in over 60 different organizations in the San Francisco Bay Area. This pattern differed from the concurrent fieldwork pattern of the other 85 percent of the students during both years. Since the first-year CO students had virtually all of their courses on campus, including some skills training in organizing and planning, the two groups rarely had any contact with each other, further reinforcing their ideological and professional separation.

Despite these differences between the two cultures, the disciples of Freud and Alinsky coexisted in the School. Typically, most of the CO students were primarily interested in learning about various strategies of social action that could benefit the poor, oppressed minorities and other "victims of the system." Perceiving themselves as "system changers" in contrast to the Direct Service (DS) students, who were seen as psychotherapists or "people changers"—and as agents of the Establishment— few CO students in the sixties were interested in the traditional forms of process-oriented, interagency planning and coordination that were once considered part of CO, and partially reintroduced in the next decade of the seventies.

As if this were not enough, interpersonal relations among faculty were also affected by a traditional Berkeley status and power stratification between professors who are member of the Academic Senate, the faculty governing body of the University of California, and all other nontenured members of the teaching staff. The latter group consisted of the entire fieldwork staff and part-time lecturers, some of whom had doctorates and taught in other schools and departments. The imbalance between the two faculty groupings is dramatized in the statistic that when Berkeley was the fourth-largest school of social welfare in the United States with 387 students in 1971, only 22 persons of the 70 faculty members were in the Academic Senate, and they taught barely a fourth of the academic courses. For at least eight or more years, relationships between these two groups of faculty—big F and little f—were soured by the resentment of being disenfranchised, and resentment was directed against The Professors, with both groups meeting separately until 1972. By then, with the consent and cooperation of the faculty, the Departmental Teaching Staff (DTS) was organized as an administrative faculty in which there was a greater sharing of governance functions.

These divisions within the faculty and among the students complicated the development of teaching materials for a relatively new and amorphous field of professional social work practice. Accordingly, beginning in 1965, I launched a series of comparative case studies on the participation of the poor in nine community action programs (CAP) in the San Francisco Bay Area. I saw this as an opportunity to observe at first hand in cities where I had lived and worked all of my life, an unprecedented range of sponsored efforts to develop citizen participation in governmental program planning and development. This project was also suitable for my own research, as a new and somewhat overaged entrant into the world of Berkeley's scholarly professionals and its high expectations of faculty.

Over a three-year period, a few graduate students and I observed hundreds of meetings and service programs, and I also interviewed the leading participants and officials. This research became one of the major sources of teaching material for our CO methods courses in both years, as well as the basis of one of the first books on participation of the poor.

Meanwhile, the students were getting a different message from a new faculty member who taught an elective social action course which, we later learned, included mock urban guerrilla exercises in the Berkeley hills. Another one of his elective courses that year on the black ghetto also achieved considerable notoriety by including lectures by three of the leaders of the Black Panthers in the sixties, Eldridge Cleaver, Huey Newton, and Bobby Seale.

A more conventional and longer-lasting colleague, personal friend, and subsequent dean was Harry Specht, who arrived in Berkeley in 1967 after a Brandeis doctorate and successful career at Mobilization for Youth. As assistant professors, we shared the conventional wisdom that there was so much to learn, but relatively little to teach in CO in a Berkeley graduate school. In another period of world history, another teacher, Archimedes, had asserted that he could move the world—with a prop strong enough and a lever strong enough. Because of our previous professional experience, we knew that the props and levers of CO were rarely strong or long enough to change communities or to move the world. Accordingly, from the start, we decided to collect a group of readings from the social sciences and social work that could be used by students in preparing themselves for a variety of professional roles. After five years of preparation, including testing in class, *Readings in Community Organization Practice* was first published in 1969 at the height of interest in various forms of planned change in communities and neighborhoods. On the one hand, we thought that it might be the best of times because of the profusion of new ideas and experiences in stretching the boundaries of CO practice. On the other, the unsettled period of ferment through which we were living might be the worst of times to identify the most useful concepts and principles for the emerging forms of CO.

In the end, the state of the field—the lack of suitable studies that dealt both with the know-how and the know-why of professional community work—convinced us and the publisher to proceed. At the time, we were struck by the pessimism that characterized the most theoretically sophisticated authors, and, in retrospect, the rather naive optimism of the more ideological writers. In my own comparative research at the same time on community development programs in The Netherlands and in Israel while on a first sabbatical, I was impressed with the pervasive influence abroad, in widely varying cultural contexts, of an imported American ideology and social policies for promoting citizen participation, but with its modest accomplishments in these countries.

Two more editions of *Readings in CO* with different selections, reflecting the rapidly changing scene in the United States, were later published in 1975 and 1983. While the practice and theory of CO has made considerable progress during the last 25 years, the turbulence that marked the 1960s has subsided, and its legacy of unreal promises and expectations has almost been forgotten. Instead, work in the community has become more pluralistic, political, and professional, paralleling the changes in the CO program at Berkeley beginning in the seventies, toward a primary emphasis on social planning, social policy, and the management of organizations. Partly a response to the growing student interest in organizational behavior, these curriculum changes may also have reflected less optimism about the process of organizing neighborhood residents and/or bringing about major changes in the community power structure. Indirectly, some of these changes may also have been influenced by the suggestion in the second edition, published in 1975, to think of two interrelated *contexts*—of community, and of organization—to avoid the confusion of multiple definitions of CO as a field, method, process, and goal.

In the last decade, as we noted in the Introduction to the third edition in 1983, the welfare state was already in decline, if not in retreat, in most countries, and the traditional core constituency of CO—the poor—were even worse off in the United States as legislators could, with relative immunity, seek balanced budgets and reduced taxation as their top priorities.

Some early warnings of this change in the zeitgeist appeared in the previous decade of the seventies and were also reflected in the subsequent transformation of the CO program. Originally linked expediently with administration in the mid-sixties, the sequence was (perhaps naively) advertised as preparation for practice in either field or for movement between them. Few students were interested in administration then, but over the next decade, CO went through a series of name changes that reflected the growth of student interest in the macro aspects of social work in social policy, planning, and the management of organizations. By 1974, the title was modified to Social Welfare Organization, Planning and Administration (OP/A), drawing on courses in social planning, community organization, and social agency administration. Nine years later, in 1983, the two methods' concentrations in the new Indirect Services track were called Social Agency Management (SAM) and Social Welfare Planning (SWP). In 1989, these were combined again into Management and Planning (MAP), ending a 25-year period during which student interest in grassroots organizing declined drastically.

As one of the early schools of social welfare to adopt CO as a full-fledged specialized method in 1964, Berkeley's experience may have reflected major trends in public policy and in the economy, as well as lessened demand from students. The drop in applications for admission to the CO program could be ascribed to the following: (1) The lack of jobs for CO graduates in the early seventies due to the cutbacks in federal spending when, for first time in 25 years, the growth rate in all governmental spending for social welfare slowed considerably relative to GNP. Until then, social welfare spending grew at a rate twice that of the GNP in the previous decade. The grants economy which supported student stipends and most CO programs entered a recession from which it never recovered. (2) Contributing to the fading of CO at Berkeley, or as a factor in its own right, was the belief of some of the mayors and other local officials in the San Francisco Bay Area that CO might be a disruptive threat to the power structure, as it was viewed in the experience of Mobilization for Youth in New York. Similar struggles for power took place in the SF Bay Area in most of the Community Action Programs, and the outcomes also added to the disenchantment with some of the results of neighborhood organization. (3) Another possibility suggested was that both the CO methods and its practitioners may have been inadequate for the assigned tasks. Professionalism did not seem to make a significant difference, particularly in attempts to organize ethnic communities, where indigenous leadership was usually preferred to paid outsiders. (4) The "crowding out" of CO may also have been part of the climate since the sixties, reflecting changing social and political trends and the disillusion with programs of the Great Society and the negligible results of CO. The latter, in turn, may have been due to unrealistic expectations, inadequate knowledge and/or skill, the parallel development of newly discovered ethnic, gender (feminist), and sexual (gays, lesbians) communities of identity, as well as the tremendous growth in neighborhood and self-help groups, each with its own agenda of social, political, racial, or economic goals.

A contrary and more positive explanation could be, of course, that CO was a victim of its success in influencing professional education, which has become increasingly sensitive to the importance of community, now a major component of many other courses, and perhaps decreasing the need for such a specialization in a school of social welfare.

Yet, during its first seven years (1964–71), 150 students received their MSWs, the majority with two years of CO methods courses, in a class and field program that was regarded as pioneering and innovative for its time. For example, an NIMH grant was used to establish an Urban Community Development Center in Oakland headed by faculty field consultants who supervised students placed for the first time in a wide range of new organizations such as redevelopment agencies, human relations commissions, housing associations, community action programs, neighborhood service centers, and welfare rights organizations.

In the early 1970s, "community laboratories" were also established for first-year students for observation, analysis, and skills training in organizing and planning; small-group workshops were scheduled on specialized topics with outside speakers; and at the conclusion of the second year, integrative seminars and student-initiated courses were scheduled for the third quarter. At its peak in the spring of '71, among the 66 block placements in the second year were those in Washington, D.C., with NIMH, the Urban Institute, and the Health & Welfare Council of the National Capitol Area. In Sacramento, students were placed in the capitol with the California Department of Education, Bureau of Community Services and Migrant Education, and the offices of two state senators.

While some students saw themselves in the field as pioneering in the development of new forms of community action, one of the most popular and successful courses in the School was program development, which required intensive study of social planning concepts and methods. The course culminated in the presentation of a proposal for a social service program prepared by teams of two to three students, which was critiqued by the class. Adding to the reputation of the course was the fact that many student proposals were subsequently funded by local foundations or governmental agencies.

The next two decades of CO, or of the Indirect Services track as it became known, were periods of consolidation of the macro elements in social work education at Berkeley. Student participation on the School's faculty committees became less strident and contentious, and many student curriculum recommendations were adopted by the School. These included special CO sections of the basic courses in Growth and Development, the added requirement of a course on ethnicity for all students, and admission of CO students to electives in the other professional schools of Public Policy, Public Health, and City and Regional Planning.

But echoes of the stormy beginnings of CO still recurred from time to time, as in the early seventies. In the midst of additional cutbacks, personnel losses, and lowered graduate enrollment ceilings, the School was again accused of "institutional racism" in separate formal complaints filed by its Chicano, Asian-American, and black students. Because it had to defend its affirmative action policies before the Council on Social Work Education, NIMH, the Graduate Division of the University of California, and the Social Services Union, CSWE reaccreditation was delayed for over a year. A similar incident occurred later, in the nineties.

Underlying some of these conflicts was a clash between the two professional cultures in the School of Social Welfare. The Direct Services model was based on a social worker in a public or nonprofit agency trying to help individuals or families with their problems, and for some students, it also served as an introduction to preparation for private practice as psychotherapists. In contrast, some of the Indirect Services students perceived themselves as organizers of a process of empowerment for marginalized or victimized groups. Other students, however, saw themselves as the executive of a community-based organization, or as a social planner, while still others who had received a public welfare training grant would be returning to a higher administrative position in their county welfare departments. All three types of students in the Indirect Services also felt marginalized because of their small numbers, as well as the sharp contrasts between the different client-systems and professional ideologies reflected in the School. Both students and faculty often felt as if there were two separate Schools in Haviland Hall. Yet by the seventies, after a reduction in the number of both CO students and field teachers, a more collaborative pattern of work developed among the students, academic and field faculty, and agency supervisors who participated in the CO curriculum committees.

Underlying some of the academic skirmishing was the resistance of the faculty to implement a major policy recommendation that would have altered the balance of power in the School. Culminating almost a decade of successive and often disruptive change, the first MSW curriculum policy was officially adopted by the faculty on May 21, 1973, although informal discussions began as early as 1966. The two years immediately preceding the final vote were among the most decisive for the School because of the conjunction of a series of threats described earlier, including the possible loss of accreditation because of a politicized CSWE procedure considered by many faculty members to have been hostile and inappropriately interventionist.

Given the temper of the times, it was not clear to what extent these actions were related to this curriculum policy statement then being considered by the faculty, which placed more emphasis on social welfare and indirect interventions than in the past, by dividing the resources of the School equally between the two tracks. Berkeley would provide graduate education for social planners, administrators, and supervisors in a social problem–centered MSW program, while the California state colleges would specialize in educating social workers for the line jobs. This was, of course, unacceptable to the Direct Service faculty, who were aware of the decline in CO applications, and whose voting power made it easy to stop this initiative.

These persistent divisions between the two tracks, however, took a different turn following the retirement of Dean Chernin in 1977 after 30 years, and the appointment of Professor Harry Specht, who continued to teach a CO course each semester. Under his influence, some members of the faculty, including several in the Direct Services track, became increasingly concerned about the trends in the profession toward psychotherapy and private practice, regarding it as a desertion of the historic mission of social work. Dean Specht, who was later to write a book critical of this movement of social workers into private practice, persuaded the faculty to reevaluate the purposes of the School in the light of these developments. By the end of 1982, the faculty had reformulated its primary mission as the education of social workers for professional careers in the public social services. This policy gave a positive lift to the School in many ways. There was a significant increase in applications for admission, in stipends for students, and in faculty research grants relating to the public social services. Major collaborative partnerships were forged with state and county agencies, and all students were required to complete at least one year of field work in a public agency.

The new mission statement of the School during the late seventies coincided with the establishment of a new School of Public Policy at Berkeley, and we were successful in adding some of their courses as electives for our students, in addition to those already approved in public health, city and regional planning, and law. In response to the increasing interest in these professional schools on the role of nonprofit organizations as providers of public social services, some of my research on purchase of service contracting and other forms of privatization in the SFBA and several European countries was used in courses on social policy, planning, and administration. These studies also related to a parallel emphasis in other new MSW courses on organizational behavior, and influenced the direction of my next research project. I began a series of studies as a follow-up to my earlier doctoral dissertation on the social policy implications of governmental-voluntary agency relationships in social welfare. This was followed several years later by an international comparative study of a group of social agencies in the context of the blurred boundaries between state, market and civil society in four countries. Some of this research was useful in developing teaching materials on recurrent practice issues confronting CO staff and the executives of both large and small voluntary nonprofit organizations.

One of the lasting benefits of the emergence of CO in the sixties was a fortunate congruence in its timing and the subsequent availability of several useful texts and case material. In addition to the books of Berkeley faculty, the newly published CSWE-sponsored text, *Community Organization and Social Planning*, by Robert Perlman and Arnold Gurin, as well as the Brager and Specht volume on community organization, were required items for many years. As locality-based community organization receded in interest, faculty redesigned their methods courses to help students learn how to analyze both organizational behavior and the processes and strategies used by professionals in trying to bring about changes in community and agency policies. Greater emphasis was placed on a more systematic and conceptual approach to professional practice, including evaluation and learning from experience.

I started this chapter with some recollections and I conclude with a few personal reflections on more than 50 years at Berkeley as a former student and faculty member. In reviewing the other articles in this volume, I found similar examples of the seminal and continuing influence of the sixties on the teaching and learning of CO. Those were indeed years of anger and of hope for both students and faculty. Making sound judgments under conditions of uncertainty is an art that cannot be reduced to a technique which one can learn from books. Perhaps not, but we believed that there was much that CO students could learn from books, and fortunately some of them agreed with us. Yet there were also a few with an anti-intellectual and antiestablishment bias characteristic of the era who were impatient with ideas that did not clearly relate to the mystique of grassroots organizing. Despite this ideological baggage that might have encumbered them, they have also had perhaps unanticipated but successful careers in social planning and administration, in addition to others who became faculty members or deans, including five at Berkeley.

In looking back on those early days of CO when the climate was a "heady mixture of idealism and destruction," there was little interest in the history of CO in social work. Yet, many years later, it was one of the first CO graduates, Professor Michael J. Austin, now on our faculty, who coauthored *The Roots of Community Organizing, 1917–1939* with Neil Betten. While they were primarily concerned with the formative years of CO, in recent years there has been a proliferation of CO courses in education, public health, sociology, psychology and psychiatry. Today there are few social sciences, interdisciplinary studies, or professional schools that do not also have a community component that is part of their educational program.

In addition, there has been an enormous "natural" growth of indigenous community organizations and other voluntary associations in the last 30 years, particularly in urban areas, as a spontaneous process of volunteer citizen action, rather than as a sponsored and professionally assisted mode of planned change. This includes, of course, the explosion in the number and types of new, voluntary associations based on self-help such as those organized by feminists, persons with AIDS, the homeless, gays, or the disabled.

The widespread prevalence of these multiple forms of citizen participation is part of a continuing challenge to the professionalization of CO. After all, one of the enduring themes in the history of CO—at least in social work—has been a search for identity and legitimation as a distinctive professional method. The success of this quest is still open to question, and it will certainly continue in the twenty-first century.

ENDNOTE

1. Todd Gitlin, *The Sixties: Years of Hope, Days of Rage* (New York: Bantam Books, 1987), p. 242.

BIBLIOGRAPHY

Betten, Neil, and Michael J. Austin. 1990. *The Roots of Community Organizing, 1917–1939*. Philadelphia: Temple University Press.

Brager, George, and Harry Specht. 1973. *Community Organizing*. New York: Columbia University Press.

Kramer, Ralph M. 1966. "Community Organization and Administration: Integration or Separate But Equal?" *Journal of Social Work Education* 2:2 (Fall), pp. 48–56.

Kramer, Ralph M. 1969. *Participation of the Poor: Comparative Community Case Studies in the War on Poverty*. Englewood Cliffs, NJ: Prentice-Hall, Inc.

Kramer, Ralph M., and Harry Specht, eds. 1969, 1975, 1983. *Readings in Community Organization Practice*. Englewood Cliffs, NJ: Prentice-Hall, Inc.

Perlman, Robert, and Arnold Gurin. 1972. *Community Organization and Social Planning*.New York: John Wiley and Sons.

Specht, Harry, and Mark Courtney. 1994. *Unfaithful Angels: How Social Work Has Abandoned Its Mission*. New York: Free Press.

PART THREE

REFLECTIONS ON THE REFLECTIONS: COMMENTARIES FROM DIVERSE VANTAGE POINTS

The Role of Ideas, Interests, and Institutions in Community Organizing

Susan E. Clarke

These reflections are a subtle reminder of the limits of disciplinary understanding. The stories told here weave together a rich fabric of fervent beliefs, high expectations, ethical dilemmas, rough realities, strong values, and a true sense of history and the significance of the moment in which one lives. But disciplinary boundaries separate and unravel these strands. This is part of the essential nature of disciplinary thought but, for contemporary political science, it too often means trying to understand social and political change by focusing on material interests without accounting for passions (Hirschmann, 1977) and institutions.

In this commentary, I would like to broaden that perspective to acknowledge how ideas and values—the passions of public life—as well as interests and institutions shaped the experiences recalled here and the prospects for political change during this period. The aim is not to test which is more determinative of policies but to ask how they mesh—and how and why this changes over time. As Reich (1988) indicates, broad public philosophies play a central role in organizing politics, but their ca-

pacity to direct policy is limited unless they are transformed into programmatic ideas. This transformative process marks these recollections;
nearly every author speaks to the struggle to translate values and moral
principles into programmatic approaches, and their ability to do so often
depended on the institutional settings and political context in which they
worked.

Even though structural interests and organized groups are central to
politics, political change cannot be fully understood without considering
the triangular relation of ideas, interests, and institutions. Bringing these elements together sharpens the focus on the processes by which new programmatic ideas, such as the notion of community organization presented
here, become dynamic elements of political change. The innovative programmatic ideas advocated by these authors introduced new definitions of
community problems and promoted distinctive solutions giving residents
a voice and role in solving community problems.

COMMUNITY ORGANIZERS AND AGENDA-SETTING PROCESSES

Simply characterizing such notions as "an idea whose time had come"
masks the dynamic processes shaping policy choices and agendas prior to
the actual decision stage (Kingdon, 1995, 1). In particular, this slights the
critical if often invisible role played by activists and specialists, such as the
authors here, in crafting and advocating new policy alternatives. Agenda-
setting models of predecision policy processes portray streams of problems
and political dynamics as shaping agendas, but credit policy advocates
and specialists with distinctive roles in generating policy solutions. In
contrast to pressure-group approaches, agenda-setting notions incorporate
the interactions of ideas, interests, and institutions; they highlight the
processes by which policy alternatives are generated and the dynamics
by which issues move onto the public decision agenda (e.g., Kingdon,
1995; Baumgartner and Jones, 1993). Kingdon argues that this is neither a
linear decision process nor a series of predictable stages. Rather, issues
gain agenda status when problems, policy solutions, and politics inter-
sect: this is especially likely when issue advocates act entrepreneurially to
frame a problem, take risks in promoting solutions that challenge conventional wisdom, and overcome resistance as well as the competition of
other ideas.

In many ways, the narratives here depict just such efforts. Community organization issues gained agenda status despite being supported by
groups with little political power on behalf of those with even less. The
agenda-setting approach offers an insightful framework for weaving together the authors' accounts of how this occurred and for placing these

community organizing narratives in a larger theoretical and political context. It directs our attention to four consequential elements in these narratives: (1) how activists framed community problems and formed coalitions, (2) the entrepreneurial strategies used in advocating unconventional solutions to persistent problems, (3) the responses to "windows of opportunity," and (4) the institutional factors shaping and limiting their effectiveness. Without question, the agenda-setting framework also increases our appreciation for those seeking to change the way we understand our social setting and to reframe our sense of what is possible.

ADVOCATES AND IDEAS: FRAMING PROBLEMS AND FORMING COALITIONS

As Bob Perlman recalls his thoughts on entering the social work school at Western Reserve in 1946, community organization sounded more appealing than group work because it seemed to involve social justice and social change. Part of the self-definition for many in this cohort emerged from their high expectations for social change and their rejection of the apolitical stance of many social work practitioners in the early postwar years. It is impossible to understand community organizing without recognizing this discontent with inequities in material resources and political power in American society. Nor can we fathom the motives driving these advocates without acknowledging their concern for distributive justice.

Although most of these accounts comment on the structural biases sustaining these injustices, the impetus for community organizing stemmed from a pragmatic assessment that enough change is possible to justify the effort. Cloward and Piven recount assessing mobilization strategy choices by asking whether they would "get poor people more, if only a little more." As Barrington Moore (1972) put it, we do not understand how to increase human happiness but we do know how to reduce human misery. For many of the activists in this volume, this meant both enhancing the material resources available to those they were working with, as well as strengthening their political voice. This definition of the problem lead to strategies involving more than simple addition of resources in order to reduce inequalities. In programmatic terms, it required strengthening the families and communities in which individuals lived by working with those groups to solve problems.[1]

Ideas Framing Problems

Reflections on how to think about particular problems and what to do are integral to these narratives; as Spergel graphically argues, these problem-solving processes are value-laden, often entailing moral dilemmas as well.

Trying to account for the evolution of community organization without focusing on such problem definition processes would be misleading. In these personal histories, the politics of ideas is central: it includes competing stories defining community problems and effective solutions, the networks and coalitions among community organizers sharing similar concerns and ideas, the evolution of a community able to influence policy and practice, and activists' roles as entrepreneurs within the profession as well as within the community.

Agenda-setting models assume that not all intolerable conditions are recognized as problems and few problems gain the sustained attention of policy makers. Recall John Turner's point (also noted by Kingdon, 1995) that situations or conditions are not problems: Poor community conditions become problems only if there is a sense that something can, and must, be done. Advocates use causal stories (Stone, 1989) to define community problems as amenable to intervention and prescribe what can and should be done. These causal stories attribute "blame" to certain aspects of the situation, they resonate with other values and beliefs important to citizens and decision makers, and they privilege some solutions over others. In doing so, they define problems and frame issues for both citizens and decision makers.

This emphasis on the cognitive and social dimensions of problem definition does not deny the reality of inequities and needs. It does, however, suggest that people try to make sense of these complex realities by selecting, organizing, and interpreting knowledge and information into "frames" or stories that explain situations and guide actions (Rein and Schon, 1993; Snow and Benford, 1992). Kingdon (1995) argues that some problems (and not others) come to the attention of policy makers through these definitional, or framing, processes. Thus, problem recognition and definition is a critical process. By providing a frame, or central organizing idea, linking solutions to recognized problems, advocates increase the likelihood that issues will gain attention. This also allows decision makers to select certain dimensions of the situation, or context, for attention and problem-solving efforts. Note that in many of the cases recounted here, the community organizer's key role was getting people to recognize new problems, or perceive old problems in new ways, and providing causal stories that ascribe blame and prescribed particular solutions.

Competing community organization models reflect alternative ideas, or frames, identifying problems and prescribing solutions. Turner, Rothman, and Austin's accounts note many of frames referred to by these activists: early "tripartite" community organization models linking case work, group work, and community organization; the Pittsburgh model of the "community organization specialist as a planning specialist"; the Cleveland model of interagency councils; the Ford Foundation's "grey areas" model of independent, community-based organizations with citizen participation and the MFY exemplar; Rothman's "trinitarian" model of locality development, interorganizational social planning, and social action; the Industrial Areas Foundation's Alinsky-like model using churches and neighborhood issues for mobilization of cross-neighborhood coalitions; and various adaptations of these approaches. Zald reminds us, too, of the spontaneous, volunteer community groups emerging in the absence of sponsored, planned change.

This repertoire of community organizing models introduces both opportunities and constraints. In adopting any one of these definitions of community problems, the decision process will be changed in ways that affect the eventual outcomes. That is, the different definitions influence the type of information collected about problems, the venues in which problems are addressed and solutions pursued, the types of alternatives considered and officially adopted, how results are evaluated, and whether programs are considered successes or failures. Several authors remark on the limitations posed by the causal stories or problem definitions characterizing community organization during this era. As Austin contends, these frames limited the potential for effective community based action by their partial perspectives on community problems. In particular, Turner, Rothman, and others note the slighting of race, ethnicity, and economic dynamics in early community organization models and curriculum. Few authors claim long-term impacts; many note that framing community organization in terms of residential mobilization in "one neighborhood at a time" provided only partial understanding of the context and prompted the eventual "derailment" of projects by larger dynamics.

Forming Coalitions

Ideas or frames are revealed in political struggles. Advocates use casual stories to manipulate how problems are defined, even while making them seem like descriptions of facts (Stone, 1989). As Stone notes, causal stories both assign responsibilities as well as legitimate and empower some actors as fixers for a problem. They, therefore, can become the basis for new political alliances among those sharing problems or between those sharing problem definitions—groups with problems and groups, such as community organizers, with solutions.

Ideas define the grounds for cooperation. The shared notion of community organizing as a process of citizen mobilization for problem solving, with organizers acting as change agents, transformed local politics across American communities. The broad consensus among activists on the purpose of community organizing—a "master frame"—permitted discussion of the more technical and substantive issues of what to do and what works. The sense of debate and contestation is palpable in these accounts; the historical arenas including a range of remarkable organizations such as SASS at Western Reserve University, the Heller School, the Columbia School of Social Work, the Cleveland Welfare Federation, various New York City youth agencies, CSWE and later ACOSA, among others.

Ideas also generate oppositional coalitions. The ideas of citizen participation and empowerment underlying new community organization approaches redefined poor people's interests and understanding of their problems in ways that challenged established interests. Local responses to new ideas were shaped, however, by the institutional settings rather than by universal, mechanistic forces. Perlman's account of resistance to the initiatives of Action for Boston Community Development (ABCD), Brager's analysis of the opposition stirred by Mobilization for Youth, and numerous other vignettes presented here underscore the importance of the political context of community organization. As these authors make clear, this context varies considerably, sometimes depending on the local government structure; in many northeastern and midwestern cities (the focus of nearly all of these narratives), mayors and district-based city councils were quick to recognize potential threats from new community organizations and to mobilize resources to resist these incursions.[2]

Policy Networks and Epistemic Communities

These narratives feature advocates motivated to act, causal stories promoting community organization interventions, and coalitions sharing a common understanding of community problems. Yet it could be argued that community organization alternatives did not gain agenda status until policy networks and an incipient epistemic community—community organizers with recognized expertise, shared values, and authoritative claims to policy-relevant knowledge (Haas, 1992)—emerged around community-organizing notions. Policy networks reflect the increased linkages, exchanges, interdependence, and integration of some members of a larger policy community sharing specific interests that set them apart from other community members. From these narratives, it is clear that a similar world view, including a body of ideas about community organizing, brought these activists together and distinguished them from mainstream social work professionals. The authors thoughtfully describe the origins and evolution of community organization in social work; as their accounts reveal, this process generated tensions within the social work profession as well as efforts to promote new policy interventions. In contrast with the apolitical stance of many in the profession at this time, community organizers were committed to engaging the political process and making it more responsive to the problems facing their communities. These policy networks are essential aspects of the agenda-setting process: they generate new problem definitions, develop a shared knowledge base, form consensus on appropriate solutions, and provide expertise to policy makers on problems and plausible solutions.

In a sense, these recollections collectively describe the evolution of a community-organizing policy network. Many of the authors are linked together in a generational cohort by overlapping personal and professional ties that must appear remarkable and enviable to today's younger practitioners. This policy network supplied a solid core for an epistemic community. In addition to supporting this policy network, CSWE and NASW self-consciously recognized their responsibilities for building the epistemic community—developing and sharing a knowledge base about community-organizing practice. Not only did these organizations seek to stimulate ideas, they also brought together academics from diverse disciplines and practitioners. Promoting expertise and talent served to attract new supporters and recruit new members to the community organization field. As Schwartz puts it, there was an implicit understanding of the need to "sell" Community Organization as a profession and source of authoritative knowledge.

In turn, these professionals developed a community organization framework capable of providing practical alternatives for policy makers. From acting as "an informal resource for the President's Committee on Juvenile Delinquency," to taking on government positions, to numerous accounts of testifying before congressional groups and local audiences, these activists engaged in the issues of the day. The fragmented and partial institutional context for policy making on community problems enhanced the importance of these epistemic communities. In a more coherent and centralized government structure, such communities might hold less sway; but in the American setting of decentralized, shared decision-making authority, they proved an invaluable source of expertise and skills to decisionmakers.

COMMUNITY ORGANIZERS AS ENTREPRENEURS

Thinking of community organizing in entrepreneurial terms is not a familiar perspective. Yet if we think of entrepreneurs as characterized by particular activities rather than as personality types or roles (Schneider and Teske, 1992), there are many ways in which the activists here acted entrepreneurially. Similar to their counterparts in business and government, they were willing to take risks and to mobilize resources to shift the conventional balance in ways that advanced their agendas. In many instances they operated outside conventions: Rothman's description of the marginalization of certain approaches and the diffusion of alternative ideas illustrates the roles entrepreneurs play in bringing new ideas into practice.

In the agenda-setting perspective, policy entrepreneurs bring together problems and solutions; they recognize the opportunities political events create for highlighting particular problems and couple preferred solutions to currently visible problems. As community activist Preston Wilcox has commented informally, these are "golden moments." To Mildred Barry, it is the nature of community organization: Matching problems with answers based on professional knowledge but tempered by contextual realities. For those working in programs such as MFY, it meant recognizing when windows of opportunity open and promoting new approaches as feasible solutions to persistent problems. As Rothman puts it, this may be less an "enabling" role and more an aggressive advocacy stance. MFY illustrates entrepreneurial coupling of interests through causal stories: The juvenile delinquency issue and MFY's solution attracted NIMH and Kennedy administration support not only because it seemed plausible but because it met other needs for each group.

Within the community organization profession, Mildred Barry, Chauncey Alexander, and others acted as organizational entrepreneurs. They continuously reshaped organizational arenas, redefined the organizational rules of the game, and sought to create new intellectual and organizational "capital." Indeed, Barry presents a straightforward account of the mix of advocacy and brokering demanded of entrepreneurs: She describes efforts to redefine health issues, to create new meanings for health as a goal, and to broker resources and expertise in an ambitious community health-planning enterprise. Her metaphor of the canoe on the river illustrates an agenda-setting process of constructing initiatives and watching for windows of opportunity to put them into play. This resonates with the governance and collaborative leadership themes sounded by Austin and Perlman and underscores the continuing need for entrepreneurial initiatives that encourage "getting things done." To several authors, the apparent absence of this entrepreneurial capacity in contemporary settings reflects a declining influence on shaping understandings of what is feasible and possible.

POLICY WINDOWS AND POLICY CHANGE

From an agenda-setting perspective, agendas change when policy windows open: Entrepreneurs take advantage of political opportunities to couple new alternatives such as those advocated by community organizers with salient problems. These policy windows represent opportunities to make choices among alternatives; the windows open in response to political changes or the rise of new pressing problems but can close quickly for many different reasons. Occasional windows of exceptional opportunity (Kingdon, 1995) allow new issue frames and participants to emerge and alternative solutions to gain visibility. In Kingdon's view, the scarcity and volatility of policy windows puts a premium on advocates' being in a position to act quickly to take advantage of these opportunities. Policy makers will be seeking policy alternatives they can claim as solutions, but these proposals must be well developed and credible if they are to be coupled to pressing problems.

The credibility of new ideas can be undermined by the path-dependency inherent in political processes. All communities have an institutional and structural legacy in which previous decisions and existing institutions dominate and channel activities. These become the focusing devices for subsequent decisions and "lock-in" a master frame, set of solutions, and affected interests. Spergel describes this dilemma as dealing with echoes or myths—that is, continuing to repeat problem definitions and solutions (also see deNeuville and Barton, 1987). Over time, the odds of continuing on the same path increase and odds of significantly deviating or starting a new path decrease (Wilsford, 1994). As a result, policy processes are limited to "bounded innovations" (Weir, 1992): New ideas are entertained to the extent they fit within familiar patterns. Cloward and Piven's animus toward organizational strategies implicitly recognizes these path-dependent tendencies; they illustrate their concerns with many examples of grassroots organizations attempting to stymie spontaneous mobilization and protest movements.

For these and other reasons, new ideas are likely to go nowhere unless windows of opportunity occur and entrepreneurial initiatives take place. To Perlman, Zald, Brager, and others, the early 1960s represented such a window: Initiatives and funding by the Ford Foundation and the President's Committee on Juvenile Delinquency coincided with the civil rights movement and the political mobilization of African Americans to create, in Perlman's words, a national climate of "resurgent liberalism." Nurtured by political realignments, this political climate supported a reappraisal of existing national policies; the subsequent redirection gave more emphasis to poverty, legitimated national leadership and funding, and introduced citizen participation processes in program planning and implementation.

Brager's appraisal of Mobilization for Youth details how a new idea—Ohlin and Cloward's opportunity structure theory of youth delinquency—took advantage of the window opened during the political realignments of the Kennedy administration. This window of opportunity was preceded by years of advocacy and promotion by many of these authors to "soften up" the policy process and make it more receptive to planned intervention addressing poverty and delinquency issues. The causal story presented by community organizers "blamed" poverty and lack of opportunities for community problems; planned intervention strategies in support of community mobilization were the solutions advocated by many of these practitioners. As the juvenile delinquency problem garnered increasing attention and a sense of urgency, this causal story became more plausible. As several of these authors imply, juvenile delinquency was the "hook" to justify funding of numerous community initiatives aimed at ameliorating poverty. Advocates of the Mobilization for Youth used his hook to couple poverty problems (including juvenile delinquency) with their preferred, innovative, intervention solution.

Introducing such new solutions requires taking advantage of windows and/or seeking to open them through strategies creating "shocks" or crises in the normal routines of local politics. To Cloward and Piven, disruptive protest and political realignments create shocks and crises that historically reinforce each other in opening the window for poor people's gains. They identify just two such five-year windows in the industrial age: 1933–1937 and 1963–67. Several activists see these changes in political climate and windows of opportunity as cyclical; by Perlman's count, this window remained open about 15 years at the most, but it was only five to Cloward and Piven. Brager and others advise that community organizers' effectiveness is shaped by these cycles: At best, organizers can push limits but must anticipate windows and be ready to take advantage of the opportunities as they arise. Or as Cloward and Piven put it, the intervals between the times of turmoil are times to organize.

Ideas are often borrowed and recombined. As Brager's essay illustrates, the MFY approach became the model for the War on Poverty; even though the organization itself suffered, the causal story behind MFY became accepted as a legitimate definition of community problems and possible policy solutions. The innovative strategies introduced by MFY significantly influenced social work thinking and were adopted as solutions to myriad other problems: notions of employing local low-income residents in community programs, of seeing social workers as advocates of the poor, of providing legal assistance to the poor, of restoring subsidized work training for youth and of focusing on structural change as well as individual adaptation.

MFY is a prime example of the politics of ideas, the importance of windows of opportunity, and the activities of policy entrepreneurs in linking problems and solutions. But the authors offer numerous other examples of coupling new ideas to political opportunities and continuing problems. Mildred Barry, for example, describes how the planning process that was developed in the Cleveland Health Goals project prompted the new community-wide planning orientation for the Cleveland Welfare Federation; these innovative changes came in response to 1974 federal legislation and funding providing for local "health systems agencies." This mandate created incentives—opened policy windows—for institutional changes but did not determine the local outcomes; Barry alludes to the many struggles over whether to form a new agency or to convert existing agencies into these new entities.

But even when windows open and new ideas gain support, there are many instances where groups' claims are rejected or distorted and no policy change occurs. We can accurately attribute this familiar result to the systematic bias in American politics, but that is a limited explanation. Instead, consider the argument that policy makers not only choose among available solutions but also identify target populations and ascribe policy benefits and costs accordingly (Schneider and Ingram, 1994). This approach emphasizes the process by which policy makers "construct" policy targets; by depicting groups in terms of certain positive and negative attributes, they can distinguish among groups and legitimate their responses to some demands and not others. Those groups that are seen as powerful or at least positively viewed gain disproportionate rewards, those characterized as weak and negatively perceived are punished. Cloward and Piven argue for mobilizing "pools" or aggregations of poor people, but policy makers will struggle to break down these pools into those deserving of benefits and others perceived less negatively.

Cloward and Piven, for example, cite the 1960s urban riots as prompting enaction of civil rights legislation and Great Society programs. But closer examination of the legislative hearings on those programs reveals continuous efforts to design policies in ways that target benefits so as not to reward "rioters." As Cloward and Piven acknowledge, national Democratic political leaders *did* respond to the national mobilization to flood the welfare rolls but "their remedy was not quite what we had expected." Rather than nationalizing the welfare system, political leaders targeted the indigent elderly and disabled for benefits in a new federally financed Supplemental Security Income (SSI) program. Similarly, the riots hampered passage of fair housing legislation until policy makers effectively distinguished between helping middle-class minority professionals and potential homeowners—but not all minorities, which could include "rioters" (Sidney, 1997). The state's capacity to manipulate policy responses independent of group resources and mobilization strategies by constructing target populations is an important constraint on community organizing strategies, whether based on "normal" or dissensus politics.

Finally, new ideas lose momentum when windows close as public attention shifts to other problems. Although most problems that are recognized as amenable to intervention remain salient, their priority declines. Cloward and Piven attribute this to the effects of repression, co-optation, concessions, channeling, and other demobilizing forces. Indeed, the apparent addressing of problems, symbolic or otherwise, can act to demobilize advocates (Reed, 1995; Lipsky, 1968) as well as instigate mobilization of counter forces.

INSTITUTIONS AS OPPORTUNITIES AND CONSTRAINTS

A dense constellation of formal organizations and agencies crowds these narratives. Nevertheless, the seemingly obvious importance of institutional elements is an elusive concept. Although it narrowly refers to the formal institutional venues for community organizing, it also encompasses the ways in which rules and norms embedded in institutions can shape preferences and policy choices. Thus it is difficult to generalize about the institutional context for community organizing other than to comment on fragmentation and complexity. The myriad ways in which institutional frameworks of norms and rules influence community organizing seem to defy generalization. But an analytic focus on institutions as a strategic context that both enhances and limits the effects of community organizing, independently of groups' numerical strength or resource base, can help explain the waxing and waning of community organization initiatives. In reflecting on the accounts here, certain themes stand out: Institutions played a particularly important part in shaping community organizing experiences by creating both veto points and access at different levels, by acting as incentive structures that privileged some interests over others, and by articulating certain "rules of the game" that gave advantages to particular types of grassroots organizations.

Access and Veto Points

Community organizing operates within a decentralized federal framework; this appears to permit access to policy makers at numerous levels but also acts to hamper coherent or coordinated policy responses. Cloward and Piven contend that electoral institutions in America historically limited the access of poor people to power. Even as the Voting Rights Act of 1965 and the "motor voter" legislation of the 1990s removed institutional barriers to access, actual voting rates increased little. Thus they conclude that a vision of a different world—alternative frames or causal stories, in the terms used here—is as critical to mobilization as removal of barriers to access.

Fragmentation and decentralization often make change more difficult because they extend the decision chains—the sequence of affirmative decisions necessary for action—to more institutional arenas and more actors (Immergut, 1992). In doing so, they expand the number of veto points involved in policy formulation. In itself, this makes cooperation more difficult because each veto point reflects areas of strategic uncertainty in the decision process. Each also reflects distinctive political configurations and different rules for reaching decisions and transferring decision to the next arena (Immergut, 1992).

Perlman's experiences with ABCD in Boston in the 1960s offer vivid examples of these abstract points: the decision chain in which ABCD was embedded featured Boston Redevelopment Authority (BRA) director Logue, the mayor, city hall staff, urban renewal neighborhood residents, the Ford Foundation sponsors, and the President's Committee on Juvenile Delinquency sponsors. Not only did the sheer number of potential veto points constrain ABCD's choices and dampen the momentum for change, but also the political interests represented by each point resisted any changes threatening their position and saw few gains from cooperation. Not surprisingly, ABCD was criticized for reacting continually to these diverse pressures and emphasizing process at the expense of product. Perlman's retrospective observations on ABCD, however, can be seen as an argument for democratic institutional designs in which decision chains are less vulnerable to strategic uncertainty and potential vetoes.

Incentive Structures

Institutions also shape agenda-setting processes by providing the grounds for groups' calculations of political strategies (Immergut, 1992, p. 85). These multiple access points encourage groups to "venue-shop"—to seek the most receptive arena for their demands. In a decentralized federal system, these arenas can be at the national, state, or local level and in the executive, legislative, or judicial branches. Although this appears to offer multiple opportunities for being heard, it also creates complexity and uncertainty. Since it is likely to be impossible to gain necessary support in any one arena, this generates governance dilemmas: how to overcome uncertainty and fragmented authority to get things done. This governance task is precarious: Public officials face some electoral accountability and have incentives to manipulate negotiations to accommodate their dual constituencies of economic and electoral interests (Friedland, Piven, and Alford, 1978).

To some, this appears a one-sided process: Economic and government interests control the resources that sustain current inequalities and see mutual gains from cooperating with each other to support the status quo, while there are few incentives to respond to community groups demanding change. They define what is negotiable and can threaten to exit the negotiations at their will. By controlling the "rules of the game," they can ensure that policy responses to community organizing are nonthreatening to their interests. Cloward and Piven refer to this view as dissensus politics, contrasting it with the governance argument that consensus politics and coalition building are paths to power. From their perspective, protest efforts that take advantage of fragmentation and disarray are more likely to produce gains for poor people than are coalition efforts.

Rules of the Game

Most social science accounts of institutions characterize them as configurations of rules and norms, but few consider how discourse itself—the frames and stories—is driven by the institutional context. That is, we adopt particular frames or problem definitions depending on the institutional conditions and circumstances—the rules of the game. Thus, institutions channel discourse in selected ways: Mandates for citizen participation or public hearings, for example, ensure that this channeling does not always advantage the most powerful.

The misgivings about sponsorship in many of these narratives reflect this concern about the effects of institutional channeling. Or, as succinctly put in Margaret Berry's narrative, the simple question of "who pays you" raises concerns for integrity and accountability for community organizations. Berry's account of the Pittsburgh Community Chest crisis in the late 1940s, Perlman's recollection of sponsor pressure at ABCD, and Brager's presentation of the byzantine scenario of sponsor intrigue undermining MFY are examples where external funding pressures directly challenged the agendas and activities of community organizations. These instances highlight the paychecks and practice dilemma: Margaret Berry wryly comments that militant 1960s organizations eventually found out that those holding political or economic power are not likely to finance threats to that power.

Anxieties persist about how this external funding dependency alters the ways problems are perceived and alternatives considered. It seems to be more than a question of sponsorship. As groups scramble to package diverse revenue sources into a funding "portfolio," they must contend with multiple, inconsistent, and often contradictory decision rules promulgated by sponsors. Bob Perlman continually returns to this theme in his description of the early years of (ABCD).

Similarly, the accountability needs of funding organizations and agencies create demands for program evaluation. But demonstrated improvements that can be attributed to program intervention are rare indeed. This is a troublesome theme in many of these recollections of lives dedicated to social action. Austin recognizes the institutional imperatives for program evaluation but argues it is nearly impossible to satisfy these concerns given the "untidy" models used in community organization. The MFY experience suggests, too, that specific problems may be used strategically to draw attention to broader concerns and larger strategies; the more effective these problem definitions in garnering support and funding for these broader goals, the less likely there will be demonstrated intervention effects of the specific problem serving as the "hook." Furthermore, as Perlman recognizes, the "action-research" model builds in tensions between researchers committed to useful evaluations and planners and program staff willing to compromise evaluation procedures for program results. Even the question of how to define "success" remains vexing; Spergel's essay emphasizes the pitfalls of trying to do so and the need to consider both policy and individual effects. As we see in Perlman's narrative, the benefits may be unanticipated and initially invisible: He and others recognize the important role played by community organizations during this period in facilitating black leadership skills and experience.

INTERESTS, IDEAS, AND INSTITUTIONS: LINKING THE PAST TO THE FUTURE

Changing Interests

The needs and concerns at the heart of the community organizing efforts described here are rooted in a declining industrial economy. Although many of these stories start in the buoyant post–World War II economy, the seeds of economic transition are already apparent. Family structures are beginning to transform, new economic interests are emerging as a postindustrial economy begins to take shape, the stability of manufacturing jobs is threatened by the internationalization of the labor force, and suburbanization is drawing jobs and middle-class families away from the center city. The activists here struggled with the consequences of these trends and changing conditions even though a full sense of the transformations at hand remained elusive.

In Austin's and Perlman's account of the Glenville case in Cleveland, and in many of the other experiences presented here, community organizing used territorial boundaries of communities as natural settings for organizing. Territorial identity became key to overcoming conflicts related to interests that were not shared. And as Turner's narrative demonstrates, this territorial voice can translate into political influence when residents and homeowners mobilize. Reaching across neighborhoods and beyond class boundaries, however, is a relatively rare event in the accounts here. The most frequent nonterritorial organizing in these historical accounts is coordination of agencies and social work professionals.

The communities featured here now differ dramatically on social, racial, and economic dimensions. The industrial economy structures that Cloward and Piven see as aggregating people and providing collective capacities for mass political action are giving way to production systems that fragment work settings and isolate workers. Whether these changing work regimes and increased job and wage instability provide grounds for linking poor people, the working poor, and the newly vulnerable middle class remains to be seen.

In many communities, these postindustrial economies and globalization trends mean the absence of work and the attendant social isolation and disorganization (Wilson, 1996). Draining communities of the economic and social resources necessary for civil society leaves few grounds for organizing. Mobilizing communities by appealing to neighborhood identity or shared concerns is problematic under these conditions. A public philosophy of meritocracy explains inequities as a result of lack of merit or effort rather than because of discrimination or structural forces (Bluestone, 1995). This often precludes coalitions with sympathetic third-party allies, as well as constrains protest activities. Indeed, Spergel argues that those working in fragmented or disorganized communities should promote further collaboration and coherence rather than greater conflict and isolation.

These trends lend further significance to the continuing question of organizing geographic communities or communities of interest. In Austin's view, community organization historically gave priority to organizing neighborhoods, based on "an idealized model of relatively stable residential districts"; this neighborhood strategy was embedded in liberal democratic theory's notions of decentralized, self-reliant governance as the basis for a good society. Not only do contemporary trends call into question the viability of such areas and the likelihood of such positive outcomes, they also challenge this "master frame" as too narrow. By considering neighborhoods independently of the larger economic and social dynamics in which they exist, this master frame generated solutions continually overwhelmed by larger trends. Perhaps, as Austin argues, contemporary organizing must begin to develop an alternative master frame incorporating different causal stories, drawing on more inclusive interpretations of changing conditions, and utilizing symbols that bring together cross-neighborhood or cross-class coalitions.

Changing Ideas

Perhaps the most significant but intangible change is the shift in the climate for organizing. The heady postwar climate described by these activists swirled around how, not whether, to use public authority for social good. Those returning from the war brought a vivid sense of the fragility of life, the role of fate and life chances, and a conviction that purposeful action could change the course of events. For many, the GI Bill provided the opportunity to gain necessary skills and different perspectives. There were many different definitions of salient problems and competing notions of how to go about addressing the societal problems that were so evident, but little question that this was an appropriate venture. In branching out from the social work profession, community organization approaches signaled the arrival of a new idea about societal problem solving and the evolving professional identity of those committed to it. There is no way to explain the rise and fall of these community organization ideas by looking to the interests involved or even the self-interests of early community organization leaders. It is necessary to examine the zeitgeist—the spirit of the times—and the shifting political terrain in order to appreciate these developments.

The current climate of ideas offers dramatic contrasts. The terrain is deeply influenced by notions of markets and using competition to allocate resources. Rather than the focus on community and government intervention, the policy paradigm emphasizes individuals, defines social capital as links among those individuals, and puts a primacy on economic solutions. The symbols and metaphors supporting these approaches center on voluntarism, self-help, and obligation rather than community, public goods, and citizenship rights. As several authors recognize, the focus is now on using the market rather than state agencies to address problems.

It is ironic that the Chapel Hill gathering where these recollections were initially presented occurred as President Clinton's April 1997 Volunteer Summit was about to take place. Margaret Berry puts this current "romance" with local effort and mutual aid in historical perspective by reminding us that the earlier experiences with building local self-reliance in the 1960s involved substantial national commitment and funding. The current nostalgia slights these distinctions as well as the historical roots, political networks, and stable financial assets of many settlement houses and other voluntary welfare organizations in the past. In the view of Alexander and Spergel, among others, the trajectory has moved beyond community organizing to an emphasis on public policies aimed at changing situations by changing the incentives guiding people's choices. Thus, even when windows open, as Perlman dryly comments, new and effective ideas about complex social problems may be hard to find or to recognize, even in practice.

Finally, the causal stories emphasizing structural and systemic definitions of community problems and solutions now are joined by causal stories centered on the cultural identities of groups as salient aspects of both the problems and solutions considered. Margaret Berry recounts earlier encounters with these frames as settlement houses faced charges of "welfare colonialism." This reinvigorates the issue of what types of communities to organize and, perhaps, whether it is necessary to develop a new view of "the good society," as Austin advocates. Given the barriers to new ideas noted above, rethinking community organization models is fraught with pitfalls. Nevertheless, the changing terrain of interests and institutions pushes us toward this undertaking.

Changing Institutional Context

Not only is the interest group terrain changing, the political opportunities for effective community organizing have shifted dramatically. With the retrenchment of the so-called welfare state and state devolution trends, there seems little chance that notions of planned intervention and funds for citizen empowerment will gain access to national policy agendas. And any slack resources that cities may have had available to respond to distressed communities and groups dwindled and became a source of competition among groups. Most central city governments now are in a state of permanent fiscal austerity. Their struggles to balance revenue and expenditure needs are constrained by the intensified interjurisdictional competition for private investment. This competition encourages a "bottom-line" mentality in which those sectors and groups seen as productive receive benefits and others are rejected. There are few electoral incentives for local officials to act compassionately or with a concern for social justice.

Mildred Barry's narrative emphasizes the dynamic institutional changes during these postwar years as local welfare councils and community chests' coordinating roles shifted toward community-based planning efforts. In the mid-1970s, these public planning orientations began to be displaced by market-oriented perspectives and community development corporations. These blossomed during the Reagan-Bush years (Vidal, 1996) and persist as key implementing organizations for Clinton's urban programs. In contrast to the resident mobilization around local problems integral to the community organizing recounted here, Community Development Corporations (CDCs) are more likely to rely on a corporate structure to carry out large-scale housing and economic development projects. CDCs and other market-oriented community organizations rose in response to national incentives and reflect a changing national policy climate; their "success," and the success of groups adopting these organizational strategies, must be seen in this context. Questions remain as to whether these are representative organizations and whether they are amenable to operating only in relatively stable neighborhoods. Not that these questions are restricted to contemporary CDCs: Margaret Berry recalls the representation issues challenging settlement houses in the 1960s, and Bob Perlman emphasizes the tensions between service and advocacy roles in neighborhood service centers during this period. Similarly, Berry's rendition of a 1967 report on neighborhood corporations in one of the California settlements highlights how the political aspects of entrepreneurial leadership displaced the service priorities.

Community organizers now work in a dense institutional setting of complex organizational structures and decision rules. In recognizing the significance of institutional changes over time, we accept that the fortunes of different community groups and organizing models can be traced to the context of decision-making processes as much as group resources or other factors exclusive to the group (Immergut, 1992, p. 66).

CONCLUSION

A number of these authors note with regret the relative decline of community organization since the 1970s. They attribute this to the changing political climate, the shifting institutional context, the erosion of the knowledge base, and the undermining of the historical "master frame" of community organization by demographic, economic, and social trends. While all these factors surely play a role, the most poignant and persuasive argument is the need for rethinking the "master frame" in ways that more comprehensively map out the contemporary trends and conditions facing community organization. Metaphors, frames, and causal stories are not right or wrong, true or false; it is a question of how well they fit the context. These recollections describe the construction and elaboration of a community organizing frame appropriate for a particular historical era. The authors are sensitive to the fact that their experiences were shaped by the political and social circumstances prevalent during those years. So, as Rothman concludes, the intellectual and organizational agendas for community organization now center on finding a robust intellectual framework and viable organizational niche appropriate for these new times.

ENDNOTES

1. In normative terms, these accounts are steeped in canons of liberal democracy, with goals of individual rights and decentralized, self-reliant, community governance. In many cases, they tend to reflect Walzer's (1983) notion that we exist in a political and economic setting where simple equality of all citizens is unlikely but complex equality is desirable. This presumes that we strive for a world in which one's standing in the political community—citizenship—is not determined by one's position in economic, educational, religious, racial, and other settings. Thus, building community coherence and viability strengthens citizenship and political voice, even though inequities persist within different spheres. But this perspective is troubling to several authors. Spergel and Austin note that community organization often appears to be an end in itself rather than a means to achieving well-being and a liberal democratic order. Also, Margaret Berry's account of the community control struggles of the 1960s provides a sobering reminder that decentralized democracy in the absence of complex equality can be an exclusionary

rather than inclusionary process. And, as Cloward and Piven argue, complex equality is impossible in the face of stratification and entrenched coercive power: what they refer to as "normal politics" is imbued with class biases in political resources, particularly the capacity to start and sustain mass organizations.

2.   The implication is that cities with city-manager structures and/or at-large elections were less likely or able to respond in this fashion. There isn't enough variation here to support that proposition, but the ready opposition of competitive social agencies and organizations in New York City and Boston indicates that more than electoral incentives are involved.

BIBLIOGRAPHY

Baumgartner, Frank R., and Bryan D. Jones. 1993. *Agendas and Instability in American Politics*. Chicago: University of Chicago Press.

Bluestone, B. 1995. "The Inequality Express," *The American Prospect* (Winter) no. 20: 81–93.

Cox, F. M., J. L. Erlich, J. Rothman, J. E. Tropman, eds. 1970. *Strategies of Community Organization*. Itasca, IL: F. E. Peacock Publishers.

deNeuville, Judith I., and Stephen E. Barton. 1987. "Myths and the Definition of Policy Problems." *Policy Sciences* 20:181–206.

Friedland, Roger, Frances Fox Piven, and Robert R. Alford. 1978. "Political Conflict, Urban Structure, and the Fiscal Crisis." Pp. 197–225 in *Comparing Public Policies*, edited by Douglas Ashford. Beverly Hills: Sage.

Haas, Peter M. 1992. "Introduction: Epistemic Communities and International Policy Coordination." *International Organization* 46:1–35.

Heclo, Hugh. 1994. "Ideas, Interests, and Institutions." Pp. 366–392 in *The Dynamics of American Politics: Approaches and Interpretations*, edited by Lawrence C. Dodd and Calvin Jillson. Boulder, CO: Westview Press.

Hirschmann, Albert. 1977. *The Passions and the Interests*. Princeton, NJ: Princeton University Press.

Immergut, Ellen M. 1992. "The Rules of the Game: The Logic of Health Policy-Making in France, Switzerland, and Sweden." Pp. 58–89 in *Structuring Politics: Historical Institutionalism in Comparative Analysis*, edited by Sven Steinmo, Kathleen Thelen, and Frank Longstreth. Cambridge: Cambridge University Press.

Ingram, H. "Constructing Citizenship: The Subtle Messages of Policy Design." In *Public Policy for Democracy*, edited by Helen Ingram and Steven R. Smith. Washington, DC: Brookings.

Kingdon, John. 1995. *Agendas, Alternatives, and Public Policies*. 2nd ed. Boston: Little, Brown.

Lieberman, Robert C., Anne Schneider, and Helen Ingram. 1995. "Social Construction (Continued): Response." *American Political Science Review* 89:437–446.

Lipsky, M. 1968. "Protest as a Political Resource." *APSR* 62:1144–1158.

Moore, Barrington. 1972. *Reflections on the Causes of Human Misery and Upon Certain Proposals to Eliminate Them*. Boston: Beacon Press.

Reed, Adolph, Jr. 1995. "Demobilization in the New Black Political Regime: Ideological Capitulation and Radical Failure in the Post-Segregation Era." Pp. 182–208 in *The Bubbling Cauldron*, edited by M. P. Smith and J. R. Feagin. Minneapolis: University of Minnesota Press.

Reich, Robert. 1988. "Introduction." Pp. 1–12 in *The Power of Public Ideas*, edited by R. Reich. Cambridge: Harvard University Press.

Rein, Martin, and D. Schon. 1993. "Reframing Policy Discourse." Pp. 145–166 in *The Argumentative Turn in Policy Analysis and Planning*, edited by F. Fischer and Forester. Durham, NC: Duke University Press.

Rochefort, D., and Roger W. Cobb. 1994. "Problem Definition: An Emerging Perspective." Pp. 1–31 in *The Politics of Problem Definition*, edited by D. Rochefort and Roger W. Cobb. Lawrence: University Press of Kansas.

Schattschneider, E. E. 1960. *The Semi-Sovereign People*. New York: Holt, Rinehart and Winston.

Schneider, Anne, and Helen Ingram. 1994. "Social Constructions and Target Populations: Implications for Politics and Policy." *American Political Science Review* 87:334–347.

Schneider, Mark, and Paul Teske. 1992. "Toward a Theory of the Political Entrepreneur: Evidence from Local Government." *APSR* 86 (#3 September).

Schumpeter, Joseph. 1942. *Capitalism, Socialism, and Democracy*. New York: Harper & Row.

Sidney, Mara. 1997. "The Origins of Fair Housing Policy: Uncovering Images of Race and Class." Presented at the Conference on Housing in the 21st Century: Looking Forward. International Sociological Association, Research Committee 43, June, Alexandria, VA.

Snow, D. A., and R. D. Benford. 1992. "Master Frames and Cycles of Protest." Pp. 133–155 in *Frontiers in Social Movement Theory*, edited by A. D. Morris and C. M. Mueller. New Haven, CT: Yale University Press.

Stone, D. 1989. "Causal Stories and Formation of Policy Agendas." *Political Science Quarterly* 104:281–300.

Vidal, Avis. 1996. "CDCs as Agents of Neighborhood Change: The State of the Art." Pp. 149–163 in *Revitalizing Urban Neighborhoods*, edited by W. Dennis Keating, Norman Krumholz, and Philip Star. Lawrence: University Press of Kansas.

Walzer, Michael. 1983. *Spheres of Justice: A Defense of Pluralism and Equality*. New York: Basic Books.

Weir, Margaret. 1992. *Politics and Jobs*. Princeton, NJ: Princeton University Press.

Wilsford, W. 1994. "Path Dependency, or Why History Makes It Difficult but Not Impossible to Reform Health Care Systems in a Big Way." *Journal of Public Policy* 14:251–283.

Wilson, W. J. 1996. *When Work Disappears*. New York: Vintage.

Some Lessons on Community Organization and Change*

Stephen B. Fawcett

Community Organization is the process of people coming together to address issues that matter to them. The goals of improving understanding of Community Organization—and its practice—have been embraced by a variety of related disciplines including *political science* (e.g., Cuoto, 1990; Gaventa, 1980), *action anthropology* (Stull and Schensul, 1987; Tax, 1952), *public health* (e.g., Bracht, 1990; Fawcett,

*Some ideas in this chapter are based on work supported by grants from the Kansas Health Foundation and the John D. and Catherine T. MacArthur Foundation to our Work Group on Health Promotion and Community Development. Thanks to Bill Berkowitz, Jannette Berkley-Patton, and Tom Wolff, whose feedback on an earlier version helped improve this manuscript. Thanks also to my colleagues at the Work Group, and the community-based organizations and grant makers with whom we collaborate, whose work and wisdom have deeply influenced my ideas about community organization and change. Correspondence should be directed to the author, Department of Human Development, 4001 Dole Center, University of Kansas, Lawrence, KS 66045.

Paine-Andrews, Francisco, Schultz, et al., 1995; World Health Organization, 1986), *community psychology* (e.g., Fawcett, 1991; Rappaport, Swift, and Hess, 1984), *history* (e.g., Fisher, 1987), *sociology* (e.g., Zald, 1987), and *social welfare* (e.g., Brager and Specht, 1973; Cox, Erlich, Rothman and Tropman, 1987; Dunham, 1963; Perlman and Gurin, 1972; Ross, 1955). In the field of social welfare, in particular, there was an influx of young professionals following World War II who specialized in working within and between groups of people. These and other community organization practitioners attempt to enhance self-determination (a process goal) and improve community life (produce tangible outcomes).

In the United States, the latter half of the twentieth century was a period of marked change in the context of community organization practice. The late 1950s saw a mass migration of low-income families, especially African Americans, from the South to northern cities. This contributed to a political instability in which the Democratic party attempted to attract new urban black voters (Piven and Cloward, 1977). Following mass disruption and protests of the 1960s, there was an unprecedented flurry of federal legislation, including the Civil Rights Act of 1964 and the Voting Rights Act of 1965, and a flood of antipoverty programs such as food stamps and legal assistance for the poor. Increased racial tensions, and a rollback of government supports for poor people in the 1980s and 1990s, further defined the evolving context of community organization practice.

Community Organization occurs in the variety of contexts that define "community." First, people come together who share a common geographic *place* such as a neighborhood, city, or town. Problem solving through community-based organizations (CBOs), neighborhood associations, and tenants' organizations represent common forms of place-based practice. Second, community organizing occurs among those who share a *work situation* or workplace. For instance, union organizing, such as among industrial or farm laborers, brings together those concerned about working conditions, job security, wages, and benefits. Finally, community organization arises among those who share a common *experience or concern*. For example, organizing occurs among people who are poor (Piven and Cloward, 1977), have concerns about issues such as substance abuse or violence (Fawcett et al., 1995), share a common ethnicity (Branch, 1988; Morris, 1984), or have physical disabilities (Suarez de Balcazar, Bradford, and Fawcett, 1988).

Societal critics sometimes debate whether community organization should feature collaboration *or* confrontation—a false dichotomy that ignores the context of the work. Several models of practice emerged in the various contexts of community organization work (Rothman, 1995). First, *social planning* uses information and analysis to address substantive community issues such as substance abuse or crime. For example, planning councils or task forces engage professionals in setting goals and objectives, coordinating efforts, and reviewing goal attainment. Although social planning may occur in a context of either consensus or conflict, its use may help build agreement on common ends. Illustratively, information about high rates of adolescent pregnancy, and factors that contribute to it, may help communities focus on the goal of preventing teen pregnancy, and even on controversial means, such as using sexuality education and enhanced access to contraceptives.

Second, *social action* involves efforts to increase power and resources of low-income or marginalized people (Alinsky, 1969). For example, an advocacy organization, such as a disability rights or tobacco control advocacy group, may arrange disruptive events—including lawsuits, sit-ins, or boycotts. These aversive events can be avoided or escaped by accommodations from those in power, such as employers modifying policies that discriminate against people with disabilities or tobacco companies eliminating advertising directed to minors. Social action tactics fit a context of conflicting interests (and discrepancies in power) that are not easily reconciled by conventional means of negotiation.

Third, *locality development* involves bringing people together to discuss common concerns and engage in collaborative problem solving. For example, people in urban neighborhoods or rural communities may cooperate in defining local issues, such as access to job opportunities or reduced violence, and in taking actions to address them. This strategy of group problem solving fits a context of consensus about goals and means.

Finally, there are also a variety of hybrid models that combine elements of the above approaches. For example, *community partnerships* or coalitions combine elements of social planning and locality development when people who share common concerns, such as child well-being or substance abuse, come together to change community conditions—specific programs, policies, and practices—that protect against or reduce risk for these concerns (Fawcett, Paine, Francisco, and Vliet, 1993; Fawcett et al., 1995). These models, and their variations, may be implemented at local, state, regional, and even broader levels.

This chapter reflects on the work of community organization and change in the United States during the latter half of the twentieth century. First, a brief description of the author's background and experience might help clarify the perspective offered. Second, lessons learned from community work are outlined based largely on the reflections of the authors in this book. Finally, the article concludes with a brief discussion of some issues in the work of community organization and change.

BACKGROUND AND COMMUNITY ORGANIZATION EXPERIENCE

I was born in 1947 in Providence, Rhode Island. As an Irish Catholic, my childhood included stories of discrimination against the Irish and others. My academic career spanned the disciplines of applied behavioral psychology, with an emphasis on changing the environment to affect behavior, and community psychology, with its ecological orientation and values of collaboration and respect for community assets and strengths. In the 1990s my colleagues and I became more active in public health, particularly with a network of community health researchers, practitioners, and grant makers involved in community initiatives for health and development.

In the late 1960s, while a VISTA volunteer, I did community organizing in low-income public housing. In addressing issues that mattered to our neighbors, we drew on social action strategies and disruptive tactics used at the time. During the 1970s and 1980s, my colleagues and I helped develop and apply interventions for community-based organizations including training programs, e.g., for job-finding (Mathews and Fawcett, 1984), agency-based voter registration (e.g., Fawcett, Seekins, and Silber, 1988), lifeline utility rates (Seekins, Maynard-Moody, and Fawcett, 1987), and advocacy organizations in the disability rights and independent living movement (Balcazar, Seekins, Fawcett, and Hopkins, 1990). In the 1980s and 1990s, we developed an agenda-setting and social planning approach, known as the Concerns Report method, for people sharing a common place or neighborhood (Schriner and Fawcett, 1988), concern (e.g., about community health, Paine, Francisco, and Fawcett, 1994), or experience such as being low-income (Seekins and Fawcett, 1987) or having a physical disability (Suarez de Balcazar, Bradford and Fawcett, 1988). In the 1990s, my colleagues and I worked closely with community partnerships and grant makers involved in initiatives to prevent substance abuse (Fawcett, Lewis, et al., 1997; Paine-Andrews, Fawcett, et al., 1996), cardiovascular diseases (Paine-Andrews, Harris, et al., 1997), and adolescent pregnancy (Paine-Andrews, Vincent, Fawcett, et al., 1996); and to promote child well-being and urban neighborhood development.

Family background as an Irish Catholic and first-generation college student contributed to my embracing social justice as a goal, and social action (and related conflict) as a sometimes necessary means of change. Professional training as a behavioral scientist predisposed me to see societal problems in the *behavior* of people—both those experiencing problems and those in power—and to focus on changing the *environment*, the conditions under which people act (Fawcett, 1991). Practice in community psychology highlighted the value of collaborative partnerships; and work in public health, the value of making an impact at the level of the whole population (e.g., neighborhood, city or town, county). Finally, collaborating with foundations and other grant makers helped clarify the importance of changing the broader context or system in which communities attempt to address what matters to them.

SPECIFIC LESSONS ON COMMUNITY ORGANIZATION AND CHANGE

This section summarizes some lessons learned from the author's experience with community organization practice, and especially from senior practitioners who wrote reflections for this book. The citations appearing without dates refer to those background papers. Lessons are stated as propositions, assumptions, principles, and values related to the work. They are highlighted in italics and organized by broad topics related to community organization and change. They need to be weighed against one another in particular contexts.

Lessons on Community Context

The propositions that follow reflect accumulated wisdom about how context affects community work.

High-profile commissions and reports create conditions for experimentation and optimism about public problem solving (Brager, Perlman). For example, during the 1960s, the President's Commission on Juvenile Delinquency helped spawn innovative efforts such as those of Mobilization for Youth in New York City. Such commissions help set the public agenda by highlighting what should be addressed and how (Cobb and Elder, 1972; Kingdon, 1995). Prominent reports frame explanations for societal problems—for example, by focusing attention on poverty as a "root cause" of many societal problems. They also feature promising alternative solutions—for instance, identifying legal assistance for the poor as an innovative model for problem solving.

Multiple models of community organization practice may be necessary to fit the variety of contexts in which community work is done (Rothman). For example, social planning or locality development strategies may fit contexts of consensus about common purposes such as working together to reduce violence. By contrast, the strategy of social action, with its disruptive activity and related conflict, may be more appropriate in contexts of conflicting interests, such as organizing to change wages and other conditions of the workplace.

Crosscutting issues are good contexts for community organization practice (Barry). Some community issues—for example, neighborhood safety or substance abuse—affect the majority of people who share a common place. As such, they offer a solid basis around which a critical mass of local people can work together. When community organization efforts involve people of diverse income and power—such as crime and violence that affects people across income—prospects for substantive change are enhanced.

Community organization cannot be completely divorced from politics, or from controversy (Austin, Rothman, Turner). Consider the case of people coming together in a rural community to address issues of toxic waste and environmental pollution. Public debate may focus on both the economic interests of affected businesses and the health concerns of local residents. When the interests of different parties cannot be maximized simultaneously, community organization efforts inevitably invoke politics: the art of reconciling or adjusting competing interests.

Poor people can make substantial gains (or losses) during periods of tumultuous change, and related realignment of political parties (Cloward and Piven). Would there have been a Civil Rights Act of 1964 without rioting (and a realignment of the Democratic party)? Political parties seek to avoid or terminate mass protest—and other apparently unorganized behavior—by changing (or appearing to change) policies, programs, and practices related to voiced concerns. Since mass protest is something those in power act to avoid, it is an important means by which poor people—with otherwise limited resources—can achieve power and influence.

Strategies used in Community Organization should match the times. In times of turmoil, mobilizing those affected by the issues, such as through protests or other disruptive action, may yield maximum gains (Cloward and Piven). By contrast, in those (often long times) between periods of mass mobilization, community organization might use less conflict-oriented approaches, such as locality development or collaborative partnerships, to define and pursue common purposes.

Mass protest and grassroots Community Organization can work together (Cloward and Piven). When public protests and other forms of disruption increase, so do the grassroots organizations that address prevailing issues. For example, protests regarding pro-life (antiabortion) interests were associated with increases in local organizations supporting this and other related causes. When public concern declines, so does organizing at the grass roots. Although protest nourishes organization, the reverse does not hold; organization does not engender protest (it may even retard it).

Community organizations form when (and not before) people are ready to be organized (Turner). Although organizations may exist to promote interest in an issue, such as child hunger, people come together only when significant numbers of people care about the issue and feel that their actions can make a difference. A particular challenge is discovering (and engendering) those conditions in which issues—such as child hunger or homelesness—matter to large numbers of people who share a common place or experience.

Those institutions that seek to avoid conflict and controversy make a difficult base from which to do community organization work (Austin). Consider the case of a school-community initiative to prevent adolescent pregnancy or HIV/AIDS. Although schools are well positioned to deliver information and health services to youth, school officials often oppose providing sexuality education or enhanced access to contraceptives for those who choose to be sexually active. Human service agencies and educational institutions that rely on public monies may be poor choices as lead agencies in controversial community organization efforts.

Lessons on Community Planning

Societal and community problems are evidence that institutions are not functioning for people (Spergel). Much of the framing of societal problems in the 1980s and 1990s focused on personal attributes of those immediately affected. For example, stated "causes" of high rates of youth crime may highlight the values and behavior of youth and their families such as "poor anger control" or "bad parenting." Such analyses rarely emphasize the contribution of broader environmental conditions, such as nonavailability of jobs or chronic stresses associated with low income, and the institutions responsible for them. In addition to individual responsibility, public institutions—such as schools, business, religious organizations, and government—should be held accountable for widespread problems in living.

We must set realistic goals for community organization efforts (Perlman). Community-based initiatives often overpromise, particularly with grant makers. Establishing unrealistic objectives—for example, to reduce academic (school) failure by 50 percent in the next two years—sets the group up for perceived failure. Organizations should carefully assess the feasibility of their proposed aims.

If we set (only) modest goals, we will likely achieve less (Brager). Although goals ought be achievable, they should also be challenging. Objectives can be overly modest, for example, to reduce rates of school failure (now at 80 percent) by 10 percent within three years. Insufficiently challenging objectives may not bring forth the necessary effort, resources, or degree of change needed to address the community's concern.

Social planning can engage experts in helping address societal problems, particularly when there is consensus on the issue (Barry, Rothman). We can advance locally valued purposes by engaging technical experts *and* local citizens in defining problems and solutions. Outside experts, such as university-based researchers or public officials, can assist in obtaining and interpreting data, facilitating the process of setting priorities, and identifying promising alternatives. Planning need not be limited to the traditional roles of facilitating coordination and communication among health and human service agencies (Barry).

Locality development or self-help efforts can also assist in addressing community issues (Rothman, Turner). Local people have the experiential knowledge to come together to define local issues, such as neighborhood safety or jobs, and take action in addressing them. Such self-help efforts have their roots in the settlement house movement in urban neighborhoods. They are guided by respect for the autonomy of local people to decide (and act on) what matters to them (Berry).

Local control can hinder collaboration at broader levels of planning (Berry). Planning at higher levels than the neighborhood, city, or town may be necessary to address the broader conditions that affect community organization efforts. For example, the growing concentration of poverty in the urban core, a result of regional planning decisions and other broader policies, is a structural issue that affects community development efforts within inner-city neighborhoods (Jargowsky, 1997). Although desirable for community building, strong local control may actually hinder the broader planning and coordination necessary to address local issues.

Lessons on Community Action and Mobilization

Each individual has the capacity for self-determination, self-help, and improvement (Berry). A basic assumption of community organization is that people most affected by local concerns can do something about them. This "strengths" perspective highlights people's assets and abilities, not their deficits and limitations. While acknowledging personal and community competence, we also recognize the importance of environmental supports and barriers that affect engagement in community life such as the opportunities for, and consequences of, community action.

You can't do it by yourself (Barry, Turner). Addressing what matters to local people—good health, education, and jobs, for example—is beyond any one of us. The idea of "ecology"—interactions among organisms and the environment—helps us see community action as occurring within a web of relationships. Community life is enhanced when individual strengths are joined in common purpose, an expression of the principle of interdependence. We are interconnected: Each of us has a responsibility to make this a world we all value.

Strong leaders are present in even the most economically deprived communities (Turner). Authentic leaders—those who enable constituents to see higher possibilities, and pursue them together—are among us, although not always acknowledged by those in authority. When doing community organizing in low-income public housing, I found that a simple question helped in "discovering" local leaders: "To whom do children go when they are hurt (and their parent or guardian is not home)?" Such questions help us discover the "servant leaders" (Greenleaf, 1997) among us: those who "lead" by addressing the interests of their "followers."

Community practitioners should never get used to the terrible conditions they see in their community work (Schwartz). Those doing community work, particularly in low-income communities, are exposed to horrible things: children in uncaring and unhealthy environments; adults without adequate food, clothing, and shelter; and the absence of other components essential for a decent life. Practitioners need to know how they are feeling about what they see and hear, perhaps disclosing experiences and feelings with colleagues to help support each other. They must also decide how to use those feelings—such as anger about conditions in which some people live—to energize and sustain the work.

People's beliefs and values enable them to stay committed (Barry, Spergel). To make a difference, those doing community work must be in it for the long haul. People's values, such as fairness or respect for the dignity of others, help sustain their efforts. For instance, a personal or family history of discrimination—a common experience for many ethnic minorities—may predispose us to embrace the value of social justice, and to work for equality of opportunity.

The work of Community Organization is like that of a "secular church" (Berry). Religious institutions help shape our beliefs about what is right and good, such as our responsibility to care for others. Community-based organizations, such as a homeless coalition or tenants' rights organization, call us to serve the common good—things beyond ourselves. As such, they enable us to devote our lives to higher purposes, while working in this world.

Community practitioners have few opportunities to reflect on their work (Perlman). Those doing the work of community building are often consumed by its demands. For example, leaders and staff of community-based organizations rarely take time to consider lessons learned about community action, barriers and resources, or other features of the work. Personal reflection journals and periodic group retreats help leaders and groups to reflect, to literally "bend back" and review initial purposes and recent directions. As such, they promote "praxis": the joining of understanding (theory) and action (practice).

Responding to events and opportunities to build community often takes us beyond what we know (Rothman). Community practice is largely an art form. Effective intervention is shaped more by trial and error than by tested general statements about the conditions under which specified interventions (the independent variable) effect desired behavior and outcome (the dependent variables). Yet, attention to the conditions that matter to local people—crime, drug use, and poverty, for example—cannot await the findings of research trials. We must be decisive in the face of uncertainty, even when the scientific evidence for a chosen course of action is inadequate (Schwartz).

Lessons on Opposition and Resistance

Societal problems sometime serve the interests of those in power (Brager, Spergel). For example, a regulatory policy that permits environmental polluters to go unpunished serves the economic interests of businesses that pollute, as well as those elected and appointed officials who may benefit from campaign contributions or bribes. Similarly, the existence of drugs and violence may indirectly benefit elected officials since they often gain public support when they rant against perpetrators of drugs and violence. When those in authority oppose community action efforts (or ignore appeals for substantive intervention), there may be a disconnect between the public interest (common good) and the private interests of those with disproportionate influence.

Racial and ethnic tension and controversies have disrupted and destroyed many community organization efforts (Austin). Race and ethnic differences matter in this work. For instance, most African Americans share a common history of discrimination based on race—such as being followed more closely in a store or being ignored by cabs in a city. When you are an ethnic minority, people may assume they can think and speak for you, even if they have given no evidence that they care about you. Distrust of the "other" (the majority or minority culture) may breed conflict that disrupts reciprocity and social ties among people of different races and cultures (Shipler, 1997).

Social action tactics, such as disruptive protest, have many detractors (Brager). Participating in (or supporting) protest can be dangerous, especially for those who remain in the community. For example, following a school boycott launched by residents of a low-income public housing project, it was my friend Myrtle Carter, a welfare mother and visible leader, who was subjected to police harassment. She was arrested and jailed for a minor parking violation while we outside organizers who were also part of the effort experienced only small inconveniences. Those using protest tactics should expect those in power to retaliate, even by establishing criminal penalties for particularly effective disruptive actions such as strikes (Cloward and Piven).

Less in-your-face social action approaches can produce a strong political base from which to make change (Austin). For example, the Industrial Areas Foundation (IAF) currentlyappears to be relatively effective in attracting support (and avoiding opposition) for its causes. Consistent with the *I Ching* and other statements of Eastern philosophies, less direct or forceful actions may be less likely to beget opposition and adverse reaction.

Opposition and resistance may come in a variety of forms (Brager). An analysis of the advocacy literature suggests different ways in which change efforts may be blunted. These include deflecting attention from the issue, delaying a response, denying the problem or request, discounting the problem or the group, deceiving the public, dividing and conquering the organization, appeasing leadership with short-term gains, discrediting group members, or attempting to destroy the group with slur campaigns through the media (Altman et al., 1994). Skilled practitioners can help group members recognize (and avoid or counteract) sources and modes of opposition.

Community organizations may respond to opposition with appropriate counteractions (Austin, Cloward, and Piven). Consider the case of local welfare officials (the opposition) who discount claims of a disability rights group (the advocates) that people with disabilities are being denied assistance unfairly. To counteract this opposition, disability advocates might document the number and kinds of cases denied, and use media advocacy about the consequences of denying eligibility to arouse public concern. Depending on the nature and form of opposition, appropriate counteractions may include reframing the issues, turning negatives into positives, going public with opponents' tactics, concentrating the organization's strength against the opponents' weakness, and knowing when to negotiate (Altman et al., 1994).

Opposition to change may be like peeling an onion. Advocates should expect multiple layers of opposition and resistance to community and systems change (Brager). For example, community organizations working for better schools may face resistance initially from school board officials; later, from local principals; and still later, from teachers. Peel off one layer, and another form of resistance or opposition may be there to protect vested interests.

Lessons on Intervention and Maintenance of Efforts

The lessons that follow note assertions about implementation of strategies and the maintenance of community organization activities.

The strategy of Community Organization should fit the situation (Alexander, Rothman). The broad and specific means of intervention should match the context and the goals. For example, social planning—

using technical information often with the guidance of outside experts—may assist in defining goals when people share common interests. Similarly, locality development—featuring self-help efforts of local people—may be appropriate for reducing a particular problem, such as substance abuse or neighborhood safety, around which there is widespread agreement. By contrast, social action—with its disruptive tactics and related conflict—may be needed in contexts of opposing interests, such as in reducing discrimination or disparities in income or power.

Using multiple strategies usually has advantage over any single strategy. Some initiatives—for instance, a campaign for school reform—get stuck using one preferred means of action, such as collaborative planning or disruptive tactics, even when the goals or conditions shift. By invoking only one strategy, the organization's actions may be easier to ignore and the benefits of complementary approaches may go untapped. For example, the threat of disruptive tactics (social action) may make support for self-help efforts (locality development) more likely (Perlman). Flexibility in strategy, and use of multiple means, may enhance community efforts and outcomes.

Being in two cultures promotes creativity (Rothman). Some community practitioners operate in more than one system of influence. For example, those who combine research *and* practice must respect the influences of both academic disciplines and members of community-based organizations. Being open to different audiences helps integrate disparate ideas, discover novel solutions, and transform practice.

The work of Community Organization takes time, and follow-through (all). Mobilizing people for action requires substantial time and effort (Perlman). Making the calls and personal contacts to bring about a change in school policy, for example, cannot be done solely by volunteers. The stimulation and coordination community work, like any other valued work, should be paid for (Turner). Without salaries for community mobilizers or organizers, follow-through on planned actions suffers.

External support may be both a necessity and a trap for community organizations (Cloward and Piven). Community organization efforts are seldom sustained without external resources. Yet, financial support usually has strings attached. For example, accepting money from foundations or the government may restrict advocacy efforts. Although often a necessity, outside resources may come at the price of compromising the group's goals or available means of action.

Community organizations often fade away (Cloward and Piven, Perlman). When the issues around which community organizations were initially formed begin to fade, so may the organizations. For example, a taxpayer rights organization may dissolve when its goal of blocking a particular public expenditure, such as a school bond issue, is resolved. Those

326   REFLECTIONS ON THE REFLECTIONS

organizations that endure after the issues subside may lose members unless they reinvent themselves to address other emerging issues.

Organizations need small wins. "Small wins" are shorter-term, controllable opportunities to make a tangible difference (Weick, 1984). For example, a good neighborhood organizer might work for improved trash pickup or more streetlights to provide (literally) visible benefits of group action. Without victories, community organizations can neither retain their members nor attract new ones (Cloward and Piven).

Lessons on Community Change

The central ideal of community organization practice is public benefits, not certification (Schwartz). Practitioners' interests should always be subordinate to those of the people served. Yet, when disciplines such as social welfare or public health market training for "professionals" in the work of Community Organization, they risk creating professions in which practitioners benefit more than clients. Those professions that certify people—and not promising practices or demonstrably effective methods—may give primacy to the interests of professionals (or guild interests), not those experiencing the concerns.

Community Organization must go beyond the process of bringing people together. For some practitioners, dialogue among representatives of different groups is a sufficient "outcome" of community development efforts. Yet, local people who come together to address what matters to them are usually interested in going beyond talk to action and results. Community organization efforts should bring about tangible benefits such as community change, problem solving, and enhanced social justice (Rothman).

The primary need is not for individuals to adjust to their world, but for environments to enable people to attain their goals (Schwartz). Much framing of societal problems focuses on the deficits of those most affected. For example, prominent labels for causes of academic failure might include "poor motivation" (of youth) or "poor monitoring" (by parents). Alternatively, analyses of academic failure might address such environmental conditions as few opportunities to engage in academic behavior (in schools) and limited opportunities for employment (following school). Community health and well-being are private *and* public matters, calling for both individual *and* social responsibility (Barry).

Community-based organizations can function as catalysts for change. Effective community organizations transform the environment; they alter programs, policies, and practices related to the group's mission (Fawcett et al., 1995). For example, a disability rights organization might modify policies regarding employment discrimination against people with disabilities or establish new job training programs that accommodate people with different impairments. In their role as catalysts for change, community organizations convene others, broker relationships, and leverage resources for shared purposes.

Lessons on Systems Change

The following propositions regarding systems change refer to alterations in the broader conditions that affect community work at the local level.

Interventions should include systems changes that reflect the "root causes" of the problem. Consider the typical interventions for most societal problems—for example, job training to address unemployment or drug awareness programs to counter substance abuse. Such initiatives usually try to change the behavior of those with limited power who are closest to the "problem," for instance, low-income adults (unemployment) or youth (substance abuse). When used alone, service programs and targeted interventions, such as those for so-called "at risk" adults or youth, may deflect attention away from more "root" causes, such as poverty and the conditions of opportunity that affect behavior at a variety of levels. Resolution of many societal issues, such as crime or unemployment, requires systems changes, including changes in decisions made by corporate and political decision makers, at levels higher than the local community (Turner).

Systems change does not necessarily occur simply by reporting felt needs to appointed or elected officials. For those with high economic or political status, simply expressing a concern may have influence on decisions that affect them. Available to such groups are a variety of traditional means of exerting influence including petitioning, lobbying, influencing the media, supporting political candidates, and voting in large numbers (Cloward and Piven). These means are largely unavailable to those most affected by many societal problems, however, such as children and the poor. Marginalized groups lack the resources to exert influence in conventional ways.

The great power of social movements is in communicating a different vision of the world (Cloward and Piven). Marginalized groups use the drama of protest—and the conflict it provokes—to display realities not widely understood or regarded as important. For example, the media may cover a strike and related protests by farm workers or coal miners, and the violence it often evokes from owners, the police, or others in power. Media coverage helps convey the story of conditions faced by those protesting and the unfairness of the action (or inaction) of private and public institutions that are targeted. The dramatic nature of protest and related conflict can help politicize voters who, through enhanced public support of the positions of marginalized groups, can exert influence on those in power.

Community organizations should seek changes commensurate with their power. Since ignoring them is likely and retaliation is possible, small organizations with limited power should avoid seeking fundamental changes in the system (Austin). For example, a single grassroots organization in a low-income neighborhood may not be positioned to effect systems changes such as altering the priorities of grant makers who support work in the community. However, sometimes small and scrappy organizations may succeed in bringing about community change when their bulkier counterparts do not.

Community (and broader systems) change can be effected through collaboration (Barry). Collaboration involves alliances among groups that share risks, resources, and responsibilities to achieve their common interests (Himmelman, 1992). For example, local community-based organizations interested in the well-being of children can link with each other to effect local programs (e.g., mentoring), policies (e.g., flextime to be with children after school), and practices (e.g., adults caring for children not their own). In addition, broader partnerships with grant makers, government agencies, and business councils can affect the conditions in which change occurs at the community level—for example, by altering grant-making programs to support collaborative work or promoting child-friendly business policies through industrial revenue bonds or new corporate policies. Collaborative partnerships help bring about community and systems change when they link local people to resources and institutions, at the multiple levels in which change should occur, to address common interests.

Lessons on Community-Level Outcomes

The lessons that follow summarize insights about indicators of societal problems, substantive change at the community level, and expectations we should have about such change.

Societal problems often reoccur. Consider the problem of gang violence that occurred after World War II and reoccurred in the 1990s (Spergel). Broad social conditions—wide disparity of income, weak social ties, and related mistrust of others—appear to affect the likelihood of societal problems such as increased death rates, infant mortality, and perhaps youth violence (Wilkinson, 1996). Improvements achieved in one era may need to be reestablished by future generations who must again transform the environmental conditions that support the reoccurrence of societal problems.

Most community efforts "chip" away at the problem. The majority of community interventions do not match the scale of the problem (Perlman, Turner). For example, a welfare reform program may prepare ten unemployed people to compete for only one available job, or create 100 jobs in a community with thousands of unemployed. We often effect small changes in a context that itself remains unchanged (Watzlawick, Weakland, and Fisch, 1974).

Real change is rare. Significant improvements in community-level outcomes—reducing rates of adolescent pregnancy or academic failure by 50 percent or more—are rather unusual. Yet, in requests for grants, community-based organizations often promise (and grant makers expect) statements of objectives that indicate significant improvements as a result of only modest investments over a short time. We should not perpetuate myths about what most interventions can actually accomplish (Spergel).

Development of community leadership may be a positive by-product of even "failed" community efforts (Austin, Turner). Although an initiative may "fail" to produce statistically significant changes in community benchmarks or indicators, it may develop new leaders or build capacity to address new issues in the future. For instance, a public health initiative that produces only modest reductions in rates of adolescent pregnancy may develop the capacity to effect changes that matter, such as four years later when the group switches its efforts from adolescent pregnancy to HIV/AIDS or to child abuse. Community documentation and evaluation should help us see what is actually achieved by community initiatives, including evidence of intermediate outcomes (e.g., community and systems change) and other indicators of success or "failure" (i.e., community capacity over time and across issues) (Fawcett, Paine-Andrews, Francisco, et al., 1997).

Optimal health and development for all people may be beyond the capacity of many communities to achieve, but it is not beyond what we should seek (Barry). Most community-based efforts, such as to create healthy environments for all our children, will fall short of their objectives. Yet, justice requires that we create conditions in which all people can make the most of their inherently unequal endowments (Adler, 1981). Support for community initiatives should be guided by what we must do for current and future generations, not by what limited gains we have made in the past.

CONCLUSION

The fundamental purpose of Community Organization—to help discover and enable people's shared goals—is informed by values, knowledge, and experience. This article outlined lessons distilled from experience, particularly that of an earlier generation of community organization practitioners (each with an average of over 40 years of experience) who embraced the value of social justice. The insights were organized under broad themes of community organization practice.

Most community work proceeds unaided by a clear theory of action. Emerging models of Community Organization and change (e.g., Fawcett et al., 1995) may evolve into testable frameworks for practice. Multiple case study designs (Yin, 1988), and interrupted time series designs (Cook and Campbell, 1979), could help examine several key scientific questions including: What combinations of strategies, such as social planning and social action, effect community (and systems) change optimally? Under what conditions? What amount and kind of community (and systems) changes effect community-level outcomes? Under what conditions? More refined theories of action—particularly those further informed by data from field research—might help guide the practice of community organization.

To remain viable, the multidisciplinary field of Community Organization must improve its science base, and its legitimacy as an area of scholarly inquiry (Rothman). Many of those drawn to community work are predisposed to "doing" or action, not systematic research or reflection. Time for even disciplined reflection is severely limited by demands of the work. Knowledge of community ways may be lacking in many trained researchers, and skill in methods of community research and intervention may be rare among practitioners. Environmental factors—such as lack of recognition and reinforcement from peers (including promotion and tenure)—make community research a potentially risky path for academic researchers. Without grants and others resources for community research, its practice may remain limited. Finally, insularity—separation from others doing the work, both within and between communities, and across disciplines—is another barrier to understanding, support, and effectiveness of community research and practice.

Community Organization often has a *bottom-up* or grassroots quality: people with relatively little power coming together at the local level to address issues that matter to them. For example, grassroots efforts may involve planning by members of a neighborhood association, protests by a tenants' organization, or self-help efforts of low-income families to build local housing. Yet, Community Organization may also function as a *top-down* strategy, as when elected or appointed officials—or others in power—join allies in advancing policies or resource allocations that serve their interests. Bottom-up and top-down approaches to community organization may work in conflict, such as when appointed officials conspire to make voter registration of emerging minority groups more difficult. Top-down and bottom-up efforts may also work in concert, as when grassroots mobilization, such as letter writing or public demonstrations, help support policy changes advanced by cooperative elected or appointed officials working at broader levels.

Community organization strategies may be used to serve (or hinder) the values and aims of particular interest groups. Consider the issue of abortion: Those organizing under the pro-choice banner may use protest tactics to advance policies and practices that further individual freedom (a woman's "right" to choose whether to have an abortion). Alternatively, those working on the pro-life side may organize to seek changes consistent with the value of security and survival (an unborn child's "right" to life). Depending on our values and interests, we may applaud (or denounce) the use of similar disruptive tactics by proponents (or opponents) on the issue.

What is the relationship between personal values and qualities—and the experiences and environments that shaped them—and the work of community organization and change? Personal background, such as a basic spirituality or a history of discrimination associated with ethnic minority status, can predispose a practitioner to embrace particular values, such as social justice or equality, consistent with the work of community organization. What qualities and behaviors of community organizers, such as respect for others and willingness to listen, help bring people together? Many of these attributes (and behaviors)—including clarity of vision, capacity to support and encourage, trustworthiness and tolerance of ambiguity—are similar to those of other leaders (Gardner, 1990; Heifetz, 1994). How do we cultivate such natural leaders, and nurture and support their work in bringing people together? Further research may help clarify the relationship between personal qualities and behaviors, such as those of the "servant" (Dass and Gorman, 1985) or "servant leader" (Greenleaf, 1997), the broader environment that nurtures or hinders them, and the outcomes of community organization efforts.

Finally, leadership in community work may begin with a *few good questions*: What is desired now, in this place, by these people? What is success? Under what conditions is improvement possible? How can we establish (and sustain) conditions for effective community problem solving—over time, and across concerns? How would we know it? Imagine a "living democracy" (Lappe and DuBois, 1994): large numbers of people, in many different communities, engaged in dialogue about shared concerns and collective action toward improvement. Perhaps these lessons—inspired by reflections of an engaged generation of community organization practitioners—can help us better understand and improve the essential work of democracy: people coming together to address effectively issues that matter to them.

BIBLIOGRAPHY

Adler, M. 1981. *Six Great Ideas: Truth, Goodness, Beauty, Liberty, Equality, Justice: Ideas We Judge By, Ideas We Act On.* New York: Macmillan.

Alinsky, S. 1969. *Reveille for Radicals.* Chicago: University of Chicago Press.

Altman, D. G., F. E. Balcazar, S. B. Fawcett, T. Seekins, and J. Q. Young. 1994. *Public Health Advocacy: Creating Community Change to Improve Health*. Palo Alto, CA: Stanford Center for Research in Disease Prevention.

Balcazar, F. E., T. Seekins, S. B. Fawcett, and B. L. Hopkins. 1990. "Empowering people with Physical Disabilities Through Advocacy Skills Training." *American Journal of Community Psychology* 18, 281–295.

Bracht, N., ed. 1990. *Health Promotion at the Community Level*. Newbury Park, CA: Sage Publications.

Brager, G., and H. Specht. 1973. *Community Organizing*. New York: Columbia University Press.

Branch, T. 1988. *Parting the Waters: America in the King Years 1954–63*. New York: Simon and Schuster.

Cobb, R. W., and C. D. Elder, 1972. *Participation in American politics: The Dynamics of Agenda-Building*. Baltimore: The Johns Hopkins University Press.

Cook, T. D., and D. T. Campbell. 1979. *Quasi-Experimentation: Design and Analysis Issues for Field Settings*. Chicago: Rand McNally.

Cuoto, R. A. 1990. "Promoting Health at the Grass Roots." *Health Affairs* 9, 145–151.

Dass, R., and P. Gorman. 1985. *How Can I Help?: Stories and Reflections on Service*. New York: Alfred A. Knopf.

Dunham, A. 1963. "Some Principles of Community Development." *International Review of Community Development* 11, 141–151.

Fawcett, S. B. 1991. "Some Values Guiding Community Research and Action." *Journal of Applied Behavior Analysis* 24, 621–636.

Fawcett, S. B., R. K. Lewis, A. Paine-Andrews, V. T. Francisco, K. P. Richter, E. L. Williams, and B. Copple. 1997. "Evaluating Community Coalitions for the Prevention of Substance Abuse: The Case of Project Freedom." *Health Education and Behavior* 24, 812–828.

Fawcett, S. B., A. L. Paine, V. T. Francisco, and M. Vliet. 1993. "Promoting Health Through Community Development." Pp. 233–255 in *Promoting Health and Mental Health in Children, Youth, and Families*, edited by D. S. Glenwick and L. A. Jason. New York: Springer Publishing Company.

Fawcett, S. B., A. Paine-Andrews, V. T. Francisco, J. A. Schultz, K. P. Richter, R. K. Lewis, E. L. Williams, K. J. Harris, J. Y. Berkley, J. L. Fisher, and C. M. Lopez. 1995. "Using Empowerment Theory in Collaborative Partnerships for Community Health and Development." *American Journal of Community Psychology* 23, 677–697.

Fawcett, S. B., A. Paine-Andrews, V. T. Francisco, J. A. Schultz, K. P. Richter, J. Berkley, J. Patton, J. Fisher, R. K. Lewis, C. M. Lopez, S. Russos, E. L. Williams, K. J. Harris, and P. E. Evensen. "Evaluating Community Initiatives for Health and Development." In *Evaluating Health Promotion Approaches*, edited by I. Rootman, D. McQueen, et al. Copenhagen: World Health Organization–Europe. In press.

Fawcett, S. B., T. Seekins, and L. Silber. 1988. "Low-Income Voter Registration: A Small-Scale Evaluation of an Agency-based Registration Strategy." *American Journal of Community Psychology* 16, 751–758.

Fisher, R. 1987. "Community Organizing in Historical Perspective: A Typology." Pp. 387–397 in *Strategies of Community Intervention: Macro Practice*, 4th ed., edited by F. M. Cox, J. L. Erlich, J. Rothman, and J. E. Tropman. Itasca, IL: F. E. Peacock Publishers.

Gardner, J. W. 1990. *On Leadership*. New York: Free Press.

Gaventa, J. 1980. *Power and Powerlessness: Quiescence and Rebellion in an Appalachian Valley*. Champaign: University of Illinois Press.

Greenleaf, R. 1997. *Servant Leadership*. New York: Paulist Press.

Heifetz, R. A. 1994. *Leadership Without Easy Answers*. Cambridge, MA: Belknap Press of Harvard University Press.

Himmelman, A. T. 1992. *Communities Working Collaboratively for a Change*. Monograph available from the author, 1406 West Lake, Suite 209, Minneapolis, MN 55408.

Jargowsky, P. 1997. *Poverty and Place: Ghettos, Barrios, and the American City*. New York: Russell Sage Foundation.

Kingdon, J. 1995. *Agendas, Alternatives, and Public Policies*. 2nd ed. Boston: Little, Brown.

Lappe, F. M., and P. M. DuBois, 1994. *The Quickening of America*. San Francisco: Jossey-Bass.

Mathews, R. M., and S. B. Fawcett. 1984. "Building the Capacities of Job Candidates Through Behavioral Instruction." *Journal of Community Psychology* 12, 123–129.

Morris, A. D. 1984. *The Origins of the Civil Rights Movement*. New York: The Free Press.

Paine, A. L., V. T. Francisco, and S. B. Fawcett. 1994. "Assessing Community Health Concerns and Implementing a Microgrants Program for Self-Help Initiatives." *American Journal of Public Health* 84(2):316–318.

Paine-Andrews, A., S. B. Fawcett, K. P. Richter, J. Y. Berkley, E. L. Williams, and C. M. Lopez. 1996. "Community Coalitions to Prevent Adolescent Substance Abuse: The Case of the 'Project Freedom' Replication Initiative." *Journal of Prevention and Intervention in the Community*.

Paine-Andrews, A., K. J. Harris, S. B. Fawcett, K. P. Richter, R. K. Lewis, V. T. Francisco, J. Johnston, and S. Coen. 1997. "Evaluating a Statewide Partnership for Reducing Risks for Chronic Diseases." *Journal of Community Health*.

Paine-Andrews, A., M. L. Vincent, S. B. Fawcett, M. K. Campuzano, K. J. Harris, R. K. Lewis, E. L. Williams, and J. L. Fisher. 1996. "Replicating a Community Initiative for Preventing Adolescent Pregnancy: From South Carolina To Kansas." *Family and Community Health* 19(1):14–30.

Perlman, R., and A. Gurin. 1972. *Community Organization and Social Planning*. New York: John Wiley.

Piven, F. F., and R. A. Cloward. 1977. *Poor People's Movements: Why They Succeed, How They Fail*. New York: Random House.

Rappaport, J., C. Swift, and R. Hess, eds. 1984. *Studies in Empowerment: Steps Toward Understanding and Action*. New York: Haworth.

Ross, M. G. 1955. *Community Organization: Theory and Principles*. New York: Harper and Brothers.

Rothman, J., ed. 1998. *Reflections on Community Organization: Enduring Themes and Critical Issues*. Itasca, IL: F. E. Peacock Publishers.

Rothman, J., J. L. Erlich, and J. E. Tropman, ed. 1995. *Strategies of Community Intervention*. 5th ed. Itasca, IL: F. E. Peacock Publishers.

Schriner, K. F., and S. B. Fawcett. 1988. "A Community Concerns Method for Local Agenda Setting." *Journal of the Community Development Society* 19, 108–118.

Seekins, T., and S. B. Fawcett, 1987. "Effects of a Poverty Clients' Agenda on Resource Allocations by Community Decisionmakers." *American Journal of Community Psychology* 15, 305–320.

Seekins, T., S. Maynard-Moody, and S. B. Fawcett. 1987. "Understanding the Policy Process: Preventing and Coping with Community Problems." *Prevention in Human Services* 5(2):65–89.

Shipler, D. K. 1997. *A Country of Strangers: Blacks and Whites in America*. New York: Alfred A. Knopf.

Stull, D., and J. Schensul, 1987. *Collaborative Research and Social Change: Applied Anthropology in Action*. Boulder, CO: Westview.

Suarez de Balcazar, Y., B. Bradford, and S. B. Fawcett. 1988. "Common Concerns of Disabled Americans: Issues and Options." *Social Policy* 19(2):29–35.

Tax, S. 1952. "Action Anthropology." *American Indigena* 12, 103–106.

Watzlawick, P., J. H. Weakland, and R. Fisch. 1974. *Change: Principles of Problem Formation and Problem Resolution*. New York: Norton.

Weick, K. E. 1984. "Small Wins: Redefining the Scale of Social Problems." *American Psychologist* 39, 40–49.

Wilkinson, R. G. 1996. *Unhealthy Societies: The Afflictions of Inequality*. London: Routledge.

World Health Organization. 1986. The Ottawa Charter for Health Promotion. *Health Promotion* 1, iii–v.

Yin, R. K. 1988. *Case Study Research: Design and Methods*. Newbury Park, CA: Sage.

Zald, M. N. 1987. "Organizations: Organizations as Polities: An Analysis of Community Organization Agencies." Pp. 243–254 in *Strategies of Community Organization: Macro Practice*, 4th ed., edited by F. M. Cox, J. L. Erlich, J. Rothman, and J. E. Tropman. Itasca, IL: F. E. Peacock Publishers.

The Importance of History and Context in Community Organization

Robert Fisher

> All great science, indeed all fruitful thinking, must occur in a social and intellectual context.... History does not unfold along a line of progress, and the past was not just a bad old time to be superseded and rejected for its inevitable antiquity.
> —Stephen Jay Gould, naturalist

History and context matter. While the importance of history to Community Organization seems obvious, it has not overly impressed most social workers or community organizers. It's not that social workers and community organizers don't know the importance of history. They've just had little time for it, always overwhelmed as they are by contemporary events, and have not valued it as much as other research or organizing tools. This collection of autobiographical essays presents implicit and explicit arguments for the value of history to social work in general and community organizing in particular. As the book's title promises, historical reflection reveals enduring themes and offers critical insight into contemporary practice.

Community Organization as a formalized body of social work knowledge and practice, as these essays document, is only a few generations old. As Wayne McMillen, an early pioneer in community organization, noted in 1947, "education for this field of practice [Community Organization] is in the infancy of its development" (McMillen, 1947). And so it was when the participants in this volume began to get involved with and reshape it. In a field where we can still capture much of its past in the voices of the people who made it, we owe it to ourselves and our successors to chronicle our roots, to write our history. This was Jack Rothman's intention from the outset, to contribute to the history of community organization practice in social work, to the history of academic training in Community Organization, to the intellectual history of theories and ideas about Community Organization, and to the professional history of the relationship between social work associations and Community Organization.

Context, as well as history, matters. Organizing and organizers are always shaped by a myriad of factors, including national events, local context, leadership, and resources. Because organizing efforts and writings about organizing are always specific to a particular time and place, analysis of such work should situate the work in the context of the varied social sites that generated it. While the selected participants in this volume pursued unique paths into Community Organization, they represent a cohort of organizers and analysts who primarily came of age during and after World War II and held positions of at least modest influence at the start of the sixties. The prior generation of community organization professionals had come of age in the twenties and thirties. The succeeding generation of organizers and analysts of organizing came of age in the student, anti–Vietnam War, and feminist movements of the sixties and early seventies. While these cohorts overlap, each was heavily influenced by the events, precedents, debates, experiences, opportunities, and barriers of their era. This commentary emphasizes the importance of context, both to the cohort of organizers whose reflections we've read and to enduring themes and critical issues for contemporary organizing. Initially, however, let me situate myself in terms of history and context with a bit of autobiography.

PERSONAL HISTORY AND CONTEXT

In the early 1970s I was completing a Ph.D. thesis, teaching in Boston, and working with a neighborhood organizing effort in Cambridge. My work with the Alinsky-style Cambridgeport Homeowners and Tenants Association (CHTA) was an initial opportunity to assume some leadership and responsibility in a political organizing effort. My political education derives mostly from growing up in a working-class Jewish neighborhood in Newark, New Jersey, in the 1950s and 1960s, with struggles around race, poverty, and war forming the backdrop of my high school, college, and graduate school years. But grassroots organizing in CHTA was my first hands-on opportunity at organization building.

From 1973 to 1976, CHTA held hundreds of meetings in people's homes, in churches, and in neighborhood food co-ops. We protested university (M.I.T. and Harvard) expansion into, and destruction of, the working-class neighborhood. We walked in support of local labor strikers. We picketed City Hall for improved recreational facilites in the neighborhood. We successfully blocked evictions and traveled on Sunday mornings to the suburban homes of Cambridgeport slumlords, where we passed out leaflets to neighbors and passersby exposing the slumlord in their midst. CHTA had some obvious weaknesses: Despite countless hours and effort to build a multiracial, indigenous-led, working-class organization, it was still disproportionately directed by young, college-educated, white men and women active in the peace and women's movements who were relatively new residents in Cambridgeport. Over time, however, CHTA's commitment to democratic process and building relationships had begun to develop a solid base among long-term neighborhood residents. In 1976, the organization was growing, winning battles, uniting with other efforts, and continuing to be both self-critical and proud of its accomplishments.

In that year, activists associated with the Boston Fightback and October League, a Marxist/Leninist/Maoist organization, became more involved with and critical of CHTA's limits, specifically its "nonideological" approach. Believing that the "correct line"—anticapitalist, anti-imperialist, antiracist—would not only provide direction for the organization, it would get working people more involved in the effort to build a multiracial working-class organization, the more left activists prompted first a split in CHTA and then its demise. The lead organizer and founder of CHTA, as well as others, went off to do union-oriented factory organizing in the shipyards of Quincy, Massachusetts (returning years later to community-based organizing in Cambridge). Others, put off by the undemocratic nature of Maoist politics, continued work in the neighborhood, though not within CHTA. Everyone was forced to take sides.

I saw merit in both. The multiracial, antiracist organizing of the Boston Fightback dared to take on the segregationist forces—very active and visible at that time in Boston. Their commitment to the cause of social justice and working-class advancement was impressive. For years we had struggled in CHTA with the role of ideology—having and sharing an analysis. Alinsky organizing since the 1960s emphasized a "nonideological" approach; let the people decide; ideology was seen as manipulative and undemocratic. A lesson of the late sixties instructed that ideology divided the New Left from potential allies in the working class. The communist-style efforts, even with obvious flaws, said that both ideology and a political analysis were critical to the organizing process. On the other hand, the good work done in Cambridgeport had been based on democratic process and on carefully building relationships over time—playing softball with neighborhood residents, developing a community garden, working in the neighborhood food cooperative together—efforts designed not only to build a community organization for social change but to build a "prefigurative" community: democratic, cooperative, egalitarian, honest, trusting, caring, and solidified by simply living, relaxing, and doing grassroots politics together. I worked for only a short time more in Cambridgeport, ending up on a different path. Another academic position took me in 1977 to Schenectady, New York. I clearly needed to step away from the struggle in order to make sense of it.

CHTA's experience, not uncommon in the political ferment of the mid-1970s, guided and influenced my research for many years. Trained as a social and urban historian, I turned to the past to make some sense of the present. I sought roots to ground my work. I sought precedents to guide contemporary organizing—that is, examples of community organizing efforts that were affected by ideology and political struggle, efforts that helped win more power and democratic rights for the poor and powerless. I looked first to the history of activism, the arena of community organizing with which I was most familiar and concerned. I turned to the history of Alinsky organizing, the Old and New Left, civil rights and Black Power, and so forth. Here was organizing tied to political parties, programs, social movements, and progressive ideas. Here were efforts, I presumed, that understood that, for America to accomplish its goal of democracy, it would take radical and transformative change—radical social movements, struggle to win state power—not incremental reforms. Here I would find models from the past to inform the present. I did and I didn't, and that is discussed at length elsewhere (Fisher, 1994a).

I also discovered that the history of community organizing consisted of more than social movements and Old and New Left roots. Another aspect, social work community organizing—the focus of this volume—kept forcing its way into my research. First, it appeared in writings on the social settlements, most notably Allen Davis's (1967) history *Spearheads for Reform*. Davis, however, framed the settlements in terms of the history of American social reform, not Community Organization. Then it appeared for me in thesis research on The People's Institute, a social reform organization on the Lower East Side of New York City in the early twentieth century. The Institute's work included public school-based community centers, which were consciously *neighborhood organizing* efforts. In the mid-1970s I came across the seminal work of Jack Rothman, not only the typologies of community organizing (Rothman, 1968) but also his effort to codify social science principles for social change (Rothman, 1974). Both challenged me to think more analytically and systematically about the history of community organizing and social change. The former legitimized the diversity in the history of community organizing that I was beginning to discover; the latter, which has received less attention despite—perhaps because of—its depth and breadth, reinforced the importance and utility of theory to organizing and social change.

A chance meeting with Rothman in 1977 at the University of Michigan opened up a wider history of community organizing within the profession of social work, as he suggested I meet with Arthur Dunham, who was at that time retired and professor emeritus at Michigan. Dunham encouraged my interest in the history of community organizing. He pointed to varied efforts in social work community organization, including the Association for the Study of Community Organization (ASCO) and the brief, excellent history by Meyer Schwartz (1965) in the *Encyclopedia of Social Work*. Increasingly evident to me was a strand of community organizing in the social work tradition. Rooted in the social settlements, emerging slowly in the 1920s in the work of people such as Mary Parker Follett, Jesse Steiner, Michael Davis, Leroy Bowman, and Edward Lindeman, it was superseded in the 1930s by the focus on centralized federal programs but expanded dramatically after World War II and especially in the 1960s through the writings of many of the people in this volume.

My research also led me to another strand of community organizing. More reactionary and conservative in impulse, these neighborhood improvement associations, now even more widely proliferated, proved that community organizing existed outside of both political activist/left and social work/social reform traditions. It also underscored that community organizing was not inherently progressive. Despite contentions that simply the process of bringing people together in democratic decision making would produce progressive goals and programs, the history of neighborhood maintenance efforts illustrated that democratic process—letting the people decide—was an essential element in community organizing, but not its sole one. Other factors, including context, social movement activity, leadership, and ideas, in addition to democratic process, I concluded, helped produce community efforts focused on social change.

The book I wrote, *Let The People Decide: Neighborhood Organizing in America* (1984) concluded with other lessons regarding the wider history of community organizing. Three of them seem most pertinent to this collection. First, neighborhood organizing has a long and important history. It is not simply a product of the past generation, not a transitory phenomenon. It is a means of democratic participation, a means of extrapolitical activity, a way to build community, obtain resources, and achieve collective goals. Neighborhood organization has been an integral, ongoing, and significant basis of civil life *and social work* in the United States for more than a century. It is most American to turn readily to organizations at the grassroots level to build community, meet individual and collective needs, and participate in public life. This is as true today as it was more than a century ago (de Tocqueville, 1969). Weil (1996) supports this point, proposing five major periods in the development of practice approaches and models in social work community organization: (1) proto-models, 1890s–1910s; (2) definitions and practice method development, 1920s–1930s; (3) practice method specification, 1940s–1950s; (4) articulation of basic models, 1960s–1970s; and (5) expansion and specification of models, 1980s–1990s. Rothman, Brager, Perlman, Spergel, and others were the prime movers of the fourth historical period, critical players in the codification and expansion of social work community organization, as well as contributors in the 1980s–1990s.

In the second lesson, neighborhood organizing cuts across the political spectrum. While all neighborhood organizing is a public activity, bringing people together to discuss and determine their collective welfare, it is not inherently liberal or radical, reactionary or conservative. Nor is it inherently inclusive and democratic. It is, above all, a political method, an approach used by varied segments of the population to achieve specific goals, serve certain interests, and advance clear or ill-defined political perspectives. The form an organization takes depends on a number of factors, especially the ideology and goals of its leadership, the constituency organized, funding, and local and national context. The diversity of political stances within the three traditions—the social work, Alinsky, and neighborhood-maintenance traditions—is not as great as the difference between them. Nevertheless, even among the community organization practitioners and analysts invited to participate in this volume, despite similarities in experience and a nearly common core of social work training and values, a diversity of beliefs and analysis is evident.

In the third lesson, neighborhood organizing efforts develop in a larger context that transcends local borders and determines the dominant form of neighborhood organizing in any era. Conditions at the local level directly spawn and nurture neighborhood organizing projects. The organizers, residents, local conditions, and many other factors at the grassroots level combine to forge consistently unique neighborhood organizing experiences. While neighborhood organizing projects have a significant origin, nature, and existence of their own at the local level, they are also the products of national and even international political and economic developments. To no small degree, the larger political-economic context determines the general tenor, goals and strategies, even the likelihood of success, of local efforts. I will return to this issue of context, after discussing the importance of history to contemporary practice.

HISTORY MATTERS

Despite the general view of activists and social workers that history is important, it is also seen as a luxury, and a highly subjective one at that. The emerging history of community organization (Fisher, 1994a; Piven and Cloward, 1977; Mooney-Melvin, 1986; Weil, 1996; Betten and Austin, 1990; Delgado, 1986) has begun to make a critical contribution to the literature and practice. In this volume alone, the historical recollections demonstrate how people make history, build collective memory, and develop enduring themes and critical analysis to inform the present, as well as illustrate how context heavily informs our work. Making history is the act of affecting change in public life. Flacks (1998) distinguishes between two arenas of human action: action directed at the sustaining of everyday life and action directed at the making of history. The former is the important work we all do in activities relevant to the "survival, maintenance, and development of self and one's dependents"(p. 2). Others call this private, as distinct from public, life (Fisher and Karger, 1997). Public life, that is history making, is action focused on the survival, maintenance, and development of society. "What we mean by history making," Flacks proposes, "are activities that have the effect of changing one or more features of the patterned everyday ways of life characteristic of a community or a society. ...*History is constituted by activity that influences the conditions and terms of everyday life of a collectivity* [original emphasis]" (Flacks, 1988, p. 3).

The reflections in this volume constitute history not only as recollections of the past but as history making: Brager at MFY; Rothman's creation of a model of contemporary community organization; Piven and Cloward's influential and pioneering intellectual and activist work covering the past four decades; Berry's leadership in the settlement movement and Alexander's at NASW; and Austin's continued activism in social work, Texas electoral, and grassroots politics. While most of the people in this volume made their primary contribution as social work academics, they also made history beyond the university. The predominant trend in our contemporary world pushes people into private life, away from the public world. Not accidentally the trend even proposes the end of history (Fukuyama, 1992), as if significance can now only be found in private life and as if the problems of the modern world had been resolved or are soon to be. In today's world people do tend to focus on everyday life, primarily on how to survive it. Bellah et al. (1985), Specht and Courtney (1994), Lasch (1978), Putnam (1996), and Fisher and Karger (1997) blame the decline of public life on individualism, psychotherapy, narcissism, TV, and global capitalism, respectively. Relatedly, people increasingly fear and retreat from arenas of power—"power corrupts," "power oppresses," "power is the problem." Because the participants in this volume understand public life and power differently, they have all spent a great deal of their lives in public, engaged in public issues, debates, causes, and institutions. As Flacks (1988) underscores, making history is tied to recognizing the significance of power to social change. Ernesto Cortes (1993), the lead organizer for the Texas Industrial Areas Foundation and part of a different tradition of community organizers, proposes that one of the primary goals of organizing is to "give people a thirst for power." Cortes understands, as do the participants in this volume, that, as Flacks (1988) puts it, power is "the capacity to make history—to influence the conditions and terms of everyday life in a collectivity" (p. 5). Many of the recollections—those of Austin, Piven and Cloward, Berry, Perlman, Spergel, Brager, and others—focus squarely on the issue of power. There is little doubt as to the importance to community organization of the struggle to develop, maintain, and advance power in order to make history.

In chronicling how people make history, reflections such as this volume help build collective memory. This is a second aspect in which history is valuable to contemporary practice: It provides roots. Community organizing is almost always an audacious act. Claims for social change, let alone social action, require legitimation; if the needs were understood as legitimate and acceptable, then social action would not be necessary. Social change finds ways to legitimate claims and needs, and history—that is, building a collective memory of prior struggles—provides critical ammunition for legitimating efforts. In his own writing, Meyer Schwartz (1965) offers roots dating back to the 1920s. While community organizers must always seek resources in the present, the possession of a collective memory is also a valuable, if intangible, resource. It is one, moreover, that becomes increasingly valuable toward the end of the 1990s, as other resources for social action continue to shrink and as the opposition intentionally undermines connection with social change efforts in the past. Much of the thrust of neoconservatists in the 1980s was to delegitimate the claims, and roll back the gains, of social movements and social change efforts in the 1960s and 1970s. History was not dead for them; they knew that one of their primary tasks was to delegitimate the claims and voices of that social activist era.

The struggle over history, of reclaiming and building a collective memory of community organization and social activism, occurs in the present and influences contemporary and future practice. The autobiographies in this volume provide countless "lessons from the past" that are critical to contemporary organizing. At the least, with a knowledge of the history of community organization, organizers feel less alone, less marginalized, and more connected to others in the past who contributed to building a foundation in social work for community practice. The autobiographies provide shoulders to stand on. Social action requires commitment for the long haul—that's another lesson from this volume—and having a sense of this work beyond the present. Having roots in the past and a vision for the future helps sustain and mobilize people for the long haul.

A third importance of historical analysis to community organization emphasizes linkage between past and present. The events or lessons of the past in the volume are inextricably tied to and selected to inform the present. History is not what happened in the past; it is the selection of data and interpretation of events from the past. This is obvious throughout this volume. We don't find in the relatively brief biographies definitive histories of people's lives, or definitive histories of their community organization experience. Their lives and experience are richer and deeper and more valuable than an article can relate. They have each chosen aspects of their work—an intellectual framing of community organization, a specific formative event, a few lessons learned, an overview of changes in the profession or in academia, and so forth—to serve as vehicles for enduring themes and critical analysis from the past. For example, Rothman is interested in the intellectual roots of community organization *and* chooses to write about them as the central focus of his recollection. He obviously thinks readers should know about them. His present interest pulls from the past and targets an audience in the present. Brager chooses to write about the difficulties and challenges faced in Mobilization for Youth. As with Austin and others, Brager thinks contemporary organizers need to understand that all organizing is political, and that political opposition should not be overlooked or underestimated. Or, as in the case of Perlman's essay, politics and ideology are seen as the problem, a different lesson that links to the present and informs the choice of historical material as well as its analysis.

Or history helps to build bridges in the present, as in settlement worker Berry's speaking fondly of SDS and New Left organizing in the 1960s. Then and even now there were major divides between settlement/social workers doing community organization and political activist community workers, such as those with the New Left or Alinsky. Alinsky, for example, juxtaposed his approach to community organizing against the settlement/social work model. He said they had turned the exciting and important work of community organizing into the boring field of Community Organization. Those in social work Community Organization thought Alinsky was full of hot air, and that the New Left organizers who followed him were terribly inexperienced and naive. But here in Berry's piece she intentionally includes a positive analysis of the organizing approaches of SDS and wishes it could have had more success. Her writing of history seeks to acknowledge bridges not built in the past, and it informs the building of such in the present. On the flip side, Kramer's piece criticizes the radicalism of the sixties at Berkeley and proposes that its ending and the return of Community Organization to management and administration concerns was a most positive change. History is never simply the past, but an interaction between the past and the present. The reflectors in this volume, involved in a lifelong work in this field, have some strong ideas about both the past and present, and their pieces connect one with the other.

CONTEXT MATTERS

In the words of renowned English social historian, E.P. Thompson (1971, p. 45), "The discipline of history is, above all, the discipline of context; each fact can be given meaning only within an ensemble of other meanings." Contextualization assumes that "different historical events can be regarded as going together to constitute a single process, a whole of which they are all parts and in which they belong together in a specially intimate way. And the first aim of the historian, when asked to explain some event or other, is to see it as part of such a process, to locate it in its context by mentioning other events with which it is bound up" (Walsh cited in Berkhofer, 1995, p. 34). Certainly issues of human agency—leadership, ideology, daily choices regarding strategies and tactics, and so forth—all play a critical role in the life of any effort, but the larger context heavily influences what choices are available, what ideology or goals are salient, and what approaches seem appropriate or likely to succeed. By its very nature, history puts the actions and work of individuals into a larger framework, interweaving the local with the more global, the particular with broader trends, events, and developments in society.

Social work has always seen itself as a discipline that valued context. Whether the call was for social diagnosis, putting the person in the environment, ecological and systems theory, or, more recently, empowerment theory, the understanding was that *social* work was about the interaction of individuals with the larger world in which they lived. Of course, as many others have proposed, in terms of contextualizing practice, social work has talked the talk more than walked the walk. Gutierrez's (1992) study of empowerment practitioners, for example, reveals most practitioners engaging in a relatively narrow practice beginning and ending with individuals. Specht and Courtney (1994), in a polemic against the asocial nature of social work, detail how it became preoccupied with the individual, lost sight of the contexts in which people live, and grew less and less interested in Community Organization. Community Organization, by its very collective nature, explicitly acknowledges that context is critical. Individuals are critical to the success of a community effort, but so are the larger contexts—economic, political, social, cultural, and so forth—in which the community operates. It is not by accident that so many of the reflections, especially Piven and Cloward's and Austin's, discuss in detail the contexts that shaped their work.

Throughout the history of neighborhood organizing there has been a direct and dialectical relationship between the national context and local community organizing efforts. In each era since the 1880s, national context has given shape to a *dominant* type of organizing practice. Organizing is always shaped by a myriad of factors, including local context, leadership, and resources. Nevertheless, whether it was community work in settlement houses during the "progressive era," oppositional class-based organizing of the Communist Party and Saul Alinsky in the 1930s, conservative organizing in the decade after World War II, or social reform initiatives and grassroots insurgencies in the 1960s and 1970s, discourse, policies, and programs at the national level substantially determined the overall nature of community organizing, and which types would develop, survive, attract attention, or have an impact (Fisher, 1994a). That is not to underestimate the important role local efforts played in affecting these national developments. Grassroots insurgency, for example, pushed the national political economy left during the 1930s and 1960s. But it was nonetheless this national political economy, in turn, that profoundly structured the broader context for and nature of grassroots activism.

In the neoconservative 1980s and 1990s, the impact of the national political economy on local organizing has been vivid. While a wide variety of efforts continue promoting social change and democratic resistance, it is the neoconservative political economy that largely determines the choices of most community organizers, pushing them into community economic development, moderate strategies, and proliferated bases (Fisher, 1994b). A discussion here of all three developments would be inappropriate, but brief attention to the first—community economic development—illustrates how national context affects local community organizing.

Contemporary Context and CDCs

In general, during the 1980s concern with broader social issues and social action receded. In the economic crisis of the past few decades, economic survival became the paramount issue for most individuals, organizations, businesses, and cities. As economic support for social services and solving social problems declined due to opposition at the federal level and shrinking local tax bases, and as political discourse in the nation revolved around neoconservative solutions to all problems, community organizing efforts moved increasingly away from social action and into the business of economic development (Pierce and Steinbach, 1990). This trend is nowhere more evident than in the rapid growth and spread of community development corporations (CDCs). While CDCs first sprang up in the 1960s and caught on with modest government support during the Carter administration of the late 1970s, after 1980 CDCs found government support drastically cut. The new, "third wave" of CDCs that developed in the privatization campaigns of the Reagan years were forced into becoming much more businesslike than their predecessors. They had to exhibit "business talent and development skills once thought to be the exclusive province of the for-profit-sector" (Pierce and Steinbach, 1987, 30). The Community Services Administration and the Office of Neighborhood Development were dismantled. Other sources of federal funds were dramatically cut back. The bottom line for CDCs, as with almost everything else in the decade, was economic success. Most of the new CDCs have become less like Community Organization and more like small businesses and investment projects, evaluated on the bottom line and heavily constrained by prerogatives and demands of the business world. Unlike community organizing I did with CHTA, or those efforts chronicled here by Austin, Brager, and Cloward and Piven, for example, most avoid political controversy, are dominated by professionals with a largely technical orientation, have narrow membership bases, and reject social action activity.

Forced to focus on economic success, most CDCs are not able to sustain their work for community empowerment. But they do not always give up on this goal by choice. The absence of public support, newly rigid interpretations of IRS restrictions on political activity of nonprofit groups, the necessity of seeking funds from and joining in partnerships with private-sector leaders, and the orientation of the CDC approach to economic investment and development decisions, all push contemporary CDCs away from politics and an analysis of power. "This lack of fiscal and political support," Marquez (1993) concludes, "has forced CDCs to accommodate themselves to rather than redirect the course of the free market."

To simplify a complex matter, for many efforts in the 1980s community economic development has become virtually synonymous with community organizing, as if organizing and empowerment were rooted in economic development issues, as if neighborhood struggles were always the same as community economic development, as if foundation support for building a house would help a poor community more than foundation support for social action organizers, as if working in partnership with local banks to develop "sweat equity" demonstration projects were the answer to urban poverty and housing shortages. "If the primary success story of the last 25 years has been the development of a legitimate, skilled nonprofit development sector with the proven capacity to create and preserve housing, jobs and businesses," Bill Traynor (1993) of the Community Training and Assistance Center in Boston sums up the problem, "the major failure has been the proliferation and dominance of a narrowly focused—technical—production related model of community development which is estranged from strong neighborhood control or direction and which does not impact the range of issues which affect poor neighborhoods." The prerogatives of a conservative, corporate-driven political economy heavily affects the nature of contemporary community organizing.

Contextualizing the Reflections

The authors in this volume operated in varied contexts and, accordingly, have chosen to organize their narratives by focusing on different contexts that reveal something about community organizing past and present. According to Berkhofer (1995), because historical practices and texts are always specific to particular times and places, analysis must situate a history in the context(s) of the numerous and varied social sites that generated it. While context is a multilayered construct, it may be helpful to see it not only in terms of time and space—that is, vertical and horizontal contexts—but also in terms of identity, association, and ideas. In such a five-part construct of context, there are, first, temporal contexts such as past, present, and future; or the 1930s, the 1960s, or the year 1959. Second, there are spatial or geographic contexts such as urban, suburban, and rural; the North, South, and Midwest; or Cleveland, Chicago, New York, and Pittsburgh. Third, there are contexts of primary identity such as class, race, gender, ethnicity, religion and work; being African American, a working-class Jew, a university professor, social work professional, community organizer, or settlement worker. Fourth, there are contexts of association such as an individual, family, group, organization, or institution; or, more specifically, NASW, Case Western Reserve School of Social Work, University of Michigan, Columbia, Mobilization for Youth, and so forth. And fifth, there are ideological or philosophical contexts in which concepts—a set of animating and legitimating ideas such as social justice, democracy, participation, conflict, cooperation, or feminism—form a frame of reference for people's lives and work. While there is more to context than these aspects, they help identify the diversity of contextual factors that shaped the work discussed in this volume. Brager's context just after McCarthyism on the Lower East Side of Manhattan working with Mobilization for Youth, fueled by social justice ideology and the theories of Olin and Cloward. Perlman doing social planning work with ABCD in Boston in the early 1960s. Spergel teaching at the University of Chicago and doing community organizing and delinquency work in Hyde Park. Alexander making advances as NASW. Rothman engaged in community life and steeped in the intellectual world of the social sciences and community organization. Schwartz developing the first community organization curriculum at the University of Pittsburgh in the late 1950s. Kramer engaged in curriculum battles at Berkeley and in creating community organization materials. Piven and Cloward, activist intellectuals throughout the generation, referencing the periods 1933–38 and 1963–68 as the only temporal contexts in the twentieth century truly supportive of mobilization, at the same time they were deeply involved in initiating, developing, and leading organizing efforts such as the National Welfare Rights Organization and the Human SERVE voter registration project. Austin focused on the importance of context with his discussion of social work in Cleveland and Texas over 50 years. There is indeed a wide diversity of contexts and experiences evident in these reflections.

Despite the diversity of contexts, however, participants have a good deal in common, and this relates to shared contextual factors. The selected participants form a rather distinguishable cohort characterized by, though not exclusively, a high percentage of white men of working-class origin, disproportionately Jewish, who were participants in World War II, who went to universities on the GI Bill, who were trained or worked as professional social workers in a few cities—most notably Cleveland, Pittsburgh, New York, Chicago, and Boston—and who had their most substantial impact as university educators and social work practitioners in the 1960s and 1970s. Like any generalization, this one falters on close inspection. Three are women. Two of the three women participants (Berry and Barry) and one of the men (Alexander) did not go into academia primarily, but instead worked as practitioners and leaders in the field. Three of the participants (Berry, Barry, and Schwartz) were born earlier, receiving their university education prior to World War II. One, Turner, is African American. Nevertheless, the common threads that unite their voices dominate over their differences, and these commonalities result largely from shared contexts. The broadest context that unites the participants and forms a common basis for the choices and opportunities available to them encompasses the central events and currents of the years 1941–1973. It was this larger context that shaped this cohort and helped it move Community Organization in social work from its infancy to greater sophistication, from being a modest effort to coordinate agency resources to an expanded vision of Community Organization that included social action and grassroots organizing.

Time Inc. magnate Henry Luce (1969) pronounced near the close of World War II the start of the American Century. Just as the prior one had belonged largely to the British, the next century, he opined, would be dominated by a relatively unchallenged American hegemony in economics, politics, and culture. The forecast hit the mark in the generation after World War II. The years from approximately 1945 until 1973 in the United States were ones of tremendous economic growth and opportunity as well as political and cultural change. Initially there was the enthusiasm of the postwar atmosphere—with individuals returning to peace and civilian life after years of delaying school and work, after years of disturbing personal life. The atmosphere was buoyed for social workers by the social justice *zeitgeist*. Fascism had been defeated abroad; democracy had prevailed. Of the approximately three million students in universities after the war, one-third were there on the GI Bill. And many were there studying to become social workers, as social work, like other professions, was about to undergo a major expansion. At the same time, however, elites sought to cement U.S. economic and political power worldwide and fashion a conservative consensus at home for the Cold War through economic growth and political repression. The former opened up opportunities and career advancement for young adults, but the latter heavily curtailed the kind of social justice work that interested the cohort of social workers represented in this volume, many of whom were Jewish and had just fought in a war against racism and injustice. The late forties and early fifties, on the other hand, were characterized by a right-wing politics, including McCarthyism, opposed to any criticism or dissent of a liberal or more left nature, with the effect that Community Organization during these years was terribly quiet. As David Rosenstein, then president of the National Federation of Settlements put it in 1953, at the height of the repression: "People in the neighborhoods are afraid to join anything" (quoted in *New York Times*, 1/31/53).

In response to the imperialism and repression during the late fifties and sixties, nationalist and socialist rebellions in the Third World (e.g., Vietnam, Iran, Guatemala, much of Africa) challenged imperialism abroad, and the civil rights movement resisted apartheid and oppression of people of color at home. As the Cold War political economy experienced resistance on a host of fronts, more liberal elites came to power in the early sixties, seeking at least to modestly address social problems at home. In this more liberal context, the cohort of community organization professionals found, at least at first, a more comfortable and supportive home. Stymied for years by a reactionary context and a social work profession that pursued more traditional (micro) and more conservative (adjustment-oriented) forms of social work, the new reform context of the sixties expanded the audiences and opportunities for this new group of social work professionals interested in Community Organization. The sixties were exciting, vibrant, and progressive.

Contrary to accounts that portray college professors as depressed by events of the day and under siege by anti-intellectual students, universities were booming and blessed with lots of students and money. It was an exciting time for most faculty, an atmosphere, at the least, of financial support for their work, and at best, of support for progressive change. It is not accidental that many of the participants in this volume played very influential roles and made substantial contributions to the public issues of the day. Cloward, with Ohlin, heavily influenced first the course of juvenile delinquency projects and then the whole community-based, participatory model that came to be characteristic of both government and grassroots efforts during the decade. Brager, with Cloward, lead Mobilization for Youth. Piven and Cloward helped mobilize a National Welfare Rights Organization. Perlman worked at the innovative ABCD antipoverty project in Boston in the early sixties. Berry did civil rights and settlement work in the South. Schwartz initiated the first community organization curriculum at Pitt. Rothman developed his typology of Community Organization in social work in 1968. Alexander successfully took NASW down a more social reform road in 1969. And so forth. As the ferment of the sixties generation burst on the nation, the cohort that had gone to school in the late forties, finished their education in the fifties, and were at influential social work agencies or first-rate universities were situated well to provide leadership in a context and to a new cohort more open to their goals and ideas.

While this group did not experience lives of ease, they seem twice blessed by good timing: being part of the social work expansion and GI Bill support after World War II and being well-positioned as reformers and community organizers as the ferment of the sixties and early seventies burst forth. As Clarke Chambers (1996), a history professor and founder of the Social Welfare History Archive at the University of Minnesota, describes it:

> You talk about luck. You come back [from the war] and Congress in its wisdom had passed the GI Bill. . . .Certainly in the liberal arts, which I know best, any number of my generation who were working class families, poor hard scrabble farming families, second generation immigrant families would never have gone to school without the GI Bill. When they come into the profession in the 1950s, it takes awhile to get established. But by the 1960s they're all in place and they change the nature [of things], at least in social science and the humanities. It's a remarkably lucky and exciting kind of breakthrough that takes place. . . .The things that excited me [about the 60s and early 70s] were the Women's movement, and the environment, and the anti-war movement. [Others] it turns out were excited by lots of money. [One colleague, for example] got into the Center for Urban and Regional Affairs. There was money there and he was its first director. He could reach out into depressed ghetto neighborhoods and establish effective programs, and housing, and transportation. I'll tell you, it was exciting.

Understanding the importance of the macro political economy in affecting people's lives, work, opportunities, and choices should not undermine the impressiveness of the individuals, their work, and their choices. The field of Community Organization was significantly advanced by the efforts of the group in this volume. But a look at the larger political economy and political struggles of the day helps illustrate how and why this group of individuals were able to achieve what they did and helps clarify why they share so much in common.

This group is representative of social work Community Organization professionals of their generation. Others are no longer alive—Harry Specht and Charles Grosser come most quickly to mind. The voice of those who achieved less illustrious careers and labored at less-supportive institutions is not here. Neither are those community organizers outside of social work Community Organization. Nevertheless, we have a select group of community organization practitioners and academics in social work whose contribution to the process of developing social work Community Organization has been seminal.

It seems propitious that we now rediscover and celebrate their work at a time when public life seems in decline, progressive social movements seem absent or at best fragmented, and a neoconservative context rules in direct opposition to many of the social change gains and values of the social work profession and the social movements of the sixties and seventies. In those decades, a political economy of liberalism and social change provided room for Community Organization, within and without social work. Since the mid 1970s, at least in social work, there has been little interest in Community Organization, as society and its social work professionals increasingly turned inward and toward private matters. Social work now seems to be changing, with an apparent renewed interest in Community Organization. Whether social work retreats into the personal and private or returns to its focus on the social and public remains to be seen. What is clear is that the reflections in this volume can help people rediscover the roots of Community Organization, and they offer important building blocks and lessons for those who take the time to read them.

BIBLIOGRAPHY

Bellah, R., R. Madsen, W. Sullivan, A. Swidler, and S. Tipton. 1985. *Habits of the Heart: Individualism and Commitment in American Life*. New York: Harper & Row.

Berkhofer, R. 1995. *Beyond the Great Story: History as Text and Discourse*. Cambridge, MA: Harvard University Press.

Betten, N., and M. Austin. 1990. *The Roots of Community Organizing*. Philadelphia: Temple University Press.

Chambers, C. 1996. Interview by Karen Strauss, 3/15/96 and 3/18/96. Unpublished. University of Minnesota Library Archive.

Cortes, E. 1993. "Politics of Social Capital." *The Texas Observer* (January 29), 16–17.

Davis, A. 1967. *Spearheads for Reform*. New York: Oxford University Press.

Delgado, G. 1986. *Organizing the Movement: The Roots and Growth of ACORN*. Philadelphia: Temple University Press.

de Tocqueville, A. 1969. *Democracy in America*. New York: Doubleday, Anchor Books.

Fisher, R. 1994a. *Let the People Decide*. 2nd ed. New York: Twayne Publishers. First edition 1984.

Fisher, R. 1994b. "Community Organizing in the Conservative '80s and Beyond." *Social Policy* 25, no. 1 (Fall):11–21.

Fisher, R., and H. Karger. 1997. *Social Work and Community in a Private World: Getting Out in Public*. New York: Longman.

Flacks, R. 1988. *Making History: The Radical Tradition in American Life*. New York: Columbia University Press.

Fukuyama, F. 1992. *The End of History and the Last Man*. New York: Free Press.

Gutierrez, L. 1992. "Improving the Human Condition Through Empowerment Practice." Paper presented at the NASW/IFSW World Assembly.

Lasch, C. 1978. *The Culture of Narcissism*. New York: W. W. Norton.

Luce, H. R. 1969. *The Ideas of Henry Luce*. New York: Atheneum.

Marquez, B. 1993. "Mexican American Community Development Corporations and the Limits of Directed Capitalism." *Economic Development Quarterly* 7(3): 276–298.

McMillen, H. W. 1947. "Community Organization for Social Welfare." *Social Work Year Book, 1947*, edited by R. H. Kurtz. New York: Russell Sage Foundation.

Mooney-Melvin, P. 1986. *American Community Organization: A Historical Dictionary*. Westport, CT: Greenwood.

New York Times. 1953. Clipping, untitled (January 31), no page. Social Welfare History Archive, Minneapolis, United Community Defense Services folder.

Pierce, N., and C. F. Steinbach. 1987. *Corrective Capitalism*. New York: Ford Foundation.

Pierce, N., and C. Steinbach. 1990. *Enterprising Communities: Community-Based Development in America, 1990*. Washington, DC: Council for Community-Based Development.

Piven, F. F., and R. Cloward. 1977. *Poor People's Movements: Why They Succeed, How They Fail*. New York: Pantheon.

Putnam, R. 1996. "The Strange Disappearance of Civic America." *American Prospect* 24 (Winter).

Rothman, J. 1968. "Three Models of Community Organization Practice." National Conference on Social Welfare, *Social Work Practice 1968*. New York: Columbia University Press.

Rothman, J. 1974. *Planning and Organizing for Social Change: Action Principles from Social Science Research*. New York: Columbia University Press.

Schwartz, M. 1965. "Community Organization." Pp. 177–189 in *Encyclopedia of Social Work*, Fifteenth Issue, edited by Harry Lurie. New York: National Association of Social Workers.

Specht, H., and M. Courtney. 1994. *Unfaithful Angels: How Social Work Abandoned Its Mission*. New York: The Free Press.

Thompson, E. P. 1971. "Anthropology and the Discipline of Historical Context." *Midland History* 1(3):41–55.

Traynor, B. 1993. "Community Development and Community Organizing." *Shelterforce* 68 (March/April), p. 4.

Weil, M. 1996. "Model Development in Community Practice: An Historical Perspective." *Journal of Community Practice* 3(3/4):5–67.

What Kind of Professional?
Community Organization
in and Beyond Social Work

Mayer N. Zald*

These very interesting essays on the development of Community Organization in social work practice and teaching are written largely from the perspective of each writer's own career and experiences. Similarly, I comment on them from my own scholarly interests and perspectives. I have had an interest in the relationship of social science theory and research to social work since my doctoral student days at the University of Michigan during the late 1950s. My dissertation data were drawn from a project housed in the School of Social Work, and members of my dissertation committee and senior colleagues were attempting to integrate social science into social work curriculum developments and practice. Intermittently, over this 40-year period I have written on topics

---

*I am indebted to Barry Checkoway and John McCarthy for discussions of several of the ideas discussed here. Jack Rothman provided useful editorial and substantive guidance.

related to the sociology of social welfare. Also, I have had an abiding interest in the study of social movements and the study of professions and organizations. Since Community Organization and social movements share some common issues—in particular the problem of mobilizing participation and resources, and the problem of sustaining participation and resources once mobilized—my interest in social movements may help illuminate issues in Community Organization.

CO within social work also has professional aspirations: It aims to provide college graduates with a knowledge base, skills, and a professional credential that are useful to society and to careers. The literature of the sociology of professions can illuminate the problems of CO as a profession.

Finally, in recent years I have been increasingly concerned with the historical embeddedness of social action and the need to have theories and concepts that take history seriously, that ask how institutions and practices are shaped by historical forces and their historical origins. Community Organization as it is currently practiced is shaped both by its embeddedness in social work and by its historical embeddedness in American society. Thus, some comments on that history are in order.

The papers can be read in many lights—as a set of commentaries on the history of social-work based CO over the last half century; as reflections on the personal development and careers of prominent community organizers, mostly with academic attachments for much of their careers; as commentaries on the professionalization of liberal reformism; as an indicator of the limits of professionalization and of organization; and so on. Without attempting to be exhaustive, I comment on three large issues. First, what do these papers tell us about the historical development of social work and Community Organization within social work in the United States during the last half-century? What was distinctive about this period? Second, what ought to be the relationship of the CO curriculum and CO-related research to social science theory and research? Finally, an issue that is not at the center of any of these papers, although raised in at least one or two, what do we make of the prospects of CO as a profession or occupation, related to social work or outside of its jurisdiction?

THE HISTORICAL PERIOD

These papers are by a very senior group of social workers who developed CO expertise. Most of them also became leaders in social work education, especially in the development of the CO curriculum. In many cases they drifted into social work and then into CO either because they had some prior agency/summer camp experiences, or because they had a general sense that the world was out of kilter and they wanted to try and help change it. CO was not a well-defined practice or profession. (As an aside, unlike some professions, social work in general and Community Organization in particular are not professions that have clear images in the population and are unlikely to be chosen as professional careers in early adolescence or even early in college.) In several cases, especially the most senior ones, these professors ended up constructing the first curricula in Community Organization for their schools. Textbooks for CO had already been published, but a curriculum track rarely existed or was subsidiary to the casework or group work track.

This group is part of the second generation in the process of the institutionalization of social work in academia. Members of the first generation (1920–1950) were even more likely to have come to academia after years of practice and were much less likely to have Ph.D. degrees. In this regard, the careers of this generation parallel the careers of those in other practice professions in the United States that moved into the sometimes negative embrace of the American higher education system. During this same period, schools of nursing and education were also beginning to emphasize the importance of the doctoral degree. All of the practice professions have had to confront the relationship of wisdom garnered from practice to the legitimating claims of science and scholarship fostered within university settings.

Although all of the three major types of CO practice that Rothman identifies (i.e., interagency coordination and planning, locality development, advocacy/social justice) had roots in earlier parts of the development of social work, the advocacy/social justice form of CO was relatively absent in social-work based CO during the early years of the older members of this group. The advocacy/social justice forms of CO had their roots in the settlement house movement, itself part of the larger Progressive Movement. It had later embodiment in the writings of other professors of social work such as Grace Coyle. But CO in social work did not have much connection to the major form of protest mobilization of the 1930s—labor unions and labor organizing—nor to labor unions in the forties and fifties. Although one could find occasional social workers with close ties to the labor movement, and although schools of social work identified with and built into their curriculum an explication of social welfare/welfare state policy, a strong advocacy/mobilization focus was not found in practice nor in teaching of the older members of this group. (Part of the irony here is that in the 1930s, as casework was displaced from public welfare and as intellectual developments focused on intrapersonal dynamics, parts of social work were out of phase with the major social problems of the day.) That advocacy/social justice practice is relatively absent in the 1950s is not surprising, given the relative quiescence of the political scene immediately following WWII and until the upsurge of mobilization surrounding the

Civil Rights Movement. There is an advocacy voice of CO in the fifties represented by Saul Alinsky and the IAF. But the social workers who authored these essays had no connection to Alinsky, partly because, as we know, Alinsky had little use for social work.

It is clear that the coming of the Civil Rights Movement and the election of John F. Kennedy changed the potential for one form of CO practice. It is probably not surprising that CO identifies with the poor and takes on local power structures in the sixties in a way that it did not earlier—or it does today. After all, segments of many professions became conscious of the ways in which professional practice ignored poverty and injustice and were complicit with power/practice relations of dominant groups. Urban planners, lawyers, doctors, social workers, and educators were alerted to the way in which institutions were not working for the poor and minority groups. Curricula changed and different kinds of professional practice were affirmed. Possibly it was a case of old wine in new bottles, but it appeared to be a large change.

What is a bit surprising, in retrospect, is that for CO the professional window of opportunity to engage with advocacy and social justice appears in the guise of juvenile delinquency prevention. (See especially the chapters by Brager, Spergel, and Cloward and Piven.) Of course, group work with juveniles had a prior history in settlement house and community center activities. But group work in the 1950s was not especially reform-minded. It did not attempt to change community structures.

The late fifties and early sixties were characterized by an emerging critique of American society that saw the problems of the poor not in their personal characteristics, but in the educational and employment opportunities and institutional structures of the larger society. The emerging critique was facilitated by philanthropic foundations, especially the Ford Foundation, and by programs of research funded by NIMH. As Helfgot (1981, ch. 2) shows, it drew on older traditions in the sociology of gangs as well as contemporary efforts of settlement houses. The conjunction of Cloward and Ohlin's (1960) theory of social structure and delinquency, Lloyd Ohlin's role in the President's Committee on Juvenile Delinquency and Youth Crime, headed by Robert Kennedy, and the Justice Department's role as a fulcrum of the war on poverty probably explain what in retrospect appears to be an overly optimistic attempt to reform community structures and policies through delinquency prevention programs. I say "overly optimistic" because we learned just how much resistance to these programs could be mobilized by politicians and community leaders. Overly optimistic or not, it is the case that if you were going to mobilize the poor for attack on community institutions, especially in urban ghettos, a rapprochement with young black males was essential. As often occurs, professionals conjoined a funding source and a theory to create an expanded role for advocacy/social justice practice. CO flourished in this period.

(A personal note: In 1960 I finished a dissertation at Michigan and took a position at the University of Chicago. My first major research project after the dissertation was a study of the YMCA of Chicago [Zald, 1970]. What had peaked my interest was that this traditional "gym and swim club for the lower middle class" had embarked on an innovative program of street work with gangs. For the YMCA in Chicago, as for CO, work with gangs provided an entre for the organization to severe problems of the ghettos that broke the traditional mode of practice.)

Events of the sixties not only challenged models of professional practice, they changed the bases of recruitment to schools of social work, especially to CO. As Ralph Kramer documents in his chapter, students became more diverse in terms of their class and racial backgrounds. They also challenged the received wisdom of the field and the criteria for evaluation of students. Berkeley may have experienced the sixties in a more tumultuous way than many other schools, but others had to come to grips with the changing demands of students in similar—if more attenuated—fashion. Those changes are a harbinger of the ethnicity/identity issues that have come to play an increasing role in schools of social work, as well as in the larger society.

Community Organization enrollments swelled at this time, as both middle-class and working-class students saw CO as offering a promise of social reform and a paying professional job. It would be very interesting to know what has happened to the careers and lives of this sixties generation of practitioners. The social movement literature (Fendrich and Tarleau, 1973; Fendrich and Lovejoy, 1988) documents the extent to which activists' lives are changed by their participation in movements, affecting later careers. While some CO practitioners recruited in the sixties for advocacy roles may now be indistinguishable from practitioners recruited earlier and later, I suspect that traces of their activism can be found in careers and in their ideology.

It is clear from these papers that, by the middle of the seventies, the period of street advocacy is over. The enrollment bulge ends and fewer schools of social work sustain a viable CO curriculum. CO becomes, again, a marginal player in schools of social work, though, I will argue later, playing an increasing role in the larger society.

This recounting of some of the historical backdrop reflected in the chapters suggests how much the changes in CO are reflective of the changes in the larger society, not technology or internal intellectual developments although Clarke stresses the importance of the latter. Moreover, the institutionalization of professional training that is reflected will certainly continue. Now the Ph.D. degree is indispensable for academic positions. Finally, I am struck by how much some of these papers reflect a tension between the institutionalization of social work and the changing potential markets for social work skills.

SOCIAL SCIENCE RESEARCH AND CO RESEARCH THEORY

The papers are very good at describing careers. They are also good at describing contributions to curriculum change and contributions to specific Community Organization practice efforts. On the other hand, although several of these authors have made significant contributions to scholarship, only two or three focus on that aspect of their careers here. For instance, you would never know from his chapter that Ralph Kramer (1981, 1993) has written some of the most important work there is on how the nonprofit sector is organized in different countries. Except for Rothman and for Austin, there is little sense here of how the CO educators have changed their theories or modified their perspectives on practice. Would a comparable book written by interpersonal practice educators look the same? There, new treatment modalities (e.g., family systems theories, behavioral learning paradigms, brief treatment models, etc.) and new problem categories (e.g., child abuse and neglect, wife abuse, etc.) have drastically changed the modalities and setting of practice. Except for identity-based CO practice, no such changes in modality and setting are apparent.

Assuming that I am right that there has not been much intellectual change in CO, to what can that absence be attributed? Several factors may be at work: The changing fashions of social science research and its but fitful engagement with Community Organization relevant issues may make it irrelevant to CO practice. It is difficult to develop cumulative theory and research when your case base is small and it is impractical to develop generalizations that in fact are based upon systematic research. There is a disjunction between practice professions necessarily concerned with training to handle particular cases and a theoretical social science that is not very good at talking about particular cases. Moreover, it is possible that forms of Community Organization and the sites of practice are so shaped by law and ongoing institutions that we do not see Community Organization innovation, even when it is widespread. For instance, the diffusion of community development banks that provide a cooperative mechanism for financing enterprise in low-income communities seems not to be widely recognized in the CO literature as a form of CO practice.

These issues deserve greater elaboration, but it is not possible to deal with each of them here. Briefly, I would like to comment on two issues that bear on the integration of social science and social work research. On the one hand, presumably relevant social science fields may be changing in directions that are not useful for or irrelevant to social work theorization. On the other hand, how are we to evaluate the effectiveness of CO practice, at the local and macro levels?

First, some comments about the relevance of social science research to Community Organization. Of course, since CO is not all of a piece, different aspects may require meshing with vastly different literatures in social science. The beauty of *The Dynamics of Planned Change* (Lippitt, Watson, and Westley, 1958) was that it provided an overarching frame for integrating attempts at planned change at various levels. Yet, since the forms of CO are quite different, Lippitt, Watson, and Westley provide at best a scaffolding that has to be filled in by detailed analysis from specialized literatures. For instance, I would assert that the bodies of literature in organizational theory that deal with interorganizational exchange and coordination are quite different than the literatures in social psychology, political sociology, and social movements most relevant for understanding advocacy-oriented community organization. More importantly, current theory and research in a specialized area may be conducted in such a way that it is not at all clear what it's implications are for practice fields.

Take developments in organizational theory. The two dominant schools in the sociology of organizations for the last two decades have been population-ecology and neoinstitutional theory. For much of this period they have been relentlessly antiagentic. They have had a kind of macro determinism to them. Only recently have some younger scholars opened up pathways to adaptation and choice within these theories. It would have been hard for a Community Organization professor to find a lot of help here, compared to the apparent clear help of earlier organization-environment relations theory or contingency theory.

One implication is that, while social science training may be important for CO academics, current social science theory and research may be less relevant for practice-oriented fields than a relentlessly problem-oriented approach that scans for useful approaches, regardless of their current fashionableness. Of course, disciplinary-based academics might find such work old-fashioned, but CO academics should not be concerned.

A second area in which social science research and CO practice is implicated is in the evaluation of CO practice, conducted by social workers or others, at both the locality and macro level. Most of the chapters in this volume do not address the issue directly, even when the authors implicitly assume some level of effectiveness. Among the merits of the paper by Cloward and Piven is that they have a clear conception of what they think ought to be the goals of CO practice, whether conducted by academics or practitioners in the field, and they have come to an assessment of how CO can contribute to "disruptive dissensus," which in turn may play a large role in short-term and long-term gains for poor people.

On at least three issues, Cloward and Piven have come to conclusions that deserve attention from CO academics and practioners. First, what should be the goals of CO during periods when there is little momentum to disruptive activity? For them, CO should be devoted to keeping ideals of social justice alive. Some CO practitioners might see the goals of CO as developing community infrastructures and obtaining concrete programs and facilities, regardless of their explicit relationship to ideas of social justice. But the issue needs to be directly on the table.

Second, Cloward and Piven have come to the conclusion that a focus on membership organizations and building organization is misguided. Exactly what is the role of organizations and what kinds of organizational activity are necessary to capitalize on and contribute to disruptive dissensus is a matter of some debate. One good statement of the issues is found in a paper by Gamson and Schmeidler (1984) and the reply by Cloward and Piven (1984). But that they have identified a central issue is beyond dispute.

Finally, Cloward and Piven raise a macro issue that none of the other papers address: What is the contribution of CO and disruptive dissensus to the long-term transformation of industrialized societies, especially American society? Here they confront alternative theories of the emergence and transformation of the welfare state. (For some of the relevant approaches see Esping-Andersen [1985, 1990]; Wilensky et al. [1985]; and Weir, Orloff, and Skocpol [1988].) The alternative approaches emphasize the ideologies of state elites, the relative structures of corporatist inclusion, interclass coalitions, and state-bureaucratic processes to a greater extent than Piven and Cloward do. Yet, certainly CO needs to have addressed the issue of the relationship of CO-related practice to macro societal change.

CO PRACTICE AND THE SOCIOLOGY OF PROFESSIONS

What kind of profession does CO represent? Possibly because of the charge that was given them, the authors do not say much about the problem of building a profession. What kinds of jobs are there for what kinds of people with what kinds of skills, certifications, and degrees? How have these changed? What are the potentials?

This is not the place to describe the history of professions or the history of the sociology of professions. Suffice it to say that, currently, students of the professions ask somewhat different questions than would have been asked two or three decades ago. At one time, sociologists devoted much effort to describing the phases of professionalization—as occupations standardized training, developed professional associations, and established certification and licensing procedures—or documenting the role types and role conflicts within professions. Today there is a greater tendency to see professions within a matrix of competing occupations attempting to claim a mandate over certain services and skills in relationship to clients. Professions have collective projects in which they attempt to assert their status and protect their boundaries in relation to other competitors or symbiotically related occupations (Larson, 1977). Successful professions—successful in that they are recognized by salient groups as having the cognitive tools, theories, and associated techniques to be able to best handle the uncertainties of specified problems—come to dominate occupational settings and tasks (Abbott, 1990). Even if parts of the task become routinizable and are spun off to subprofessions, or technicians (e.g., nurse-practitioners, paralegals, etc.), the profession dominates the terms of practice of the subordinate occupation.

A training route and credential can come to dominate an occupation even without the action of the state. No law or accrediting agency requires that CEOs and middle managers of large corporations have the MBA. But employer demands for credentials have clearly increased, and, except for selected high-tech industries, access to managerial positions and advancement are increasingly dependent on having the MBA.

Several questions are suggested. What are the skills of the CO practitioner? Does social work command the training of these skills in relationship to other training sites? Are there distinctive advantages in some work sites for the MSW? Since there are several models of CO, is there a distinctive patterning of the recruitment and career line associated with different modes of practice?

A profession that once dominates a work setting may lose that control to other professions, if employers believe that some other occupation delivers the goods "better" or cheaper. Consider how, at the end of the nineteenth century, doctors and psychiatrists took over the direction of institutions for the "insane" from ministers. Consider how "case management" transforms the skill base and educational requirements claimed to be needed for the delivery of services to welfare clients or to the mentally ill.

Of course, the competition among occupations and professions is often not a pure market competition, in which paying clients choose among purveyors of services with different credentials and skills, but it is a blockaded or mediated political competition. First, professional/client relationships are mediated by hierarchical third parties. Thus, employing agencies, managers, boards, and politicians determine what kinds of skills are needed. Second, these employing agencies often have to confront certification criteria and standards set by negotiation between professional associations, accrediting agencies, and the state. For instance, no matter how qualified medical technicians may be, the medical profession has attempted to control their interpretative role in the use of their reports. Similarly, HMOs may decide to recognize the counseling/clinical skills of psychologists, even though clinical social workers may have the same basic skills.

Community Organization may draw on a variety of intellectual and interpersonal skills. At the most general level these include an ability to diagnose community/group needs, design intervention programs, build and maintain organizations for drawing together groups and individuals in the pursuit of community objectives, work with groups, establish communication linkages, and the like. It also depends on a certain resonance between the personal characteristics and background of the worker and the group or community being served. If you want to organize in the Hispanic community, you need to be able to speak the language and be able to evidence an identification with that community. At an abstract level, Community Organization draws on a variety of academic disciplines and professional formulations. But for much of CO practice the more abstract formulations may not be necessary. Much can be learned on the job or in workshops of short duration. A college graduate can be taught to do union organizing in a summer. A community activist can be helped to expand the definition of his or her role in workshops and brief courses. Of course, the skills necessary for street organizing may be different from those necessary for writing proposals for grants from government agencies, or administering large budgets, or designing information-gathering instruments. These latter sets of skills are facilitated by formal educational training, whereas street organizing may depend upon field experience to a greater extent.

My thesis is twofold: First, in modern America there is an increasing demand for the skills involved in community organizing. Second, practitioners with an MSW will be useful for meeting only a small part of the demand, even if schools of social work were geared up to meet more of it.

As to the first proposition, there is a growing demand for community organizing skills, because the achievement of social goals is increasingly seen as dependent upon the mobilization of locality-based, ethnically or racially based, or specific-interest based identities. There is both a widespread belief that mobilization is efficacious (that is, mobilization is useful in achieving specific goals), and an institutionalization of requirements that groups participate in some formal way in decisions that are made affecting them. Whether it is attempts of local groups to empower citizens in relationship to city bureaucracies, or the attempts of health agencies to create networks for health education, or the attempts of labor unions to galvanize recruitment, or the attempts of local public utilities to establish linkages to community groups, CO skills are in greater and greater demand.

Funding for the jobs may come from corporations, from government grants, from membership dues, from philanthropic foundations and from church-related agencies. Training will often be in short courses and seminars. Local activists with some training may become salaried employees of small agencies; and, if they are skilled enough and articulate enough, may themselve become trainers and consultants to other programs. The Industrial Areas Foundation has more projects going today then ever before. The Campaign for Human Development funds projects throughout the nation. Community development projects abound. Church-based community organization is at high tide. Labor unions have attempted to buck the antilabor tide by developing new careers for organizers.

This discussion leads to the second proposition. The MSW degree in Community Organization is most likely to be useful in relationship to employment settings that use educational credentials as a surrogate for social/organizational competence. The larger the organization and the more its managerial cadres have avanced degrees, the more the MSW will be used as a filter in recruitment. Moreover, where positions require coordination with others from middle-class backgrounds or middle-class appearances, those with advanced degrees and middle-class modes of communication will be advantaged. Conversely, where the employing organization is small, and demands direct interaction with disadvantaged clientele, a premium will be placed on street smarts and cultural markers of community identification.

Of course, there is a paradox in all this. Social work has often been uncomfortable when it affiliated with power. Ideologically, it has identified with the poor and with an advocacy mission, even while it made its peace with the established order. Community Organization need have little to do with advocacy or righting injustices. And the "best" jobs, from the point of view of money and prestige, may have little to do with advocacy. It may well be that, increasingly, advocacy CO is done by community organizers with little connection to social work. From their perspective, the MSW in CO may look increasingly irrelevant. At the same time, advocacy has become institutionalized. Many welfare and nonprofit advocacy groups need representatives who can speak to power. A niche for MSWs interested in advocacy may be found here.

I have argued that CO in social work is in competition with short-term programs that train in basic skills in identifying community problems and in mobilizing community participation. It also faces competition from other sources—master's programs in public policy analysis and in the management of nonprofit organizations. Both provide alternative routes for obtaining the analytic, information-gathering, and administrative skills that have been part of the CO program. Whether they will come to dominate these arenas remains to be seen.

Before concluding, let me comment on another issue of professional practice that is not explicitly raised as a problematic in these papers: Who is the client of CO?

When we speak of professional mandates, it is often with an implicit understanding of who the clients of the profession are. This implicit understanding is often not problematic. For instance, we usually assume that the client of the physician is the patient. Only when the physician is subsumed in a bureaucratic structure that has partially conflicting goals (e.g., the military, which needs to be concerned with triage and returning soldiers to the battlefront; or HMOs, which are concerned about overall efficiency matters) do we begin to ask who is really the client. But for CO, which is practiced in so many different kinds of settings, and with so many different kinds of funding arrangements, the matter of who is the client, or at least who can control the professional and the organization, becomes central to understanding the fate of practice. As the story told in both the paper by Spergel and that of Brager indicates, an analysis of the dependencies of practice on legitimation and funding flows is central to understanding the viability of practice. Of course, academics, with their support in tenured positions, can devote their efforts to any cause they want, at least in the short run.

CONCLUSIONS

These papers have opened an interesting window through which to think about the history and functioning of social-work based CO in the last 50 years. In my commentary, I have focused upon how the decade of the sixties helped shape the next thirty years, on the relationship of social science scholarship to practice, and on what these papers have to say, or might have to say, about CO as a profession. Community Organization practice is deeply dependent upon a fabric of institutional rules and organizational processes for creating the demand for its services. Moreover, the forms of practice are related to cycles of advocacy and protest as well as changing interorganizational and community structures. I have argued that there is an increasing demand for CO practice, whether or not it is based upon MSW training.

What about the present and the future? While not exactly in the doldrums, it is clear that CO within social work is not as vibrant as it once was. Moreover, it faces competition from below and from the side— from short-term training programs and from other professions that train in many of the intellectual skills that MSWs in administration and CO receive.

Nevertheless, whether in social work or not, the demand for community organization practice is likely to grow. Moreover, if history is any guide, we are likely to have other protest cycles in the decades ahead. Such protest cycles create the conditions for CO invigoration.

BIBLIOGRAPHY

Abbott, Andrew. 1990. *The System of Professions: An Essay on the Division of Expert Labor*. Chicago: University of Chicago Press.

Cloward, Richard A., and Lloyd E. Ohlin. 1960. *Delinquency and Opportunity: A Theory of Delinquent Gangs*. New York: The Free Press.

Cloward, Richard A., and Francis Fox Piven. 1984. "Disruption and Organization: A Rejoinder to Gamson and Schmeidler." *Theory and Society* 18:587–99.

Esping-Andersen, Gosta. 1985. *Politics Against Markets: The Social Democratic Road to Socialism*. Princeton, NJ: Princeton University Press.

Esping-Andersen, Gosta, 1990. *The Three Worlds of Welfare Capitalism*. Cambridge, England: Polity Press.

Fendrich, James Max, and Kenneth L. Lovejoy. 1988. "Back to the Future: Adult Political Behavior of Former Student Activists." *American Sociological Review* 53:780–84.

Fendrich, James Max, and Alison Tarleau. 1973. "Marching to a Different Drummer: The Occupational and Political Orientations of Former Student Activists." *Social Forces* 52:245–53.

Gamson, William A., and Emilie Schmeidler. 1984. "Organizing the Poor: An Argument with Frances Fox Piven and Richard Cloward, 'Poor People's Movements: Why They Succeed, How They Fail.'" *Theory and Society* 13:567–85.

Helfgot, Joseph H. 1981. *Professional Reforming: Mobilization For Youth and the Failure of Social Science*. Lexington, MA: D. C. Heath.

Kramer, Ralph. 1981. *Voluntary Agencies in the Welfare State*. Berkeley: University of California Press.

Kramer, Ralph. 1993. *Privatization in Four European Countries: Comparative Studies in Government–Third Sector Relations*. Armonk, NY: M. E. Sharpe.

Larson, Magali Sarfatti. 1977. *The Rise of Professionalism: A Sociological Analysis*. Berkeley: University of California Press.

Lippitt, Ronald, Jeanne Watson, and Bruce Westley. 1958. *The Dynamics of Planned Change: A Comparative Study of Principles and Techniques*. New York: Harcourt Brace.

Weir, Margaret, Ann Shola Orloff, and Theda Skocpol, eds. 1988. *The Politics of Social Policy in the Untied States*. Princeton, NJ: Princeton University Press.

Wilensky, Harold J., et al. 1985. *Comparative Social Policy: Theory, Methods, Findings*. Berkeley, CA: International Studies Research Series, p. 62.

Zald, Mayer N. 1970. *Organizational Change: The Political Economy of the YMCA*. Chicago: University of Chicago Press.

Current, Emerging, and Future Trends for Community Organization Practice

Lorraine Gutiérrez

Over the past decade, community practice has gained increasing attention in social work, the human services, and society at large. A confluence of economic and social forces has led to increasing interest in the prevention of mental illness, child abuse, and other social problems through community-based education and development. Major foundations and governmental funding to improve social welfare have placed emphasis on ways in which business, citizens, and the nonprofit sector can collaborate to work toward the resolution of persistent social problems. Community methods are also particularly significant in light of current and emerging efforts to transfer the administration of federal programs to local control. This growing interest in community focuses attention on the degree to which existing models of community practice adequately address community needs. This book will be an invaluable resource to those of us who are interested in creating effective Community

Organization methods by understanding historical, current, and emerging issues for practice.

LOCATING THE NARRATOR

It was with pleasure that I received the invitation to participate in this ambitious and exciting project. My role in this volume is to speak from the perspective of a current educator and practitioner in Community Organization. The role of educator/organizer is one that I share with many of the authors here. However, given the nature of this book, I think it is important that I share the ways in which my voice is reflective of my own unique life experiences.

A concern with community and social justice is a large part of my heritage. A significant part of my "family narrative" is focused on community participation. My maternal grandfather was a Mexican Methodist missionary who was sent from Mexico to the southwest to minister to Spanish-speaking communities. A large part of his work, and that of my grandmother, included what would be considered social services. For example, they organized schools, arranged community care for the sick, and advocated for Mexican immigrants as part of their ministry. In the oppressive environment of Texas and Arizona in the early twentieth century, they provided one of the few sources for social care in their communities.

More formal social work played a significant role in my parent's lives as well. As struggling college students, they were brought together in the 1930s by social group workers with the YMCA who created programs to support Mexican American youth in their education. In their work with this organization, the Mexican American Movement, they developed skills and means that enabled them to stay in school and become public school teachers, but they also were involved in supporting other students. As part of this work, my father edited one of the first newspapers for Mexican American youth, *The Mexican Voice* (Muñoz, 1989). Both were actively involved in organizing annual conferences for young men and women of Mexican descent who faced many economic, social, and family struggles in order to remain involved in higher education. As I grew up, many of the adults in my social world were individuals of different races and backgrounds—Mexican American, Anglo, Asian American, and African American—who were involved in such activities as settlement work, teaching, legal advocacy, union organizing, and Chicano activism.

The feminist and civil rights movements were also significant influences on my development as an activist/scholar. As a child of the 1960s I had directly observed ways in which groups of individuals working in communities could organize to make major changes in race relations. I saw

King's March on Washington and Chavez's mobilization of farmworkers on TV, and discussed the significance of this work within my family. Members of my extended family were directly involved in different aspects of the Chicano movement. As a Mexican American child in a politically liberal family, the message I got was that only through community participation could social change take place. However, as a child and young adolescent, I had no idea of how this activity could translate into a career.

I came to my interest in Community Organization practice as a social work student at the University of Chicago School of Social Service Administration during the late 1970s. I had gone directly from an undergraduate degree in history to the master's program, with the notion that by going into social work I could be an "actor" in history in some way. In my B.A. program I had focused on American urban history and had been fascinated by the progressive movement and ways in which American society had dealt with issues of urbanization and immigration in the early twentieth century. I had seen Jane Addams, Sophenisba Breckenridge, and Lillian Wald as examples of ways in which *women* could contribute to the improvement of society.

Upon graduation from college I was deeply affected by growing media coverage of issues related to violence against women. Although my concentration at Chicago had been in "social treatment," I had taken an advanced generalist track that had included Community Organization and administration methods. I began to work, first as a volunteer then as a social worker, with new organizations focused on ending wife abuse through education, advocacy, and alternative services. In this capacity, I began to consider issues of empowerment and multiculturalism and other ideas that led me into a Ph.D. program and a career in social work research and education. Both my heritage and my work experiences have deeply affected my current work on multicultural issues in community practice. One expression of this interest is my current position, which includes coordinating the Detroit Initiative in Psychology, a program that brings University of Michigan graduate and undergraduate students into partnership with community workers in Detroit.

This brief description of who I am and where I come from suggests that I bring multiple lenses to this work and to my essay. My voice, that of a Latina, a fifth-generation Californian, a baby boomer, a feminist organizer, and advanced generalist MSW may distinguish me from most of my fellow authors in this book. However, my concern with social justice and interest in the power of social participation can be something that we all share. In some respects, my work in Community Organization, which has brought together feminist or multicultural themes in the mixing and phasing of different models, may exemplify the ways in which CO practice has evolved. It represents a challenging yet exciting amalgam of more traditional and emergent perspectives on practice.

ISSUES AND TRENDS IN CONTEMPORARY COMMUNITY ORGANIZATION PRACTICE

Today a paradox exists for community organizers in social work. Currently only 15 percent of all MSW programs offer a concentration in Community Organization (Pine and Mizrahi, 1996). Although CO methods may now be part of the foundation methods in some schools, there are few opportunities to develop advanced or specialized skills. However, an interest in community practice is growing both in social work and in other human service professions. This is evidenced by the increase in literature on Community Organization. For example, both *Families in Society* (formerly *Social Casework*) and *Social Work* have recently dedicated special issues to community-based approaches. The *Journal of Community Practice* began publication in 1994 and, on a quarterly basis, publishes articles on a range of CO methods and practices. Books on community organization, both theoretical (Mondros and Wilson, 1994) and practical (Hardcastle, Wenocur, and Powers, 1997), are also being published. This has been mirrored by similar trends in education, public health, and community psychology—all of which are documenting both the methods and dilemmas for community practitioners.

This growth in the literature corresponds with increasing funding opportunities for community-based practice. The Ford, Kellogg, and Carnegie Foundations currently have active funding programs that are focused on community-level interventions. These funding programs most often are oriented toward community development or community planning efforts. Similarly, governmental funding through the Centers for Disease Control and Prevention, the National Institute for Drug Abuse, and the National Institute of Mental Health is supporting research and development efforts testing the effectiveness of community-based interventions to improve health, to reduce the use of drugs, and to improve the accessibility of mental health services for children and families. Most often, these government funds are focused on community education and collaborative community projects.

These trends, in both research and practice, fly in the face of commonly held notions that community organization is nonexistent. Instead, they demonstrate that CO continues to develop and grow *in spite* of trends in social work. In many respects, these programs look very similar to the work conducted by the authors of this volume 30 to 40 years ago. They involve the coordination of services, the participation of community members in programs, and efforts to develop consensus about working toward alleviating community problems. However, in other respects, these programs differ in significant ways. There is more attention to dynamics of race, gender, and ethnicity; there is more collaboration with both formal and informal community workers; and CO work is often carried out by public health nurses, community police officers, or teachers. The community organizer often acts in a consultant role, with the actual organizing work conducted by community members and volunteer programs (Delgado, 1996; Gutiérrez, Rosegrant Alvarez, Nemon, and Lewis, 1996; Wang and Burris, 1994; Lucky, 1995).

Given the limited and marginal nature of education for CO, where are the leaders and workers in these programs being educated? Often these programs are being developed by people educated in other fields or those who have not had CO education in social work. Some of these individuals may have attended specialized training in CO at free-standing schools, such as the Midwest Academy or Center for Third World Organizing, or through work with international development programs such as the Peace Corps. And in some cases, they are developed by those of us who participated in CO programs in social work. Clearly there is a need for current social work education to be preparing students for this work as well.

This brief discussion suggests that CO practice has changed since 60 years ago, when these narratives began. And this growth and evolution is evidence of the significance of CO both in our society and in the helping professions. A question for this volume relates to the relevance of these narratives for contemporary practice: How can the experiences of our fore-parents inform our work today? In thinking of current practice, I believe that these narratives can be helpful in assisting us to identify enduring themes as well as emerging challenges for CO practitioners.

ENDURING THEMES IN COMMUNITY ORGANIZATION PRACTICE

Upon reading these reflections, I am struck first by the enduring themes about community organization practice that emerge from this work. Many, if not most, of the issues discussed by these authors are relevant to my students today. These narrative essays can inform current practice not only by identifying these issues and conflicts but also by providing information about how they have been handled in the past.

A critical issue for these authors was *understanding and defining what we mean by community organization practice*. They were significantly involved in the field at a time in which it was being developed and specified. They participated in the evolution from group work to a field that encompassed a range of different roles and skills. Therefore, these authors were intimately involved in identifying and defining what we mean by Community Organization, what is the knowledge base, and how it relates to other forms of social work practice. Their experience in this process helps us understand where CO practice has come from and its relationship with other methods of practice.

One theme that emerges in respect to this issue is the notion of the purpose and goal of CO practice. Perlman's example of ABCD and Brager's example of MFY raise the question of the level of change we work toward. Do we, as organizers, work toward the remediation of community problems through collaborative strategies with those in power, or do we focus on more fundamental change that challenges authorities? In the example of MFY, the use of heightened conflict may have contributed to the demise of some critical programs. However, without the use of conflict, Community Organization risks simply being the handmaiden of the current power structure. ABCD and MFY in particular highlight the importance of understanding power dynamics and the strategic use of conflict. These are important issues for current organizers to be aware of and think about in their work, especially with large foundations or other funders expressing interest in community practice. In what ways can our role as organizer be used to challenge the systems that support us?

In the second important theme, *the role of the organizer*, is the organizer the "intergroup worker," a community member, a planner, or activist? Each author places different emphasis on these roles based on his or her orientation to community work, community, and area of expertise. For example, the work of Margaret Berry in social settlement work and community development is different in context and role from Brager's work in building multiethnic coalitions and engaging in social action. These different roles involve different relationships and skill sets. However, across all situations, the community organizer is most often an individual who is bringing expertise to a specific bounded context rather than an indigenous member of the community. Very few of these authors specifically discuss ways in which grassroots community members were collaborating in this work. This issue is of concern to organizers today, especially in identity-based organizing in which the assumption is often made that only community members can be involved in direct organizing (Rivera and Erlich, 1995).

A third theme relates to the auspices of the work. *The significance of the organization that sponsors and sanctions the work* is clear in all of the narratives. This is particularly true in the examples of neighborhood organizing. In some, the relationships appear harmonious and supportive—for instance, Mildred Barry's example of community-based health planning or Turner's example of neighborhood stabilization work in Cleveland. In others the relationship is contentious, such as Brager's example of MFY. Contentiousness is also present in the example of the development of the

Community Organization curriculum and the battles that ensued at Berkeley regarding the focus and purpose of education for community organizing. This dynamic with sponsoring organizations remains, and will always remain, a significant element of CO work.

A final theme relates to *the place of community organizing in the social work curriculum*. Schwartz, Kramer, Austin, and Barry all discuss how it was that the CO curriculum was developed. In some schools, the process of curriculum development reflected conflicts involving those with a social casework orientation. In others, the CO curriculum developed, grew, and then was subsumed into a more generic "macro" or CO and management track. In all instances, CO was most often marginal and, perhaps something that only "oddballs" went into. This marginal status continues to exist within the social work curriculum. What is interesting is the degree to which CO has developed in fields outside of social work. Most schools of public health and many programs in psychology or human services are now offering courses in Community Organization. Community policing has now become a standard element of the criminal justice curriculum. An optimistic view of these trends would see these pioneers in the CO curriculum as having moderate impact on our own profession, but greater impact indirectly on other fields.

What was unexpected for me when reading these narratives was the influence of social group work on the development of CO practice. It is difficult to assess how representative this is of the field at large. Most of these authors had initially been educated in the social group work tradition, and this orientation influenced their community organizing teaching, research, and practice. Many of their practice examples utilized skills closely associated with group work—the ability to bring people together, to identify common goals, to move toward collaborative work, and to build relationships with each other. Over the past 50 years, social group work has been marginalized to an even greater degree than Community Organization, with only 7 percent of all MSW degree programs offering a group work concentration and 19 percent of the MSW programs requiring courses on groups (Birnbaum and Aurbach, 1994). As I read these pieces, I was struck by how these two substantial approaches to social work have both been infused into our curriculum, but how at the same time their distinctive methods may be lost.

The identification of these "enduring themes" provides some comfort and context for those of us currently engaged in practice. They are comforting in that they validate the many contradictions involved in our work: Questions regarding who we work for, what our work is about, and where we "belong." They suggest that these questions are inherent in this work and that there are dynamics and tensions that we need to be aware of and to manage if we are to be effective. By providing a context to our work, they also help us to understand how it is that these issues exist. We are in precarious positions—in the community, in the organization, and in the academy—because we are about being outsiders. Effective CO practice requires the ability to question the current order and how the world might operate differently. It should come as no surprise that those in power may see us as threats and work to undermine our efforts.

EMERGING CHALLENGES FOR CO PRACTICE

These narratives have been helpful for identifying the enduring themes that can be instrumental in locating our practice in the broad sweep of social welfare history. However, these narratives can also promote useful thinking about emerging issues for social work practice. By understanding the efforts of the past, we can bring new lenses to challenges of the future. For this section I have identified six issues from among the many that will face community organizers into the next century.

A current trend in social welfare arrangements is *the devolution of policies and programs to state control*. A wide range of federally funded programs—from public assistance to child welfare programs—are now being administered by state and local authorities, with input from community members. This move from centralization to localization of programs presents a challenge and opportunity for community practitioners. It suggests that there will be increasing importance placed on community-based planning, programming, and service provision.

A lesson from these narratives that has direct relevance for this trend is the importance of defining, understanding, and supporting community participation when working on local issues. The practice examples from the Kennedy/Johnson years—MFY, ABCD, and Model Cities—demonstrate the ways in which strategies for community participation can either support or undermine programs. They indicate the challenges involved when a broad range of community members are truly supported to make decisions on important program issues, and they demonstrate the importance of understanding and defining community. The backlash experienced by some of these organizations was an indication of the degree to which community members had been empowered.

If community organizers do not see devolution as an opportunity for building broad-based community participation, these decisions will be left in the hands of those who do not have the best interests of the community in mind. We have already seen this in the creation of "empowerment zones" in some communities, in support of corporate projects, that may not translate easily into improving employment opportunities. Organizers in communities need to take a close look at these new programs and at ways in which citizen input and participation are structured. If they have been controlled by "insiders" then, as Austin points out, grassroots neighborhood organizations such as the IAF can play a role in bringing more individuals and voices to the table.

A second significant trend is *increasing inequality in our society*. Over the past two decades, a greater proportion of wealth has become concentrated within a smaller segment of our society. Some economists and sociologists fear that the United States will become a two-class society made up primarily of the very rich and very poor. This is a significant difference from the practice world of these authors, which occurred during an expansion of the middle class. In stark contrast, youth today can no longer assume that their economic lives will be better than, or even as good as, those of their parents.

Community organizers must play a role in addressing the challenges inherent in these social trends. We must find ways to work toward social justice and, in working, to expand economic, educational, and other types of opportunity. The narratives in this volume that reflect work in community development are helpful in thinking of ways in which we can play more meaningful roles in this very challenging arena. Both Margaret Berry and John Turner discuss neighborhood-based work that was focused on a desire to improve economic opportunity through community participation and grassroots organizing. As they review their work they recognize the degree to which dynamics of power and conflict needed to be involved if change was to occur. These examples, and others in this book, point to the limitations of community strategies that work only to ameliorate situations without creating opportunity. Indeed, Cloward and Piven's chapter argues that any efforts by social workers to increase social justice are minimal if not futile. If we as social workers are to make a real difference in the structure of our society, we will need to work creatively in building community assets (Page-Adams and Sherradin, 1997), increasing economic opportunity (Naperstek and Dooly, 1997), and challenging existing political and economic arrangements (Medoff and Sklar, 1994).

The *increasingly multicultural composition of our society* is a significant emerging issue for community organizers. This trend impacts on how we define the concept of "community" and strategies on community issues (Rivera and Erlich, 1995). Some models for community organization practice currently focus on the need for separate programs and services for specific ethnic groups, or what Jenkins (1980) termed, the "ethnic agency." Others have looked at the challenges involved in bringing together neighborhoods that are diverse in respect to race and ethnicity, as well as national origin (Anner, 1996; Heskin and Heffner, 1987). In these situations, organizers have used such technologies as simultaneous translation devices and other methods to bring community members together.

Discussions of race, ethnicity, and multiculturalism are glimpsed only briefly in these narratives. Many of these authors may have been motivated by a desire to improve the condition of a community they identified with, but only Turner and Schwartz describe work that is focused centrally on issues identified with their race or ethnicity. Although most were working in multicultural coalitions, only Turner describes the potential involved in bringing together community members across identities that may otherwise divide them. The relative silence on this topic is perhaps generational, and our current interest in multiculturalism is a reflection of the influence of identity politics in the organizing of the late 1980s. The ways in which these organizers worked across differences in race or ethnicity by identifying common community goals provide one vision for those of us currently working in this multicultural context.

A related trend is the degree to which current community organization practice involves *communities of interest* rather than localities. This shift in practice is highlighted by Rothman, as he describes ways in which his "tripartite model" did not adequately reflect a world in which groups such as women, gay men and lesbians, people with disabilities, or older people are often involved in community-organizing efforts. Communities comprised of individuals with shared interests and different localities present different challenges from neighborhood-based organizing.

The examples in this book by Chauncey Alexander that document the struggles involved in organizing NASW have direct relevance for identity-based community organizing. Alexander identifies the challenges involved in bringing together a group of professionals who shared many similar goals and values into a professional organization that required them to set aside some of their individual interests and priorities. As a membership organization with no geographical location, the organizers of NASW focused on creating a mission and code of ethics, as well as opportunities for local participation, as ways to build a viable "community" of social workers. These initial organizers also used the media, through the television program *East Side/West Side*,[1] to communicate to the broader society the identity of social workers. There are important lessons to be learned for those of us organizing communities of interest.

As CO has ceased to be taught and practiced as a separate method, in many cases it is integrated into what all social workers learn and do. There are increasing *linkages between CO and other methods of practice such as policy, direct practice, and social work administration*. In my experiences in curriculum development at two schools of social work, we went to field instructors and other practitioners to ask them what kind of skills our graduates needed. In all cases, social workers discussed the ability to practice multiple methods and to be able to use multiple methods in the field. Social work administrators spoke of the need for graduates who could work effectively with community boards and develop programs with community members. Direct-service workers described the need for graduates who could develop and conduct community education programs or form self-help and mutual aid groups to support their clients. Consequently, many schools teach CO as one of many methods for all students.

Although this is an "emerging trend," this integration of methods is well represented in these narratives. Turner, Spergel, and Barry describe ways in which CO and social group work were linked in the work of social settlements. Their roles and skills as group workers and community workers were integrated in all they did. Alexander, Austin, and Kramer provide examples of how CO and administration have been integrated— Austin and Kramer through discussions of curriculum and education for practice, Alexander through his discussion of how CO methods were used in the organization and management of NASW. The examples from Brager and Perlman of community development programs indicate that these linkages between levels of practice were a critical element of the war on poverty programs. These examples from the past provide support for the need for integration, but also a caution. If CO is seen as one of many skills in our "bag of tricks" as social workers, it can also be lost among the options available to us. Learning when and how to bring CO methods into a practice situation is an advanced skill and therefore should be integrated throughout the social work student's career not just presented at the foundation level.

As the sixth issue, our current and emerging social reality is bringing Co into *new problem areas and new arenas for practice*. During the decades covered by these narratives, Community Organization was primarily focused on the problems and issues faced by post–World War II urban communities. The problems and arenas for practice included neighborhood stabilization, reducing gang activity and juvenile delinquency, and building the social infrastructure. The operating assumption for many of these practitioners was that our society was resource-rich, and one role for organizers was to develop the means so that more citizens could participate fully in social and economic opportunity.

Since that time, CO practice has moved into many new arenas. Grassroots groups have engaged in identity-based organizing around race, gender, ethnicity, and other social statuses. These efforts often involved collaborations between paid professionals and unpaid community volunteers. For example, my work in the 1970s and 1980s in the battered women's movement used CO methods to bring communities of women together to confront violence against women with action research, community education, and the development of programs such as emergency shelters and crisis lines. Some of us did this work as an outgrowth of our jobs at YMCAs or victim-support programs, but others worked as volunteers. This type of practice has been the basis of work done by other groups, such a disability rights organizations, HIV/AIDS groups, and others.

Community Organization is also becoming an integral element of practice in child welfare. As workers in child welfare have looked at the context of child abuse and neglect, they have argued for efforts to improve the social and economic conditions of communities and to provide opportunities for broader family support (Adams and Nelson, 1997; Kagen and Weissbourd, 1994). The creation of community-based family support programs in child welfare focuses on working with families in partnership to improve conditions in communities. This includes such efforts as the creation of family drop-in centers, early childhood co-op programs, and toy and resource libraries. This has called for the education of child welfare professionals as workers who can collaborate with community members and work as community workers rather than as case workers. This work requires CO skills.

The creation of community-based partnerships and collaboratives around specific issues such as homelessness, community violence, or substance abuse is also a growing arena for community practice (Bailey and Koney, 1995). These efforts reflect both an interest in community input and a desire to develop ways to utilize existing community resources more "efficiently." The operating assumption has changed from a society with ample resources to one of scarcity. These current partnerships are descendents of the community-planning efforts practiced by Barry, Spergel, and other authors in this volume. And, as indicated by Spergel, when efforts are put forth with skill, they can be effective in impacting the targeted problem or condition. New practitioners in this arena would benefit from reading these narratives as well as other accounts by these authors to understand ways in which this work can be made most effective.

CONCLUSION

In this article I have attempted to identify ways in which current social work students and community organizers can learn from these narratives. In reading them, I have been impressed by their richness and the ways in which the work that is represented speaks to current practice. This reflects, in part, my perspective as a former student of history, but it also reflects our lineage as social workers and members of a profession. Much of our current CO theory and methods was conceptualized and created by these authors, and we carry on this tradition in the work we do today.

There is a subtheme in these narratives that I have not yet addressed. Many of these authors describe the contrast between the idealism of their youth and the actual impact that they may have had on the communities in which they worked. Community stabilization did not stem the disinvestment in Cleveland, MFY did not eliminate juvenile delinquency, *East*

Side/West Side was canceled after one season, and, in my example, battered women's programs have not eliminated violence against women. We all enter these CO efforts with high levels of idealism and are usually confronted with the reality of social and economic systems characterized by inequality that is deeply embedded in our society. These larger forces will continue to impact on the results we eventually achieve. Perhaps, as Piven and Cloward point out, it is unrealistic to expect CO practice to have much impact on conditions that reflect the global economic order.

Yet we should not let the modest outcomes that we do achieve prevent us from engaging in efforts to increase social justice. Instead, we must recognize how our efforts have had impact in improving the human condition on multiple levels. Spergel's work over five decades has decreased the rate of juvenile delinquency, Alexander's work spurred the development of a national organization for social workers, Turner's work increased the capacity of individuals to participate in community life, and most of these authors (including the commentators) have contributed to the development of CO theory and practice. Current conceptualizations of social justice are now focusing on its manifestations on multiple levels, even in interpersonal practice. I believe that the authors in this volume must recognize how their efforts have made this a better world through their work in both their public and private lives.

One of the greatest gifts these narratives provide to us as current practitioners is this sense of perspective. To some of these authors, their accomplishments seem modest in the face of their initial idealism. To me, their careers have made major contributions to our field, and any organizer would be proud to have done half of what most of them have accomplished. Yet, this balance of idealism and pragmatism, vision and reality, is critical when organizing—idealism and vision to motivate us and pragmatism and reality to keep us grounded. If we recognize the relationship of this inherent dialectic to the work we do with communities, we understand how individual efforts are part of a larger struggle. Our greatest leaders and community organizers—Moses, Ghandi, Anthony, King, Chavez—kept their "eyes on the prize." Many did not live to see the fruits of their labors, yet this did not diminish their impact. These narratives can be critical implements for helping us all to see the significant roles we can play in the sweep of social history.

ENDNOTE

1. This program was also a feature I remember from my childhood, and I clamored to watch it even though it was past my bedtime. I remember the episodes as being compelling and interesting, and they, too, formed my image of what the profession of social work might be.

BIBLIOGRAPHY

Adams, P., and K. Nelson. 1997. *Reinventing Human Services: Community- and Family-Centered Practice.* New York: Aldine de Gruyter.

Anner, J. 1996. *Beyond Identity Politics: Emerging Social Justice Movements in Communities of Color.* Boston: South End Press.

Bailey, D., and K. Koney. 1995. "Community Based Consortia: One Model for Creation and Development." *Journal of Community Practice* 2(1):21–42.

Birnbaum, M. L., and C. Aurbach. 1994. "Group Work in Graduate Social Work Education: The Price of Neglect." *Journal of Social Work Education* 30(3):325–335.

Delgado, M. 1996. "Puerto Rican Food Establishments as Social Service Organizations: Results of an Asset Assessment." *Journal of Community Practice* 3(2):57–77.

Gutiérrez, L., Rosegrant Alvarez, A. H. Nemon, and E. Lewis. 1996. "Multicultural Community Organizing: A Strategy for Change. *Social Work* 41(5):501–508.

Hardcastle, D., S. Wenocur, and P. Powers. 1997. *Community Practice: Theories and Skills for Social Workers.* New York: Oxford.

Heskin, A., and R. Heffner. 1987. "Learning About Bilingual, Multicultural Organizing." *The Journal of Applied Behavioral Sciences* 23:525–541.

Jenkins, S. 1980. "The Ethnic Agency Defined." *Social Service Review* 54, 249–261.

Kagen, S. L., and B. Weissbourd. 1994. *Putting Families First.* San Francisco: Jossey-Bass.

Lucky, I. 1995. "HIV/AIDS Prevention in the African American Community: An Integrated community Based Practice Approach." *Journal of Community Practice.* 2(4):71–90.

Medoff, P., and H. Sklar. 1994. *Streets of Hope: the Fall and Rise of an Urban Neighborhood.* Boston: South End Press.

Mondros, J., and S. Wilson. 1994. *Organizing for Power and Empowerment.* New York: Columbia University Press.

Muñoz, C. 1989. *Youth, Identity and Power: The Chicano Movement.* London: Verso.

Naperstek, A., and D. Dooly. 1997. "Countering Urban Disinvestment Through Community Building Initiatives." *Social Work* 42(5):506–514.

Page-Adams, D., and M. Sherradin. 1997. "Asset Building as a Community Revitalization Strategy. *Social Work* 42(5):423–434.

Pine, B., and T. Mizrahi. 1996. "A Memo to ACOSA Members." New York: Association for Community Organization and Social Administration.

Rivera, F., and J. Erlich. 1995. *Community Organization in a Diverse Society.* 2nd ed. Boston: Allyn and Bacon.

Wang, C., and M. Burris. 1994. "Empowerment Through Photo Novella: Portraits of Participation." *Health Education Quarterly* 21:171–86.

Biographies of the Contributors

CHAUNCEY A. ALEXANDER

Chauncey A. Alexander graduated in psychology from the University of California at Los Angeles and earned a master's degree in social work at the University of Southern California. He completed academic work and examinations for a doctoral degree.

Alexander's career affiliations include associate director for Health Planning, Regional Medical Programs, UCLA School of Medicine; executive director, Los Angeles County Heart Association; Southern California Society for Mental Hygiene; Los Angeles Veterans Service Centers; and many years as a psychiatric social worker, community organizer, and educator. Founder of the Orange County Health Care Council—a 100-organization coalition—he continues as an active member of the executive committee. As president of the nonprofit First Amendment Foundation, he heads a board of directors of nationally prominent civil liberties leaders.

Author of more than 80 professional publications and numerous studies, reports, and special articles, Alexander has lead in the unification of the social work profession, practice analysis, and political and community organization for the improvement of health and social services. He has been accorded international recognition by voluntary and governmental officials and social work leaders in 52 countries during his decade of officerships and presidency of the International Federation of Social Workers (IFSW) . He authored the International Code of Ethics for Professional Social Workers and the International Policy on Human Rights, among other policy documents.

DAVID M. AUSTIN

David Austin holds a bachelor of arts from Lawrence College, a master of science in social administration from the School of Applied Social Sciences, Western Reserve University, and a Ph.D. from the Florence Heller Graduate School of Brandeis University.

Austin has taught at Brandeis University, has been visiting professor at the University of Tennessee College of Social Work, and since 1973 has been on the faculty of the School of Social Work, The University of Texas at Austin. In 1986 he was awarded the Bert Kruger Smith Centennial Professorship, and from 1991 to 1993 he served as acting dean.

Austin has been a member of the board of directors of the National Association of Social Workers; the Educational Planning Commission of the Council on Social Work Education; the board of directors of the American Public Welfare Association; and the board of directors of the Unitarian Universalist Service Committee. He chaired the NIMH Task Force on Social Work Research (1988–1991). In 1992 the Association for Community Organization and Social Administration awarded Professor Austin its first ACOSA Award for Lifetime Achievement in the Teaching of Social Administration. In July 1992, Austin received the President's Award for Outstanding Achievement in Research. In 1997 he received the Significant Lifetime Achievement in Social Work Education Award of the Council on Social Work Education.

MILDRED C. BARRY

Mildred Creighton Barry was born of missionary parents in Guangzhou (Canton), China, attended high school in Shanghai, graduated from Wooster College, and received her master's degree in social work from Western Reserve University. Her professional career was primarily in Cleveland, where her husband was a practicing physician, and included a variety of positions beginning with settlement house work. She was instructor and assistant professor of community organization at the School of Applied Social Sciences, Western Reserve University, from 1951 to 1954, following which she was on the staff of The Welfare Federation, holding executive positions in departments on older persons and chronically ill, the Cleveland Health Council, and the Health Planning and Development Commission. Her work contributed to changes made at the Federation and the renaming to The Federation for Community Planning.

She is the author of more than a dozen professional articles including: "Community Organization Process: An Approach to Better Understanding," *Social Work Journal*, October 1950; and "A New Model for Community Health Planning," with coauthor Cecil G. Sheps, M.D., *American Journal of Public Health*, February 1969.

Barry served on the Board of the National Conference on Social Welfare from 1966 to 1969, and on the National Association of Social Workers as chair of the Council on Social Work in Community Planning and Development from 1968 to 1969. Her awards include: Outstanding Achievement and Service Recognition, on the occasion of the Fiftieth Anniversary of School of Applied Social Sciences, Western Reserve University, 1966; and Community Leaders and Noteworthy Americans Award, Bicentennial Edition, 1975–76.

MARGARET E. BERRY

Born in Michigan's Upper Peninsula in 1915, Margaret Berry was drawn to social work through early volunteer work in West Virginia's mining towns, in Detroit's welfare department at the height of the Great Depression, and at Bryn Mawr's labor education school. She received her B.A. from Albion College in 1935, and an M.S.S.A. from Western (now Case Western) Reserve University in 1937. She worked in Cleveland for four years in the Industrial (workers) Department of the YWCA.

In 1941 Berry went to Soho Community House in Pittsburgh, where she developed the program in Terrace Village whereby Soho was the first private agency in the United States to work in public housing. She was a field instructor for the University of Pittsburgh's School of Social Work. She was director of Soho from 1947–51.

After a year in Germany as consultant to youth leadership training schools, under a Rockefeller Foundation grant, Berry joined the staff of the National Federation of Settlements in 1952, and was the executive from 1959–71. She was elected president of the National Conference on Social Welfare in 1971, and became its executive in 1972, retiring in 1979.

Berry's international interests were expressed as president of the International Federation of Settlements from 1964–72, and through the U.S. Committee of the International Conference on Social Welfare. She was a recipient of the Grace Coyle international award from Case Western Reserve's School of Applied Social Sciences. Other honors include the Jane Addams Award from the National Federation of Settlements, distinguished alumnae awards from Albion and Case Reserve, and a special citation from the National Conference. She has written numerous articles and papers and has been active in NASW and the Association for the Advancement of Social Work with groups.

GEORGE BRAGER

George Brager received his M.S. in social work (1948) from the University of Pennsylvania School of Social Work, with a specialization in group work, and his Ph.D. from the New York University Center for Human Relations and Community Studies (1968). Prior to his appointment as a planner and codirector for Mobilization for Youth, a demonstration community development effort and model for the antipoverty program, he worked in a variety of youth-serving agencies as teen supervisor, program director, and executive director. He followed Mobilization with a stint at the U.S. Department of Labor, as special assistant to the manpower administrator, after which he was appointed to the faculty of the Columbia University School of Social Work.

Brager was at Columbia from 1965 to 1992, part of which time he served as the School's associate dean and dean. He also planned and supervised a university-initiated multidisciplinary project of services, training, and research whose focus was the mentally ill homeless population. Over a ten-year period, the project expanded and ultimately became an independent, free-standing social agency. On his Columbia retirement, Brager was employed as the director of the agency's training and technical assistance arm.

Brager has authored numerous volumes, monographs, and articles, among them *Community Organizing* (with Harry Specht), *Changing Human Service Organizations* (with Stephen Holloway), and *Supervising in the Human Services* (with Stephen Holloway).

SUSAN E. CLARKE

Susan E. Clarke is professor of political science at the University of Colorado at Boulder. Her research on urban politics and community development has been supported by the National Science Foundation, the U.S. Economic Development Administration, and other granting agencies. In addition to academic positions at Northwestern University and University of Colorado, she spent two years as a visiting scholar in the Policy Development and Research Division at the U.S. Department of Housing and Urban Development. In 1991–92, she served as president of the APSA Urban Politics Section and is a nationally elected member of the Governing Board of the Urban Affairs Association.

Recent international urban research activities include a visiting faculty position at the University of Essex (1993–94), a lecture tour in South Africa on local economic development strategies (1997), and designation as a Distinguished Fulbright Chair, the Thomas Jefferson Chair in the Netherlands (1999). She is on the editorial board of the *Journal of Urban Affairs*, *Economic Development Quarterly*, and *Government and Policy*;

she is currently coeditor of *Government and Policy*. She is coauthor (with Gary Gaile) of *The Work of Cities* (University of Minnesota Press, 1998).

RICHARD A. CLOWARD

Richard A. Cloward has a master's degree in social work and a Ph.D. in sociology, both from Columbia University, and an honorary doctorate from Adelphi University. He has taught at the Columbia University School of Social Work since 1954 and has won two teaching awards.

Cloward has been particularly interested in applying social theory to the formation of organizations to promote social change. He helped found Mobilization for Youth and developed the rationale for the protest movement of welfare recipients that led to the National Welfare Rights Organization. He helped form the Human Service Employees Registration and Voter Education Campaign (Human SERVE), a national voter registration reform organization that promoted the idea that people—particularly poorer and minority groups—should be registered to vote when they apply for Welfare, Food Stamps, Medicaid, unemployment benefits, and driver's licenses. Human SERVE's program was incorporated in the National Voter Registration Act of 1993—popularly known as the "motor voter" bill—which was signed by President Clinton. The National Voter Registration Act is producing the greatest rise in voter registration in American history.

His books include: *Social Perspectives on Behavior* (1958); *Delinquency and Opportunity* (1960); *Regulating the Poor* (1971, Updated Edition 1993); *The Politics of Turmoil* (1974); *Poor People's Movements* (1977); *The New Class War* (1982, Updated Edition, 1985); *The Mean Season* (1987); *Why Americans Don't Vote* (1988); and *The Breaking of the American Social Compact* (1997). *Delinquency and Opportunity* won the Dennis Caroll Award of the International Society of Criminology (1965), and *Regulating the Poor* won the C. Wright Mills Award (1972), conferred by the Society for the Study of Social Problems. Professor Cloward also won the Society's Lee/Founders Award (1991) for "distinguished career-long contributions to the solution of social problems." He received the Eugene V. Debs Foundation Prize for "published work which evidences social vision and commitment to social justice" (1986). In 1992, he won the Herman D. Stein Distinguished Social Work Educator Award, Case Western Reserve University. For his work in the field of voter registration reform, he received the 1994 Award of the National Association of Secretaries of State. In 1995, he was the recipient of the Lifetime Achievement Award for Social Administration and Policy Practice, given by the Association of Community Organization and Social Administration, and he was the first recipient of the Lifetime Achievement Award in Political Sociology, given by the American Sociology Association.

STEPHEN B. FAWCETT

Stephen B. Fawcett holds an endowed professorship at the University of Kansas where he is Kansas Health Foundation Professor of Community Leadership and University Distinguished Professor of Human Development and Family Life. He is also director of the Work Group on Health Promotion and Community Development of the Schiefelbusch Institute for Life Span Studies. In his work, he uses behavioral science and community development methods to help understand and improve health and social concerns of importance to communities. A former VISTA volunteer, he worked as a community organizer in public housing and low-income neighborhoods.

Fawcett has been honored as a Fellow in both Division 27 (Community Psychology) and Division 25 (Experimental Analysis of Behavior) of the American Psychological Association. He received the Distinguished Practice Award of the Society for Community Research and Action and the Higuchi/Endowment Award for Applied Sciences. He is coauthor of over 100 articles and chapters, as well as several books in the areas of health promotion, community development, empowerment, self-help, independent living, and public policy. Fawcett has been a consultant to a number of private foundations, community partnerships, and national organizations, including the John D. and Catherine T. MacArthur Foundation, the Ewing Kauffman Foundation, the California Wellness Foundation, the U.S. Commission on National and Community Service, the Institute of Medicine of the National Academy of Sciences, and the U.S. Centers for Disease Control and Prevention.

ROBERT FISHER

Robert Fisher is professor and chair of political social work at the Graduate School of Social Work, University of Houston. He is, most recently, the coauthor with Howard Karger of *Social Work and Community in a Private World: Getting Out in Public* (Longman, 1997); author of *Let the People Decide: Neighborhood Organizing in America*, 2nd edition (Twayne, 1994); and coeditor with Joe Kling of *Mobilizing the Community: Local Politics in the Era of the Global City* (Sage, 1993).

A social historian by training, Fisher has published numerous articles in scholarly and popular journals on urban policy, community organizing, and social welfare history. He is the recipient of two Fulbright fellowships to Austria, in 1986 and 1994. As discussed in his essay in this volume, Fisher has been active in various social justice and community organizing efforts since the early 1970s, most recently an effort organized by a vibrant coalition of community, union, and social work activists to raise the minimum wage in Houston and another to fight the dire air pollution problem in that city.

LORRAINE GUTIÉRREZ

Lorraine Gutiérrez is affiliated with the University of Michigan, where she has a joint appointment with the School of Social Work and Department of Psychology and is a faculty associate in Latino Studies. She co-coordinates the Detroit Initiative in Psychology, an undergraduate community psychology program in partnership with community-based organizations in Detroit. This program of education, scholarship, and service involves students in service and research activities with youth serving programs and projects.

Within the School of Social Work, her teaching focuses on multicultural and community organization practice. She brings to her teaching over 20 years of social work practice and research in multiethnic communities in New York, Chicago, San Francisco, Detroit, and Seattle.

Her research focuses on multicultural issues in communities and organizations. Current projects include identifying methods for multicultural organizational development and community practice, defining elements of culturally competent mental health practice, and identifying the linkages between gender ideology and attitudes toward race and racism. She has published over 20 articles, chapters, or books on topics such as empowerment, practice, and women of color.

RALPH M. KRAMER

Ralph M. Kramer is a professor emeritus, since 1991, in the School of Social Welfare at the University of California at Berkeley. He was appointed to the faculty after receiving its first doctorate in social welfare in 1964. Prior to returning to the University of California, where he also received his B.A. and M.S.W. degrees, he was employed for 17 years in the San Francisco Bay Area as a psychiatric social worker, family service agency executive, and the director of the Social Planning Council in Contra Costa County. In the School of Social Welfare, he was responsible for the establishment of the master's degree programs in community organization, social planning, and management.

Kramer is the author of over 80 publications on the voluntary sector, social planning, and citizen participation. His books include: *Privatization in Four European Countries: Comparative Studies in Government–Third Sector Relationships* (M.E. Sharpe, 1993); *Government and the Third Sector: Emerging Relationship in Welfare States*, with Benjamin Gidron and Lester M. Salamon (Eds.) (Jossey-Bass, 1992); *The Welfare State in Israel: The Evolution of Social Security Policy and Practice*, with Abraham Doron (Westview, 1991); *Voluntary Agencies in the Welfare State* (University of California Press, 1981); *Readings in Community Organization Practice*, with Harry Specht, 3rd edition (Prentice-Hall, 1982); and *Participation of the Poor* (Prentice-Hall, 1969).

Portions of his research on governmental–voluntary relationships have been published in Italian, Dutch, French, Catalan, Hebrew, and Hungarian. His most recent research publications since 1987 have focused on social service contracting in the San Francisco Bay Area, in the U.S.A., and in several West European countries.

In 1991, prior to his retirement, Kramer was the recipient of the Berkeley Citation for "distinguished achievement and for notable service to the University of California." In 1994, he also received one of two Annual Awards for Distinguished Contribution to Nonprofit Organizations and Voluntary Action Research from the Association for Research on Nonprofit Organizations and Voluntary Action (ARNOVA).

ROBERT PERLMAN

Robert Perlman is professor emeritus at Brandeis University, where he was engaged in teaching and research at the Heller School from 1965 to 1982. When he completed the doctoral program at the Heller School, he served as program director of Boston's antipoverty program during the early 1960s. Before that and following his graduation from social work school at Western Reserve University, he worked in supervision and administration in Jewish Centers.

In the late 1960s, Perlman served as director of field studies for the project on Community Organization Curriculum in Graduate Social Work Education sponsored by the Council on Social Work Education. As part of that project he coauthored, with Arnold Gurin, *Community Organization and Social Planning*.

Since retiring from Brandeis, Perlman has been writing on the social history of Jewish immigrants at the turn of the century.

FRANCES FOX PIVEN

Frances Fox Piven earned a Ph.D. in political science at the University of Chicago in 1962, was awarded an Honorary Doctor of Humane Letters at Adelphi University in 1985, and was the recipient both of a Guggenheim Fellowship in 1973 and of a Council of Learned Societies Fellowship in 1982. Piven has held visiting professorships in various European countries, including a Fulbright Distinguished Lectureship at the University of Bologna in 1990. She is presently Distinguished Professor of Political Science and Sociology, Graduate School and University Center, City University of New York.

In addition to numerous articles on political theory and institutional analysis published in professional and popular journals, Piven has written numerous books: *Regulating the Poor* (1971, Updated Edition 1993); *The*

Politics of Turmoil (1974); *Poor People's Movements* (1977); *The New Class War* (1982, Updated Edition, 1985); *The Mean Season* (1987); *Why Americans Don't Vote* (1988); *Labor Parties in Postindustrial Societies* (1992); and *The Breaking of the American Social Compact* (1997). *Regulating the Poor* won the C. Wright Mills Award (1972) conferred by the Society for the Study of Social Problems; Piven also won the Society's Lee/Founders Award (1991) for "distinguished career-long contributions to the solution of social problems" (1991). She received the Eugene V. Debs Foundation Prize for "published work which evidences social vision and commitment to social justice" (1986). She was also the recipient of the 1993 President's Award of the American Public Health Association. For her work in the field of voter registration reform, she received the 1994 Annual Award of the National Association of Secretaries of State. Piven was the first recipient in 1995 of the Lifetime Achievement Award in Political Sociology, given by the American Sociological Association.

Professor Piven has been interested in applying social theory to the formation of organizations to promote social change. She developed the rationale for the protest movement of welfare recipients which led in the mid-1960s to the National Welfare Rights Organization, and she helped form the Human Service Employees Registration and Voter Education Campaign (Human SERVE), a national voter registration reform organization that promoted the idea that people should be registered to vote when they apply for Welfare, Food Stamps, Medicaid, unemployment benefits, and driver's licenses. Human SERVE's program was incorporated in the National Voter Registration Act of 1993—popularly known as the "motor voter" bill—which was signed by President Clinton. The National Voter Registration Act is producing the greatest rise in voter registration in American history.

Piven has served on the board of directors of the American Civil Liberties Union and has chaired their Committee on Poverty for many years. She has been both co-chairperson of the Annual Program and vice president of the American Political Science Association, as well as both vice president and president of the Society for the Study of Social Problems.

JACK ROTHMAN

Jack Rothman is professor emeritus at UCLA's School of Public Policy and Social Research. He was on the social work faculty at the University of Michigan for over 20 years. Rothman received a master's degree in social work at Ohio State University, and a Ph.D. with an emphasis on social psychology at Columbia University. Prior to entering academia, for almost ten years he was a community organization and group work practitioner in New York City.

A major theme in Rothman's work has been the application of social science research to issues of intervention and change. He has engaged in numerous research utilization projects and played a leading role in developing the methodology of intervention research/design and development. Areas of interest and research activity have included community mental health, culturally relevant intervention, innovation in organizations and communities, runaway and homeless youth, and case management. He is currently conducting a study of variables related to high achievement among social work researchers.

Rothman has authored some 20 books, as well as numerous journal articles and book chapters. He was the recipient of the Outstanding Lifetime Achievement Award of the Association for Community Organization and Social Administration (ACOSA), and also the Myrdal Award for Distinguished Contributions to Research in Human Services, granted by the national Evaluation Research Society.

MEYER SCHWARTZ

Meyer Schwartz received a master of social administration degree from Western Reserve University, following his earning a bachelor of social science from the College of the City of New York. He was dean of the Simmons College Graduate School of Social Work and associate dean and professor at the University of Pittsburgh. While at the University of Pittsburgh, he established the Community Organization Program, which was the first contemporary two-year concentration in the country. Prior to his positions in academia, he was a social planning specialist at the United Jewish Federation of Pittsburgh and a group work supervisor at the Irene Kaufman Settlement House in that same city.

Schwartz served in a leadership capacity in various social work professional groups. He was chair of the National Committee on Community Organization, Council on Social Work Education; chair of the section on Community Organization of the National Conference on Social Welfare; and project director, Community Organization Curriculum Study of the Council on Social Work Education. He wrote a major report for NASW on "Defining Community Organization Practice."

He served widely as a consultant to significant social welfare organizations. In the governmental sphere he was advisor to the Government of Israel and the Republic of China (Taiwan), both in conjunction with the United Nations, and also aided the U.S. Senate subcommittee on Office of Economic Opportunity policy, and Commonwealth of Pennsylvania Department of Welfare. Among voluntary organizations he advised were the Ford Foundation; Council of Jewish Federations, New York; and Project Jamaica.

Schwartz has written articles for the Encyclopedia of Social Work and the Journal of Jewish Communal Services, and reports for the United Nations and the National Association of Social Workers.

IRVING A. SPERGEL

Irving A. Spergel is George Herbert Jones Professor in the School of Social Service Administration (and the Department of Sociology), University of Chicago. He received his doctorate in social work from the Columbia University School of Social Work in 1960. His major teaching areas have been group work, community organization, and social research.

His practice experience has been in the Jewish community center, settlement house, mental health, and gang work fields (New York City Youth Board and Lenox Hill Neighborhood Association). He has been a consultant on youth work, street gangs, and social work education to the Ford Foundation, U.S. Departments of Labor, Justice, and Health and Human Services, and the United Nations, as well as to the Hong Kong and Russian governments.

Spergel's most recent book is *The Youth Gang Problem. A Community Approach,* Oxford University Press, 1995. He is currently engaged in multiyear gang and community mobilization research funded by the Illinois Criminal Justice Information Authority (State Planning agency) and the Office of Juvenile Justice and Delinquency Prevention, U.S. Justice Department.

JOHN BRISTER TURNER

John B. Turner is dean and Wm. Kenan, Jr., professor emeritus of the School of Social Work at the University of North Carolina at Chapel Hill. Before coming to North Carolina he was professor and dean of the Mandel School of Applied Social Sciences, Case Western Reserve University.

In 1946, he earned a B.A. degree from Morehouse College. In 1948, he received the M.S.S.A. degree and in 1959 the D.S.W. degree from Case Western Reserve University.

Among the other assignments and posts held by Turner are the following: Program Director–Butler Street YMCA (Atlanta), Area Field Worker and Director of Field Services–Cleveland Welfare Federation, Instructor–Atlanta University School of Social Work. He was also visiting professor and lecturer at the University of Georgia, Smith College, The University of Toronto, McGill University, The University of Minia, Cairo University, and American Universities (Cairo and Beirut). Over a period of several years he worked with A.I.D. in Egypt as a consultant to social development programs. He also consulted with the National Urban League when Whitney Young was its director.

Among his honors and affiliations are: CSWE Significant Lifetime Achievement Award in Social Work Education; NASW Presidential Award for Excellence in Social Work Education; Grace Coyle Award, Case Western Reserve University; Martin Luther King Jr. Citizenship Award, Orange County, N.C.; Afro-American Family and Community Service National Leadership Award; and The National Honor Society. He was the editor of the Encyclopedia of Social Work, 17th Edition, and has authored or edited numerous articles, chapters, and books.

MAYER N. ZALD

Mayer N. Zald (Ph.D. 1960, University of Michigan) is professor of sociology, social work, and business administration at the University of Michigan. He has published widely on complex organizations, social welfare, and social movements. In 1990, he edited (with Robert L. Kahn) a volume of essays titled *Organizations and Nations: New Perspectives on Conflict and Cooperation* (Jossey-Bass). In 1996 (with Doug McAdam and John McCarthy), he edited a collection of essays, *Comparative Perspectives on Social Movements: Political Opportunities, Mobilizing Structures and Cultural Framings* (Cambridge University Press). Aside from essays on social movements, he is currently engaged in a reformulation of social science as science and humanities. Several recent publications reflect this theme.

Zald has served as chair of the Department of Sociology at Vanderbilt University (1971–75) and at Michigan (1981–86, 1990–92). He has been chair of the Section on Occupations and Professions and of the Section on Collective Behavior and Social Movements, both of the American Sociological Association, a member of the ASA Council, and has held numerous editorial positions. Among his honors are fellowships at the Center for Advanced Studies in the Behavioral Sciences (1986–87, 1994) and selection as Distinguished Scholar of the Organization and Management Theory Division of the Academy of Management (1989). In 1986, he served as vice president of the American Sociological Association. In 1994, he was elected to the American Academy of Arts and Sciences.

Name Index

Subject Index

REFLECTIONS ON COMMUNITY ORGANIZATION
Edited by John Beasley
Production supervision by Kim Vander Steen
Designed by Jeanne Calabrese Design, River Forest, Illinois
Composition by Point West, Inc., Carol Stream, Illinois
Printed and bound by McNaughton & Gunn, Saline, Michigan
Paper, Writers Natural